Advance praise for

VOICE MALE

"Rob Okun is a founding father of the profeminist men's movement in this country. His important book combines decades of boots-on-the-ground activism with worldly-wise psychological insight, presenting the voices of men also fighting the good fight. Profound, inspiring, and full of surprises, this anthology is a must read for anyone committed to peace."
—Mark Matousek, author of *Ethical Wisdom: The Search for a Moral Life*

"Here is a book for women to feel hopeful about men. Longtime editor of *Voice Male* magazine Rob Okun and a chorus of writers tell the story of a movement of men standing with women in the struggle to end violence against women. But this brave book does more, revealing an emerging man culture where men are reclaiming their tears and their hearts as they join women in creating a world where we are all safe and free."
—Eve Ensler, playwright of *The Vagina Monologues*, author of *In the Body of the World*, founder of Vday

"When your children and grandchildren ask what men were doing when women were changing the world, tell them to pick up this book. *Voice Male* tells the story of men—across class, race, and sexual orientation—who responded to feminism not defensively but with support. *Voice Male* deserves a place alongside such classics as *Sisterhood is Powerful* and *The Feminist Papers*."
—Jackson Katz, PhD., author of *The Macho Paradox* and creator of the awarding-winning film *Tough Guise*

"*Voice Male* chronicles the contemporary profeminist men's movement, providing a documentary record of activism, engagement, and personal reflection… At its best, *VM* is a journey, not a destination, a shared space in which men can listen to each other, listen to the women who shared their experiences in its pages, and, most of all, feel heard by others. It is also a place to explore the meaning of gender equality, or feminism, in our personal lives, offering painful self-reflection, some exhilarating, and some merely an exhale into a richer emotional life."
—Michael Kimmel, author of *Manhood in America, Guyland,* and *Angry White Men*, from the Foreword

"Rob Okun and his colleagues offer a striking rationale—profeminism—to address the powerlessness, shame, and patriarchal values that underpin abusive behavior. This book recasts the struggle to produce better boys and men and should provoke the thinking of every professional charged with keeping our families and communities strong and safe."
—Eli H. Newberger, M.D., Pediatrician and author of *The Men They Will Become: The Nature and Nurture of Male Character*

"In chronicling the commitment of anti-sexist men, Rob Okun continues his long legacy of redefining American manhood. This book helps feminists and their male allies to deconstruct patriarchy, shifting the paradigm of what it means to be a real man. *Voice Male* is both a guide and a searchlight for future generations of boys and men."
    —Byron Hurt, director of *I Am A Man: Black Masculinity in America* and *Hip-Hop: Beyond Beats and Rhymes*

"Thank you to Rob Okun for chronicling a better way—where men are recognizing their humanity, reconnecting their hearts to their heads, vanquishing stereotypes, and proving themselves healthier role models. At long last, there is hope for my son and daughters' generation."
    —Jennifer Siebel Newsom, filmmaker, *Miss Representation* and *The Mask You Live In*

"This book is a critical tool in dismantling what's oppressive in male culture."
    —Renner Wunderlich and Margaret Lazarus, producer/directors of the Academy-award winning *Defending Our Lives, Rape Is, and Rape Culture.*

"*Voice Male* inspires men to think more deeply about what it means to be a man. From working to end gender-based violence to examining their roles as partners and fathers, it's an invaluable tool for removing obstacles keeping men from reclaiming their full humanity."
    —Judy Norsigian, coauthor, executive director Our Bodies Ourselves

"We are unaware of some of the most powerful ideas that shape our lives because they seem second nature, obvious. Which is all the more reason to hold them up for scrutiny, to… see what they really are. Masculinity is one of those ideas, and anyone looking for a place to begin this journey of discovery can do no better than this book."
    —Allan Johnson, author of *The Gender Knot: Unraveling Our Patriarchal Legacy* and *Privilege, Power and Difference.*

"Why are almost all the stone throwers in the world male? How do boys become men? What does it mean to be a man? What happens when men come together without women? Can you imagine men building a beloved community? Maybe it begins with *Voice Male*…a manual for good living [and] a book thinking about answers."
    —E. Ethelbert Miller, director of Howard University's African American Resource Center, and author of *Fathering Words*

"Insights about 'changing men' are abundant in *Voice Male* and this comprehensive book is essential reading for anyone wanting to understand those changes. Rob Okun and his contributors make a compelling case for men not only challenging violence against women but also for challenging themselves to be better men."
    —Sut Jhally, Ph.D., professor of communication, UMass-Amherst, founder-executive director, Media Education Foundation

VOICE MALE

THE UNTOLD STORY OF THE PROFEMINIST MEN'S MOVEMENT

Edited by Rob A. Okun

Foreword by Michael Kimmel

Interlink Books

An imprint of Interlink Publishing Group, Inc.
Northampton, Massachusetts

First published in 2014 by

INTERLINK BOOKS
An imprint of Interlink Publishing Group, Inc.
46 Crosby Street, Northampton, Massachusetts 01060
www.interlinkbooks.com

Library of Congress Cataloging-in-Publication Data

Voice male : the untold story of the profeminist men's movement / edited by Rob A.
Okun ; foreword by Michael Kimmel. -- First edition.
    pages cm
ISBN 978-1-56656-944-6 (hardback) -- ISBN 978-1-56656-972-9 (paperback)
1. Men's movement. 2. Masculinity. 3. Feminism. I. Okun, Rob A.
HQ1090.V65 2013
305.32--dc23
                            2013032689

Cover images, Silhouette of men © Jana Kopilova |Dreamstime.com
Cover design: Julian Ramirez
Book design and production: Pam Fontes-May

Printed and bound in the United States of America

10 9 8 7 6 5 4 3 2 1

To request our complete 48-page, full-color catalog, please call us toll free at 1-800-
238-LINK, visit our website at www.interlinkbooks.com, or send us an e-mail:
info@interlinkbooks.com

In memory of my father, Joseph Okun, the first man to teach me about tenderness and tears.

"To be hopeful in bad times is not just foolishly romantic. It is based on the fact that human history is a history not only of cruelty, but also of compassion, sacrifice, courage, kindness. What we choose to emphasize in this complex history will determine our lives. If we see only the worst, it destroys our capacity to do something. If we remember those times and places—and there are so many—where people have behaved magnificently, this gives us the energy to act, and at least the possibility of sending this spinning top of a world in a different direction. And if we do act, in however small a way, we don't have to wait for some grand utopian future. The future is an infinite succession of presents, and to live now as we think human beings should live, in defiance of all that is bad around us, is itself a marvelous victory."

—Howard Zinn

TABLE OF CONTENTS

CHRONICLING MEN'S ROLE IN THE GENDER JUSTICE MOVEMENT

[T]he struggle for women's liberation is the struggle for men's liberation as whole feeling persons capable of equal relationships. We say flatly: the women's movement is the best thing that has ever happened for men.

—Statement issued at the Fifth National Conference on Men and Masculinity, Los Angeles, December 30, 1978

My first job out of college was as a reporter for a daily newspaper. Two decades later, when I arrived at the Men's Resource Connection (MRC) in Amherst, Massachusetts, I had edited two magazines—one promoting alternative energy, *New Roots*; and one celebrating Yiddish culture, *The Book Peddler*; and had served as publisher of another, *Workplace Democracy*. Working at a male-positive, profeminist, antiviolence men's center, I didn't initially know I'd be circling back to magazine editing. I shouldn't have been surprised, though. When I was 23, one of my early mentors was the night city editor at the daily paper where I was writing obituaries in the afternoon and chasing police cars and fire trucks after dark. "Once you get printer's ink in your veins," Steve Pappas told me, "it's impossible to get it out." Fortunately, I've always liked that inky feeling—it's like having another blood supply coursing through your veins.

Soon after coming on board at the MRC (renamed twice as the Men's Resource Center of Western Massachusetts and Men's Resource Center for Change), I began writing for and helping to edit the center's periodical—then called *Valley Men*. I saw the publication had potential to be more than a newsletter for a single organization. I successfully lobbied to increase its size and circulation—adding more pages and increasing the number of copies printed from a thousand to 10,000. Then I suggested we rename the publication, a decision we announced on the cover of the fall 1998 issue. *Voice Male* remained the publication of the Men's Resource Center until I began publishing it independently a decade later.

The first issue came out in May 1983. It was just four pages long, carried no graphics, and featured listings of local, regional, and national events including "a march against rape... co-sponsored by Men Against Violence Against Women, and Sisters in Health" and an announcement for "the Eighth National Conference on Men and Masculinity... in Ann Arbor, Michigan." The back page featured a poem, "Thoughts on Withdrawal" by David Grief.

It included these lines: "I hide behind my walls, my moat, my boiling oil, my drawbridge: a man's heart is his castle, mine is secure. . . " At the end of the poem he writes, "I am scared, frightened . . . what if I die in my castle all by myself . . . I think I'll let the drawbridge down." This book is about both the men trapped behind the castle walls and those who have let the drawbridge down.

As the magazine that gave rise to this book, *Voice Male* has been long committed to chronicling profeminist men's work. That commitment remains as strong today as it did at the publication's birth three decades ago. Among our most important allies have always been women and men working to end gender-based violence; promoting active, engaged fathering and caregiving; mentoring boys on the journey to healthy manhood; encouraging men to better care for our physical, emotional, and spiritual selves; and collaborating with women to improve the lives of women and girls and boys and men.

Voice Male exists because of the women's movement; it was born out of women's struggle for liberation. From *off our backs* and *Ms.* four decades ago to *feministing, Women's eNews,* and *Bitch* today (to name just a few of our foremothers and present-day sisters), *Voice Male* unambiguously locates itself within the gender justice movement, a movement that recognizes that not just a publication—but all men—can be both "male positive and profeminist."

Trying to better understand men—from our acts of violence to our acts of compassion, from our emotional restrictiveness to our capacity to nurture—brings into focus two key pieces essential to completing the social justice puzzle I've long been working on: making clear to a wide audience how conventional expressions of masculinity have a devastating, negative impact on all the issues facing society—from racism to war, gay rights to the prison industrial complex, from women's health to the health of the planet. It is in more than just men's self-interest to articulate a new, collaborative and emotionally expressive definition of manhood and masculinities. It is central to creating a peaceful world.

In *Voice Male: The Untold Story of the Profeminist Men's Movement* you will find essays, commentaries, articles, and poetry published over the long history of the magazine. The book chronicles a wide swath of contemporary men's lives—from men as bystanders to and perpetrators of domestic and sexual abuse; to men as activists against violence and men sharing the dreams and challenges of active, engaged fathering. In these pages also are stories articulating a vision of an openhearted masculinity, a vision that begins with recognizing how men both benefit from and are damaged by the privileges we enjoy simply because we identify as male in a patriarchal society. Along the way, men's health—emotional, physical, and spiritual—is also explored, as is boys becoming men, and—central to our vision—men developing a positive relationship with feminism. The travails and triumphs of male abuse survivors, men of color, and GBTQ men are also woven into the *Voice Male* tapestry.

Introduction

Some stories in the book refer to the Men's Resource Center of Amherst, Massachusetts. As one of the early men's centers in North America, the MRC was long a source of inspiration, ideas, and writers for *Voice Male*. It was a touchstone for many women and men in the gender justice movement, and *Voice Male* shares and proudly amplifies its mission of "supporting men and challenging men's violence." While there are many voices to pay attention to in the pages of this book, when I listen most deeply the ones I always hear clearest are the ones I heard first—those of the men and women in the MRC family.

I invite you to consider all the voices, though—from the call and response of young men to tender stories of fathers and children; from the *do* tell and *do* ask of gay men to the courageous truth-telling of male abuse survivors; from the loving challenge of our sisters to the march for liberation of men of color. Think of *Voice Male* as a field guide for exploring a vibrant new expression of men and masculinities. Lace up your hiking boots. Let's get going.

—Rob Okun
Amherst, Massachusetts
June 17, 2013

FOREWORD
AGAINST THE TIDE: PROFEMINISM IN THE TWENTY-FIRST CENTURY

By Michael S. Kimmel

The quotes that serve as the epigraphs for this book's preface and initial chapter are separated by only about 60 years, yet they span the arc of a social movement: two moments defining the first two waves of feminist activism. Floyd Dell, the Greenwich Village bohemian writer, was among the founders of the Men's League for Woman Suffrage, a group of prominent public figures who led men's contingents in the great suffrage parades and organized men's support of women's suffrage. Sixty years later, that message echoed across continents and decades, finding a new generation of men who saw in feminism an opportunity to live richer, fuller lives, animated by intimacy, emotional expressiveness, and equality.

In a sense, this book chronicles that movement. Just as *Against the Tide: Pro-feminist Men in the United States, 1776–1990* documented the history of men who had supported gender equality since the founding of the country, *Voice Male* chronicles the contemporary profeminist men's movement, providing a documentary record of activism, engagement, and personal reflection. That first wave only glimpsed the ways that political activism and personal life were intertwined. If the watchwords of that first wave were the motto of *The Revolution*, the newspaper of the National Woman Suffrage Association— "Men their rights, and nothing more; women, their rights and nothing less"—the motto of that second wave was, and continues to be, "the personal is political." That is, the dynamics of our personal lives articulate and reproduce the larger structural dynamics of inequality. Feminist engagement requires political activism, but it also inspires personal engagement.

If the personal is political, so, too, is the political personal. And for two decades, under Rob Okun's able stewardship, *Voice Male* has provided an outlet for the full range of men's engagement, from moral outrage to personal anguish, from political passions to, well, passion itself. At its best, *VM* has been a journey, not a destination, a shared space in which men could listen to one another, listen to the women who shared their experiences in its pages, and, most of all, feel heard by others. It has also been a place to explore the meaning of gender equality, or feminism, in our personal lives, offering painful self-reflection, some exhilarating, and some merely an exhale into a richer emotional life.

It has also been a place of celebration of the rich diversity among men, helping to bridge the barriers of race, class, and sexuality that separate men, as well as engaging men in the work of dismantling those same social barriers that are hierarchical and oppressive to some, even as they impoverish us all.

Voice Male is a respite, a haven, a community. A place to see old friends, to recharge the batteries, and to get inspired and outraged all over again. Equal parts comforting and challenging, Rob uses his talents as a writer, a therapist, and an activist to offer what always feels like just the right mix: the cold political analysis, the warm therapeutic community, the heat of political outrage and exhortation—never tepid, but always "just right."

I think what I like best about *Voice Male* is its balance of personal and political. We often read writers who talk a good line and wonder if they are able to walk their own talk. We wonder perhaps if they are only saying the right thing to ingratiate themselves, to be good boys. Moral exhortation borne of political outrage often gives me the queasy feeling that the writer is saying, "Do as I say, not as I do."

But just as *VM* has been a place for men to engage, to take their first steps, it is also a public space, a place where they could declare themselves—their politics, their personal struggles—publicly. (Many *VM* writers were writing for a public for the first time—a hallmark of any editor's patience and skill and dedication). That is, *VM* is also a place for men to talk their walk—to publicly express the sorts of changes they were already implementing in their lives, changes as fathers, as partners, as friends, as allies. There are many who are engaged in the political activism and personal transformations that together comprise what I often like to call the Gentleman's Auxiliary of the Women's Movement. Most do so quietly, in their interactions with those they love, work with, and interact with in their daily lives. Yet all around us, antifeminist activists troll the Internet, attempting to shout down any male voice that dares to support gender equality.

Plus ça change. Profeminist men have always faced the derision of other men who question their manhood, their sexuality, their motives. The great abolitionist Frederick Douglass was ridiculed as an "Aunt Nancy Man" by the Syracuse newspapers on the morning after his rousing speech in favor of suffrage at Seneca Falls in 1848. And during those mass women's voting-rights demonstrations in the 1910s, marchers behind the Men's League banner were routinely pelted with debris and insults. Those who break ranks and stand with the marginalized are often seen as traitors.

Which is why we need more of us to not only walk our talk, but also to talk our walk, to state publicly our opposition to gender inequality, to be allies to women, and to support and challenge one another in bringing our political commitments and our personal transformations into public view. For more than two decades, *Voice Male* has been one of our most cherished shared spaces.

We men have a choice, and most men, in fact, choose to stand with women—because we believe, as men, that women's equality will not only make it possible for us to be free, but also to be happy.

A SHORT HISTORY OF ONE OF THE MOST IMPORTANT SOCIAL JUSTICE MOVEMENTS YOU'VE NEVER HEARD OF

Feminism is going to make it possible for the first time for men to be free.

—Floyd Dell, 1914

Looking through the wall of windows behind the podium, I can sense spring coming to New England. On stage a group of male students hold banners that call for an end to violence against women. Flanking them like bookends are a male district attorney and male college president. The band of men surveys the large crowd assembled to commemorate International Women's Day 2013 by celebrating the accomplishments of the New England Learning Center for Women in Transition (NELCWIT), founded in 1976 and one of the oldest organizations in the region providing services for survivors of domestic violence and sexual assault. From the stage Dave Sullivan, the Northwestern Massachusetts district attorney and Bob Pura, president of Greenfield Community College, are beginning a men's pledge. I stand with the other men and recite the words the pair alternately lead us in, promising "never to commit, condone or remain silent about violence against women and girls" and to be "part of the solution to ending all forms of this violence."

It is a poignant moment: men taking the White Ribbon Campaign pledge in the presence of a largely female audience at an International Women's Day event. There was a time when it would have been unthinkable that even a single man would be part of the program (let alone a stage full of them) at an event to honor the work of a feminist organization founded by women sitting around a kitchen table not far from where we are tonight. That the White Ribbon Campaign—initiated by Canadian men after a man stormed a college in Montreal and murdered 14 women—is given a central place in an evening celebrating International Women's Day is an expression of how far the movement for gender justice has come. This, I think, is the under-the-radar profeminist men's movement beginning to come into view.

VOICE MALE

TAKING THE PLEDGE: Men affirm their commitment "to be part of the solution in ending violence against women" at Jane Doe Inc.'s Massachusetts White Ribbon Day, commemorated annually at the statehouse in Boston on or near International Women's Day. *Voice Male* editor Rob Okun is in center with notepad. *Photo courtesy Jane Doe, Inc.*

For nearly two generations a growing number of men of all races and ethnicities in the United States and around the world have followed women both in working to prevent domestic and sexual violence and in redefining and transforming traditional ideas about manhood, fatherhood, and brotherhood. We've been called all kinds of names, but many of us describe ourselves as members of the profeminist* or antisexist men's movement. This collection of writings from *Voice Male* magazine is an introduction to our work.

It has been nearly four decades since modern-day men began this transformative work, embracing many of the ideas (if not always the label) of profeminism. Through this wide-ranging collection of articles, essays, and commentary that appeared in *Voice Male* magazine over a quarter century, the breadth and depth of the profeminist men's movement is revealed: from

---

* Why the term "profeminist" rather than "feminist man" or "male feminist"? "Stripped to its essentials," sociologist Michael Kimmel wrote in answering that question nearly a quarter century ago, "feminism involves the empirical observation that women and men are not equal in either the private or the public sphere and also the moral stance that such inequality is wrong and ought to be changed. Men may agree with this empirical assessment of women's subordinate status and the moral imperative to work toward equality. In that sense men *believe* in feminism. But to *be* a feminist," Kimmel wrote, "requires another ingredient: the felt experience of oppression. And this men cannot feel because men are not oppressed but privileged by sexism."

boys to men and fathering to male survivors and men of color; GBTQ men and men overcoming violence; men's health and men and feminism. Woven together, they create a multilayered tapestry revealing a wide, rich swath of one of the most important social change movements you've probably never heard of.

Profeminist men hold the simple "radical" belief that gender and sexual equality are fundamental democratic goals and that women and men should each have the same rights and opportunities. Although marginalized and largely absent from the national conversation about gender in the mainstream media, modern-day profeminist men have been engaged in a sweeping critique of manhood and masculinity since the 1970s. The first large-scale organized effort was by the National Organization for Changing Men—now known as the National Organization of Men Against Sexism (NOMAS). It described its origins as "a loose-knit spontaneous social movement."

In 1975 a group of male students in a women's studies class at the University of Tennessee organized "The First National Conference on Men and Masculinity," not in Boston, New York, or San Francisco but in Knoxville. Since that time, groups and organizations have sprung up across North America and in many parts of the world, following in the footsteps of the idealists in NOMAS, men in their twenties and thirties who had been inspired by the women's movement. (Some early NOMAS figures went on to make important contributions to profeminism through books such as *Refusing to Be a Man: Essays on Sex and Justice* and *The End of Manhood: A Book for Men of Conscience* by John Stoltenberg, and *The Making of Masculinities* and *A Mensch Among Men* by Dr. Harry Brod.) What may have begun in part as a kind of "gentlemen's auxiliary" to the women's movement—providing childcare in part so mothers could participate in demonstrations—soon became an inquiry into a panoply of men's experiences, in many cases reluctantly addressing the elephant in the room: male privilege.

Learning to Speak "Emotionalese"

Despite media messages that lag far behind on-the-ground truth, a progressive transformation of men's lives is under way. As you will read in this chapter's profiles of pioneering profeminist organizations, men's involvement in antisexist activism grew out of a sense of justness and fairness heightened by men's involvement in the civil rights and antiwar movements of the 1960s. For many those feelings easily carried over to women's call for liberation, itself nothing less than a social justice imperative of obvious historical importance. (Acknowledging gay rights would come later.)

Many men simultaneously felt threatened by and envious of women's groups, women's politics—the entire women's movement. Most of us couldn't keep up. Women's bilingual fluency—speaking both "Emotionalese" *and* "Politicalese"—certainly made it challenging, but not impossible, for men to understand what was happening in those dizzying times, especially once we relinquished our heretofore unquestioned belief that in the world of gender there was only one official language: "Manspeak." In those early days, some of us were confused and angry; some tuned out, choosing to ignore multiracial women's marches toward liberation. Still, a small number of men began tuning in.

Acknowledging women's fluency in Emotionalese, some of us haltingly began to talk about our struggles, our feelings, our inner lives. Trouble was, we were primarily doing so with the people we believed could hear and understand us best—women. Slowly, over time, more of us realized (often with a firm push from our partners, wives, or women friends) that who we really needed to be talking to was other men.

Despite the modest number of men involved, chinks in the armor of conventional manhood are visible, and, as our numbers grow, the chinks grow larger, threatening to crack open. Since the late 1970s, besides activities in the US and Canada, profeminist men's work has been ongoing in Great Britain, Scandinavia, Brazil, Australia, New Zealand, South Africa, Mexico, and Central America. In more recent years India and Nepal have joined the growing list, as have a number of African nations. The roots of profeminist men's work are deep. (See the Resource section, page 396).

In North America, antiviolence men's centers and men's programs have offered general-issue support programs for men, as well as groups for young men of color and GBTQ men. Fathers groups and a variety of programs for boys on the journey to manhood also are on the rise, as are programs addressing men's health, including groups for male survivors of child sexual abuse. Groups for men acting abusively, known as batterers' intervention, began in the late 1970s and now operate in most US states, often overseen by state departments of public health. There are also numerous educational initiatives engaging men in gender violence prevention efforts on college and high school campuses, in sports culture, and through a variety of community-based organizations.

Since the late 1970s, profeminist men's activities have ranged from op-eds and letters to the editor to newspaper signature ads, rallies, demonstrations and advocacy campaigns, as well as books and films—all aimed at offering an alternative to conventional notions of masculinities. As time and technology marched on, listservs were created, websites launched, electronic publications introduced, and social media campaigns inaugurated. (One of the most wide-ranging and comprehensive Internet resources is XYonline: Men, Masculinities and Gender Politics, long maintained by internationally respected profeminist scholar-activist Michael Flood.) As a sign of the growth of the movement, there are today ongoing collaborations with long-established women's programs across North America and internationally, often through women's initiatives at the United Nations. (Eve Ensler, the activist and author best known for writing *The Vagina Monologues,* made sure there was a "V-Men" page when she launched her organization's V-Day website.)

In 2009, nearly 500 men and women allies from 80 countries met for four days in Rio de Janeiro at a symposium, "Engaging Men and Boys in Gender Equality." The growing global movement, united under an alliance called MenEngage, now operates on every continent. Major conferences on related themes of men and women collaborating to prevent violence against women and promoting healthy masculinity for boys and men have been held in recent years across the globe. In North America there are numerous such events occurring each year from coast to coast, in our largest cities and at many of our most prestigious colleges and universities.

Recognizing the movement's growth and potential to become even more of a force for social change in addressing gender justice issues, in 2013 the John D. and Catherine T. MacArthur Foundation awarded a two-year grant to establish the first Center for the Study of Men and Masculinities. Headquartered at the State University of New York, Stony Brook, it is being led by the sociologist and writer Michael Kimmel. The profeminist movement is beginning a new chapter. It's been a long road to get here.

Author or editor of more than 20 books on men and masculinities, in 2013 Stony Brook University sociologist Michael Kimmel was named founding executive director of the Center for the Study of Men and Masculinities initially funded by the John D. and Catherine T. MacArthur Foundation. *Photo courtesy Michael Kimmel*

MEN ALLIED NATIONALLY FOR THE EQUAL RIGHTS AMENDMENT: Chapters of M.A.N. for the ERA dotted the national landscape in the late 1970s when men like those pictured in this 1979 flyer campaigned for the amendment to the US Constitution. Although both houses of Congress passed the bill in 1972 and 35 of the 50 states ratified it, the ERA fell short of the requisite three-quarters needed to become law. *Image courtesy the Sophia Smith Collection (Gloria Steinem Papers), Smith College*

The Making of a Movement

As feminists in the mid-1970s worked to ratify the Equal Rights Amendment (ERA), its straightforward call for justice and fairness brought forth an outpouring of male support (as had the struggle for women's right to vote so many decades before). "How long can we stand by and watch qualified people excluded from jobs or denied fair payment for their labor?" asked actor Alan Alda in an article in the July 1976 issue of *Ms.* "How long can we do nothing while people are shut out from their share of economic and political power merely because they are women?" Today, with women still earning seventy-seven cents for every dollar a man earns, there is still much work to do.

Among the proponents of women's drive for equality was an organization called Men Allied Nationally for the Equal Rights Amendment (M.A.N. for the ERA), which had active chapters in a number of states. M.A.N. marched

A Short History of Profeminism

behind its banner at ERA rallies—just as the Men's League for Woman Suffrage had paraded at gatherings on behalf of women's enfranchisement in an earlier era. As this brand of men's activism was promoting women's rights generally, a number of grassroots men's organizations were starting up to explicitly challenge men's violence against women. Emerge in Cambridge, Massachusetts, was the first batterer intervention program in the United States, founded in 1977. RAVEN (Rape and Violence End Now) began in St. Louis in 1978, followed by the Oakland Men's Project (1979); Manalive (1980) and MOVE (Men Overcoming Violence), (1981), all in the San Francisco Bay area. From the Chicago Men's Gathering to the New York Center for Men; from the Pittsburgh Men's Collective to Men Stopping Rape in Madison, Wisconsin to Santa Cruz (California) Men Against Rape and the Men's Resource Connection in Amherst, Massachusetts, profeminist organizations worked closely with the women's agencies in their communities. All of these organizations have had an impact, some locally, some nationally, some internationally, from those begun in the 1970s and early 1980s to those founded in the 1990s and the early years of this century. In the latter group are Mentors in Violence Prevention (1993); Institute on Domestic Violence in the African American Community (1993); Men Can Stop Rape (1997); Promundo, (1997); Dads & Daughters (1999); A Call to Men (2003); Men's Resources International (2004); Sonke Gender Justice Network (2006); and Man Up Campaign (2010). Since the work of these organizations is so transformative—despite being largely unknown to the wider public—it seemed important to profile some of the diverse profeminist men's organizations that have contributed to the movement's rich history.

You may notice as you read their stories how many of these organizations almost exclusively address men's violence against women (as opposed to, say, advocating for improving women's economic circumstances or their reproductive rights). Many nascent profeminist activists were either reading or reading about Susan Brownmiller's book *Against Our Will: Men, Women and Rape*, published in 1975, and Andrea Dworkin's *Woman Hating: A Radical Look at Sexuality*, which came out the year before. Radical feminism was the driving force behind the women's movement in those days, ratcheting up women's demands for equality, and eclipsing the milder liberal message espoused by Betty Friedan, author a decade earlier of *The Feminine Mystique*.

The 1970s and early eighties were a time of explosive awareness of men's violence against women, and over and over the organizers of profeminist men's projects and founders of profeminist men's organizations reported that the women in their communities were alternately imploring and demanding that men make men's violence against women their top priority. As Gloria Steinem famously said, "Women want a men's movement. We are literally dying for it."

OAKLAND MEN'S PROJECT: At its 30th anniversary reunion in 2010, alumni of the pioneering organization recalled their commitment to being a racially diverse social change organization. OMP's cofounder Paul Kivel is seated in first row, third from right; cofounder Allan Creighton is standing in the next-to-last row, third from right (leaning forward). He died in 2013. *Photo courtesy Paul Kivel*

The Oakland Men's Project, Oakland, California

When the Oakland Men's Project (OMP) began in 1979, "most men interested in ending men's violence worked with men who batter," said longtime profeminist activist David Lee, director of prevention services for the California Coalition Against Sexual Assault. "OMP decided to take a different tack; they would be dedicated to social change through prevention and education. Their work blended exercises, role plays, and an analysis exploring the links between ending oppression and male violence." The men and women at the racially diverse OMP were more interested in being a social change organization than a social service agency.

The male roles "[we] had been trained to follow didn't work. Even without identifying it as a box, we knew we wanted out," said OMP cofounder (with the late Allan Creighton) Paul Kivel, activist and author of a number of books including *Men's Work: How to Stop the Violence That Tears Our Lives Apart* (Ballantine Books, 1992). Kivel, Creighton, and others were inspired by the women's movement in general and by a 1978 national conference in San Francisco on violence against women. "For years," Kivel recalled, "women's groups had been responding to the needs of women survivors of male violence by operating shelters and rape crisis centers. One result of this organizing was to make the public aware of the tremendous need for shelter, counseling, advocacy, and legal intervention. During this period the devastating effects of the violence on women, children, and even on men became more and more visible. *Some men began to see that we could no longer discount sexual harassment, battery, and rape as women's problems* [emphasis added] . . . We could see that the effects of past violence and the threat of future violence were keeping women off the shop floor, out of the corporate office, and out of public office. It was keeping them in dangerous marriages and in poverty. The women, understandably angry, said, '*You're doing the violence. You are men. Take responsibility for your actions and address other men.*'

"We assimilated much of their anger," Kivel continued. "Partly motivated by self-hatred, we took the anger directed toward us and directed it at other men for not seeing what was happening to women. We used that anger to encourage other men to acknowledge their complicity in the violence."

Kivel and others in the OMP put together a slide show to show men's groups. It combined images from pornography, album covers, magazine ads, and comic books. Most depicted women being humiliated—bound, beaten, or raped. "Our motivation was to convey horror, shock, and outrage at how violent the images were." As part of their presentation, they read the poem "With No Immediate Cause" by Ntozake Shange, which includes these lines:

> every 3 minutes a woman is beaten
> every five minutes a
> woman is raped/ every ten minutes
> a lil girl is molested . . .
>
> every day
> women's bodies are found
> in alleys & bedrooms/at the top of the stairs
> before i ride the subway/buy a paper/drink
> coffee/i must know/
> have you hurt a woman today

Painful, raw, and real, the poem was upsetting for men to hear. Kivel recalled that when men heard it at those early slide shows in the late 1970s and early 1980s, "some [men] felt angry, guilty, or ashamed. When presented with facts about the costs of male violence against women—as we are in this poem—we could not escape the horror of [women's] reality . . . We need[ed] only open the daily newspaper to read the stories. We need[ed] only listen to the women we know talk about their experiences to know the truth.

"The fact that it was safe enough for women to publicly express their anger was an indication of an important change under way in society," Kivel said, echoing the conclusions others were making at fledgling men's centers and projects around North America. Women were challenging male perceptions of sex, gender, rape, exploitation, and abuse.

OMP's workshops in the San Francisco Bay area with racially and ethnically diverse groups of middle schools boys, college-age men, and males spanning the age spectrum went deep, asking difficult questions about men's violence against women, as well as about the intersections of race, class, and sexual orientation. The Oakland Men's Project's legacy includes many books such as *Helping Teens Stop Violence, Young Women's Lives,* and *Making the Peace.* Exercises they created, including the "Act Like a Man Box," have become workshop staples at gender socialization gatherings addressing domestic and sexual violence throughout the country and the world.

Emerge, Cambridge, Massachusetts

The Emerge Center for Domestic Abuse was founded in Cambridge in 1977. It was the first abuser education program in the United States. Emerge's mission is short enough to memorize: "to eliminate violence toward women." To achieve its goal, Emerge educates individual men who batter, works with young people to encourage them not to accept violence in their relationships, advocates for improving institutional responses to domestic

EMERGE: The first batterer intervention program in the US, Emerge staff gathered in April 1978 to celebrate the group's first anniversary. Back row, from left: unidentified, Ken Busch, Harry Jung, Andrew McCormick, David Adams. Front row: Bob Wald, Dore Penn, Joe Morse. *Photo courtesy David Adams*

violence, and promotes increasing public awareness about the causes of and solutions to violence against women. Today it is recognized as a national and international training and resource center on domestic violence.

"The nine men who founded Emerge with me included a bunch of social workers, two students, a teacher, and a cab driver," the organization's longtime coexecutive director David Adams recalled. "What we had in common was we all had been involved in various social causes of the 1970s, including the antiwar movement, civil rights movement, and the burgeoning men's movement. We were also friends of women who had started some of the nation's first battered women's programs in Boston. They asked us if we would be willing to talk to abusive men who had started calling their hotlines. We said yes."

One of the rallying cries of the women's movement in the late 1970s was "the personal is political"—a way of calling attention, as Adams saw it, to the male domination of the antiwar and civil rights movements and how those movements reproduced some of the same abuses of power men and women were protesting. By working with individual men who abused women, the founders of Emerge felt "we were also helping to create a wider dialogue about male-female relationships as well as the idea that there is a reciprocal relationship between the larger 'isms' and interpersonal forms of 'power tripping.'

"Having worked with abusive men for 35 years," Adams recalled, "I still find deep meaning and value in the kinds of conversations we help to bring about with men. Over and over, men tell us that they have had very few opportunities to talk with other men about their relationships with intimate partners and children. By coming to value this kind of dialogue—and by engaging in a process of self-examination—we hope these men will serve as community ambassadors for this new way of thinking among their male peers, and also to serve as better role models for their children."

With its development over the years of parenting education groups for fathers, Emerge has expanded its mission to include a goal of helping men to become more responsible parents.

RAVEN, St. Louis, Missouri

A handful of men from St. Louis met while attending an early conference on men and masculinity in Des Moines, Iowa. Craig Norberg-Bohm, who along with Don Conway-Long, was one of the founders of RAVEN (Rape and Violence End Now), remembers how he ended up at the gathering. It was early 1977 and he was walking the streets of St. Louis when he came across a poster that made him stop mid-stride: "Straight White Male Wrestling with the Master Culture" it read in bold letters, announcing the Third National Conference on Men and Masculinity in Des Moines. "It was on brown poster paper," Norberg-Bohm remembered, "and featured a pen-and-ink drawing of a young adult

RAVEN (Rape and Violence End Now) was founded in St. Louis in 1978, less than a year after the fourth National Conference on Men and Masculinity. In addition to running groups for men acting abusively, RAVEN shared its work at retreats where men gathered from groups throughout the Midwest planning similar antiviolence initiatives. At a retreat in 1982 are RAVEN cofounders, from left, Don Conway-Long and Craig Norberg-Bohm, Mick Addison-Lamb, a colleague, and RAVEN member Mark Robinson. *Photo courtesy Don Conway-Long*

white male shivering in a cold wind. Whoa. They were talking about *me*. I couldn't get to the conference fast enough."

While in Des Moines, Norberg-Bohm and the other men from St. Louis attended workshops offered by the Men's Task Force Against Rape and Sexism from Champaign-Urbana, Illinois. "There was an antirape workshop and another on the connection between US imperialism and men's approach to relationships," Norberg-Bohm said. Among the St. Louis attendees was a man named John Paul, "who had the gumption to announce *we* would host the next conference in St. Louis!" Conway-Long recounted. (And they did, the following Thanksgiving weekend.)

"Women we knew in the community who worked at the Women's Self-Help Center—which trained women to work hotlines for survivors of men's violence—urged us to do something about men who were violent," Conway-Long said. "We pondered, we read, we took workshops. We determined challenging men's violent behavior through both intervention and public education was the right direction."

Within a year, RAVEN had started running batterers' groups, crafting a program influenced by the Emerge program as well as eclectic sources, such as the theories of psychologist Carl Rogers, reevaluation counseling, and other peer counseling. Therapist Harv Leavitt and Norberg-Bohm led the first group in the fall of 1978. Six months later they added a second group, and for many years they operated as many as four groups a week. Three and a half decades later, RAVEN is still running groups for men acting abusively. Norberg-Bohm went on to lead the Men's Initiative for Jane Doe, Inc. in Boston where he has established a model White Ribbon Day campaign across Massachusetts.

Manalive, San Francisco and Northern California

The Manalive approach to batterer intervention was developed in 1980 and still operates today. To get an idea of the group's approach in action, consider this story from 2001. The day after the September 11 attacks, participants in a Manalive group were discussing what happened. "A young man from San Francisco started by saying he was sad for the victims and their families," recalled Hamish Sinclair, Manalive founder. Then he offered a blunt big-picture analysis: "America got a punch in the nose. It's a *fatal*."—shorthand for "fatal peril," a pivotal Manalive concept: the moment of shock when a man fears that his male-role authority has been challenged. Sinclair said the group member saw America as a long-time violator that had finally been challenged.

During the discussion, the young man went on to say, "There's going to be some serious resubstantiating going down the other way now."

"'Resubstantiating' is our program's word for giving the male-role authoritarian image substance again after it's been challenged," Sinclair explained. "Substance, though, is the problem with the male-role image. It has none. It's like any image. It's just a picture, an idea that the whole society has supported for millennia that we have to get into our head to be a 'real' man. It's a gender-based fantasy, so flimsy that a funny look can challenge it."

An acronym for Men Allied Nationally Against Living in Violent Environments, Manalive is a community-organizing program distinct from other social service, community, prison, and jail programs, Sinclair explained. It is a peer program that engages program veterans to mentor beginners.

New members have just fifty-two weeks of three-hour classes to unlearn a lifetime of behaviors. "They learned to violate from other guys," said Sinclair, "and they learned well. They got good enough at it to be noticed. So, chances are, they'll learn the new stuff from other guys in the class and get just as good at stopping it." In Manalive's more than three decades of work, more than 10,000 men have attended its classes. Today, local Manalive programs offer more than fifty classes in rural, suburban, and urban Northern California, including classes in Spanish and Cantonese. The Manalive Education and Research Center has also developed three additional tracks for women and youth.

MEN STOPPING VIOLENCE: Founded in Atlanta, Georgia, in 1982, Men Stopping Violence's founding director, the late Kathleen Carlin, invited clinicians Dick Bathrick, left, and Gus Kaufman to lead the organization's initial batterer intervention groups. *Photo courtesy Men Stopping Violence*

Men Stopping Violence, Atlanta, Georgia

When Kathleen Carlin, then-executive director of the YWCA Women's Resource Center of Cobb County, Georgia, hired Dick Bathrick and Gus Kaufman to facilitate a newly funded court-mandated batterers' program, they didn't know that within a year, in 1982, they would be launching a new organization, Men Stopping Violence. "We were an unlikely combination," Bathrick recalled. "Gus was a Jew from Macon, Georgia, and a clinical psychologist. I was a WASP from Connecticut working as a marriage and family therapist. Kathleen was a Methodist from Maywood, Nebraska, and a social worker." All three had been powerfully influenced by the social change movements of the 1960s and 1970s, Kathleen carrying out a YWCA imperative to eradicate racism, and Gus and Dick actively working in the antiwar and civil rights movements.

While in New England, Gus had made a connection with the staff at Emerge, the Boston-area batterer intervention program. To give them a better sense of the challenges abused women were facing—and in preparation for starting their group in Atlanta— Bathrick and Kaufman were invited to listen in on hotline calls lighting up the phones at the local council on battered women.

"The raw truths in those calls were riveting and heartbreaking for us," Bathrick remembered. "It brought an urgency to our efforts to start working with men. Those first groups were powerful and challenging. It was unheard of

MEN AT WORK TRAININGS: Men Stopping Violence staff members conduct innovative multidisciplinary trainings on building safe communities. Staff (in front row), from the left, ramesh kathanadhi, internship coordinator, Sulaiman Nuriddin, director of men's education, Ulester Douglas, interim executive director, and Lee Giordano, training coordinator. *Photo courtesy Men Stopping Violence.*

for men to talk together about the ways they view and treat women . . . knowing that their discussions would be taped, listened to, and commented on by women." As daunting as it was, "we continued to hold open classes and learned that men were more likely to change when they were continually reminded of the impact their actions were having on the women in their lives."

As classes and community education efforts grew, the group incorporated as Men Stopping Violence with a mission "to engage men in ending male violence against women." John Lewis, the iconic civil rights activist who a few years later would become a member of Congress representing Atlanta, was the first president of its board of directors. The organization's commitment to incorporate fundamental social change as a key to preventing violence against women has never wavered, and today it conducts trainings and other educational work in Atlanta, elsewhere in the US, and overseas.

Men's Resource Center for Change, Amherst, Massachusetts

In 1981, several men in their twenties from western Massachusetts attended the Seventh National Conference on Men and Masculinity at Tufts University near Boston. "We watched in dismay as heated arguments played

MEN'S RESOURCE CONNECTION (Men's Resource Center for Change): One of the earliest profeminist men's centers in North America, the MRC was founded in Amherst, Massachusetts, in 1982. Founders and steering committee members who gathered in 1983 include (back row from left,) Rob King, Mark Nickerson, John Breckenridge, and David Thompson. Front row, from left, the late Sam Femiano, Steven Botkin, Billy Yalowitz. *Photo courtesy Steven Botkin*

out on stage and later in the lobby," recalled Steven Botkin, a cofounder of what was first named the Men's Resource Connection. "Men who believed sexism gives men privilege and power over women were fighting with men who believed sexism damages and disempowers men."

Returning home, the young men made a pivotal decision: they would create an antisexist men's network in their community that would both support men's healing from the damaging effects of sexism *and* hold men accountable for perpetuating the individual and institutional oppression of women.

The following year, guided by the voices of feminist women and their own personal experiences in men's support groups, they created the MRC. Starting from the principle that connection is fundamental for both men's personal change and antisexist activism, the founders—Botkin, David Thompson, and Mark Nickerson—began organizing informal gatherings, support groups, and multiday retreats. And men showed up.

"In 1983 we organized the Northeast Regional Men's Conference expecting several dozen men to attend," recalled Botkin. "Instead, several hundred came." Soon after, they began publishing the *Valley Men*'s newsletter. From its early days of cutting and pasting typewritten text, the publication eventually evolved into *Voice Male* magazine.

MOVING FORWARD: The Men's Resource Center's innovative batterer intervention program, Moving Forward, pioneered support services for female partners and former partners of men in the batterers' groups. Back row, from left: Steve Trudel, Karen Fogliatti, Eve Bogdanove, James Arana, Steve Jefferson. Front row, from left: Jan Eidelson, Dot LaFratta, Gary Newcomb, Sara Elinoff Acker, Joy Kaubin, Russell Bradbury-Carlin, Susan Omillian. *Photo: Steven Botkin*

"At that time there were very few models for engaging men on issues of gender and sexism. In addition to feminist texts," Botkin said, "we devoured the early writings of men like Bob Brannon (theories of masculinity's restrictiveness) and John Stoltenberg (essays on sexuality and justice). The Oakland Men's Project certainly served as an inspiration and resource in the formation of the Men's Resource Center. Although we were on opposite sides of the country, there was a sense of being pioneers together in building a movement."

As the need for a sustained community presence and activities expanded, the early organizers decided to incorporate the MRC, eventually changing its name from Men's Resource *Connection* to Men's Resource *Center*. Responding to requests from local women's organizations, the group developed the High School Education Project to train men to colead workshops with women on respect and abuse in relationships. Other youth programs included the Young Men of Color Leadership Project and Socially Active Youth. The Men Overcoming Violence program (MOVE) was also developed, based on a MOVE program operating in San Francisco, to work with men who had been violent or abusive with their partners. The program was among the first to offer services to the women whose partners attended the groups. A Men's Support Program was also created with facilitated weekly drop-in groups for all men, including GBTQ men and male survivors of childhood abuse. Community activism included men's peace walks, vigils commemorating victims of domestic and homophobic violence, standing in support of women during Take Back the Night marches, newspaper signature ads challenging men's violence against women, and organizing a statewide fathers' conference. Recognizing growing interest in sperm donations to lesbian couples, the group held informational meetings that were the genesis for the booklet *Lesbians, Babies and Men.*

Over the years, individuals and organizations from around the country and the world requested workshops and trainings from the MRC, and many other men's resource centers have been created based on the MRC approach. Individuals who developed their knowledge, skills, and leadership at the MRC are now working as leaders locally, nationally, and internationally. (*Voice Male* magazine and Men's Resources International emerged from the MRC as independent initiatives with global impact.) Reflecting on the past 32 years, Botkin said, "The seeds of change, planted more than thirty years ago, have blossomed in many ways. The vision of the MRC has opened into an emerging global vision of men as powerful role models and full partners with women working together for healthy families, strong communities, gender equality, and peace."

Real Men, Boston, Massachusetts

At a time when Massachusetts was becoming known as a profeminist hub, Real Men, a grassroots antisexist activist men's group, formed in Boston in 1988 and remained active for a decade. The group specialized in street theater activism and public education through media and distributing leaflets. According to men's antiviolence activist and author Jackson Katz, who started the group, "We were pamphleteers in the revolutionary Boston tradition."

The name was chosen "both for its media-friendly quality," Katz recalled, "and to satirize the idea that progressive, nonviolent men were not 'real men,' a powerful and damaging aspect of the narrow definition of manhood promoted in mainstream culture." Real Men had 10 to 20 active members—men and women—and a supporters list of a couple hundred. They included graduate students, rock musicians, professors, engineers, human service professionals, businessmen, a furniture mover, and an astrophysicist.

Their first public action was handing out quiche in front of the Boston headquarters of the 1988 George H.W. Bush presidential campaign, to call attention to how the Bush campaign's major strategy (ultimately successful) was to attack the manhood of his opponent, Massachusetts governor Michael Dukakis. The tongue-in-cheek pronouncement that "real men eat quiche" was actually part of a serious national conversation about men.

"Real Men leafleted [Boston] Red Sox and [New England] Patriots games, talking about what men of all races and ethnicities who were in positions of influence with young men and boys could do to prevent violence," Katz recalled. The group also held vigils outside popular Boston sports bars on Super Bowl Sunday to draw media coverage of the ongoing tragedy of men's violence against women and to encourage men in the sports culture to play a constructive role in preventing it.

From informational picketing actions at the concerts of misogynist comedians such as Andrew Dice Clay and Sam Kinison to organizing the first men's fundraiser for the Massachusetts Coalition of Battered Women's Service Groups (later Jane Doe, Inc.), Real Men dedicated itself to consciousness-raising and educational activism. Other activities included organizing high-profile panel discussions such as "Beyond Wimps and Warriors," which featured the voices of veterans, antiwar activists, and feminists discussing issues of masculinity in the first Gulf War. Real Men also organized one of the first public speak-outs in the country for pro-choice men.

White Ribbon Campaign, Toronto, Ontario

If it were between countries, we'd call it a war. If it were a disease, we'd call it an epidemic. If it were an oil spill, we'd call it a disaster. But it is happening to women, and it's just an everyday affair.

—Michael Kaufman, November 1991

The White Ribbon Campaign (WRC) is the world's largest movement of men and boys working to end violence against women and girls and to promote gender equity, healthy relationships, and a new vision of masculinity. Its story is worthy of a book of its own. It was created by men in response to the December 6, 1989 Montreal massacre when a disgruntled man brandishing a gun stormed into the city's École Polytechnique, specifically aiming at women. He murdered 14 and wounded 10 others.

"Three of us, Jack Layton, Ron Sluser, and I, came up with the idea for this campaign," recalled the writer and activist Michael Kaufman, "but we were quickly joined by several dozen other men in a handful of Canadian cities in time for our late November launch in 1991." Within days it mushroomed across Canada and, within years, around the world.

At its core, the group calls on men to pledge "never to commit, condone or remain silent about violence against women and girls" and to make that commitment known by wearing white ribbons or taking part in WRC activities.

The first WRC office was in the bedroom of cofounder Layton's son Michael. "The bed would just get cleaned off when Mike came home from school," Todd Minerson, WRC executive director, wrote in a remembrance of Layton, who died in 2011. From the WRC's humble beginnings in a boy's

WHITE RIBBON CAMPAIGN: Jack Layton, left (who died in 2011), and Michael Kaufman, along with Ron Sluser (not pictured), founded the White Ribbon Campaign in 1991 after a man opened fired at a polytechnic institute in Montreal murdering 14 women and wounding 10 others on December 6, 1989. *Photo courtesy Michael Kaufman*

bedroom, "Men have taken up the dream of ending gender-based violence," Minerson said. It has spread from Canada to more than 60 countries.

"Millions and millions of men and boys, from Brazil to Pakistan, China to England, Namibia to Russia, Cambodia to the United States, Chile to Japan, Norway to Argentina have worn a white ribbon, put up a poster, signed White Ribbon pledges, taken part in White Ribbon ceremonies, marches, services, and meetings," Kaufman recounted.

Among its wide-ranging programs and activities is White Ribbon's education and action kit, used by hundreds of thousands of teachers and students in 3,000 schools across North America. The kit, which combines in-class lessons with schoolwide projects, has been used to raise awareness about violence against women and to promote ideals about gender equality and healthy relationships. White Ribbon is helping create tools, strategies, and models that challenge negative, outdated concepts of manhood and inspire men to understand and embrace the incredible potential they have to be a part of positive change.

Why has the campaign traveled the globe? "White Ribbon spread first of all because of the tremendous impact of the women's movement around the world," Kaufman believes. "It has spread because most men don't use violence in our relationships and because we are finally ending our long

MUSLIMS FOR WHITE RIBBON: Since 1991 the men's antiviolence initiative has spread to more than 60 countries around the world and its pledge to be part of the solution in ending violence against women has been signed by millions of men on every continent, including Dr. Hamid Slimi, chair of the Canadian Council of Imams. *Photo courtesy White Ribbon Campaign*

silence." It spread, too, Kaufman added, "because from the start, we decided the WRC should be a campaign like no other—a campaign that aimed to be totally mainstream and which was completely decentralized because we believed that men and women knew best how to reach the men and boys in their own communities."

When Minerson was feeling overwhelmed by the daunting work of the campaign, "Jack [Layton] told me, 'Always have a dream that will outlast your lifetime.' I have thought about our work to end violence against women in that way ever since. Our vision is for a masculinity that embodies the best qualities of being human. We believe that men are part of the solution and part of a future that is safe and equitable for all people."

Chronicling the Movement

Some men found their way into the fledgling movement after perusing the eye-opening anthology *For Men Against Sexism: A Book of Readings*, edited by Jon Snodgrass (Times Change Press, 1977). In the book's introduction, "Men and the Feminist Movement," Snodgrass, a working-class man who attended college on the GI Bill, earned a Ph.D., and moved to California to teach sociology, wrote: "While . . . aspects of women's liberation . . . appealed

FOR MEN AGAINST SEXISM: One of the first books to offer men a window into women's plight and men's interior lives was the classic *For Men Against Sexism*, edited by Jon Snodgrass and published in 1977.

to me, on the whole my reaction was typical of men. I was threatened by the movement and responded with anger and ridicule. I believed men and women were oppressed by capitalism, but not that women were oppressed by men . . . I was unable to recognize a hierarchy of inequality between men and women . . . nor to attribute it to male domination. My blindness to patriarchy, I now think, was a function of my male privilege."

Among the essays in the anthology are: "How Pornography Shackles Men and Oppresses Women" by Michael Betzold; "Men Doing Childcare for Feminists" by Denys Howard; "Homophobia in the Left" by Tom Kennedy; "The Socialized Penis" by Jack Litewka; and "Black Manliness: Some Fatal Aspects" by Sedeka Wadinasi. Publication of the book marked a critical moment in the chronicling of the evolving movement.

That chronicling was also found in the pages of early profeminist magazines from Great Britain, the United States, and Australia. *Achilles Heel*, published in London, began in 1978. *M: Gentle Men for Gender Justice*, in Madison, Wisconsin (later renamed *Changing Men*), released its first issue in 1979. *XY: The Magazine for and about Men*, came out of Canberra, Australia, beginning in 1990. Although *Achilles Heel* and *Changing Men* are no longer publishing, their contributions to the movement remain invaluable. *XY* continues as the leading online space for exploring issues of gender and sexuality in men's and women's lives.

A Short History of Profeminism

EARLY PROFEMINIST MAGAZINES: *Achilles Heel* (United Kingdom); *XY* (Australia); and *Changing Men* (United States) chronicled the profeminist men's movement in the 1980s and 1990s when each published groundbreaking stories about men and masculinities.

Produced by a collective of socialist men and launched to coincide with the London Men's Conference in 1978, *Achilles Heel* published for two decades with various taglines, finally settling on "the radical men's magazine." In an editorial in the first issue the editors wrote, "For all of us it is a process of making public a very private and very important experience—that of consciously redefining and changing the nature of our relationships with women and with each other as men. In making this experience public and in beginning to develop an analysis around it, we are in a sense 'coming out' politically as men and realigning ourselves with the women's and gay movements in the struggle against sexual oppression."

XY's editorial policy affirmed "a healthy, life-loving, non-oppressive masculinity," that supported men's networks for change throughout Australia. The magazine was described as a place not just to explore gender and sexuality, but the "practical hows and whys of personal and social change." Readers could expect to find both personal stories of men's lives and discussions of masculinity and the changing relations between men and women.

Reading these publications today one can see they were recording profeminist history as its practitioners were simultaneously defining the parameters of the emerging movement. Articles ranged from "ERA: What's in It for Men? (*M/Changing Men*'s inaugural issue, Winter 1979–80); "Rethinking Men's Power" (*Achilles Heel*, Summer 1997); and "Young Men: From Emptiness to Life" (*XY*, Winter, 1995). *Voice Male* continues the work of chronicling the movement.

At the same time as publications were reporting on the doings of burgeoning profeminist activism, in the 1990s and early 2000s a new wave of

VOICE MALE

VOICE MALE MAGAZINE: What began in 1983 as the newsletter for the Men's Resource Connection evolved into a national magazine chronicling the profeminist men's movement.

organizations was emerging, including the Institute on Domestic Violence in the African American Community, Mentors in Violence Prevention, Men Can Stop Rape, Promundo, Dads and Daughters, A CALL TO MEN, Men's Resources International, Sonke Gender Justice Network, and the Man Up Campaign. From grassroots beginnings these groups and others, like Menswork in Louisville, Kentucky and the Minnesota Men's Action Network in the US, and larger ones such as the international Engender Health's Men as Partners program, are among the organizations that have been making important contributions to the twenty-first-century profeminist men's movement.

The Institute on Domestic Violence in the African American Community, St. Paul, Minnesota

Founded in 1993 by a group of scholars, activists, and practitioners in St. Paul, Minnesota, the Institute on Domestic Violence in the African American Community (IDVAAC) is concerned about the unique issues African Americans face when dealing with domestic violence—from intimate partner violence and child abuse to elder maltreatment and violence in the community. To achieve its goals, the institute collaborates with advocates, researchers, and policymakers to develop responses to domestic violence that are culturally relevant and tailored to the specific challenges of domestic violence among African Americans.

"The idea for the institute grew out of a series of informal meetings among scholars and advocates who were unsatisfied with the 'one-size-fits-all'

INSTITUTE ON DOMESTIC VIOLENCE IN THE AFRICAN AMERICAN COMMUNITY: Directed by Sheila Hankins and Oliver Williams, the institute was founded in 1993 in response to a recognition that a "one-size-fits-all" approach to domestic violence services provided in mainstream communities would not suffice for African Americans.

approach to domestic violence provided by mainstream domestic violence prevention centers," explained codirector Oliver J. Williams, Ph.D. "We felt the high rates of violence in the African American community would only change if individuals and groups came together to draw attention to the problem."

According to the institute's research, domestic violence disproportionately affects African Americans—for instance, black women comprise eight percent of the US population, but in the last year for which data was available, 2005, they accounted for 29 percent of domestic violence victims. "The challenges that African American victims face are often intensified by economic disadvantages, racial discrimination, and other stressors that particularly impact the African American community," said codirector Shelia Hankins.

Williams and Hankins each have more than 30 years of experience researching and working on the intersection of racial and domestic violence issues. Critical issues of keen interest at the institute include preventing domestic violence when men return from prison, hip-hop and domestic violence, and the intersections between religion, spirituality, and domestic violence. "Today we also are working on programs for formerly battered women, prisoners, parolees, and fathers to confront the root causes of violence in the African American community and promote healthy and positive family relationships," Williams said. "We want to see conflicts resolved in a constructive and loving manner."

Mentors in Violence Prevention, Boston, Massachusetts

One creative strategy for engaging high school- and college-age men to promote gender equality is to encourage popular athletes to become involved in that effort. The first large-scale program to do this was Mentors in Violence Prevention (MVP), a gender violence and bullying prevention program developed in 1993 at Northeastern University's Center for the Study of Sport in Society in Boston. MVP introduced the "bystander"

MENTORS IN VIOLENCE PREVENTION: MVP, founded in 1993, is credited with introducing the bystander approach to the domestic and sexual violence fields, and is noted for its work with college and professional sports teams, schools and the US military. Current and former directors and senior male trainers were reunited at a 2012 MVP conference in Boston. From the left, Don McPherson, Jackson Katz, Daryl Fort, Byron Hurt, Jeff O'Brien, and Duane DeFour. *Photo courtesy Mentors in Violence Prevention*

approach to the sexual assault and domestic violence prevention fields, and has been widely influential in the development of prevention initiatives in college and professional sports culture, schools, and the US military.

With start-up funding from the US Department of Education to create a model for gender violence prevention education that relies on the social status of male college and high school athletes and other student leaders, "the idea was to train young male student-athletes to speak out about issues that historically had been considered 'women's issues,' such as rape, relationship abuse, sexual harassment, and gay-bashing," recalled MVP cofounder Jackson Katz. "If young, socially popular men with a kind of "manhood credibility" on college and high school campuses would make it clear to their peers and younger boys that they would not accept or tolerate sexist or heterosexist beliefs and behaviors, it would open up space for young men beyond the insular sports culture to also raise their voices," Katz recounted. The program is based on the elementary premise in social justice education that members of dominant groups—men, whites, heterosexuals—play an important role in efforts to challenge sexism, racism, and homophobia. While the initial focus was on men, by the mid-1990s MVP had developed into a mixed-gender initiative, inside and outside of organized athletics

Over the past twenty years, MVP facilitators—including college and high school students—have led workshops and awareness-raising sessions with hundreds of thousands of men, women, boys, and girls across the United States and on US military installations in all branches of the armed services worldwide. MVP's gender violence prevention program for the US Marine Corps began in 1997, and MVP is a mainstay for both the Air Force and Navy sexual assault prevention programs. For the past decade, MVP has begun to expand overseas with initiatives in Canada, Australia, Scotland, Sweden, and other countries.

"MVP didn't start up in organized athletics because of problems in that subculture," Katz explained. "Just the same, the Steubenville, Ohio, rape case [in which two high school football players were convicted in early 2013 of raping a drunk 16-year-old girl] and the Penn State football child sexual abuse case more than a year before underscore why we have to examine—and transform—social norms in male sports culture."

But the impetus for MVP was proactive and positive, and had to do with the potential leadership of successful male (and later, female) student-athletes and coaches who, because they are seen as exemplars of traditional masculine success, have an enhanced level of credibility with their male peers and with younger men.

"Initiatives to prevent sexual violence that don't engage men in sports and other areas of the dominant culture are often ignored by people in the mainstream and can easily be marginalized. Why stay on the margins and not go right for the center?" Katz asks. As the Penn State and Steubenville debacles make clear, sports culture provides an unparalleled platform from which to call attention to a range of societal problems—and to catalyze efforts to change the social norms that often underlie them.

Although MVP originated in sports culture, and continues to use sports terminology in some of its curricular materials, its initial vision was to begin in athletics and then move into broader student and professional populations in colleges, high schools, middle schools, and other institutions—as it has through its work with the military. Still, athletics remains a critical arena. The organization has trained thousands of student-athletes, coaches, and athletic administrators across the racial, ethnic, and socioeconomic spectrum at hundreds of Division I, II, and III programs and with professional sports organizations and teams in the NFL, CFL (Canadian Football League), NBA, WNBA, MLB, and NASCAR.

The original training specialist for MVP was Byron Hurt, hired just after he graduated from Northeastern University (where he had been the quarterback on the university's football team). Hurt is now a renowned documentary filmmaker. He credits MVP with shaping many of his ideas about masculinity, misogyny, and homophobia, ideas he incorporated in his acclaimed 2007 documentary, *Hip-Hop: Beyond Beats and Rhymes*. The person who succeeded Katz as director of MVP was Don McPherson, a star quarterback at Syracuse University, member of the College Football Hall of Fame, and NFL veteran, himself a powerful antisexism speaker and advocate since the mid-1990s.

VOICE MALE

CALLING ON ALL MEN TO TAKE THE FATHER'S DAY PLEDGE

CONNECT: Founded in 1993, the New York City antiviolence organization aims to promote healthy relationships, positive masculinities, and awareness of domestic violence. Its coexecutive director Quentin Walcott, seated, second from left, says the group's annual Father's Day rally attracts thousands of men who pledge to end violence in their homes and communities. *Photo courtesy CONNECT*

CONNECT, New York City

"I am committed to working with men because it is important to move them from being bystanders to allies to activists in ending violence in our communities, no matter if it takes place in the home, school, workplace, or on the street," said Quentin Walcott, co-executive director (with Sally N. MacNichol) of CONNECT, a New York City-based interpersonal-violence-prevention-training, educational, and advocacy nonprofit organization founded in 1993.

"Our mission is to prevent interpersonal violence and promote gender justice through a range of methods—legal empowerment, mobilizing at the grass roots, and education efforts committed to transforming the beliefs, behaviors, and institutions that perpetuate violence," Walcott explained. "We have to have all the pieces in place in order to create a society based on mutuality, respect, and social justice, including accountable institutions, peaceful communities, safe families, and empowered individuals."

To achieve its goals, CONNECT leads initiatives to transform men into allies in preventing violence and helps them recognize attitudes and behaviors that lead to domestic violence. CONNECT differs from many other violence prevention groups in its focus on changing male behavior in addition to providing support for female victims. "Men commit more than 90 percent of reported cases of domestic violence. Yet traditional domestic abuse programs focus on women and children—the victims of family violence—rather than the batterer," Walcott noted. "CONNECT's programs—from groups for abusive fathers to middle school boys on the road to manhood are all aimed at promoting healthy relationships, positive masculinities, and domestic violence awareness." CONNECT also provides safe spaces for men and women to be in dialogue and practice together through its Community Dialogue Series, demonstrating the transformative work developed in its single gender groups.

The organization works with traditionally underserved communities including undocumented immigrants and non-English speakers to extend its reach and empower individuals who otherwise might not receive help. CONNECT's programs include after-school workshops with middle- and high-school boys, roundtables, and support groups for activists and peer educators, legal assistance for marginalized communities, and workplace/union initiatives that train employees and management to recognize abuse. Additionally, CONNECT serves as a leading training center for social workers, teachers, advocates, and activists who help develop community-based programs and plans and guide specialists on self-care techniques to deal with the unique stresses and emotional challenges of working with perpetrators and victims of abuse.

Men Can Stop Rape, Washington, DC

Meanwhile, during the mid-1990s in Washington, DC, a loose collective of profeminist men had been meeting to talk about men's role in changing a culture that condones (at least through its silence) sexual assault. "We were called DC Men Against Rape," remembered one of its members, Patrick Lemmon, "and those conversations became the genesis for what today is known as Men Can Stop Rape (MCSR)."

The organization slowly began to coalesce when Lemmon and collaborators Mike Airhart, Bill Christeson, Jonathan Stillerman, and Dave Wildberger began to focus more in their consciousness-raising sessions on taking action. "We decided to focus on DC public high schools since they were frequently identified as dangerous and difficult, and because it felt like the right thing to do as members of an urban community," Lemmon said. "Jonathan and I both had an unusual amount of time on our hands, since he had just finished graduate school and I had just come back to town from working on a political campaign in my home state of Louisiana, so we took on the bulk of planning, fundraising, and moving the work forward. We used my spare bedroom as our first office."

The name the group initially chose, Men's Rape Prevention Project, seemed ideal for the effort. "Using 'Project' made it sound temporary," Lemmon recalled, "and 'Men's' made it clear that it was men's work. But it

MEN CAN STOP RAPE: Based in Washington, D.C., Men Can Stop Rape sees its mission as trying to stop violence before it happens. It focuses on helping men to use their strength in positive ways. Director of strategy and planning Pat McGann, left, has been with the organization since its founding in 1997; executive director Neil Irvin since 2001. *Photo courtesy Men Cen Stop Rape*

had two problems that haunted it from the beginning. First, most people who heard it thought that we were focused on preventing the rape of men (which of course was true, but only part of the goal), and second, the acronym read—'Mr. PP.' You can only imagine the moment when a student pointed this out to us in class. The name did not last very long."

Lemmon and Stillerman became the first codirectors in early 1997. Stillerman stayed on the job for seven years, Lemmon for a decade. For the first few years, MCSR was an entirely volunteer organization focused on giving workshops in DC public schools, but by the end of 1999 the demand was clear. "We changed our name," Lemmon said, "moved into an actual office, and expanded our focus to college students around the country and internationally. The growth of the organization was consistently just a little bit more than what we expected or thought we could handle. We always felt like we were running to catch up with MCSR's growth."

Men Can Stop Rape continues to grow. It believes traditional masculinity is still too dominant in the culture, "still too much the air we breathe," in the words of Neil Irvin, the organization's current executive director. "It's something we often take in automatically, unaware. As one of the significant sources of violence against women across the globe, as well as other forms of violence, and as an unconscious source of conflict for many men, stereotypical masculinity causes great harm, particularly when it goes unrecognized. We all benefit from consciously developing healthier, nonviolent masculinities."

Men Can Stop Rape sees its mission as trying to stop violence before it ever happens. The group focuses on helping men use their strength in positive ways in their relationships, an approach grounded in the "social ecological model" advocated by the Centers for Disease Control and Prevention (CDC) as a framework for preventing gender-based violence.

Since its beginnings, MCSR has reached more than two million youth and professionals through its an award-winning youth program, Men of Strength Club; a college program, Campus Men of Strength Club, and through "My Strength Is Not for Hurting," a public awareness campaign.

Men of Strength Club is a school-based, 22-week curriculum that teaches male teens aged 11 to 18 healthy dating-relationship skills and encourages them to show their strength in positive ways among their peers. The club's curriculum is in schools throughout California, the District of Columbia, Florida, Kansas, Maryland, Missouri, New York City, North Carolina, Ohio, and South Carolina. Meanwhile, MCSR's Campus Men of Strength Club for college and university men has eight chapters in colleges in Florida, Hawaii, New York, North Carolina, and Washington, DC.

MCSR's Strength Media public awareness materials have been distributed in all 50 states and in 20 foreign countries. "Where Do You Stand?" posters target high school- and college-age men, while the group's " Y-MOST: Young Men of Strength" posters focus on empowering middle school-aged boys to take action against gender-based harassment, teasing, bullying, and cyberbullying. "We've created materials for more than 10 state and federal agencies, created posters, video PSA's, and training materials for the military through the Department of Defense Sexual Assault Prevention and Response Office," said Pat McGann, the organization's director of strategy and planning.

"We believe all men have the capacity and desire to play a positive role in creating communities free from violence," said executive director Irvin. "As part of this belief, we believe it is essential to approach men as potential allies rather than see them only as potential perpetrators. In order for men to have empathy for themselves and women, we all must embrace and be comfortable with the full range of emotion in men that is authentically human."

Dads and Daughters, Duluth, Minnesota

The national nonprofit Dads and Daughters was the brainchild of CREDO/Working Assets CEO Michael Kieschnick, a progressive philanthropist and entrepreneur. It is Kieschnick's contention that fathers and stepfathers with female children can "see the world through their daughters' eyes" to recognize and advocate against sexism. He built Dads & Daughters

DADS AND DAUGHTERS: For a decade beginning in 1999, Dads and Daughters forged a unique niche, strengthening individual fathers' relationships with their daughters while challenging sexualized advertising aimed at girls and young women. Executive director Joe Kelly, right, conducted trainings, testified before Congress, and authored many important books, including *Dads and Daughters: How to Inspire, Understand, and Support Your Daughter When She's Growing Up So Fast. Photo courtesy Joe Kelly*

to mobilize these fathers to use their positions of male privilege in the service of battling sexism to make the world safer and better for daughters. He recruited Joe Kelly, who along with his wife, Nancy Gruver, published the girls' empowerment magazine *New Moon*, to become the organization's executive director.

Between 1999 and 2008, Dads & Daughters (DADs) organized campaigns against harmful marketing to girls through "dad-to-dad" communication. DADs members wrote letters and e-mails to corporate executives who were themselves fathers, asking: "Would you send this message to *your* daughter? If not, then stop sending it to my daughter."

This approach led several companies to pull ad campaigns and/or drop products. For example, a DADs action convinced Campbell's to remove an after-school TV ad promoting soup as a diet aid for girls, while another effort persuaded Hasbro to drop plans to create a line of dolls based on the Pussycat Dolls, a highly sexualized burlesque dance and singing act.

In addition, DADs representatives lent fathers' voices to Supreme Court amicus briefs and congressional testimony in favor of strong Title IX enforcement. DADs also launched the "See Jane" project, which oversaw groundbreaking research into gender portrayals in mainstream children's media. Under See Jane's auspices, comprehensive content analysis by the University of Southern California's Annenberg School of Communication found that only

28 percent of speaking characters in the 100 highest-grossing "G"-rated movies were female. The research also revealed distorted portrayals of males, for instance showing nonwhite male characters as far more likely than white male characters to be violent and far less likely to be fathers or in committed relationships.

DADs activism and advocacy generated substantial coverage in the mainstream media, including the *Today Show*, CNN, Fox News, NPR, *The New York Times,* and many other outlets. The fathers participating in advocacy campaigns reported increased pride in their fathering and the positive impact they could have on their daughters' lives.

Covering the personal and political, Dads & Daughters also provided resources for men to strengthen their personal relationships with their daughters and stepdaughters—including the best-selling book *Dads & Daughters: How to Inspire, Support, and Understand Your Daughter* by Joe Kelly.

A CALL TO MEN: The Next Generation of Manhood City

For Tony Porter, it was the words of a nine-year-old boy that reaffirmed his life's mission. "I was working in a very small charter school made up of predominantly African American boys in Milwaukee, Wisconsin," Porter told *Rebel* magazine. "We were talking about all the things that define being a man and I asked what would happen if we could step outside the 'man box.'" The boy looked at Porter and said, "Then I would be free."

A CALL TO MEN: Since early in this century A CALL TO MEN has challenged male socialization and men's violence, focusing particularly on the way men are trained to view and treat women. From the left, cofounders Tony Porter and Ted Bunch with staff members Danielle Erwin, Lina Juarbe Botella, and Rickie Houston. *Photo courtesy A CALL TO MEN*

Porter was caught up short. "If he—*this nine-year-old boy*—is not free, then what is he?" Porter remembered thinking. "What is his day-to-day experience from school to home, or going outside to play? What is this man box he adheres to, not just to get through the day but to *survive*? And where are we, as men, falling short in giving him his freedom?"

Porter and Ted Bunch cofounded A CALL TO MEN to work to end domestic and sexual violence against women and girls by challenging men to reconsider their long held and long-taught gender beliefs—then take those lessons back to disseminate within their respective communities and the rest of the country. Concurrent with that mission is the goal of transforming how boys become men and how men define manhood.

The pair initially held workshops in the greater New York City area. In the fall of 2003 they launched the organization with a conference, "A CALL TO MEN: Ending Violence Against Women and Becoming Part of the Solution" and shifted their focus to offering workshops and trainings around the country. In recent years, they've conducted seminars in several countries overseas, including Brazil, Democratic Republic of Congo, and South Africa, and have set up a branch of the organization in the United Kingdom.

"Domestic violence, rape, and sexual assault are the most devastating health issues and social problems facing our society," Bunch noted. "There is no other problem, disease, or illness that claims as many victims. In almost every case the perpetrator is a male. No other crime or social ill has such a destructive effect on families, children, communities, or the workplace as men's violence against women. For this reason, if for no other, it is vital that men become involved in the effort to end men's violence against women and each other."

The core of Porter's and Bunch's work is challenging, rethinking, and assailing the collective socialization by which men are trained to view and treat women. "Domestic violence is rooted in sexism, patriarchy, and male domination, and that collective socialization contributes to violent behavior," Porter explained. "One of the founding principles of most societies was that women and children belonged to men—that they were property, and that thinking still exists, to varying degrees, in many cultures."

Porter and Bunch focused much of their early work on bystander intervention. Their work has since evolved into deconstructing conventional manhood. "As we increase and promote a healthy, loving, and respectful manhood we decrease and prevent all forms of violence against women and girls. The result is, we all benefit," Bunch and Porter said.

"If we truly want to end violence against women, then we have to end it in *all* communities," Porter said. "We like to reach in and grab a man's heart and make sure he's thinking differently about this issue than when he came. But the real work is after. It is rare that I'm ever in an audience with men who disagree with my message. The hurdle is to get men to leave the room and put this newfound knowledge into action."

Bunch agreed. "We may be courageous in many respects, and the man box teaches us not to fear—we pretend we're not afraid even when we're petrified," he said. "But this is a different kind of courage. For me, the challenge is to truly step outside the confines of our collective socialization—to have [a man] leaving a training empowered and prepared to take this issue head-on and bring it to a place to make necessary adjustments in his own life and have the courage to speak with and educate other men and boys."

Men's Resources International, Springfield, Massachusetts

By the turn of the millennium, the idea that men and boys could be change agents in gender-based violence and sexual and reproductive health and community development had begun to take root throughout the world. The Men as Partners program was pioneered in South Africa by EngenderHealth; Instituto Promundo field-tested Program H with young men in Brazil (H for *homens* and *hombres*, the words for men in Portuguese and Spanish respectively); and the Men's Resource Center of Western Massachusetts was helping men's resource centers get started in various parts of the United States. Increasingly, women's organizations and programs serving women

MEN'S RESOURCES INTERNATIONAL: MRI has conducted numerous trainings, primarily on the African continent, on a range of topics from ending gender-based violence to training men as peace builders. Executive director Steven Botkin, left, and MRI's James Arana, second from right, also facilitate masculinity reflection groups, like one for staff from CARE Niger and Mali attended by Dr. Fatma Zennou, the program coordinator, and Amadou Amadou, a counselor at CARE Niger. *Photo courtesy Men's Resources International*

and girls recognized the need to engage men and boys as allies. More and more men, often inspired by women's activism, were learning about the privileges and damages of the masculinity they inherited, and exploring ways to take action to promote a new kind of positive masculinity that was healthy, compassionate, and responsible.

Out of this growing interest in engaging, educating, and organizing men, the vision for Men's Resources International (MRI) took shape: a global network of women and men working together for unity and peace in our families and communities. Incorporated in 2004 by a diverse group of men and women with many years of experience working in men's resource centers and other community development initiatives throughout the United States, MRI's mission is to use training, consulting, and organizing to mobilize networks of men, in alliance with women, to prevent violence and promote positive masculinity.

"Several of us had worked for many years at the Men's Resource Center in western Massachusetts, but we didn't know if the strategies and skills that worked in communities in the US would be effective in other cultural contexts," reflected Steven Botkin, one of MRI's founders. "MRI's popular education approach, the value we placed in indigenous wisdom and leadership, and our faith in the power of compassion and connection has, over the years, generated enthusiastic responses in communities around the world." James Arana, another MRI founder, added, "By bringing men and women together to reflect on the consequences of dominant masculinity on our families and communities, we facilitate mutual understanding, building partnerships, and promoting individual and collective action."

Over the years, MRI has conducted trainings in the United States, Liberia, Nigeria, Rwanda, Côte d'Ivoire, Tanzania, Zambia, the Philippines, Nepal, Albania, Niger, Ireland, and the Netherlands through partnerships with NGOs such as Concern Worldwide, CARE International, the International Planned Parenthood Federation, the International Rescue Committee, and the Women's Peacemakers Program, and by responding to direct requests from individuals and local organizations.

Most recently, MRI has developed a tool kit for organizing "Masculinity Reflection Groups" for men and women with CARE International in Mali and Niger; a model for women and men as partners in peace building in the central East African Great Lakes region; a Healthy Manhood curriculum for the YMCA in the United States, and a male involvement initiative for Concern Worldwide in Liberia.

"We see our work as wide-ranging," said MRI cofounder and board chair David Thompson, "from ending gender-based violence to promoting sexual and reproductive health; from training peace builders and supporting women's empowerment to improving men's health, engaging men as role models, and preventing extreme poverty."

MRI trainings of trainers, organizational and program development consultations, and leadership mentoring have supported men and women from more than 40 countries to organize their own community initiatives, create national organizations, and become trainers and leaders in their own communities. Formative trainings and consultations have been provided for NGOs in Rwanda (Rwanda Men's Resource Centre), Democratic Republic of Congo (Congo Men's Network), Nigeria (Ebonyi Men's Resource Centre), Zambia (Zambia Men's Network), and the United States (Men of Color Health Awareness).

Serving as an advisory member of the MenEngage Alliance, MRI has supported the emergence of this global network. "MenEngage is another step toward our vision of a global network of women and men working together for unity and peace in our families and communities," said Botkin. "Now we must engage in a deeper dialogue about how to create authentic and equal partnerships."

Promundo, Rio de Janeiro, Brazil; Washington, DC; Kigali, Rwanda

Founded in 1997, Promundo works to promote caring, nonviolent, and equitable masculinities and gender relations in Brazil and internationally.

"We are working to transform gender norms and power relations within key institutions where these norms are constructed," said the group's cofounder and international executive director, Gary Barker. "At our core, we are an applied research institute that tests, evaluates, and advocates for policies and programs that transform masculinities."

Promundo is known for its painstakingly thorough research on masculinities and gender equality, developing, evaluating, and scaling up gender-transformative interventions and policies, and carrying out national and international advocacy to achieve gender equality and social justice.

In 2009 Promundo hosted the first Global Symposium on Engaging Men and Boys in Gender Equality in Rio de Janeiro, a four-day conference the group organized in collaboration with diverse partner organizations. In 2011, its MenCare Global Fatherhood Campaign, organized with the Sonke Gender Justice Network, was launched in Washington, DC and South Africa to engage men in care work and fatherhood.

Both in Brazil and internationally, Promundo trains educators and provides technical advice on gender equity issues. It has rigorous standards for evaluating the impact of projects on a variety of its core themes, including gender, masculinity, homophobia, violence against women, and sexual exploitation of children and adolescents.

Promundo develops advocacy campaigns to mobilize youth, families, communities, government, and private entities to take action to promote

PROMUNDO: Promoting caring, nonviolent, and equitable masculinities and gender relations in Brazil and internationally, Promundo has offices in Rio de Janeiro; Kigali, Rwanda; and Washington, D.C. Staff reunited at a 2013 symposium organized by the US Institute for Peace, are from the left: Joseph Vess, senior program officer, Alexa Hassink, program and communications assistant, both in the Washington office; Alice Taylor, program officer, Rio de Janeiro, Gary Barker, international director based in Washington, Tatiana Moura, executive director, Rio de Janeiro, and Jane Kato-Wallace, program officer, Washington. *Photo courtesy Promundo*

gender equality and prevent violence against women and children. "Many of these campaigns are developed and implemented by young people themselves, providing them with an opportunity to express their voices and practice activism," Barker noted.

The organization also coordinates qualitative and quantitative studies in different cultural contexts in Latin America, Africa, Asia, and Europe and has provided technical support for research studies with the World Bank, the World Health Organization (WHO), and the United Nations Population Fund (UNFPA), among others.

Sonke Gender Justice Network, Cape Town and Johannesburg, South Africa

Founded in 2006, the Sonke Gender Justice Network works across Africa to strengthen government, civil society, and citizen capacity to support men and boys in taking action to promote gender equality, prevent domestic and sexual violence, and reduce the spread and impact of HIV and AIDS. *Sonke* means "all of us" or "together" in Nguni, the language of a people who were

SONKE GENDER JUSTICE NETWORK: Both innovative and practical, the Sonke Gender Justice Network employs a variety of strategies to promote gender justice in South Africa and elsewhere on the continent. Its "One Man Can" campaign supports men and boys to take action to end domestic and sexual violence and to promote healthy, equitable relationships. The campaign's tool kit is available in English, French, Xhosa, Zulu, and Afrikaans. *Photo courtesy Dean Peacock*

thought to have migrated from the north to the Great Lakes region of subequatorial central East Africa.

Sonke has an expanding presence on the African continent and a growing international profile, through its involvement with the United Nations and other international networks and affiliates. "We recognize that effecting sustained change in gender roles and relations requires addressing the forces that shape individual attitudes and community norms and practices," said founder and executive director Dean Peacock. "And that means traditions and cultures, government policies, laws and institutions, civil society organizations, the media, and the family—as well as underlying economic, political, and social pressures."

Sonke believes that an effective response to gender-based violence and HIV and AIDS require organizations to develop multifaceted strategies and build relationships with both traditional and nontraditional partners. "We work closely with a range of organizations and individuals including women's rights groups, social movements, trade unions, government departments, sports associations, faith-based communities, media outlets, university research units, and human rights advocates," Peacock said.

Sonke is committed to ensuring that its programs are informed by the perspectives and priorities of those working to advance the rights of lesbian, gay, bisexual, transsexual, and intersexual communities, people living with HIV and AIDS, and refugees and migrants. Women, sexual minorities, young people, refugees, migrants, and other relevant stakeholders are represented in Sonke's governance structures.

"Our vision," Peacock said, "is a world in which men, women, and children can enjoy equitable, healthy, and happy relationships that contribute to the development of just and democratic societies."

Man Up Campaign, New York City

"When my daughter was born, I was fully immersed in being a war journalist," Man Up Campaign cofounder Jimmie Briggs recalls. "Assuming I would be traveling for most of her childhood, I sat down and wrote her a letter. It's one I've been rewriting periodically for the last thirteen years." (She has yet to see it). Briggs, who would change his career path from one of covering men who made war to working to create a generation who make peace, once told his daughter that he had been covering wars because "these experiences must be recognized, must be honored." On an early trip to northern Uganda,

MAN UP CAMPAIGN: Jimmie Briggs, a former war correspondent and the father of a teenage daughter, launched the Man Up Campaign in 2010 in the belief that males and females working collaboratively is key to fostering gender equality. Man Up's mission is to mobilize young people to face up to violence against women and girls in their local communities. *Photo courtesy Man Up Campaign*

Briggs met an old man who told him, "If a dying person tells you their story and it's not passed on, you would be haunted." Recounting the incident, Briggs said, "Well, I did pass on the stories I heard, but the knowledge and the awareness remained to haunt me."

As the visionary of the Man Up Campaign, Briggs believes engaging youth collaboratively—both male and female—can help foster gender equality. The organization's mission is to educate and mobilize young people to address violence against women and girls in their communities.

Briggs argues that without actively working to help young people change their lives, especially young men, achieving gender equality and preventing violence against women and girls may be an impossible goal. "I am not an expert on violence against women, but as a former journalist and a newly awakened advocate, I do know the absence of men and boys, as well as the missing component of youth's ingenuity and passion, has been an impediment to lasting progress in preventing violence."

Through his work with youth in North America and globally, he holds firmly to the belief that there is hope for creating and affirming alternative masculinities and, possibly, preventing violence as a whole—whether it's child soldiers in the developing world, rape as a weapon of war, or urban violence here in America. "By no means do I—nor could I ever—hold myself up as the ideal or 'perfect' man. Through starting Man Up and being exposed to critical dialogues with young men—and young women—around the world, I recognize that the journey of transformation is a never-ending one. The key is to remain self-aware."

As a journalist, Briggs is committed to making the world a better place not just for his daughter but for all the sons and daughters in the world. "As a father, as a man, as a citizen of the world, I know we all must hold to the belief that a world can exist where I would want to live, where men stand up with—and for—women and girls. It is with that faith that I could go and leave my family for long periods of time."

Society's Text Message to Boys—and Men

Despite the inroads made in redefining manhood, it is still difficult for men to grow up without being inundated with distorted messages about what it means to be a man. Boys are regularly exposed to variations of the same text message from contemporary society: "Be tough. Use few words. Rule the roost. Get the job done. Don't complain." An alternative narrative has begun to emerge thanks to the work of social scientist and profeminist men's movement pioneer Robert Brannon, an early leader of the National Organization of Men Against Sexism (NOMAS). In *The Forty Nine Percent Majority: The Male Sex Role*, which he edited with Deborah S. David (Random House,

1976), Brannon presents four rules of masculinity that are still a cornerstone of masculinities studies today:

- *No Sissy Stuff*: Never do anything that even remotely hints of femininity. "Real" men always steer clear of *any* behavior or characteristic associated with women.

- *Be a Big Wheel*: Masculinity is measured by success, power, and the admiration of others. Consequently, men need wealth, renown, and prestige to be identified as "real" men.

- *Be a Sturdy Oak*: Manliness requires rationality, toughness, and self-reliance. A man must remain calm in any situation, show no emotion, and admit no weakness.

- *Give 'em Hell*: Men must exude an aura of daring and aggression, must be willing to take risks and "go for it" even when reason and fear suggest otherwise.

Brannon's description of the male gender role was a key to unlocking the door to men's liberation, as has been the collective work of Joseph Pleck, William Pollack, Ronald Levant, Terrence Real, Dan Kindlon, and Michael Thompson. Feminists who were breaking free of the shackles that had held women back for—well, forever—had implicitly invited men to do the same, even though most men were not even aware of their shackles. In those early days, women had neither the time nor the inclination to show men the door— we were going to have to find it on our own. For those who *did* find it, our awakening came with many small "aha" moments rather than one enormous "Eureka!" The most significant awareness that men came up with was this: *There is no single way to be a man.* Although perhaps obvious today, it was a subversive notion at a time when the socially sanctioned standard for manhood was heterosexuality and whiteness. (The term *masculinities* was not then part of the vernacular.)

In the 1970s, when men heard the word *patriarchy*—a social system that is male dominated, male identified, male centered, and organized around an obsession with control that is gendered masculine—being spoken in the women's movement lexicon of oppression, most men became defensive, not hearing that it was the *system* of patriarchy women were challenging, not necessarily men individually. Women believed patriarchy was bad for men too, and that individual men were not personally responsible for its existence. In 1973, a decade after writing *The Feminine Mystique,* Betty Friedan observed "that men weren't really the enemy—they were fellow victims, suffering an outmoded masculine mystique... " That didn't mean, men quickly learned, that standing by silently rather than actively challenging a system that privileged males was still an option. While they may quibble about many other issues, profeminist activists, academics, and psychologists all agree that men's liberation has to begin with a critical examination of the considerable benefits and entitlements men receive simply for arriving on the planet in male-identified bodies.

In every decade since, feminist women have regularly invited men to join them, from a Gloria Steinem op-ed in the *Washington Post* on June 7, 1970, "Women's Liberation Aims to Free Men, Too" to the present day's "Feminism Needs Men, Too," an article Lauren Rankin wrote for policymic.com that appeared on May 14, 2013. "Ending the patriarchal oppression of women is good for men. Patriarchy doesn't just privilege men over women, but privileges certain kinds of men and certain kinds of masculinity," Rankin wrote. "*Feminism works to free both men and women from the gender binary that imposes a strict set of acceptable gender performances*" [emphasis added].

At the same time profeminist men's work was taking root, a different kind of men's movement activity was emerging in the late 1980s and early 1990s: retreats expressly focusing on men's impoverished inner lives. Unfortunately, those personally important explorations—which got plenty of publicity—typically neglected the reality of (white) men's economic, social, and political power over women, and the deep cultural misogyny that justified it. Instead, most of those seekers, sometimes referred to as the mythopoetic branch of the men's movement, engaged in an often-painful emotional inventory in considering their personal lives, especially their relationships (or lack thereof) with their fathers and other men. This was, and remains, important emotional work. But many of these men failed to consider that their personal experiences of sadness and loss—and often violence—were directly connected to the system of male dominance and the narrow definitions of manhood it produces. Even worse, many of these men refused to join in efforts to challenge men's violence against women and children; some even went so far as to say (absurdly) that men were the "true" victims of sexism, and began organizing the nascent "men's/fathers' rights movement," which sought to fight feminist reforms on everything from rape laws to child custody issues and sexual harassment policies in the workplace.

While Robert Bly was getting the headlines leading retreats, publishing *Iron John*, and appearing on *Bill Moyers Journal*, profeminist men were educating themselves about domestic violence and sexual assault and beginning to talk with one another about the changing gender landscape they were trying to navigate. The genuine inner growth work many men in the mythopoetic men's movement were engaged in had merit—as far as it went. Looking back, some men I've spoken with have acknowledged that they were more focused on their personal growth than on weaving that growth into the fabric of greater social change, particularly as it affected the women in their lives. In the 1990s, asking leaders of the mythopoetic men's movement to focus on social justice would have required a sobering examination of male privilege, an inquiry most were reluctant to undertake. In recent years, the ManKind Project (formerly known as the New Warriors), a group that grew out of the mythopoetic men's movement, has begun to integrate gender justice concerns into its overall philosophy.

As an organization with a comprehensive approach to working with men, the Amherst, Massachusetts-based Men's Resource Center (MRC)—the center where I worked for so many years—is emblematic of the wide-ranging vision emanating from the profeminist men's movement. With a philosophy that supported men engaging in personal growth work without abdicating responsibility to address the epidemic of men's violence against women, the center worked with a cross-section of men—from groups for those seeking connection and support to a specific program for men acting abusively.

The twin aims of the organization, supporting men and challenging men's violence, seem contradictory. How can you both support men and challenge them? For the Men's Resource Center, there was no inconsistency; it was two wings of the same dove. "Of course we care about men," we would answer skeptics. "It's why we run batterer groups for men who act abusively *and* support groups for men who don't."

Because the Men's Resource Center was more a social change organization than a social service agency, on the same morning that the batterers' intervention program staff was meeting to discuss individual men's progress (or lack thereof), or fielding a call from a man in crisis searching for a support group, we also might be soliciting signatures from men in the community for a Valentine's Day newspaper ad redefining the holiday as a time to celebrate respectful and peaceful relationships. While we didn't explicitly advertise our approach, it was based on an innate understanding that the personal is political. We weren't alone.

At men's centers and gender justice organizations in North America and around the globe, men like Rus Funk of Menswork in Louisville, Kentucky, and Chuck Derry of the Gender Violence Institute in Clearwater, Minnesota, operate from a similar ethos. The particulars may vary from state to state and culture to culture, but the spirit of hope and camaraderie shared between female and male gender justice activists is ubiquitous. In its collective vision of gender equality, whether in Rio or Cape Town, Mexico City or Delhi, Toronto or Austin, "the personal is political" remains the operating principle, the guiding star by which profeminist men and their allies navigate.

As you make your way through this book, hold ever-present the image of the "man box"—the restrictive set of rules and expectations (be tough, strong, don't cry…)—that men around the world are coming together in greater numbers to dismantle once and for all. What profeminist men's work has contributed to the gender justice movement is a way out of the box. Once free from these pressures and false expectations, men can begin to see themselves as responsible, accountable, loving partners and husbands, sons and brothers, mentors and allies. The possibilities for self-care increase with the capacity to feel love and connection more than fear and isolation.

The male writers whose stories you'll read in this collection, in one way or another, have left the box. While some may have left sooner than others, all have considerable tools at their disposal. At the 2009 Engaging Men symposium in Rio there was an exhilarating moment when the gathering's "Call to Action" was shared with delegates. It includes these hopeful words:

> We speak many languages, we look like the diverse peoples of the world and carry their diverse beliefs and religions, cultures, physical abilities, and sexual and gender identities. We are indigenous peoples, immigrants, and ones whose ancestors moved across the planet. We are fathers and mothers, daughters and sons, brothers and sisters, partners and lovers, husbands and wives. What unites us is our strong outrage at the inequality that still plagues the lives of women and girls, and the self-destructive demands we put on boys and men. But even more so, what brings us together here is a powerful sense of hope, expectation, and possibility, for we have seen the capacity of men and boys to change, to care, to cherish, to love passionately, and to work for justice for all.

As more men join in such a hopeful vision, each of us must begin by acknowledging how much power and control men still exercise in society today. Not a power we earned but one we were born into by virtue of arriving on a patriarchal planet in male bodies. Relinquishing our grip on power, privilege, and entitlement is at the core of building a profeminist men's movement. Men who are reluctant to embrace its message fear losing control, having less. Most of all, we fear the unknown. *"What will my life look like if I'm not in charge?"* we wonder. Is it asking too much to trust that our lives will be enriched in ways we can't yet imagine if we loosen our grip and share the reins, or— Goddess forbid—experience our lives with women holding them? Each of us has to answer that question for ourselves as we face the fear and the excitement such a notion evokes.

Even when women were angry and frustrated at men's resistance to giving up our privilege, entitlement, and obsession with control, they didn't give up on men. As the noted feminist theorist bell hooks wrote in her 2004 book, *The Will to Change: Men, Masculinity and Love,* " . . . only a feminist vision that embraces feminist masculinity, that loves boys and men and demands on their behalf every right that we desire for girls and women, can renew men in our society. . . "

The time is at hand for more men to join women. For close to half a century women have been redefining who they are and what they want. Listening to, learning from, and asking women questions—while listening to, learning from, and asking ourselves and other men questions—is essential to our happiness and fulfillment. What are we waiting for?

Where does the profeminist men's movement go from here? This much is clear: the movement is growing, younger men are joining, women and men are collaborating in greater numbers, and our voices are beginning to be heard above the mainstream din. (Every contemporary campaign for gender equality—from the fight to reauthorize the Violence Against Women Act to the international One Billion Rising! Campaign on Valentine's Day —has included a chorus of men's voices. Men are playing key roles in state domestic and sexual violence coalitions around the country, from the trainings and technical assistance of David Lee and Chad Keoni Sniffen at the California Coalition Against Sexual Assault to Emiliano Diaz de Leon's leadership at the Texas Association Against Sexual Assault. That's real progress. Still, among the places where men's voices are especially needed today is in the national conversation about violence—a conversation engaged with renewed urgency in the wake of the mass murders at Sandy Hook Elementary School in December 2012. We still have much to do, including ensuring that mass shooters' gender and race—male and white (with a few exceptions)—become central on the agenda of activists working for gun control.

In 2012, several hundred men, women, and transgender people gathered at a "Healthy Masculinity Summit" in Washington, DC, organized by Men Can Stop Rape, Women of Color Network, A CALL TO MEN, Men Stopping Violence, the National Resource Center on Domestic Violence, and Coach for America. A two-year action project committed to fostering a new generation of "nonviolent, emotionally healthy male leaders," its goal is to greatly increase the population of positive change-makers in society. In the aftermath of the Washington summit, a series of real and Twitter town halls took place, campus conversations began, and youth leadership summits convened. That is just one example of projects and initiatives under way in North America. There are dozens around the world—from MenCare, the global fatherhood effort operating in 25 countries in Asia, Africa, Latin America, and Europe promoting equitable, nonviolent, and caring parenting; to the One Man Can Campaign in South Africa and elsewhere on the African continent, which believes "one man can love passionately, stop AIDS, end domestic violence, break the cycle, demand justice, and stop rape." The organizations profiled in this chapter and the dozens of others listed in the resource section at the end of the book are an ongoing source of inspiration. Check them out. Get involved. Join—or start—campaigns for gender equality to ensure healthy lives for boys and girls in your own community or on your campus.

People who know me say I'm a glass-half-full person, even in the face of

MENENGAGE: As a global alliance established to engage boys and men to achieve gender equality, MenEngage coordinates a range of programs including the MenCare global fatherhood campaign. The 2013 MenCare meeting in Cape Town, South Africa, brought together 100 men and women from 25 participating countries to further promote men's participation as caregivers. Fom left, Gary Barker (Promundo-US), Pancho Aguayo (CulturaSalud, Chile), Douglas Mendoza (REDMAS, Nicaragua), and Michael Kaufman (Canada). *Photo by Sipho Mpongo*

a steady diet of news reports of men behaving badly. Every day we wake up to the bad news, even though there is so much good news to report. Wouldn't we all be buoyed knowing about the amazing work of so many organizations in so many social justice arenas? That certainly was a major motivation for this book—to share the inspiring story of "one of the most important social justice movements you've never heard of."

Just days before I finished this chapter, I was asked to contribute the Fathers' Day column for Eve Ensler's V-Day website. The piece I wrote, "Male Student Athletes: Newest Profeminist Allies," described 22 young men about to graduate from prep school who had just come out as gender justice advocates.

In a letter to the editor of the student newspaper at Phillips Academy, the prestigious private school these students attended in Andover, Massachusetts, lead author Tyler Olkowski, captain of the crew team, rejected the school's longstanding sexist male athlete tradition. He wrote that the tradition "has been tainted by . . . the objectification and sexism that pervade athlete culture. This culture may not be our fault, but it is our problem to fix." The letter went on to say, "The definition of 'cool' doesn't have to be a traditional masculine figure who objectifies [his] sexual partners or who climbs . . . social ladders through hook- ups."

Wow, I thought. This letter has swung open wide more than just the locker room door; it's opened a portal to the world of gender equality. When I read that the captain of the football team and the baseball team and the basketball team, and hockey, lacrosse, and track and cross-country—*every* sports team captain on campus—had signed the letter, I blinked back tears.

Here were entitled young, primarily white men about to head off to begin privileged lives as future captains of industry, rejecting one of the linchpins of conventional masculinity: male athlete culture. I was floored. *This* is what is possible for the profeminist men's movement. *This* is what the next generation of young men is capable of. Perhaps, I thought, I got the subtitle of the book wrong: the story of the profeminist men's movement *is* being told. Maybe I just hadn't known where to look. I am hopeful these young men will only deepen their commitment to gender equality over the years and will use their platform as male athlete-leaders to reach out to their peers. It's a momentous task they're taking on.

As the poet Rilke wrote more than a century ago, these young men will need to "live the questions" that are unfolding in their lives. They will need to "liv[e] along some distant day into the answers." They—and other young men around the world who are also finding their voices and their hearts—are the ones who will record the next chapter of the profeminist men's movement and who will tell the ongoing story of the transformation of manhood into something more egalitarian, nonviolent, and life affirming.

BOYS TO MEN

Tired of holding this pose?

Cultural conceptions and expectations of masculinity begin affecting men at increasingly young ages. Sports, video games, and cartoons are seen as vital parts of boyhood, but often they function as vessels for unhealthy masculinity. From playground politics to parental choices of toys, from young men's interactions with their female peers to adult mentors' hopes for young men, Boys to Men includes a variety of perspectives about how young men express and experience their masculinities and what parents, mentors, and authorities in the gender justice movement can do to help them develop in healthy directions.

The Journey to Healthy Manhood
By Steven Botkin
Summer 2002

Once upon a time there was a baby boy. When he was born, his whole being was intent upon one goal: the expression of his need for connection. His most powerful instincts were driving him toward intimate contact with another human being. There was no fear… and there was no shame. There was only the power of life reaching to be embraced.

This baby (if he was lucky) knew many moments of safe, loving connection with others. And in these moments his sense of himself in the world took root. Through this root sense of connection with the bigness of life flowed his power—to express his needs and desires, to reach out into the world, to be open with his true self.

The violation comes in many ways, but always as a profound shock. Sometimes it is physical: Smacking. Spanking. Whipping. Beating. Sexual invasion. Sometimes it is verbal: Belittling. Name-calling. Yelling. Screaming. Threats. And sometimes it comes in other forms: Neglect. Unrealistic demands. Witnessing violence or abuse. Hunger. Oppression.

And then, when his natural instinct is to express his pain and fear and reach for contact that will confirm the violation, the situation is made infinitely worse by the words "Stop whining," "It's for your own good," "It wasn't so bad," "It was your fault," "Don't tell anyone"—or even "It didn't happen." This is profoundly confusing. His need for connection is doubly violated: first in the acts of abuse, then in the minimizing and ridiculing of his response to them. Now there is fear, and there is shame. In these moments the boy is powerless to protect himself and unable to return to the comfort of connection.

Everywhere he turns, however, there is someone selling him a product they claim will make him powerful and protect him from being a victim ever again. As he looks around he sees many examples of other males using this product who seem to be in control of their lives, getting what they want, invulnerable to being hurt or mistreated. They appear to be revered by many and to have a mysterious connection of brotherhood with others who are using the same product. He also sees that other boys and men who do not use this product continue to be targeted for ridicule and abuse.

The product label says "Masculinity." It teaches him to find power in domination and control. He learns how to be stoical about pain, to hide any fear, and to show no shame. Anything or anyone that threatens this pretense of invulnerability must be controlled, suppressed, dominated into submission in order to maintain his sense of safety and power.

And the price for this product (yes, it's in the very small print) is that he must forfeit his birthright. In order to get the "benefits" of masculinity he must be silent about having ever been hurt or scared, and pretend that he does not really need connection. His sense of himself now becomes rooted in a disconnection from much of his own internal experience and from authentic intimate contact with others.

But the natural drive toward connection—perhaps the most powerful force in life—is never completely lost or forgotten. Even as the boy grows to be a man who is hiding himself behind the mask of masculinity, he is also searching for ways to express his deepest desire for connection. In each gesture of domination or control can also be found the agonized and distorted reaching for contact that is struggling to break through the legacy of hidden pain and fear.

And this is where a place like the Men's Resource Center comes into the story. We are the men with the legacy—telling this story about ourselves, remembering our birthright, reaching for connection, reclaiming our *true* selves. We are the men and women creating safety and support for others and ourselves to speak out about how violence and abuse have affected our lives. We are a community unmasking mass-marketed masculinity, exposing the lies of power as domination, and creating a culture of compassion and connection.

This is the journey to healthy masculinity. It is a journey that is both painful and joyous. None of us can (or really wants to) travel this path by ourselves. We can only find our way as men and women embracing together the full range of our genders, rooting our lives again in the true power of our connection to ourselves, one another, and life itself. Join us.

VOICE MALE

Searching for a New Boyhood
By Michael Kimmel
Winter 2000

There's no question that there's a boy crisis. Boys are four to five times more likely to kill themselves than girls, four times more likely to be diagnosed as emotionally disturbed, three times more likely to be diagnosed with attention deficit disorder, and 15 times more likely to the victims of violent crime. The debate concerns the nature of the crisis, its causes, and, of course, its remedies.

One voice in the debate, epitomized by therapist Michael Gurian (*A Fine Young Man, The Wonder of Boys*), suggests that boys are both doing worse than ever and doing worse than girls—thanks to feminists' efforts. Gurian argues that as feminists have changed the rules, they've made boys the problem. By minimizing the importance of basic biological differences, and establishing girls' standards as the ones all children must follow, feminists have wrecked boyhood.

To hear these critics tell it, we're no longer allowing boys to be boys. We've misunderstood boy biology, and cultural meddling—especially by misinformed women—won't change a thing. It's nature, not nurture, that propels boys toward obnoxious behavior, violence, and sadistic experiments on insects. What makes boys boys is, in a word, testosterone, that magical, catch-all hormone that drives them toward aggression and risk-taking, and challenging this fact gives them the message, Gurian says, that "boyhood is defective."

This facile biological determinism mars otherwise insightful observations. Gurian adroitly points out the nearly unbearable pressure on young boys to conform, to resort to violence to solve problems, to disrupt classroom decorum. But he thinks it's entirely due to biology—not peer culture, media violence, or parental influence. Steve Biddulph (*Raising Boys*) agrees: "Testosterone equals vitality," he writes. All we have to do is "honor it and steer it into healthy directions." This overreliance on biology leads both writers to overstate the difference between the sexes and ignore the differences among boys and among girls.

More chilling, though, are their strategies for intervention. Gurian suggests reviving corporal punishment both at home and at school—but only when administered privately with cool indifference and never in the heat of adult anger. (He calls it "spanking responsibly.") Biddulph, somewhat more moderately, advocates that boys start school a year later than girls, so they'll be on a par intellectually.

The problem is, there's plenty of evidence that boys are not "just boys" everywhere and in the same ways. If it's all biological, why aren't Norwegian or French or Swiss boys as violent, homophobic, and misogynist as many are in the US? Boys are not doomed to be victims of what Alan Alda once facetiously called "testosterone poisoning." They can become men who express their emotions and treat their partners respectfully, who listen as well as act, and who love and nurture their children.

But how do we get there? Another group of therapists, including Dan Kindlon and Michael Thompson (*Raising Cain*), and William Pollack (*Real Boys*), eschew testosterone-tinged testimonials and treat masculinity as an ideology to be challenged. For them, we need to understand the patterns of boys' development to more effectively intervene and set boys on the path to a manhood of integrity.

To do that, Kindlon and Thompson write, we must contend with the "culture of cruelty" that forces a boy to deny emotional neediness, "routinely disguise his feelings," and end up emotionally isolated. Pollack calls it the "Boy Code" and the "mask of masculinity"—a kind of swaggering attitude that boys embrace to hide their fears, suppress dependency and vulnerability, and present a stoic front.

Unfortunately, these therapists' explanations don't always track. For one thing, they all use examples drawn from their clinical practices but then generalize casually from their clients to all boys. And, alas, "all" is limited almost exclusively to middle-class, suburban white boys.

If all the boys are white and middle class, at least they're not all straight. Most therapists treat homosexuality by casually dropping in a brief reference, "explaining" it as biological, and urging compassion and understanding before returning to the more "important" stuff. Only Pollack devotes a sensitive and carefully thought-out chapter to homosexuality, and he actually uses the term "homophobia."

The cause of all this posturing and posing is not testosterone, of course, but privilege. In adolescence, both boys and girls get their first real dose of gender inequality, and that is what explains their different paths. Of the male therapists, only Pollack and James Gilligan (*Violence*) even seem to notice this. For the others, boys' troubles are all about fears suppressed, pain swallowed.

Books by Myriam Miedzian (*Boys Will Be Boys: Breaking the Link Between Masculinity and Violence*) and by Olga Silverstein and Beth Rashbaum (*The Courage to Raise Good Men*), published several years ago, offer critiques of traditional boyhood and well-conceived plans for support and change. These books see in feminism a blueprint for transforming both boyhood and manhood. Feminism encourages men—and their sons—to be more emotionally open and expressive, to develop empathic skills, and to channel emotional outbursts away from violence. And feminism demands the kinds of societal changes that make this growth possible.

The real boy crisis usually goes by another name. We call it "teen violence," "youth violence," "gang violence," "violence in the schools." Let's face facts: men and boys are responsible for 85 percent of all violent crimes in this country, and their victims are overwhelmingly male as well. From an early age, boys learn that violence is not only an acceptable form of conflict resolution but also one that is admired.

As their title, *Challenging Macho Values*, suggests, Jonathan Salisbury and David Jackson want to take issue with traditional masculinity, to disrupt the facile "boys will be boys" model, and to erode boys' sense of entitlement. And for Paul Kivel (*Boys Will Be Men*), raising boys to manhood means confronting racism, sexism, and homophobia—both in our communities and in ourselves. These books are loaded with hands-on practical advice to help adolescents raise issues, confront fears, and overcome anxieties, and to help teachers dispel myths, encourage cooperation, and discourage violent solutions to perceived problems. "We believe that masculine violence is intentional, deliberate, and purposeful," write Salisbury and Jackson. "It comes from an attempt by men and boys to create and sustain a system of masculine power and control that benefits them every minute of the day."

Gilligan and Miedzian, along with James Garbarino (*Lost Boys*), understand that the real boy crisis is a crisis of violence—specifically the cultural prescriptions that equate masculinity with the capacity for violence. Garbarino's fortuitously timed study of youthful offenders locates the origins of men's violence in the way boys swallow anger and hurt.

Gilligan is even more specific. In his insightful study of violence, he places its origins in "the fear of shame and ridicule, and the overbearing need to prevent others from laughing at oneself by making them weep instead." The belief that violence is manly is not carried on any chromosome, not soldered into the wiring of the right or left hemisphere, not juiced by testosterone. Boys learn it. Violence, Gilligan writes, "has far more to do with the cultural construction of manhood than it does with the hormonal substrates of biology."

That's where feminism comes in. Who, after all, has offered the most trenchant critique of that cultural construction but feminists? That's why the books by women and men that use a feminist perspective (Gilligan, Kivel, Miedzian, Pollack, Salisbury and Jackson, and Silverstein and Rashbaum) are far more convincing than those that either repudiate it (Gurian, Biddulph) or ignore it (Kindlon and Thompson).

Frankly, I think the antifeminists such as Gurian and Biddulph (and the right wing in general) are the real male bashers. When they say boys will be boys, they mean boys will be uncivilized animals. In their view, males are biologically propelled to be savage, predatory, sexually omnivorous creatures, hardwired for violence. As a man, I find this view insulting.

Feminists imagine, and demand, that men (and boys) can do better. Feminism offers the possibility of a new boyhood and a new masculinity based on a passion for justice, a love of equality, and the expression of a full range of feelings.

Yo, Boyz: It's About Respect
By Aviva Okun Emmons
Winter 2003

As a 17-year-old woman, an activist and feminist with parents who hold the same values, I grew up hearing that men could change—that they could stop acting inappropriately toward women and treating women badly; that they could learn to empower women and break out of stereotypical gender roles. I believe men can change too, but the fact is they haven't changed enough: at least not enough of them have changed, not yet.

I observe many different behaviors among my peers. Many of these are negative behaviors, which adults often criticize and characterize as being specific to the teenage years. As I have discovered, though, many of these behaviors continue on into adulthood. If not corrected early, they can develop into patterns that can be destructive to yourself and those with whom you interact.

What am I talking about? I'm talking about sexism. I'm talking about men. Boys. Guys. Dudes.

I'm talking about violence, name-calling, and degradation of women, domestic abuse, rape, sexist remarks, and the fear that these instill in women, ladies, sisters, chicks, babes, and girls. What you call yourself, or how others define you, doesn't matter here. The only thing that really matters is the fear. And it's got to stop.

Men make women afraid. That's what I'm talking about. They make me afraid. Passing a man on the street at night makes me afraid. The rapes that were reported at the University of Massachusetts three years ago still make me afraid. The fact that so many other rapes go unreported makes me afraid. The fact that so many women live with men who treat them poorly—or worse, violently—and that these women have no power to stop the abuse makes me afraid.

I feel caught in a double standard. All the facts and statistics, and even my gut intuition, tell me to fear men, but I don't want to. I believe that men are inherently good, kind, and humane and that they have been stereotyped as rapists, wife beaters, and sexual predators because of the small percentage of them who do these horrible things.

However, men do have the power in our society. That's an irrefutable, undeniable fact. And as the people with power, they can change these stereotypes and consequently make the world a safer place for women.

So here's what I'm asking. Men: you have the power to stop this cycle of fear and violence. Do it. Stop it. And keep in mind that taking steps toward safety also means taking steps away from abuse, assault, and the mistreatment of women. Challenge violence and aggression toward women wherever you see it. It comes in many forms and is often disguised as something as innocent as a joke or a passing comment. But these small incidences of sexism are what make this world an unsafe place for women. So be a role model for other men. Tell them their sexist jokes aren't funny, that you don't appreciate hearing women being degraded. Avoid situations where such talk may be going on. Or simply walk away from them. It's not always easy to intervene when this sort of conversation occurs; it's difficult to do in the heat of the moment. You make yourself vulnerable to ridicule and aggression directed at you for challenging it. But you've got to do it. Because the situation only gets worse when men cross lines of acceptable conduct and are not challenged or criticized for doing so.

Men learn from boyhood that sexist behavior is acceptable, and that there are no consequences for it. Then they grow up, become teenagers, and have girlfriends, friends who are girls, sisters, and female peers. And they think that it's acceptable to treat them as less than they are. To degrade them. To call them names. To objectify them. To criticize them. To hit them. To rape them. To kill them. And this is not acceptable! I won't stand for it. And neither should anyone else.

But men are only part of the problem. Women also need to change their perspective and their behavior. Every time women complain, "Men don't listen, they're impossible," or "All men are pigs. I hate men," or "All men want is sex," they are taking away men's opportunity to change, to improve, to make the world a safer place. Women are degrading men, saying that they aren't capable. And as long as they keep saying and believing it, men won't be capable. Instead, women need to encourage men, empower them to make the world a safer place. Women need to be the ones who say, "I was at a party and a man sat down with me and really listened and that felt great," or "My husband is so respectful of me and I really appreciate it and I tell him so." These kinds of responses are what will truly help to motivate men.

Although I've been referring to men and women, I also mean boys and girls, young people and teens. They need to get into the habit of treating each other with respect and taking responsibility for their actions and behaviors now.

For example, boys need to become aware of how they interact with girls, especially in a group setting. Sexist remarks and stares and jokes are degrading to a girl's self-esteem. Girls don't appreciate this type of behavior, and my guess is that many boys who observe this type of behavior exhibited by their male peers aren't thrilled with it either. Ignorance might be the excuse, but I think anyone with common sense knows by high school to treat people nicely, and this means with respect and decency. Also, in a group setting, people may not feel comfortable speaking up for fear of criticism. So boys, next time you are in mixed company, think before you say something crude or inappropriate—you might be offending a friend.

Negative, derogatory behavior or speech makes girls feel unsafe. We feel lost and unheard. Taking an active role as the whistleblower for sexist conduct can be a helpful thing for your girl friends who may not feel safe to do it themselves. This can make a huge difference in the way girls experience their high school social circles and helps both sexes move toward interacting on a more meaningful level, to get beyond how people look and act and get to what they're thinking.

Don't misunderstand: I'm not saying all guys are bad people who treat girls like trash. I am saying that some do and that I don't like it. I would really appreciate if other guys noticed this and did something about it—it would make high school a much cooler place to be.

I have hope that this cycle can be broken, and that young men and boys won't keep carrying sexist attitudes and behaviors into adulthood. Hearing boys say, "Hey, that's not cool, man," to their buddies, and hearing girls advocating for how they want to be treated fills me with optimism. But we all need to speak up: boys and men, women and girls. We need to stop perpetuating the old patterns, and work to make the world a safer place for all of us.

Getting Out of the Man Box
By Doug Ginn
Winter 2001

Last year, a female cofacilitator and I were leading a discussion on gender roles with a group of white, lower- to middle-class, high-school-age boys. Our first activity was to brainstorm what it meant to "act like a man." On a sheet of newsprint we wrote their suggestions inside a square box, which we said represented the traditional view of masculinity. Around the box, we wrote the consequences a man might face if he tried to step out of the "box of conformity." The result? Name-calling, threats, and violence: these kids knew what was up. They were becoming men in the same culture that produced me. Misogyny, homophobia, and even violence were a part of life. This state of affairs seemed natural to them.

For the rest of the session, we discussed the ways gender roles are reinforced. I kept emphasizing the box as a visual metaphor to show how dominant white masculinity is confining and rigid—besides being dangerous and destructive. Through the exercise, I hoped these teenage boys might glimpse what it was like to transgress their gender, to see the possibilities doing so opens. After a while, one of the older boys said something that shook the ground beneath my soapbox and made the square, visual metaphor on the newsprint behind me seem irrelevant. "I don't know," he said, "I kind of like being inside the box."

Yes, he admitted, "acting like a man" meant you often had to seek out danger to prove yourself, but the danger could be fun. Yeah, you had to disrespect girls and gays with your friends, but that's how you got to be a part of their clique. Most important, acting like a man gave you power and privileges in this society that were withheld from most other groups of people. Despite the fact that "being a man" meant dominating others and never showing vulnerability, the payoff, for this teenage male anyway, was still worth it. And, as it turned out for the group, he was not alone in feeling that way.

Only four years earlier, I had been in the same place as he was—uncertain about the world but grasping for some way of explaining it. In those four years, I have gone through many transformations; I still am, as it's an ongoing process. Yet somewhere along the line, I forgot what it was like to be numb to the pain of others. This boy's comment triggered memories of being a desensitized teenager, struggling to feel in a desensitizing culture.

My parents did as much as they could to teach me about the world and the importance of caring for other people. They tried to explain why violence was never the answer, that there was never an excuse for violence against women, that you should always respect those with different lifestyles and opinions. I am the man I am today because of them—but the hardest part of the journey had to be walked alone. There wasn't much my parents could do for me between junior high and high school. I didn't want to be shielded anymore. I wanted to stand on my own two feet, and that meant walking face-first into the oncoming wave of adolescence.

The media landscape through which I wandered was relatively the same as the one this group of teenage boys was experiencing. It's a world where society is corrupt and everyone screws everyone, so you might as well get yours while you can. The only thing that really matters is being hyper-cool. Any sort of brutality can be made acceptable if it's sexy enough. This world isn't much different from the one that most adults inhabit every day, but adults have other things to occupy their minds—paying the bills, raising kids, trying to be good role models. For young people, this corrupt world is our whole world.

We don't immediately accept it, of course. We want to believe that there is goodness in the world, but the positive role models get fewer and fewer the further we get from the world of our parents. At first, "polite society" filled me with rage because it stank of falseness, but the only outlet for this rage was mediated (and medicated)—through TV, music, and movies. The violence had to be extreme, the sex ultra-raunchy, and the music aggressive and loud. The more cracks that appeared in society's civilized facade, the more jaded I made myself. Eventually, it became a source of pride. Anyone who still cared about "saving the world" was naïve and open to ridicule. Now I can see this whole process happening at an even earlier age as I watch young people growing up.

The flipside to this depressing tale is that I eventually grew tired of being unable to feel any real emotions. The power and privilege that came from staying "inside the box" felt hollow. I wanted to try being something other than ultra-jaded and hyper-cool. When I got to college, studying history, theory, and politics stirred up the embers in my stomach, and as passion returned to my heart, I found a healthy outlet working with organizations dedicated to social change—not on a fly-by-night basis but as a long-term project spanning, I hope, the rest of my life.

Too few young adults get the chance to explore the opportunities college offers, and many young men who do get to college have already grown too accustomed to the "box" of masculinity to be able to give it up. To seriously challenge sexism, instead of just preaching, we need to acknowledge how difficult it is for young boys to adopt any other persona but the traditional, dominant, masculine one. There have to be outlets for young boys to channel their anger into healthier forms of expression, and we need to mitigate that anger by honestly engaging with them from a very early age. Most important, men, and especially young men, need to set the example of a masculinity that is lived "outside the box."

Wanted: Young White Guy to Change the World

By Ethan Smith
Summer 2004

So, what are your plans?"

That's probably the most common question I hear these days, having graduated from college a few weeks ago. Some of my friends are going to graduate school, some are working for Teach for America; one is a preschool teacher. This summer, I'm painting houses. After August, I have no plans.

I have a unique situation, an extremely privileged situation. I have an undergraduate degree, very little debt, a family that doesn't need me financially, and at the moment, health care. I've worked hard, but there is no doubt in my mind that my privilege as a white, middle-class male has helped me get to where I am.

I may not have any specific plans, but I do have some guiding principles. It sounds like a cliché, but I want to change the world. (The older I get, the more clichés make sense to me.) Leaving the protective bubble of college in 2004, I see lots of possibility, as well as a world very different from one that most of us would want to live in. I see violence on levels from personal to international; I see the largest amount of economic inequality ever; I see ecological disaster, present and future; I see oppression based on a number of social categories; I see unaccountable government, increasing corporate control, and media manipulation.

I want to help end all inequality and oppression, whether based on race, class, gender, sexuality, ability, state control, or any and all other systems of hierarchy. I want to see significant, fundamental change on a societal level. I want to work toward a world based on cooperation rather than competition, love rather than fear, community rather than isolation.

So I looked in the Help Wanted section of the newspaper. There were no headings or entries under "Revolutionary." I also checked "Freedom fighter," "Ally," and "Pro-feminist, antiracist, anticapitalist, antistatist, freedom- and peace-loving anarchist." Nothing there, either. Apparently there is more demand for jobs that keep the capitalist engine running than for social change mechanics to dismantle it. How come I can't find an ad that reads, "Wanted: Young white guy to be an ally in the struggle against white supremacy. Work with dedicated staff to end police brutality, abolish the prison system, create economic equality, and further revolution. $20K starting salary, full benefits. Call Bill at 617-555-7206?"

The problem is, the more change I want to make in the world, the harder it seems to get paid to do that work.

The challenge I see for myself is to take the privilege that I have and try to create the greatest amount of positive change while doing something I enjoy. Not everyone has the ability to do something they enjoy, and I don't expect to be enjoying myself every minute of the day. Along the lines of the saying attributed to Ghandi—"Be the change you want to see in the world"—I'm going to try not to hate my life and my work.

There are opportunities. There are "social profit" groups that do great work. There are community groups I can join, regardless of my work. There are lessons to be learned from those who have been at this crossroads before. I also have the tools and energy to be creative and chart a new course. There are an infinite number of ways to change the world every day. It is a challenge to figure out how to make a living this way. However, if this is my greatest challenge, so be it.

Call me naïve. Call me idealistic. In 10 years maybe I'll reread this, shake my head, and eat my words. In the meantime, however, this is an important time of decision for me, and for many of my peers who are serious and passionate about social and environmental justice. We look up to the generations before us, and we look beyond them, because as the Commencement Day cliché goes, we are the future.

So, do I have any plans? Well, I'm working on it. I might go to Guatemala and learn Spanish, then take auto repair classes and be a profeminist mechanic. The truth is, I've got nothing planned, and everything planned at the same time. In two weeks I might have it all laid out, or I still might have no idea in

20 years. Wherever I end up, I will keep the principles of equality and freedom close to me . . . and maybe a copy of the Help Wanted section as well.

Postscript: Nine years later, this still resonates with me, and I'm also shaking my head at myself. Figuring out how to survive within capitalism and work for change is important, and I find myself critiquing the tone of this piece and the expectation I had that it should be easy for me to find paid activist work. Today, I remain excited about my work for radical social justice, including helping to run an abolitionist organization supporting LGBTQ people in prison, working to end domestic violence, supporting local farmers, and organizing with my union. I also very much enjoy my paid work as a nurse.

The Reader's Double Standard
By Randy Flood
Summer 2010

Where was the outrage when an adult woman is depicted having sex with an adolescent boy, as was the case in *The Reader,* the 2009 Academy Award-winning movie? Was there none because of our culture's gender-constructed ideas about sexuality? For adolescent boys, it may be considered titillating—and a big compliment—to be seduced by an older woman. It's every teenage boy's fantasy, right? But when it comes to examining the implications of an adult woman initiating sex with an adolescent boy, conversation comes to a near standstill, more often dismissed or minimized than thoroughly discussed.

The Reader tells the story of Michael Berg (David Kross plays the adolescent; Ralph Fiennes, the adult), a German lawyer who, as a teenager in the late 1950s, is sexually seduced by an older woman, Hanna Schmitz (Kate Winslet). Hanna disappears only to resurface years later as one of the defendants in a war crimes trial stemming from her actions as a guard at a Nazi concentration camp in the later years of World War II.

A benevolent, lonely woman seeking connection, closeness, and intimacy, Hanna finds it with Michael. Her Achilles heel is that she is illiterate, a sharp contrast with well educated Michael who "entertains" her by reading aloud. In the world of emotions it is Michael who is illiterate and vulnerable—just as he is also horny and sexually inexperienced. Older, more powerful, wiser, and skilled sexually, Hanna initiates a "relationship" that is depicted as acceptable, even romantic; some saw it as a unique, endearing love story.

Missing from any serious consideration of the film is the toll this emotionally lopsided "affair" might have had on the young man, in large part because of society's gender-constructed views about sexuality. The audience gets a peak at how hurt and sad Michael is after Hanna temporarily rejects him. As his preoccupation with the sex they're having grows, he becomes estranged from his age-appropriate peers. He forgoes swimming and other fun adolescent activities with his friends for clandestine afternoon sexual escapades. This leads to lateness at family dinners and uncomfortable silences during meals as he tries to make sense of this powerful, exciting, and confusing experience on his own. When Hanna suddenly departs, Michael feels abandoned.

Years later, Michael encounters Hanna when his law school class attends her Nazi war crimes trial. He sits in the courtroom isolated, in emotional agony. He refuses to let any of his classmates or professors reach him, donning impenetrable, emotional armor. He keeps his dark secret sequestered in the caverns of his soul, casting an ominous, harmful shadow across his life.

When we see Michael years later, he is going through a divorce caused, we're led to believe, by his emotional closedness, aloofness, and inner pain. The audience sees some of the seismic damage done to Michael, but only glimpses—subtle, ancillary, not part of any substantive commentary the film makes. As Michael's life demonstrates, although boys may not cry out and tell us about their inner turmoil, what happens to them over time is their legacy.

Imagine the outrage—and the national conversation that would have ensued—if the gender roles had been reversed: an adult male and female adolescent! The discussion would most likely have focused on the inappropriateness of the sexual relationship, the inherent power differential, statutory rape concerns, the manipulative and offensive predation of the adult male, and the insidious negative impact on the adolescent female—an impact we'd presume she'd carry throughout her life. Rather than the subtle societal ethos that suggests perhaps he was lucky to have been sexually "mentored" by an adult female. Feminist analysis and commentary may well have undermined the film's momentum and stunted its popularity.

That's what should have happened, but instead *The Reader* was acclaimed. In fact, Kate Winslet's poignant performance won her an Academy Award for best actress. Besides the blatant double standard, what is the message here? Society has a long distance to travel if we are to understand the emotional reality and naked vulnerability at the core of male sexuality and adolescent posturing. Despite their unconcealed sexual energy, adolescent males need no less respect and protection than do adolescent females.

It matters little that society says male socialization promotes men's emotional invulnerability. Younger males—indeed, all males—remain vulnerable regardless of what tough guise they may strike. Just because some boys want to drive cars fast, binge on alcohol, and skip school at 15 does not mean society should allow or condone that behavior. Just the opposite. Just because some men want to exploit adolescent girls sexually, there is still a social—and moral—imperative to protect these girls. It's pretty basic: adults have a responsibility to provide a safe and healthy environment for our children until they are old enough or mature enough to do so for themselves.

While real life provides laws and policies designed to protect girls and boys, when it comes to enforcing our cultural ethos, society's gendered view of sexuality undermines enforcing such laws equally. Try as popular culture might to use its many forms—in this case, cinema—to seek to normalize adult female sexual predatory behavior against adolescent boys, in the end it adds no more to creating a healthy and safe environment than going to Hooters does to offering a nutritious, healthy meal.

Where is the outrage? Where is the demand that society protect *all* adolescents from sexual predators—boys and girls alike?

Leaving the Team, Becoming a Man
By Nathan Einschlag
Winter 2007

Growing up in New York City in the immigrant neighborhood of Jackson Heights, Queens, by the time I was 21 I had seen things many young people have only read about or seen on television. I saw young abused girlfriends pushing strollers on the way to the local elementary school to pick up their kids. It was routine to pass prostitutes on my way to the subway late at night. I knew what happened to the drug and alcohol abusers in the 'hood: they died. I was from a neighborhood where I'd trained my senses to be aware, to stay out of harm's way. I always watched a block ahead, spotting shadows, keeping my distance from men on the corners. I walked with my head up and a swagger that can only be learned in New York City.

I made a decision when I was young to stay focused, to not be dragged into the street life. I put my heart and soul into basketball, and the senses I had honed walking those late-night blocks all my life would not fail me. It was love. Basketball embraced me and I embraced it. Sophomore year I made the varsity basketball team at Fiorello H. LaGuardia High School of Music & Art and Performing Arts. As a junior and senior I was a starter. In my senior year, the team won the division championship. It was a high point in my life, right there at the end of high school. What would leaving the city and going to college bring?

I was going to a small liberal arts college in Baltimore where I expected to walk onto the men's Division III basketball team. I thought I was ready. I had no idea that college would be so much different from high school. Things changed drastically for me my freshman year.

Girls approached me all the time. Drunk girls. Eyeliner girls, with eyes half shut, balancing red plastic cups full of beer. Those same girls would be all over the lacrosse players, who would call them sluts later that week. Girls didn't see the guy I was, just a freshman trying to get to know people. They saw the basketball logo and didn't need to know anything more about me. They thought I must be like all the other guys who pushed up the girls' skirts as they walked by or pretended to trip while grabbing girls' breasts.

"Dude, get a drink, stop being so uptight," those guys would say. I didn't want a fucking drink. Where were the kids who wanted to listen to music and get on the dance floor?

I once came back to my room and had to step over two girls lying on the floor in the hallway. They could have been waiting for me, or for anyone who walked by and was interested in quick, easy sex. College was nothing like I had expected.

The kids on my high school team were among the most creative and talented teenagers in New York City. We didn't pound 40s on a Monday night. We didn't drive drunk for fun. All we needed was a ball and a court. Nothing made us happier. Off the court we argued about who had the flyest sneakers or who was a better rapper, Nas or Jay-Z.

We didn't buy 16-ounce Miller Lites instead of 8-ounce cans, so the girls would get drunker from the doubled alcohol level. "The girls don't notice," my college teammates assured me. It wasn't fun for me to hear male dancers at my school called fags. I wasn't enjoying being affiliated with the team. To outsiders looking in, I appeared to be nothing more than a freshman on the basketball team who needed to be broken in. When I turned down drinks, girls would ask my teammates what was wrong with me, why was I such a weirdo. They called me that because I would not objectify them. The gender roles at my school were like nothing I'd experienced. Girls were doing male athletes' laundry while the players poured beer on them and called them names. Bitch. Slut.

One day it just hit me; I understood. Everything I had questions about, everything I had been stressed about for a year and a half of my life, finally seemed to have an answer. I simply wasn't like them. I stuck out like a weed in concrete. In the locker room, on the basketball court, in the words I spoke, by my actions. Everything about me was different. I saw things differently. I was from a different place. Mama done raised me different.

To make matters worse, my coach was not playing me. He hadn't seemed to take a liking to me either. At practice I was serious and I listened, two qualities I had learned from playing on other teams. The other freshmen were rowdy and rude. Some upperclassmen were hotheaded and didn't look Coach in the eye when he talked to them. It was weird for me to watch this happen, but he seemed to respond well to their bad behavior. He took my silence as a sign that I was lethargic, unmotivated. I had such desire to play, but my coach would decide instead to question my masculinity. "I need to HEAR you, NATE! TALK LOUDER!" he'd yell. "GODDAMMIT! SCREAM! . . . SOMETHING!"

Off the court people treated me differently, too. "Dude, if you weren't on the team I'd probably make fun of you too. Fuck it, though. You're cool. Bitches seem to like you." Thankfully, girls did show me attention. At least I was a cute weirdo, on the basketball team, and not some freak fag like a theater major. I couldn't tell my teammates that I was minoring in theater. I didn't need to give them any more ammunition.

I loved basketball, but it was ruining my life. At the time my desire to play was overwhelming. I wanted to show Coach that basketball was my priority. I stopped telling him I'd have to miss practice for tutoring sessions or class requirements. Often I would show up at study groups late, still sweaty from practice. I'd convince the ushers at the theater to let me in late. I feared missing practice.

Coach seemed to love most of his players' attitudes. They were rich kids who didn't think about their parents' money or care too much about education. Their father's business would hire them, so what did a C- or a D+ here or there matter? My priorities were different. I didn't have time to stay and bullshit about "bitches and beer" in the locker room. I didn't care if Susan was wearing a low-cut shirt today in Philosophy, or that she almost fell down the stairs last night at the soccer party. It wasn't their fault that they gave her the beer. No one told her to drink so much. This is college, not kindergarten. I had reading to get done; I had papers to write. I always felt like the odd man out, but now I started not to care. This isn't what I wanted from a basketball team. I didn't feel a part of a team, even if the school saw and treated me like I was. Something was changing; it was me.

I'd talk to old friends on the phone about school. I'd lie and tell them things were going well, I was adjusting fine. The next party I went to, I bought in for a red plastic cup. It was soon full of beer. Maybe they're right, and I do need to loosen up, I thought. I had practice late the next day and wouldn't have to worry about being hungover. If I teased a few girls that night, cursed and yelled, tried to be like one of the guys, maybe I'd finally get some playing time. If Coach saw that the guys liked me more, maybe he'd take notice of my game and play me more.

Not only was I slow in practice the next day, but Coach laid into me extra hard. The guys didn't see me in any new light, and I still felt like the odd man out. Nothing was going to change the situation I was in. My teammates were sexist and ignorant. It would be so easy to be like them. I could just kick back, get wasted, and blame my actions on intoxication. But I wasn't about to let that happen. I would make a decision that would have important consequences, and it would cost me one of the things I held closest to my heart.

I quit the basketball team after a year and a half. Feeling more comfortable at school now, I shed the basketball reputation. I am no longer the cute weirdo athlete on campus but Nate, "the quiet kid who I see in the library who is gonna be in the play next week." The girls are a little shyer when they approach me now, especially the ones from the parties I used to go to. I'm not like the other guys and they feel embarrassed and a little ashamed. I still hear them whispering about when I was on the team and what they thought I was like, but I also hear the truth now. "That's Nate. He's such a man."

Had I known what a shock I was going to be in for when I started college, I would not have stayed quiet around my teammates' unruliness and obnoxious behavior. Had I understood the hypermasculine jock culture that existed in Division III sports before I joined the team, I would have promised myself that I'd be more vocal, challenging the things my teammates thought were fun.

But I was silent; I let people categorize me, let them think I had the same beliefs and interests as the guys on my team. I never told my coach how I felt until the day I quit the team. He'd had the wrong impression about me, about how to approach me. I will always look back and wish I had been more honest with my teammates and the staff about how I was feeling.

Still, I will also look back at my college basketball career as one of the most influential times of my life. I learned more about myself during that year and a half of struggle than I did during my entire life before that. By turning my time on the team into a learning experience, and growing from that experience, I know I made the right decision to leave college basketball. Have the athletes at my school stopped their sexist behavior? No. But by sticking to my principles and not letting people categorize me I was able to succeed in fighting gender stereotypes with my words and my actions, and to show that there is another way for men to be.

Coaching Our Kids
By Michael Messner
Spring 2009

Campbell Weber is a single, divorced father who coaches his thirteen-year-old son Robbie's Little League baseball team. When I asked him if he would coach again the next year, for what would be Robbie's final year in Little League, he thoughtfully considered the meaning and importance of his doing so: "I'll only coach if Robbie wants me to—if he's embarrassed, I won't do it. But I'd really like to. This year would be my last year, because next year he'll be in high school, so I'm treasuring this time that I can spend with him. I'm not a well-off man, so the only thing that I'm leaving Robbie is the time that I spend with him, and that's really important to me. My dad died when I was sixteen and I was at boarding school, and I didn't get to do things with him; he wasn't a go-out-and-do-things kind of guy. We never went out and threw the baseball around, that sort of thing. I've made sure that Robbie and I do a lot of stuff together, because those are the memories he's gonna have. And that's what he gets."

When Campbell Weber punctuated his statement with the words, "And that's what he gets," it gave me a sad stab of recognition and memory. My own father had a very successful public life as a high school teacher, a coach, and a naval officer. He was very busy, so I spent far more time with my mom and sisters than I did with him. His relative absence from my life added tremendous emotional salience to the rare moments I did get to spend with him, and many of those moments were organized around sports.

I am a father now, too. Both of my sons are in their teens, but when they were younger they both played community-based youth sports. Stepping onto a soccer field, a basketball court, or (especially) a Little League baseball field with my sons immediately brought up visceral feelings and what felt like ancient memories. I felt a sense of continuity that stretched from my father, who died many years ago, through me and to my sons. I wanted the playing field to be a place where I could connect with my sons, though I did not want it to be *the only place*, or even necessarily the most important place.

I experienced these continuities from my childhood against a shifting backdrop; something fundamental had changed since I was a boy. Now there were girls—scores of them, hundreds of them—out there on our community's playing fields. Unlike my childhood in the 1950s and 1960s, when there were almost no opportunities for girls to play sports, today millions of girls participate in organized soccer, baseball, softball, basketball, and other sports. This, to me, is one of the many positive achievements of the feminist movement, during my lifetime.

Another apparent change struck me when we arrived at our then-six-year-old son Miles' first soccer practice: I was delighted to learn that his coach was a woman. Coach Karen, a mother in her mid-thirties, had grown up playing lots of sports. She was tall, confident, and athletic, and the kids responded well to her leadership. "Great, a woman coach!" I observed cheerily. "It's a new and different world than the one that I grew up in."

But over the next twelve years, as I traversed many seasons of youth sports with Miles and eventually with his younger brother, Sasha, we never had another woman head coach. It's not that women weren't contributing to the kids' teams. All of the "team parents" (often called "team moms")—parent volunteers who did the behind-the-scenes work of phone-calling, organizing weekly snack schedules and team parties, collecting money for a gift for the coaches—were women.

Women head coaches were few and far between. This stimulated the feminist researcher in me. How is it possible in this day and age, I wondered, that only 13 percent of the soccer coaches, and 6 percent of the baseball and softball coaches are women? Why was it that the women coaches were clustered around girls' teams and around the very youngest kids teams? And why did most women coach for just one year before quitting? This began for me a seven-year-long research project that explored the gender and family dynamics of youth sports coaches in my community.

Watching, and especially listening to the voices of women coaches, I learned a great deal about how an "old boy's network" makes it very difficult for women to break in to coaching, and how informal (and I am convinced, mostly unconscious) words and actions by male coaches make youth sports coaching a chilly, unwelcome climate for the few women who do coach. As you move up past coaching five-, six-, and seven-year-olds and begin to enter the intermediate and older age groups, the coaches told me, everything gets more "serious." As coaches increasingly emphasize winning, they yell at the kids more, adopt more extreme "drill sergeant" styles on the playing fields, use their bodies and voices in more intimidating ways, and most of the women coaches bail out.

More than one woman coach who quit, or cycled back to remain working with the youngest kids, told me, "I just couldn't take that." But here is the surprise I learned through my research: a lot of the men coaches couldn't take it either. The women coaches think that all of the men are uniformly "confident" in coaching. To be sure, women coaches are subjected to a great deal of gender-based scrutiny—"Is she really qualified to coach my son?"—and male coaches are usually just assumed to know what they are doing, until they prove otherwise. However, many men reported to me that they felt insecure about taking on such a public position in their kids' lives. And several told me that they opted out of coaching the older kids' teams for precisely the same reasons that the women had dropped out. When it got "too serious," when the values of the league shifted toward narrow conceptions of toughness, competition, and winning, many men bailed out, just as had most of the women. Will Solomon, a baseball coach with lots of sports experience, told me "there's no way" he would go on to coach his son's baseball team at the twelve-year-old age level.

"It gets so *serious* at that level," he said. I had observed Will to be a fun and supportive coach, very low-key and good with all the kids. I especially appreciated his style because my son Sasha had had a less than successful season before playing on Will's team. Suddenly, Sasha was swinging the bat better and making good consistent contact, sometimes ripping solid line drive hits. It seemed to me that Sasha was just more relaxed, looser, and I attributed that to the lower pressure, the fun atmosphere that Will had created on the team. I asked Will if he intended to volunteer to coach the next season, and his response was unequivocal: "Ha! There's no way I'll coach in the majors next spring. Anyway, I doubt they'd have me." When I asked him why, he said, "I figure I'd be considered not serious enough." "I don't get it," I said, "you are a great coach, and I'm not sure too many people in town have more sports experience than you." "I guess it's a couple of things," he explained. "One, I don't think they'd want me to because I'm not as focused on the baseball side of it as I am on the sort of kids side of it, and I think [in the majors] they start to get real serious about the baseball side. And the other thing is that there does form sort of a club among these coaches at the major league level which I didn't see at the [younger kids'] level. So I think probably they wouldn't want me, you know. I mean the kids would. But the coaches, the powers-that-be wouldn't."

Will Solomon's words illustrated a clear pattern that emerged in my years of research. At the younger levels, there is more elbow room for coaches—men and some women—to deploy what I call "kids' knowledge" as the underlying philosophy of their coaching strategies. As the kids get older, coaches move very noticeably to what I call "sports knowledge." This transformation radically shifts the kids' playing experiences away from a "kids knowledge" emphasis on universal participation, trying out different positions, having fun, engaging in healthy exercise, and learning to cooperate with teammates. The shift to a "sports knowledge" value system shifts the kids' experience toward a focus on perfecting skills, strategic attempts to win games and championships, aggressive competition, a decline in empathy when a kid gets hurt, specialization of kids' roles on teams, and the emergence of a star system that marginalizes the less skilled kids. This values shift—and the way it's embodied and enforced by the "inner circle" of men coaches—is what causes most women, and many men, to say "not for me."

It strikes me that this is a wonderful example of how the interests of women are congruent with the interests of many men—a majority of men, really—who are made to feel uncomfortable and are marginalized by narrow expressions of masculinity. Creating more space for women in youth sports coaching will also expand the space for more kinds of men to participate—and vice versa. I've observed this already happening on a small scale in youth soccer (although not that I can see in baseball). Women are actively trying to recruit more women coaches, are supporting each other to hang in there and thrive, and are working with male allies to instill their teams and leagues with positive coaching values and practices.

I am convinced it is important to increase the numbers of women coaches in youth sports. It matters because today's generation of mothers is rich with athletic experience and talent; many women want to coach but are discouraged from doing so. It matters because what adults do in youth sports is linked to gender divisions of labor in other realms; an "unfinished feminist revolution" in work and family life is further reinforced by such a skewed male dominance in youth sports coaching. It matters because, as preparation for the world they will inhabit as adults, boys need to see and experience the full range of women's leadership and physical abilities. It matters because women coaches can be an inspiration to today's girls, giving them a vision of what they can do when they are adults. And it matters because including larger numbers of women is an important part of broadening the field for male coaches, making it a safe place for the emergence of a more nurturing style of male coach, which will surely be a benefit for all of our kids.

Boyhood Without Weapons
By Sarah Werthan Buttenweiser
Spring 2006

I've never bought a toy gun or sword. Before our first child, gender un-known, arrived, we vowed to do what we could to keep our household weapon- and Barbie-free. Our simplistic reasoning: weapons encourage boys to emulate tough warriors, and Barbie encourages girls to value unattainable body measurements over actual accomplishments. If we could shield our kids from these toys, surely the underlying messages wouldn't filter through, or at least not so strongly. We were somewhat naïve, of course. We didn't re-ally take into account the influences of societal norms or peers' preferences. Nor did we imagine that this wouldn't be easy to pull off.

Certainly, we weren't wrong about the forcefulness with which those toys are promoted. One need only walk down the blue aisles at Toys "R" Us to confirm that from GI Joe to all types of weaponry, the explicit, prevailing no-tion is that boys and fighting go together. According to the toy industry, "boys will be boys" means boys will fight. So buy them guns.

Consider some of the most popular marketed "boy" categories of fantasy play: construction, racecars, firefighters, knights, space aliens, cowboys, and pirates—and this is leaving out media influences like the *Star Wars* franchise. Firefighters have axes, used purposefully in their work, just as construction workers require saws and drills. Knights and pirates have swords, essential equipment for their historic battles.

The first sword that entered our house, carried by a semi-smiling plastic knight prepared to slay a green dragon, measured not much more than the tip of my pinky. This gift, ripped open instantly, now belonged to the burgeoning toy collection. I grabbed the sword, hid it in my hand, and rushed it out of sight. When your first child moves from toys large enough to put in his or her mouth to toys comprising seemingly infinitesimal tiny parts, you scramble not to lose any all-important pieces. So, after this stealth operation, I hesitated. By messing with the toy's pristine intactness, I was trying to ensure that ours would become a gentle knight, or at least one wily enough to slay the dragon without weaponry. I tossed the bright plastic sliver into the garbage, and that sword was never missed.

While we've never bought any guns or swords, gun-fighting or sword-fighting toys, knights, and pirates do live in our house alongside construction guys and baby dolls. (And one lone "Glinda" Barbie. She was a prize at a baby shower for a lesbian couple. Glinda's shoes and crown are long gone, her gown resting in a bin; she appears from time to time naked with disheveled blond hair, legs usually splayed in some strange position, far from any societal ideal of beauty.)

My husband brought in his childhood Lego sets, which included knights with swords and shields. Unlike me, he didn't toss the weapons out before handing the set over. A foam pirate bath toy has the swords already in the pirate's hands. Another pirate, a gift, joined the collection recently; there was a larger knight set with more weaponry that we traded in (before it was noticed by the three-year-old) for an arctic explorer. These pirates and knights do get played with some. Over time, I've begun to understand that there's a balance to be found; while I deem weaponry bad, I also must respect my kids' interests (anyone have teens who like gangsta rap?).

Take the stick that becomes a sword or the finger a gun. I used to quash made-up weaponry play immediately. But I started to think about how essential it is to reckon with impulse, aggression, power, and even the fantasy of destruction. I flashed back to the many beaten, drowned, and dismembered Barbies brutalized throughout my childhood. Much like learning that kids need to be loud and race around even when the space to do so feels impossibly small or crowded, I wanted to create some room for this exploration. At the same time, I wanted to convey to them my feelings about violent play and about violence in general.

Nowadays, when they pretend to sword-fight, the conversation goes something like this: "Be careful, you guys. Why are you fighting?" The usual response is, "We're knights. We won't hurt each other." If, however, a sword or gun is pointed at me, I redirect the fantasy straightaway. "I don't want to be shot. I don't think it's ever fun to pretend with a weapon that in real life kills people."

My eldest son, now 10, was never into fighting. At a four-year-old birthday party where boys were wielding laser swords with frantic, gleeful fury, he endeared himself to every parent in the backyard by declaring, "Stop with all that fighting. I don't like weapons." He reads all sorts of fantasy, some with violent battles, plays with Yu-Gi-Oh cards (the game features dueling) and enjoys other conflict-oriented games such as Battleship. His values are peaceful, environmentally conscious, antiracist, against gender discrimination—in short, all I could hope for.

The seven-year-old, who says he likes how the swords and shields look on the Lego guys, recently drew an elaborate picture of an alien war machine, which also fixed the roads on Mars. He published a letter to the editor in our local paper this past summer denouncing war. He and the three-year-old love to wrestle—with his friends. None of my kids has ever asked for a toy weapon.

Do their peace-affirming values have anything to do with not having weapons or guns or television? I can't know—sample-size my one household, my three boys—but given all the studies of how prevalent violence is in children's cartoons, I can only guess that this has helped. While we do talk about gun violence, the Iraq war, and other such issues, reality in our household plays out less about morals and more about how we live: with soccer and ballet, drawing and homemade obstacle courses, lots of books and lots of hugs. And, of course, the odd pirate, knight, and alien war machine.

Rite of Passage in Nevada
By Michael Burke
Winter 2001

What do boys need to become good men? The question continues to plague us, tolling like a bell. It is especially urgent for those of us who are trying to raise sons. One partial answer that has emerged is the idea of creating structured, transformative rites of passage to actively usher boys into manhood.

It has been suggested, for example, that we take some of the rituals by which men initiated boys into adult male society in traditional cultures—some of these involving frightening and physically torturous ordeals—and replicate them today, albeit in kinder, gentler packaging. Groups of men from California to Connecticut have done this with their teenage sons: picking them up early from school unexpectedly and spiriting them off for a sort of mythopoetic camping trip, complete with animal masks, chanting, dancing, and other planned "rites." The overall effect may be more surprise (and embarrassment?) than fear. Does it do much good? I don't know. But perhaps it does no harm; at least it shows Dad cares, even if he's a little new age-y sometimes.

A more typical and traditional example of a rite of passage is the bar mitzvah, which often has been seen as a child's and family's religious obligation more than a meaningful spiritual passage on the journey to manhood. Happily, a growing number of Jewish families are making that passage more meaningful—and for bat mitzvah girls, too.

Hearing a friend's disappointing story about a bar mitzvah where the boy's family never discussed what the ritual meant got me thinking about my own experience with rites of passage. Although I was raised Catholic, for me the effect of the formal religious rite of passage was similar. At age 11, I received the "sacrament of confirmation"—sort of like a second baptism, except this time you stay dry and (supposedly) you're conscious of what's going on.

Except I wasn't. I didn't have a choice in the matter, and it didn't occur to me to question it. I don't recall feeling any different after the ceremony, though you might think that would be a byproduct. (In fact the only memorable part was the rehearsal beforehand: My adult sponsor, our next-door neighbor Mr. McCloskey, drove me not to St. Catherine's but to Temple Beth El. Mortified, I looked over at him in gaping adolescent panic, only to see him convulsed with wheezy laughter; I had forgotten it was April Fools Day. But if he'd left me at the synagogue, who knows? It all might have worked out differently for me.)

My Catholicism was confirmed—for a few years. By sometime in college I was searching for something else, and today I would not put my son or daughter through what I was made to do. Their religious beliefs, their spirituality, will be their own affair, and I don't anticipate arranging any ceremonies for them.

So my "official" rite of passage was transitory in its effect. But a couple of summers later, I found myself at the vortex of a harmonic convergence of forces which came together in the Ruby Mountains of northeastern Nevada. What happened there may have been called forth by the spirits of mountain lion and mule deer, of sagebrush and sandstone and quaking aspen; but in fact I think it was all planned by my dad—well, some of it.

It was a family camping trip, an annual event that had a certain amount of ritual attached to it already. It was the summer Nixon resigned; we heard it on the car radio when my dad started it up to charge the battery and plug in his electric razor. "Our long national nightmare is over," Gerald Ford told us. "The system worked," my dad informed me. (I was unsure.)

The campsite next to ours was occupied one day by an Indian family, come up from one of the towns to camp and fish and picnic. While the mother took their two boys down to the creek, the father, whose name was Ben, ambled over to our camp, in a straw cowboy hat and leather boots, tallboy in hand, to sit on a stump and beguile my dad and me with stories. Friendly and voluble, Big Ben, as we took to calling him among ourselves, appeared a comic character at the time, but seems a sad figure to me in retrospect: a middle-aged Navajo man adrift in the country of the Shoshone, his wife's people; he appeared to do little but drink beer and tell tales, then totter back unsteadily to his own camp when dinnertime came. He told us about his own rite of passage, though: how his wife-to-be's father handed him a rifle loaded with only one bullet and told him to go up on a ridge and shoot a deer to claim his bride. He pantomimed how he saw the big buck, aimed, and fired—and the buck went down. His prowess excited wonder among his new in-laws. "They say, 'How you do that, Ben?'" he boasted, which became our family joke.

When Ben's wife returned with their sons, they carried stringers of trout—a fact that excited my admiration and curiosity. I had been fishing too, but since I was the only one in my family who fished, I was doing it strictly solo and catching nothing. I was probably self-conscious about looking foolish, so it must have been my mother who spoke up and asked the other woman how they caught all those fish. I was using salmon eggs and getting skunked; she and her boys were using nightcrawlers and cleaning up. The next day I prevailed on my father to drive me into town, ten miles or more down winding mountain roads, to buy worms. Thereafter I spent several golden days tramping up and downstream, encountering deer and range cattle and even a scary nest of snakes—and catching a number of nice native rainbows and a few exotic brook trout (imported from the East), which I cleaned and my mother dipped in milk and coated in cornmeal and fried for dinner. Success at last— and for the first time, a feeling of competence at something useful, at which I'd previously been a miserable failure. For that I have that woman and her sons to thank.

One afternoon when I was not absorbed in fishing, my father and I hiked up the mountain nearest our campsite, leaving my mother behind in camp. That was somewhat unusual, just the two of us, but evidently I made no note of it. We hiked upward through stands of aspen, whose small green heart-shaped leaves quivered fitfully in the breeze. We could smell the urine of wild cats—whether cougars or bobcats, we never saw them—and in the dust of the trail could make out the occasional hoofprint of mule deer, and sometimes their scat, too. The stands of aspen were so thick as to be impassable to humans. As we climbed we turned to see the late-afternoon sun changing the colors of the sheer rock wall across the canyon, from red to gold and back again, as the moon rose above us in a solid blue sky.

At some point we stopped for a rest and took a drink from my dad's old army canteen. I had recently hit puberty, and somehow—I don't know what the transition was—we started talking about sex. I'm sure I didn't bring it up, but what transpired was that my dad gave me a sort of Sermon on the Mount—about the physical aspects, in particular, of human sexuality. I must have been a little embarrassed, but I was grateful, too. Partly to receive this knowledge, much of which was still literally a mystery to me (though I'd heard and read some things, both true and laughably false), but also for my father's willingness to share this aspect of life with me—for this communion, if you will—and for his openness on a subject that fills many parents with dread.

Having grown up on a farm in Idaho, my father didn't see any sense in keeping silent about our bodies, how we receive pleasure from each other while incidentally making more of our kind. He grew up seeing animals do it, he'd had five kids himself, and he must have learned from his father and become convinced by his own experience that there was no shame in it, and no reason for ignorance or prudery. I asked questions after a while, and he answered—he covered a fair amount of ground, as I recall. Looking back, I wish he had talked more about some of the "intangibles"—about emotions, being in a relationship, about the troublesome aspects of sexuality and feelings, and what it really means to love someone. But I realize that these were not things for which my father had many words—just as I didn't know how to ask.

What he had, and what he shared that day, was a vital, nuts-and-bolts sense of what his son, wavering at the trailhead into adulthood, needed to know to move forward, to deal with the feelings that would soon surge and almost overwhelm his (my) young body. That he was able to speak this—to tell me, in plain language, without embarrassment, some of the crucial "facts of life"—is something I still find moving, and for which I will always honor him. Many men and women I know were told far less growing up. (Some, indeed, were told nothing, and for them that omission had consequences, great and small.)

Unlike Moses, I don't think I was irrevocably changed coming back down the mountain (I had no commandments, for one thing—not even "Be fruitful and multiply," which might have been a nice touch). But what happened that day, and my dad's role in it, was important nonetheless. What would I say to my son in the same situation? When the time comes, will I be able to do as well? I've got a few years to think about it, fortunately, since he's only six. But time goes by fast: I was six only yesterday myself; then seventeen, having my first sexual experience; then in college, then on my own in New York City. Those were all "rites of passage" for me. Now married and a father myself, I'm still having them—only now they're called midlife crises.

A friend of mine said, when we were discussing this subject, that it would be better if all of us—parents, teachers, Big Brothers, extended family, community members—helped boys more in their journey every day, rather than just concocting a ritual for them to go through at puberty and saying "There—now you're a man." (I think the same holds true for girls as well.) I think what's important—especially for fathers—is to show our sons and daughters that we care, that we're here for them every day and for the long haul. It may be by helping them with their homework, or playing baseball with them, or just talking with them about school, about sex, about their hopes and dreams and fears. It will often involve listening to them, driving them places they need to go, and being patient with them while they figure out how, someday, to get there on their own. It may even take the form of a ritual, religious or otherwise, in which we celebrate with them their passage into adulthood. Some of their rites of passage we may never see—part of the scary letting-go process that begins at birth. The key is to stay on the path, to stay connected with them in their upward climb, and by doing so to help smooth the long ascent.

VOICE MALE

Believing in Young Men
By Rob Okun
Winter 2007

In my work encouraging men to explore options outside the constraining box of conventional masculinity there's certainly no shortage of bad news. Men's violence against women (and other men) remains at catastrophic levels; there's little chance *Voice Male* is going to be short of problems to cover anytime soon. Nevertheless, my family and friends will tell you I'm a glass-half-full person—upbeat, optimistic. Even in the face of gloom and doom—the senseless war in Iraq, the criminal neglect plaguing the Gulf Coast and New Orleans, the indifference to the tragedy in Darfur— I always seem to look for ways to connect the dots of possibility, the signs of hope trumping despair.

So where is the good news? Not long ago, I talked into the night around a fire pit in New Orleans with young men volunteering to help with the city's renewal, shared Chinese food with an inspiring group of male college students challenging sexism and violence on an elite New England campus, and met in a classroom after school with local male high school juniors and seniors, members of a "women's rights club."

It was hard to retain my glass-half-full demeanor when I arrived in New Orleans before the holidays. My wife and I came to visit one of our daughters, part of the legion of twentysomethings who'd moved to town to help with the relief effort. The mix of women and men, many volunteering with the Common Ground Collective, represents the best of our troubled, creative country. Since Hurricane Katrina and the ensuing floods overwhelmed the region, thousands of volunteers have passed through Common Ground, headquartered in a three-story brick school where floodwaters peaked above the second story.

Sitting around a fire pit in the backyard of a colorful, shotgun-style house in the Seventh Ward, with live banjo as a soundtrack, I watched the flames dance, illuminating the faces of the volunteers. I saw in their expressions and heard in their words a sensitivity to, and awareness of, the class and racial issues plaguing the city (issues predating Katrina) that stirred in me a sense of hope. We talked for a while, then joined the music making—adding guitar and harmonica, it was N'awlins after all. When we picked up the conversation, we wrestled with how to reconcile the enormity of the calamity with the limitations of an under-funded, all-volunteer, grassroots effort. These young men's compassion caught my attention—soft, understated, not an attribute necessarily associated with males. I think the scope of the devastation and the shameful neglect, plain for all to see, helped crack open their hearts. On the plane home, I was misty-eyed thinking about that night. I had been witness to a quiet, powerful expression of men's courage. Despite the struggle New Orleans faces, these young men filled my glass with more than just dregs of hope.

Back home, I went to dinner with activist-filmmaker Byron Hurt and most of the members of the Men's Project at Amherst College. Founded on principles similar to those of the Men's Resource Center for Change, adapted to a college community, the group's goal is to sustain a male-initiated, profeminist, antiviolence/anti–sexual assault presence at Amherst, even when prevailing attitudes objectify women and pressure men to strike a tough guise.

They'd invited the filmmaker to screen his new film, *Hip-Hop: Beyond Beats & Rhymes*. At dinner, one young man asked Hurt how he had gotten involved in "men's work." Byron responded by asking each of us to answer, too. As we passed around steaming platters of food, one by one we shared the spark—a teacher, parent, sister, friend, girlfriend, a training, becoming a father—a cascading series of experiences that had resulted in each of us reaching a similar conclusion: there's a better way to be a man. As we headed over to see the film, I could feel my glass of hope filling up.

A few days later, in a classroom at the regional high school in Amherst, Massachusetts, I met with the male members of the Women's Rights Club, a 40-member group, a quarter of whom are guys, 16 to 18. With little prompting, they shared why they'd joined: becoming aware of the sexual harassment female students experience; wanting to support a performance of *The Vagina Monologues*; not wanting to have to pretend they were a certain kind of guy. A starting member of a varsity sports team told how, at a team meeting, he'd announced he had to leave early to attend the Women's Rights Club. He was met with a string of derisive comments, all questioning his manhood. His response? "I don't care what you say. Being in this group is important to me." Others then shared how their male friends had teased them, too. But they'd all withstood the criticism. It was an hour after school had ended, and they were all there—a young men's group. Their voices may not be as deep as those of the men around the fire in New Orleans; their mission not yet as broad as the students' at Amherst College. Nevertheless they, too, had connected the dots clearly enough to know that there are other ways for men to be. For someone who likes to see his glass half full, I left the high school that day with mine overflowing.

VOICE MALE

"Men's Tears"
Freya Manfred
Spring 2006

Every day since school began
our ten year old bursts into tears:
"My bike is scratched! My cat is hurt!"
He pushes away our hugs, and weeps,
standing, sitting, lying in the leaves,
the great head with zinnia-petaled hair
bowed over the heaving chest.
Helpless, hopeless, wave after wave,
he weeps until he's done.
It's hard for us to listen,
but we say to each other,
"Why shouldn't a boy cry?"
Please God, why shouldn't a man?
Why shouldn't all the men in the world
lie down and cry, feet dangling,
knuckles rubbing their wet faces.
Let them stop working, stop traveling, stop talking,
and sit, in the daylight, in the dark,
in the woods and cities and deserts,
and cry, sobs filling the sky,
inhalations flooding their lungs
with other men's exhalations
connecting them together,
their bodies becoming one with rivers, lakes and seas;
while we sisters, mothers, and grandmothers
crouch down beside them, praying,
our bodies feeling their pain
as we do when our small sons cry:
sweet and strong, these men and nations,
bold enough to weep men's tears.

CHANGING MEN

Photo courtesy Lacey Byrne

In tandem and in collaboration with women's movements since the 1970s, the profeminist men's movement has been working to illuminate the unhealthy aspects of patriarchal masculinity and offer resources for moving forward. Changing Men chronicles men's efforts to articulate the damages inflicted by traditional masculinity, support other men in healing such wounds, and navigate complicated aspects of men's lives such as sex, sports, the military, and relationships. From descriptions of the unhealthy pressures of old-school manhood to hopeful visions of new models for masculinity, Changing Men paints a picture of the shifting landscape of men and masculinities.

The High Cost of Manliness
By Robert Jensen
Winter 2007

It's hard to be a man; hard to live up to the demands that come with the dominant conception of masculinity: the tough guy.

So, guys, I have an idea—maybe it's time we stop trying. Maybe this masculinity thing is a bad deal, not just for women but for us.

We need to get rid of the whole idea of masculinity. It's time to abandon the claim that there are certain psychological or social traits that inherently come with being biologically male. If we can get past that, we have a chance to create a better world for men and women.

The dominant conception of masculinity in US culture is easily summarized: Men are assumed to be naturally competitive and aggressive, and being a real man is therefore marked by the struggle for control, conquest, and domination. A man looks at the world, sees what he wants, and takes it. Men who don't measure up are wimps, sissies, fags, girls.

The worst insult one man can hurl at another—whether it's boys on the playground or CEOs in the boardroom—is the accusation that a man is like a woman. Although the culture acknowledges that men can in some situations have traits traditionally associated with women (caring, compassion, tenderness), in the end it is men's strength-expressed-as-toughness that defines us and must trump any female-like softness. Those aspects of masculinity must prevail for a man to be a "real man."

That's not to suggest, of course, that every man adopts this view of masculinity. But it is endorsed in key institutions and activities—most notably in business, the military, and athletics—and is reinforced through the mass media. It is particularly expressed in the way men—straight and gay alike—talk about sexuality and act sexually. And our culture's male heroes reflect those characteristics: they most often are men who take charge rather than seek consensus, seize power rather than look for ways to share it, and are willing to be violent to achieve their goals.

That view of masculinity is dangerous for women. It leads men to seek to control "their" women and define their own pleasure in that control, which leads to epidemic levels of rape and battery. But this view of masculinity is toxic for men as well.

If masculinity is defined as conquest, it means that men will always struggle with one another for dominance. In a system premised on hierarchy and power, there can be only one king of the hill. Every other man must in some way be subordinated to the king, and the king always has to be nervous about who is coming up that hill to get him. A friend who once worked on Wall Street—one of the preeminent sites of masculine competition—described coming to work as like walking into a knife fight when all the good spots along the wall were taken. Masculinity like this is life lived as endless competition and threat.

No one man created this system, and perhaps none of us, given a choice, would choose it. But we live our lives in that system, and it deforms men, narrowing our emotional range and depth. It keeps us from the rich connections with others—not just with women and children, but with other men—that make life meaningful, but require vulnerability.

This doesn't mean that the negative consequences of this toxic masculinity are equally hazardous for men and women. As feminists have long pointed out, there's a big difference between women dealing with the possibility of being raped, beaten, and killed by the men in their lives, and men not being able to cry. But we can see that the short-term material gains we men get are not adequate compensation for what we give up in the long run—which is to surrender part of our humanity to the project of dominance.

Of course there are obvious physical differences between men and women—average body size, hormones, reproductive organs. There may be other differences rooted in our biology that we don't yet understand. Yet it's also true that men and women are more similar than we are different, and that given the pernicious effects of centuries of patriarchy and its relentless devaluing of things female, we should be skeptical of the perceived differences.

What we know is simple: In any human population, there is wide individual variation. While there's no doubt that a large part of our behavior is rooted in our DNA, there's also no doubt that our genetic endowment is highly influenced by culture. Beyond that, it's difficult to say much with any certainty. It's true that only women can bear children and breastfeed. That fact likely has some bearing on aspects of men's and women's personalities.

But we don't know much about what the overall effect is, and given the limits of our tools for understanding human behavior, it's possible we may never know much.

At the moment, the culture seems obsessed with gender differences, in the context of a recurring intellectual fad (called "evolutionary psychology" this time around, and "sociobiology" in a previous incarnation) that wants to explain all complex behaviors as simple evolutionary adaptations—if a pattern of human behavior exists, it must be because it's adaptive in some ways. Over long stretches of evolutionary time, that's true by definition.

But in the short term it's hardly a convincing argument to say, "Look at how men and women behave so differently; it must be because men and women are fundamentally different"—when clearly a political system has been creating differences between men and women.

From there, the argument that we need to scrap masculinity is fairly simple. To illustrate it, remember back to right after 9/11. A number of commentators argued that criticisms of masculinity should be rethought. Cannot we now see—recognizing that male firefighters raced into burning buildings, risking and sometimes sacrificing their lives to save others—that masculinity can encompass a kind of strength that is rooted in caring and sacrifice? Of course men often exhibit such strength, just as do women. So, the obvious question arises: What makes these distinctly masculine characteristics? Are they not simply human characteristics?

We identify masculine tendencies toward competition, domination, and violence because we see patterns of differential behavior; men are more prone to such behavior in our culture. We can go on to observe and analyze how men are socialized to behave in those ways, toward the goal of changing such destructive behaviors. That analysis is different from saying that admirable human qualities present in both men and women are somehow primarily the domain of one gender. To assign them to one gender only is misguided and demeaning to the other, which is then assumed not to possess these qualities to the same degree. Once we start saying that strength and courage are "masculine traits," it leads to the conclusion that woman are not as strong or courageous.

Of course, if we are going to jettison masculinity, we have to scrap femininity along with it. We have to stop trying to define what men and women are going to be in the world based on extrapolations from physical sex differences. That doesn't mean we ignore those differences when they matter, but we have to stop assuming they matter everywhere.

I don't think the planet can long survive if the current conception of masculinity endures. We face political and ecological challenges that can't be met with this old model of what it means to be a man. At the more intimate level, the stakes are just as high. For those of us who are biologically male, we have a simple choice: We can settle for being men, or we can strive to be human beings.

Unnatural Embrace: Men's Fear of Hugging

By Michael Burke
Spring 2002

Last summer I hugged my brother-in-law—for the first time.

It was one small step for two men, if not "mankind." Whether or not it's ever repeated, it seemed important at the time, and still does.

A colleague got me sitting up straight in my chair recently when he said: "*Male socialization is about homophobia.*" He was speaking from his own experience as a gay man, but still I wanted to argue, Come on, "male socialization" is not reducible to such an absolute, simple formula. It's more complex than just straight men's fear of being seen as gay, or of having contact with gays, or of "becoming" gay. There's more to it than that. Isn't there?

Then I thought about that moment with my brother-in-law. I've known him—my wife's sister's husband—for a dozen years. We're not close friends, but he's had me up to his camp in the Adirondacks for "beer and bloody meat," as he delicately puts it, and we've spent time together at family gatherings.

It would be an understatement to say we're different. He's from western New York, used to be in law enforcement, and perhaps having dealt with so many criminals over the years seems, to my West Coast sensibility, to look on life with a colder eye. He likes to fish and hunt, play golf and drink beer. I've heard him say things I thought were racist or sexist.

I've also seen him seek out the one African American guy on a charter boat to smoke and have a conversation with, heard him tell how he met his wife in a way that would make the *Sleepless in Seattle* screenwriters race for their laptops. If you say to him, "You're a good guy," or "That was a nice thing you did," he's likely to growl, "Don't tell anybody." I like to think of him as the Redneck with a Heart of Gold.

Yeah, I love the guy (don't tell anybody). If I were ever lost in the woods or under attack, he's the one I'd want by my side.

So why did it take so long for us to share that hug?

It wasn't merely the passage of time or the comfort of long familiarity that finally relaxed our studied male reticence. It took the sudden and unexpected death of our father-in-law.

He was only 58 and had meant a lot to both of us (though I never hugged him either, come to think of it). At the funeral, we both grieved for this father-mentor we had loved.

Afterward, I didn't think about it—I just came over and embraced my brother-in-law. Actually, I guess I did think about it—quickly. Probably I realized just as I was about to do it that I had never hugged him before, but now it would certainly be okay.

In any case, he accepted it totally. Well, mostly totally. "God-*damn* it," he whispered, leavening any awkwardness with anger, one of the few acceptable male emotions. "It's not fair."

He's right. It's not fair people we love die young, and it's not fair we don't tell them we love them before they leave us forever. It's not fair that because they're men and so are we, we feel afraid to hug them when we see them, afraid to show them what they mean to us, afraid to reach out and hold on to that fleeting thing, human warmth and connection.

My brother-in-law and I are not alone. In the recent movie *Life as a House,* a woman asks her husband why he isn't worried that their young sons never hug him, nor he them. His response: "If I worried about everything I ought to be worried about, I'd be you."

As men we've learned to say (and believe): We'll be the soldiers, the providers, the problem solvers; we'll leave the expression of emotions—the hugging and crying—to the womenfolk. We may worry, but you'll never see it. We may feel something deep down, in a place we've almost forgotten how to get to, but you'll never know.

Putting aside how anachronistic such behavior is in light of changing gender roles—and how unhealthy it is for us—are we really afraid that hugging will make us "gay"? Or worse, that it will makes us *women*? I learned at an early age: Men only hug each other when they've won the World Series. Or the Super Bowl, NBA Finals, or Stanley Cup. Then it's permissible; then it's okay. But only teammates and coaches. Any other hugging situations were by definition the domain of sissies and wimps, actors and interior decorators. I grew up knowing this without being told. *That's* the legacy of male socialization.

And not even the relative orgies of hugging in the men's groups I belong to have entirely cured me of this ingrained hug-o-phobia. I sense it in other men sometimes—even my friends. I seem to know when not to hug. *Don't touch—we're not* gay, *after all!* Of course it's not that simple. I tell myself I don't want to make them uncomfortable; it's true. I tell myself I'm not afraid they'll think I'm gay, and that's true (I think). But then what am I afraid of?

Maybe I haven't fully come out yet—not as gay, but as a man free in my emotions and reactions, free to reach out to men and women and transgender folk, gay and straight and bisexual, in just the way I choose, the way I authentically feel in the moment, unconstrained by concerns about the perceptions of others regarding my masculinity, my identity.

One of the Zen sayings I venerate goes something like, "Walk forward or walk back, but don't wobble." That's what the true bodhisattva, the enlightened man, does. I'm not there yet. I still wobble sometimes, unsure of my actions and motives, unsure how they'll be received by others. And afraid, above all, of rejection.

Sadly, I never hugged my father-in-law, who surely merited it. (Some men have legitimate reasons to not want to be hugged, such as those who were abused as children.) There may have been other important men in my life whom I should have embraced more fully, physically and otherwise. Now I hug my father every time I see him, even though hugging wasn't really done in my family. And I've now hugged all my brothers-in-law—even the crusty, lovable Redneck with the Heart of Gold, who asks from time to time about my "men's club."

I'm not into forcing anything on anybody; not out to try to improve the species. It's me I have to work on, day after day, resocializing this strange, familiar person slowly and painfully, trying to shed my fear of other men and other people, my own homophobia, my fear of being rejected and shamed— the long, sad legacy of male rigidities I was taught. I'm working on it, in my wobbly way, one hug at a time. Other men can think me gay, or just overly men's-movementy; that's okay—I'll take it as a compliment and come out as a hugger. No, better yet: I'll come out as a man.

The National Conversation about Masculinity
By Michael Kimmel
Winter 1998

I believe that we are having a national debate about masculinity in this country—but we don't know it. For example, what gender comes to mind when I invoke these social problems currently plaguing American society: "teen violence," "gang violence," "suburban violence," "drug violence," or "violence in the schools?" And what gender comes to mind when I ask you to imagine the sneering, arrogant guards at a border crossing in Bosnia, the caravans of jeeps following their warlords in Somalia, the cheering throngs that greet yet another terrorist bombing in the Basque country, the youths slinging their automatic weapons as they swagger down the streets of bombed-out Beirut? Of course you've imagined men. And not just any men—but younger men, in their teens and twenties, and relatively poorer men, working class or lower middle class.

Now how do our social commentators discuss these problems? Do they note that the problems of youth and violence are really a problem of young men and violence? Do they ever mention that everywhere ethnic nationalism sets up shop, it is young men who are the shopkeepers? Do they ever mention masculinity at all?

Now imagine that these were all women. Would that not be the story, the only story, the only issue to be explained? Would not a gender analysis be at the center of every single story? Would they not have experts of female socialization, frustration, anger, PMS, and everything else under the sun? But the fact that these are men warrants nary a word.

Frankly, I believe that until we take on the question of masculinity we will not, as a culture, have a clue how to address these burning issues. That's not to say that all we have to do is address masculinity. Of course the issues are more complex than that, requiring analyses of the political economy of global economic integration, of the transformation of social classes, of urban poverty and hopelessness, of racism. But to ignore masculinity—to keep masculinity invisible—means that we will never completely understand these problems, let alone resolve them.

That's the missing piece here. Recognizing, acknowledging, and appreciating race or gender requires that we make them visible. In our colleges and universities we have done that with women. Now we need to integrate men into our curriculum. Because it is men—or, rather masculinity—that is invisible.

Huh? Did he just say, "integrate men into the curriculum?" That "Men are invisible?" What's he talking about?! Men aren't invisible. They're everywhere.

Quite true. Men are ubiquitous both in universities, professional schools, and in the public sphere in general. And, of course, it's true that if you look at the college curriculum, every course that doesn't have the word "women" in the title is about men. Every course that isn't in "women's studies" is, de facto, a course in men's studies. Except we call it history, political science, literature, chemistry. But it's always about men as political leaders, military heroes, scientists, writers, artists. Men, themselves, are invisible as men. Rarely if ever do we see a course that examines the lives of men as men. What is the impact of gender on the lives of these famous men? How does masculinity play a part in the lives of great artists, writers, presidents, etc? On this score, the traditional curriculum suddenly draws a big blank. Everywhere we turn there are courses on men, but no information on masculinity.

But listen to the voices of the men themselves. Cultural figures like composer Charles Ives insisting that Impressionistic music was "sissy" and that he wanted to use traditional tough guy sounds to build a more popular and virile music? Or architect Louis Sullivan describing his ambition to create "masculine forms"—strong, solid, tall, commanding respect? (Sullivan invented the skyscraper.) Or political figures, like the endless parade of presidential hopefuls who have both proclaimed their own manhood and raised questions about their opponents' manhood?

Think about the 1840 presidential campaign, during which William Henry Harrison's supporters chastised Martin Van Buren as "Little Vanny," a "used up man?" (You might recall that Harrison was actually deceived by his own hypermasculine hype, eschewing a topcoat while taking the oath of office on the coldest day in several years, and dying one month later of pneumonia.)

And what about President Lyndon Johnson's vainglorious claim during the Tet offensive of the Vietnam War, when he said that he "didn't just screw Ho Chi Minh. I cut his pecker off!" Or George Bush, boasting proudly after his vice-presidential debate with Geraldine Ferraro in 1984 that he had "kicked a little ass" and then squaring off against television commentator Dan Rather in 1988 to dispel his image as a wimp?

Gender is everywhere we look. In the past 25 years, the pioneering work of feminist scholars has made us increasingly aware of the centrality of gender in shaping social life. Gender is one of the central organizing principles around which social life revolves. Twenty-five years ago, social scientists would have only listed class and race as the master statuses that defined and proscribed social life. If you wanted to study gender in the 1960s in social science, you might have been able to study "Marriage and the Family"—which was kind of the Ladies Auxiliary of the social sciences. There were no courses on gender. Gender, we now know, is one of the axes around which social life is organized, and through which we understand our own experiences.

American men have come to think of ourselves as genderless, in part because we can afford that luxury of ignoring the centrality of gender. So we treat our military, political, scientific, or literary figures as if their gender, their masculinity, had nothing to do with their military exploits, policy decisions, scientific experiments, or writing styles and subjects. And those whom we disenfranchise and oppress are those whose manhood we come to believe is not equal to ours.

So we continue to act as if gender applied only to women. Now we have to make gender visible to men. As the Chinese proverb has it, the fish are the last to discover the ocean.

Cracking "the Bro Code"

By Chelsea Faria and Stephen Koenig
Summer 2011

Part I:
By Chelsea Faria

The Bro Code: How Contemporary Culture Creates Sexist Men, a new film by Thomas Keith, exposes the mainstream media's reinforcement and encouragement of troubling social "norms" about manhood. Unfortunately, there's a lot of bad news about men.

A prime example is the hype behind the reality television show *Jersey Shore*. The character of Ronnie epitomizes the sex-driven, misogynistic, and unemotional (or is he?) man. For Ronnie, "There are three words: beers, bitches, and the beach ... that's all you need to know about the Jersey Shore. I mean, I really don't know what love means. The whole thing about this is pretty much about getting laid. Just take your shirt off and they come to you. It's like a fly comes to shit." (Need a barf bucket?)

Ronnie's misogyny is front and center in *Jersey Shore*. Each episode attracts between *5 and 8 million* viewers. Ronnie and the rest of the cast are each paid a couple thousand dollars *per episode* to spout their sexist drivel. Power, money, and misogyny—a dangerous combination for women *and* men.

While documenting the pressures men and boys feel to conform to the tough, powerful, hypermasculine image the media perpetuates—an image considered desirable by many women—*The Bro Code* highlights the difficulties men face trying to escape. It's hard to speak out against the mainstream masculinity, especially if your role models and close friends would disapprove at best and at worst, harass and bully you.

As *The Bro Code* makes clear, classic gender stereotyping has an impact on women's psyches as well as men's. In *The Jersey Shore*, the women feel pressured to "compete with other women for the coveted prize of who can be the hottest, the sexiest, the naughtiest..." filmmaker Keith reminds us.

Watching *The Bro Code* discuss women and the cultural norms that haunt us, I found myself questioning my own identity. Where do my actions fit in with the media's expectations? Are women—myself included—really attracted to bad boys, or is that just a storyline the media plays over and over until we learn it, adopt it, live it? Some men adopt hypermasculine behaviors, *The Bro Code* suggests, because they believe women are attracted by it—that women wouldn't date but only befriend gentle, sensitive guys. But for any men reading this article, listen up: I guarantee you that women are *not* impressed by sexism, misogyny, and other acts that degrade our gender. Pay attention, guys: acknowledging emotions and displaying emotional maturity are *assets* in any relationship. Devaluing women—and placing us below men on the pedestal of power—is, well, just not sexy. It's a real turnoff, actually.

I know there are guys out there challenging this kind of behavior. But there needs to be a lot more. I'd certainly like knowing that more guys had my back. How does it feel to often be the only person in a room who's offended by a rape joke or by a stand-up comedian's steady onslaught of sexist and homophobic material? Uncomfortable. Infuriating. Isolating. If I speak up, I face belittling comments and dismissal: "*A feminist just can't take a joke, right?*" or "*Calm down, it was just a joke.*" No dialogue, no willingness to hear me out. This is the world I live in. This is what I'm up against.

I'm aware of that world every time I feel the need to dissent. Still, *The Bro Code* reminds me that I am not alone. I'm glad that documentaries like this one dissect the messages—crack the code—conveying the debilitating impact the bro code has on all of us, male, female, transgender. Hopefully, the film will persuade viewers to question their role in the struggle to create a violence-and-oppression-free society where women's rights are valued just as much as men's.

Part II
By Stephen Koenig

I love being known as a college football player on the field, but I hate being known as a college football player off it. The reputation—not to mention the image—attached to playing football is hard to carry: a misogynistic party animal who counts sexual partners and beers just as much as he counts sacks and touchdowns. While many men aspire to be a "player," for football players the expectation to uphold the core values of "real manhood" is magnified.

From early on in life, young men are directed on a different track to adulthood than our female counterparts. If we are to believe the media—in its self-appointed role representing society—boys value toughness and a strong libido as definitions of the ideal man. This reinforces the idea that mistreating or demeaning women is acceptable because it encourages men to view women as sex objects.

The Bro Code is a cinematic intervention aimed at interrupting this cycle of misogyny. It forces viewers to reconsider how men are seen and how both men and women have been harmed by a media-driven society determined to mold men according to hypermasculine ideals.

As a male college student, I can attest that harassing women for the sake of enjoyment or "male camaraderie" is an all too common occurrence on college campuses. College-age men across the country spread a message of hate and dominance over their female peers.

As a college football player, I am exposed to such behavior way more than I would like. That's not to say Amherst College football players—or any group of male college athletes—are bad people. My team is very close and supportive of one another. But it is our very cohesiveness that makes standing up for something you feel is wrong all the more difficult.

Some time at the beginning of our weekly Sunday team meetings is always dedicated to various players bragging about how much alcohol they consumed and what sexual conquests they had achieved the night before. Anyone—including me—who does not go along with this idea of masculinity is forced to sit and listen uncomfortably. Do I remain quiet, thereby suggesting that I agree or condone such behavior, or do I speak up and risk alienating my friends and teammates?

If it wasn't bad enough that the epidemic of mistreating women has infected college campuses, the media has minimized the danger of sexual violence against women by using rape or other forms of sexual violence as the punch line of jokes. *The Bro Code* portrays a scene from *Family Guy*, Seth

MacFarlane's animated hit comedy series. In the episode, main character Peter Griffin—after hearing on the news that three young women had been raped and murdered—whines, "Everybody's getting laid but me." Not only is the joke insensitive, it conveys to *Family Guy's* massive—and largely male—audience that making fun of rape is okay. Such a dangerous message perpetuates the violent, insensitive behavior that defines today's negative masculinity. *The Bro Code* exposes the disconnected dots between so-called humor and actual sexual violence against women.

The Bro Code shines a harsh light on contemporary men, exposing how difficult it is to form a positive male identity in today's society. The other guys on the Amherst College football team are not just a bunch of bad boys who get off on ragging on women. They have been taught that their view of women being subservient to men is right. A film like *The Bro Code* makes clear that the best way to prevent attitudes like this and to stop men from mistreating women is to educate them about the sexist culture into which they were born, one that continues to devalue women. It's time more men recognized our responsibility to speak up. As *The Bro Code* demonstrates, we have the tools. The question is, are we "man enough" to use them?

Male Student Athletes: Profeminism's Newest Allies

By Rob Okun
Summer 2013

In a world where too many men stay silent in the face of discrimination against women—from sexual harassment to domestic and sexual violence—the public statement of two dozen Massachusetts male student athletes not long before Father's Day offers a sliver of new hope.

Twenty-two graduating senior athletes from prestigious Phillips Academy in Andover, Massachusetts, signed a letter to the editor of the school newspaper that explicitly endorsed feminism.

Saying it was "time to speak out" about the campus male athletic environment that fosters an "imbalanced hook-up culture, classroom dynamics and even defining the gender roles of females on campus that younger students emulate and eventually internalize," Tyler Olkowski, captain of the crew team, was lead author of the letter. He said he and his cosigners—the captains and leaders of every sport on campus—"realize our athlete culture has a problem."

"This culture may not be our fault, but it is our problem to fix."

The poignant letter underscores that the male athletes' "collective character has been tainted by the objectification and sexism that pervade athlete culture. This culture may not be our fault, but it is our problem to fix . . . It is time for Andover's athletes to find new, constructive ways to bond and develop team camaraderie that aren't based on conquering [at] dances and competitively targeting females; not by prodding teammates to "hook up" and teasing those who don't. The definition of "cool" doesn't have to be a traditionally masculine figure who objectifies [his] sexual partners or who climbs [his] respective social ladders through hook-ups."

The letter, which circulated among profeminist men's organizations and on gender justice websites is a hopeful indicator that another generation of men is learning at a younger age to be allies to women. Since the signers included the captains of the football, baseball, basketball, hockey, soccer, lacrosse, track, cross-country, golf, volleyball, water polo, and squash teams, there's every reason to believe these young athlete-leaders will arrive at college and university campuses this fall primed to take their commitment to challenge sexism and male (athlete) privilege to a new level. Their bold stand is inspiring, and allies and leaders on their new campuses will surely be ready to embrace them.

All of us should join these young athletes to keep the momentum building from their courageous statement. The door to gender equality is open wider because of these young men, and their bold statement should be on the agenda at athletic departments around the country.

After reading the letter by the Phillips Academy 22, can there be any question that male awareness of gender inequality is growing? In its wake, won't it be more difficult to ignore voices advocating for a culture shift away from male domination and toward gender equality? Those of us who have been working for decades on this shift proudly stand with these young men. Their voices embolden us to continue our work.

Let's convene teach-ins to transform student-athletes into student gender justice leaders

It is time to amplify those voices by encouraging colleges and universities to convene teach-ins and trainings on transforming student-athletes into student leaders for gender justice, and conducting them every fall. Phillips Academy, which in 1996 established the Brace Center for Gender Studies, might play a leading role in organizing or hosting such gatherings. Athletic directors and school administrators in the US should consider inviting Mentors in Violence Prevention (MVP) to conduct trainings on their campuses.

I'm always on the lookout for good news about men. As the Andover group has just graduated high school, it's premature to know if any of the Phillips Academy 22 will become fathers. I hope, though, that their fathers—and mothers—don't only use Father's Day as an occasion to say how proud they are that their sons published the letter.

Its last sentence asks next year's senior class athletes to make a decision—whether to "silently perpetuate the culture we inherited, or choose the culture our teams and community deserve." They ask the rest of us to choose, too. Let's work to ensure more of us stand with the Phillips Academy 22.

Why a Men's Center?
By Steven Botkin
Fall 1997

Creating a men's center requires more than finding an office, or even offering specific programs. If a men's center is going to become part of the fabric of society, people need to understand and support the concept of such a center in their community.

We knew that many truths about men—truths we all needed to hear—were buried under the weight of the power and privilege men were offered, if only we would keep silent. We knew the oppression of women and the dehumanization of men are two sides of the same coin. We knew that homophobia is directly linked to men's fear about expressing who we really are. And we knew that racism, classism, and ableism demand that we fight for one "right" way to be a man.

Before the end of our first decade, in 1990, we had developed the Men Overcoming Violence batterers' intervention program, the High School Education Project, Gentle Warrior retreats, workshops for colleges and human service organizations, and were publishing a newsletter. Yet, in the more than two decades since our founding, there are still very few men's centers in the United States—in the world for that matter. Step by step we have created the MRC as a model of what is possible; a vibrant, grassroots, community-based men's center.

If men's centers are going to become more than a passing fad temporarily catching the eye of the media, we need to understand and support the reasons for having men's centers in our communities. Because so few people have any experience of a men's center, and because there are many voices of suspicion and fear, we need careful, and repeated, explanations of "why a men's center." Here are some of our answers to the question, "Why a men's center?"

Because Men are Hurting
Many men are in pain. This pain can be physical, mental, or emotional, often all three. Some men recognize it; many do not. Often men try not to pay attention to their pain. We have learned to "suck it up," "hold it in," "walk it off." We believe that admitting our pain to others is an admission of weakness, proof of not being a "real man," letting others down, and an invitation to be shamed and abused. We often end up isolated and afraid in our pain. Addictive and abusive behaviors are one way we attempt to cope with this hidden pain.

At a men's center, a safe place is created where men are encouraged to respect the full range of our feelings, where we do not have to deny our pain, our fear, our anger, or our joy, where men come together to witness and support each other in expressing ourselves clearly and honestly. We break through our fears and learn that our greatest strength is in our vulnerability, with ourselves and others.

Because Men are Hurting Others

Violence in our relationships, in our families, on our streets, and in our schools continues to be one of the most significant social issues of our time. Much (although not all) of this violence seems to be committed by men and teenage boys. Although we have a growing number of legal and social services for victims of violence, society has not yet developed an array of effective resources for addressing the perpetrators.

At a men's center, men join together in learning how to recognize and take responsibility for our patterns of hurtful behavior. We examine how the social and psychological dimensions of masculinity have affected us personally and created the conditions for violence and abuse. We share and support one another's efforts to change these patterns, individually and culturally. We join as allies with women in challenging cultural and institutional systems of domination and control. We offer ourselves and our society models of recovery, safety, empowerment, and hope.

Because Men Are Divided Against One Another

From an early age, males learn to compete against one another. We are taught to think about ourselves as potential soldiers fighting other men to the death in combat. We see other men as dangerous enemies from whom we have to defend ourselves and our families, and with whom we must compete for limited resources. We have used differences of race, nationality, class, and sexual orientation as battlegrounds fueling our fear of other men.

At a men's center, men come together with an agreement of honesty and respect for one another. We learn to put aside our fears and create a culture where we can practice understanding rather than winning, communication rather than fighting, sharing rather than defending. We become a place where men from different backgrounds, lifestyles, and communities can learn to feel safe with, listen to, and care for one another.

Because Masculinity Is in Transition

Our understanding of what it takes to be a successful man is going through big changes. We are being called upon to develop new ways of relating to our emotions, our partners/wives, our children, and our work. These changes can easily leave us feeling confused, disoriented, and overwhelmed. At a men's center, men find others who are facing the challenges of these changes. Together we resist the pressures to adapt to a rigid, dominating masculinity, instead supporting each other in developing diverse ways of being a man that express our highest values and visions. We are creating a new, healthier culture of masculinity.

Because Men Want to Help

Many men care about issues of violence, oppression, inequality, liberation, and healing. Although we may want to take a stand, speak out, make a difference, we often feel uncertain, scared, isolated, silenced, and powerless. At a men's center, men join together with other men who want to make a contribution to the lives of the men, women, and children in their communities. Together, we find ways to take actions that give voice to our caring and our commitment. We learn how to work collaboratively with one another and with women, developing shared power and leadership. A men's center offers training and opportunities for men's leadership and community activism.

The best answer to "why a men's center," of course, may be simply to look at the Men's Resource Center. Each week, we serve more than 100 men and women through our support groups and Men Overcoming Violence programs alone. Each year, through our youth education programs, we reach hundreds of secondary and college students. Each season we send this magazine to thousands of people throughout New England and beyond.

Why a men's center? Because it makes a unique and significant difference in the lives of individual men, women, and children, and the health of our communities and our society. Join us.

Looking at (White, Male, Straight, Middle-Class) Privilege

By Michael Kimmel

Spring 2003

> *To run or walk into a strong headwind is to understand the power of nature. You set your jaw in a squared grimace, your eyes are slits against the wind, and you breathe with a fierce determination. And still you make so little progress. To walk or run with that same wind at your back is to float, to sail effortlessly, expending virtually no energy. You do not feel the wind; it feels you. You do not feel how it pushes you along; you feel only the effortlessness of your movements. You feel like you could go on forever. Only when you turn around and face that wind do you realize its strength.*

Being white, or male, or heterosexual in this culture is like running with the wind at your back. It feels like just plain running, and we rarely if ever get a chance to see how we are sustained, supported, and even propelled by that wind. Looking at privilege is to make the wind visible.

When I present majority students with evidence of systematic discrimination, they often seem indifferent, and sometimes even defensive and resistant. "What does this have to do with me?" they ask. The more defensive of them immediately mention several facts that they believe will absolve them of inclusion into the superordinate category. "My family never owned slaves," "I have a gay friend," "I never raped anyone" are fairly typical responses. Virtually all say racism is a problem of individual attitudes and prejudiced people, not a social problem.

Such statements are as revealing as they are irrelevant. They tell us far more about the way we tend to individualize and personalize processes that are social and structural. And they also tell us that members of the majority resist discussions of inequality because it will require that they feel guilty for crimes someone else committed.

Even those students who are willing to engage with these questions also tend to personalize and individualize them. They may grudgingly grant the systematic nature of inequality, but to them, racism, sexism, and heterosexism are simply bad attitudes held by bad people. They are eager to help those bad people see the error of their ways and change their attitudes to good attitudes. This usually will come about through better education.

We who are white, heterosexual, male, and/or middle class need to go further; we need to see how we are stakeholders in the understanding of structural inequality, how the dynamics that create inequality for some also benefit others. Privilege needs to be made visible.

Researchers in a variety of disciplines are examining that which previously passed as invisible, neutral, and universal. We now can see how the experience of "privilege" also shapes the lives of men, white people, and heterosexuals. To be white, or straight, or male, or middle class is to be simultaneously ubiquitous and invisible. You're everywhere you look, you're the standard against which everyone else is measured. You're like water, like air.

People will tell you they went to see a "woman doctor," or they will say they went to see "the doctor." People will tell you they have a "gay colleague" or they'll tell you about a "colleague." A white person will be happy to tell you about a "black friend," but when that same person simply mentions a "friend," everyone will assume the person is white.

This invisibility is political. This was first made clear to me in the early 1980s, when I participated in a small discussion group on feminism. In one meeting, in a discussion between two women, I first confronted this invisibility. A white woman and a black woman were discussing whether all women were, by definition, "sisters," because they all had essentially the same experiences and because all women faced a common oppression by men. The white woman asserted that the fact that they were both women bonded them, in spite of racial differences. The black woman disagreed.

"When you wake up in the morning and look in the mirror, what do you see?" she asked.

"I see a woman," replied the white woman.

"That's precisely the problem," responded the black woman. "I see a black woman. To me, race is visible every day, because race is how I am not privileged in our culture. Race is invisible to you, because it's how you are privileged. It's why there will always be differences in our experience."

As I witnessed this exchange, I was startled, and groaned—more audibly, perhaps, than I had intended. Because I was the only man in the room, someone asked what my response had meant.

"Well," I said, "when *I* look in the mirror, I see a human being. I'm universally generalizable. As a middle-class white man, I have no class, no race, and no gender. I'm the generic person!"

Sometimes, I like to think it was on that day I became a middle-class white man. Sure, I had been all those things before, but they had not meant much to me. Since then, I've begun to understand that race, class, and gender don't refer only to other people, who have been marginalized by race, class, or gender privilege. Those terms also described me. I enjoyed the privilege of invisibility. The very processes that confer privilege on one group and not another are often invisible to those on whom privilege is conferred. What makes us marginal or powerless are the processes we see, partly because others keep reminding us of them.

Invisibility is a privilege in a double sense—describing both the power relations that are kept in place by the very dynamics of invisibility and in the sense of privilege as luxury. It is a luxury that only white people have in our society: not having to think about race every minute of their lives. It is a luxury that only men have in our society: to pretend that gender does not matter.

There are consequences to this invisibility; privilege, as well as gender, remains invisible. And it's hard to generate a politics of inclusion from invisibility. The invisibility of privilege means that many men, like many white people, become defensive and angry when confronted with the statistical realities or the human consequences of racism or sexism. Since our privilege is invisible, we may become defensive. Hey, we may even feel like victims ourselves.

I was reminded of this when I appeared on a TV talk show opposite three "angry white males," men who felt that they had been the victims of workplace discrimination. The show's title was "A Black Woman Took My Job." In my comments, I invited these men to consider what the word "my" meant in that title, that they felt that the jobs were originally "theirs," that they were entitled to them, and that when some "other" person—black, female—got the job, that person was really taking "their" job. But by what right is that *his* job? By convention, by a historical legacy of discrimination. We've needed decades of affirmative action to even begin making the playing field slightly closer to level.

Our task is to begin to make visible the privilege that accompanies and conceals that invisibility. One way to understand how privilege works—and how it is kept invisible—is to look at the way we think about inequality. We always think about inequality from the perspective of the one who is hurt by the inequality, not the one who is helped. Take, for example, wage inequality based on gender. We're used to hearing that women make about 71 cents for every dollar made by a man. In that statistic, women's wages are calculated as a function of men's wages; men's wages are the standard (the $1) against which women's wages are calculated. In this way, the discrimination against women is visible—doing the same job, they earn less, just because they are women.

But what if we changed the statistics? What if we expressed men's wages as a function of women's wages? What if we said that for every dollar earned by a woman, men make $1.34? Then it wouldn't be the discrimination that was visible—it would be the privilege. Just for being a male, a male worker received an additional 34 cents. This is what sociologist R. W. Connell calls the "masculinity dividend"—the unearned benefits that accrue to men, just for being men.

Making gender, race, class, sexuality visible—both as the foundations of individual identity and as the social dynamics of inequality—is a difficult thing to do, and there's no question but that it will make us feel uncomfortable. It's unpleasant to acknowledge that all the good things that have happened to you are not simply the result of your hard work and talent and motivation but the result of something that you had no power over. Sometimes it will make us feel guilty, other times defensive. Sometimes we just feel powerless. "What can I possibly do to change this massive system of inequality?"

In a culture such as ours, all problems are thought to be individual problems, based on bad attitudes, wrong choices, or our own frailties and addictions. When confronted with structural or social problems, we think the solutions are either aggregated individual solutions—everyone needs to change their attitudes—or that the solutions don't exist. A lone individual has no chance to change the system; we feel powerless, impotent. We can become mired in guilt. Some people argue that guilt is a negative emotion, and that we shouldn't have to feel guilty for the things that happened generations—even centuries—ago. Occasionally, someone is moved by that guilt to attempt to renounce his or her privilege. Books counsel us to become "race traitors," or to "refuse" to be a man.

And sometimes such a posture feels moral and self-righteous. Guilt isn't always a "bad" emotion after all. How would you feel about a German saying he or she really doesn't want to feel guilty about the Holocaust? "After all, I personally never sent a Jew to the gas chambers." Or a white South African who proclaimed that he or she never actually benefited from apartheid, since they got their job and their wealth by virtue of their hard work and determination?

Guilt may be appropriate, even a necessary feeling—for a while. It does not freeze us in abjection, but can motivate us to transform the circumstances that made us feel guilty in the first place, to make connections between our experiences and those of others, and to become and remain accountable to the struggles for equality and justice around the world. Guilt can politicize us. (Perhaps that's one reason why we often resist it.)

While noble in intention, however, this posture of guilty self-negation cannot be our final destination as we come to understand how we are privileged by race, class, gender, and sexuality. Refusing to be men, white, or straight does neither the privileged nor the unprivileged much good. One can no more renounce privilege than one can stop breathing. It's in the air we breathe.

And it's embedded in the social architecture surrounding us. Renouncing privilege ultimately substitutes an individual solution for a structural and social problem. Inequality is structural and systematic, as well as individual and attitudinal. Eliminating inequalities involves more than changing everyone's attitudes. Trying to rid oneself of bad attitudes, renouncing one's unearned privilege also, finally, brings us no further than the feelings of impotent despair that we often feel in the face of such overwhelming systemic problems. We feel lonely. We feel isolated from our friends, our families, or our colleagues.

The struggles against inequality are, however, collective struggles, enormous social movements that unite people across geography, race, religion, class, sexuality, and gender. Participating in these struggles to end inequality brings one into a long history of those who have stood alongside the victims of oppression, those who have added their voices to the voices of those who had been earlier silenced. Examining our privilege may be uncomfortable at first, but it can also be energizing, motivating, and engaging.

Ultimately, examining those arenas where we are privileged and those where we're not will enable us to understand our society more fully and engage us in the long historical process of change.

Poisoned Privilege: The Price Men Pay for Patriarchy
By Jane Fonda
Fall 2003

Before I turned sixty I thought I was a feminist. I was in a way—I worked to register women to vote, I supported women getting elected. I brought gender issues into my movie roles, I encouraged women to get strong and healthy, I read the books we've all read. I had it in my head and partly in my heart, yet I didn't fully get it.

See, although I've always been financially independent, and professionally and socially successful, behind the closed doors of my personal life I was still turning myself in a pretzel so I'd be loved by an alpha male. I thought if I didn't become whatever he wanted me to be, I'd be alone, and then, I wouldn't exist.

There is not the time nor is this the place to explain why this was true, or why it is such a common theme for so many otherwise strong, independent women. Nor is it the time to tell you how I got over it. (I'm writing my memoirs, and all will be revealed.) What's important is that I did get over it.

Early on in my third act I found my voice and, in the process, I have ended up "alone" but not really. You see, I'm with myself, and this has enabled me to see feminism more clearly. It's hard to see clearly when you're a pretzel.

So I want to tell you briefly some of what I have learned in this first part of my third act and how it relates to what, I think, needs to happen in terms of a revolution.

Because we can't just talk about women being at the table—it's too late for that—we have to think in terms of the shape of the table. Is it hierarchical or circular (metaphorically speaking)? We have to think about the quality of the men who are with us at the table, the culture that is hovering over the table that governs how things are decided and in whose interests. This is not just about glass ceilings or politics as usual. This is about revolution, and I have finally gotten to where I can say that word and know what I mean by it and feel good about it because I see, now, how the future of the earth and everything on it including men and boys depends on this happening.

Let me say something about men: obviously, I've had to do a lot of thinking about men, especially the ones who've been important in my life, and what I've come to realize is how damaging patriarchy has been for them. And all them are smart, good men who want to be considered the "good guys." But the Male Belief System, that compartmentalized, hierarchical, ejaculatory, androcentric power structure that is Patriarchy, is fatal to the hearts of men, to empathy and relationship.

Yes, men and boys receive privilege and status from patriarchy, but it is a poisoned privilege for which they pay a heavy price. If traditional, patriarchal socialization takes aim at girls' voices, it takes aim at boys' hearts—makes them lose the deepest, most sensitive and empathic parts of themselves. Men aren't even allowed to be depressed, which is why they engage so often in various forms of self-numbing, from sex to alcohol and drugs to gambling and workaholism. Patriarchy strikes a Faustian bargain with men.

Patriarchy sustains itself by breaking relationship. I'm referring here to real relationship, the showing-up kind, not the "I'll stay with him cause he pays the bills, or because of the kids, or because if I don't I will cease to exist," but relationship where you, the woman, can acknowledge your partner's needs while simultaneously acknowledging and tending to your own. I work with young girls and I can tell you there's a whole generation who have not learned what a relationship is supposed to feel like—that it's not about leaving themselves behind.

Now, every group that's been oppressed has its share of Uncle Toms, and we have our Aunt Toms. I call them ventriloquists for the patriarchy. I won't name names but we all know them. They are women in whom the toxic aspects of masculinity hold sway. It should neither surprise nor discourage us. We need to understand it and be able to explain it to others, but it means, I think, that we should be just about getting a woman into this position or that. We need to look at "is that woman intact emotionally," has she had to forfeit her empathy gene somewhere along the way for whatever reason?

And then, of course, there are what Eve Ensler calls Vagina-Friendly men, who choose to remain emotionally literate. It's not easy for them—look at the names they get called: wimp, pansy, pussy, soft, limp, momma's boy. Men don't like to be considered "soft" on anything, which is why more don't choose to join us in the circle. Actually, most don't have the choice to make.

You know why? Because when they are real little (I learned this from Carol Gilligan), like five years or younger, boys internalize the message of what it takes to be a "real man." Sometimes it comes through their fathers who beat it into them. Sometimes it comes because no one around them knows how to connect with their emotions (This is a generational thing). Sometimes it comes because our culture rips boys from their mothers before they are developmentally ready.

Sometimes it comes because boys are teased at school for crying. Sometimes it's the subliminal messages from teachers and the media. It can be a specific trauma that shuts them down. But, I can assure you, it is true to some extent of many if not most men, and when the extreme version of it manifests itself in our nation's leaders, beware!

Another thing that I've learned is that there is a fundamental contradiction not just between patriarchy and relationship, but between patriarchy and democracy. Patriarchy masquerades as democracy, but it's an anathema.

How can it be democracy when someone has to always be above someone else, when women, who are a majority, live within a social construct that discriminates against them, keeps them from having their full human rights? But just because patriarchy has ruled for 10,000 years since the beginning of agriculture, doesn't make it inevitable.

Maybe at some earlier stage in human evolution, patriarchy was what was needed just for the species to survive. But today, there's nothing threatening the human species but humans. We've conquered our predators, we've subdued nature almost to extinction, and there are no more frontiers to conquer or to escape into so as to avoid having to deal with the mess we've left behind. Frontiers have always given capitalism, patriarchy's economic face, a way to avoid dealing with its shortcomings. Well, we're having to face them now in this postfrontier era and inevitably—especially when we have leaders who suffer from toxic masculinity—that leads to war, the conquering of new markets, and the destruction of the earth.

However, it is altogether possible, that we are on the verge of a tectonic shift in paradigms—that what we are seeing happening today are the paroxysms, the final terrible death throes of the old, no longer workable, no longer justifiable system. Look at it this way: it's patriarchy's third act and we have to make sure it's its last.

It's possible that the extreme, neo-conservative version of patriarchy which makes up our current executive branch will overplay its hand and cause the house of cards to collapse. We know that this new "preventive war" doctrine will put us on a permanent war footing. We know there can't be guns and butter, right? We learned that with Vietnam. We know that a Pandora's box has been opened in the Middle East and that the administration is not prepared for the complexities that are emerging.

We know that friends are becoming foes and angry young Muslims with no connection to al-Qaeda are becoming terrorists in greater numbers. We know that with the new tax plan, the rich will be better off and the rest will be poorer. We know what happens when poor young men and women can only get jobs by joining the military and what happens when they come home and discover that the day after Congress passed the "Support Our Troops" Resolution, $25 billion was cut from the VA budget. We know that already, families of servicemen and women have to go on welfare and are angry about it.

So, as Eve Ensler says, we have to change the verbs from obliterate, dominate, humiliate, to liberate, appreciate, celebrate. We have to make sure that head and heart can be reunited in the body politic, and relationship and democracy can be restored.

We need to really understand the depth and breadth of what a shift to a new, feminine paradigm would mean, how fundamentally central it is to every single other thing in the world. We win, everything wins, including boys, men, and the earth. We have to really understand this and be able to make it concrete for others so they will be able to see what feminism really is and see themselves in it.

So our challenge is to commit ourselves to creating the tipping point and the turning point. The time is ripe to launch a unified national movement a campaign, a tidal wave, built around issues and values, not candidates.

That's why V-Day, the White House Project, and their many allies are partnering to hold a national women's convention somewhere in the heartland, in June of 2004. Its purpose will be to inspire and mobilize women and vagina-friendly men around the 2004 elections and to build a new movement that will coalesce our energies and forces around a politic of caring.

The convention will put forward a fresh, clear, and concise platform of issues, and build the spirit, energy, and power base to hold the candidates accountable for them.

There will be a diversity of women from across the country who will participate in the mobilization. There will be a special focus on involving young women. There will be a variety of performers and artists acknowledging that culture plays a powerful role in political action. There will be a concurrent Internet mobilization. Women's organizations will be asked to sign on and send representatives to the convention. There will be a caravan, a rolling tour across the country, of diverse women leaders, celebrities, and activists who will work with local organizers to build momentum, sign people up, register them to vote, get them organized, and leave behind a tool kit for further mobilization through the election and beyond.

This movement will be a volcano that will erupt in a flow of soft, hot, empathic, breathing, authentic, vagina-friendly, relational lava that will encircle patriarchy and smother it. We will be the flood and we'll be Noah's ark: "V" for vagina, for vote, for victory.

Conscientious Objection Is "Manly"
By Elias Sánchez-Eppler
Spring 2005

Violence is a failure of the imagination.

—William Stafford, conscientious objector during World War II
who spent 12 hours a day for three years cutting timber in remote
forests as punishment for his refusal to shoot other men in the belly.

A lot of men and women sincerely wish the US military were not in Iraq now. I count myself among them, but even I am increasingly bored with the same old rant. It's an important talk, and if you haven't heard it recently, many have gotten quite good at delivering it. One facet of the issue that came up shortly before the election last November was the potential for a draft. Again, I can't report on the likelihood of future draft legislation, but I will use the rumor of it as a call to arms, so to speak.

Many activists maintain that there is already a draft in place. It is called the "economic draft." For youth such as myself who are educated and have professional ambitions, it is easy to take our privilege and the promise of future success for granted, but for those less fortunate, the military may appear to be the only career that guarantees employment and enough pay to support a family.

Another type of draft already in place is the "culture draft." Even in times of peace, US culture and government work to create a sense of the military that is favorable to recruitment. Generally, military service is portrayed as the swiftest and surest path to financial stability, social recognition, and manhood. While women are no longer excluded from recruitment efforts, "manhood"— and all the conventional traits it embraces—is still a major attraction in joining the military. More specifically, the military claims to develop discipline, courage, camaraderie, and strength and endurance of body, soul, and mind. Many activists focus on helping young people discover these traits in civilian life. Personally, I find all of them in resisting war.

These enticements aside, no one is legally forced at present to join the military; anyone can just *not sign up*. In the eventuality of a draft, however, this is no defense. A lot of people are surprised by the idea of "defending" against a draft, but with some preparation it can be done. Fortunately, the United States Constitution includes a Bill of Rights that has withstood many previous assaults. Freedom of religion exempts some from military conscription—but what about the rest of us? Again, the law provides a loophole, albeit a small one. In the most recent draft legislation, exemption was extended to those who morally, ethically, or philosophically opposed all war as a matter of either religious beliefs or nonreligious beliefs held with religious conviction. There are two key steps in applying for this exemption. Most formidable is actually managing to prove that the exemption applies. First, however, applicants must convince themselves.

I certainly don't want to detract from the valor of citizens-in-arms, but I lack the experience, motivation, and need to add to it. That said, I would like it to apply to those of us who oppose militarism. The government claims that military service builds discipline, courage, and physical, spiritual, and emotional endurance and strength. In the event of a draft, these traits are required of those who hope to defend their claim to moral, ethical, or philosophical exemption. To formulate and live by these beliefs requires spiritual and emotional maturity and discipline. Defending these beliefs against attack necessitates courage, grace, strength, and endurance. Feminist provisions aside, conscientious objection to war is, well, "manly."

During the Vietnam War, conscientious objector status was granted by draft boards. Applicants could be exempted from combatant duties if solely opposed to killing, or from any military duty if opposed to war in its entirety. Local citizens sat on these boards and heard young men try to tell them about their beliefs, how they came to them, and how they live by their beliefs.

Personally, I love to tell audiences about my beliefs publicly. However, my experience with mock draft boards I've faced is that they are anything but sympathetic. In fact, even in role-plays it is much more like a hostile cross-examination in court than an explanation of personal beliefs conducted in a neutral atmosphere. In essence, the idea is to make the applicant contradict himself or admit to all the ways in which he betrays the beliefs that would exempt him.

The US has not had a draft since the Vietnam War, but young men are still required by law to register with the Selective Service System when they turn eighteen, and the head of the SSS maintains that full-scale military conscription of men from ages eighteen to twenty-six could get under way with less than a month's notice. In that event, the law could look like anything, and might well include young women. However, freedom of religion would certainly be grounds to appeal any charges of draft evasion if no other provisions were made. Whatever the defense, an applicant's case is made much stronger by any "material" evidence he or she might have. Material evidence to legally prove internal belief may seem a ridiculous notion—but it's crucial that anyone who is worried about the chances of a draft starting between now and when he or she turns twenty-six should seriously consider getting some.

I divide such material into four categories: articles, essays, reflections, and references. *Articles* are material proof of my antiwar convictions. For example, my file includes pictures of me demonstrating against war, certificates of participation at peace conventions, published records of my social action, and presumably will include a copy of the magazine you are currently reading. *Essays* are short pieces I put together where I talk about what I believe, why it would prevent me from participating in war, and what I do in my life in keeping with my beliefs. Between articles and essays are *reflections* on other people's writings.

Many friends have articles and information that have struck them, and these may include their various underlining, marginalia, and other reflections on the document. Finally, character *references* are a standard of complete conscientious objector files. These are letters written by family, friends, and mentors answering the same questions as essays to the best of the authors' capacities. In short, anything that shows a devotion to peace is legitimate and useful in compiling such a file.

One crucial element is time. An essay written years ago will have more bearing than one written since the applicant got called up. However, the draft board won't accept a dated document on faith. It must be authenticated. One popular and easy way of doing this is to mail it to yourself in a self-addressed envelope. This way the US Post Office date stamp is firmly on the sealed envelope, documenting the length of time one has held conscientious objector beliefs.

A mandatory draft for young people is not yet here. Will the Bush administration's adventurism overseas or further terrorist threats—real or imagined—bring it back? None of us knows for sure. But now is the time for young people who oppose the draft to speak out, and for those of us who object to war and militarism to begin documenting our beliefs and preparing ourselves for the potential trials ahead.

Becoming Green Men
By Michael Dover
Summer 2001

What does men's work have to do with saving the environment?

The best of profeminist men's work has entailed self-examination, self-discovery, and openness to change: processes that offer direct parallels to creating new paradigms for the new "green man." That applies equally well to stopping violence against women, ending racism and homophobia, and restoring the world's ecological systems. The link among all these goals is the need for men to play a critical role in countering the cultures of domination and creating instead a culture of connection. For me, these paradigms take shape in the following challenges for men (beginning, I might add, with myself).

Be in feelings. Begin where we all need to begin, in your own heart. Rediscover awe and wonder in the diversity and complexity of life. Give space for your love of the world around you and your outrage at the threats to its existence. Let go of your capacity to rationalize those threats away as "necessary," "inevitable," or "acceptable." Experience the feelings and intuitions of others as deeply as your own.

Both seek and grow connection. As boys grow into men, we are taught to isolate, to compartmentalize, to dissect. This is equally true for how we examine the world and how we treat ourselves. The real world is just the opposite. Life occurs only in connection with other life. We think we see individual trees as we walk in a forest when in fact every tree is connected through a vast network of roots and symbiotic fungi into what can't readily be described as one or a myriad of organisms. The fox and the rabbit are what they are because of each other; so too the frog and the fly, the bee and the flower. We are no different. Men in particular need to rediscover connection with one another, to see ourselves as part of an intricate web of life rather than as somehow outside of its flows and cycles. Only then can we see clearly our role in keeping that web intact.

Listen, especially to those whose voices are not usually heard. Men are so often raised to take charge, to have the answers, to "know." Attitudes such as these have contributed to the problem as much as, or more than, to the solution. Women, especially in less developed countries, often have very different experiences of environmental problems than do men. Communities of color experience environmental degradation in their neighborhood as another form of racism. Native peoples know that resource exploitation and neocolonialism are inseparable. Those of us who are used to thinking we know how to define problems and seek solutions need to step back and learn just how much we need to learn before we can be truly useful (and then, often not at center stage).

Question assumptions, including your own. Letting go of knowing the answers also means being open to being wrong—even fundamentally wrong. Wrong from the get-go. Wrong about which way is up. The holders of political and corporate power (usually men) count on the public's acceptance of their definitions of the situation: We need more oil, not fewer cars; it's owls (or salmon or ...) versus jobs; growth equals happiness. More men than women buy these assumptions, "accept" the risks, trust authority. We've got work to do with our brothers—and ourselves—so that we all begin by asking the hard questions and being prepared for uncomfortable answers.

Turn away from privilege and power toward cooperation and compassion. This is at the heart of what I believe men's work to be. Whether we have privilege and power in hand or merely the promise of them if we play the masculinity game right, it's time to recognize this as a path toward mutual destruction—of planet as well as of soul. As we listen to our feelings, seek connection, listen to others, and question assumptions, I believe we cannot help but move toward interpersonal and societal relations based on sharing among equals rather than benefiting from continued inequality.

For the next challenge, I'll defer to the eloquence of one of my heroes: the late Donella Meadows, the environmentalist, author, and columnist who reached millions with her intelligence and passion for the preservation of the planet. This is from a 1993 speech:

"Operate from love. One is not allowed to say that in public any more. Anyone who calls upon the human capacity for brotherly and sisterly love, generosity, compassion, will be met with a hail of cynicism. Once when I tried to do so, a high government official stood up to say, 'Of all scarce resources, love is the scarcest.' I just don't believe that. Love is not a scarce resource, it is an untapped one."

Honor yourself for what you do, forgive yourself for what you haven't done—yet. There's so much to do, and the problems are so difficult and complex. Nothing is enough. But any step, however small, is worth taking. Men's work—loving, generous, compassionate, respectful work—isn't easy. The profeminist men's movement has been at this work for decades and it feels sometimes as if we've only scratched the surface. And so it is with creating a sustainable world, mindful and in tune with natural rhythms. But it's the work we know we have to do. Donella Meadows closed one of her books, *Groping in the Dark* (1982), this way:

> When everyone is so sophisticated
> that they can't believe it could be so simple to be honest and to care
> And everyone is so smart
> that they know *they* don't count
> so they never try
> You get the kind of world we've got.

> Maybe it's worth thinking another way
> as if we cared and we made a difference,
> Even if it is just groping in the dark.

Meadows saw that changing the nature of human relations is essential to changing the relations of humans with nature. We can only start where we are, but we have to start.

Men's Lives: From Stubbornness to Tenderness
By Rob Okun
Spring 2006

Imagine a split movie screen: on one side a fortysomething US Navy captain in his ship's radio room; on the other, a spiritual seeker, the same age, visiting children in a crowded Indian orphanage. Now, consider the men's stories.

A decade ago, the following radio exchange occurred between a US Navy captain and Canadian authorities off the coast of Newfoundland. (The US chief of naval operations released the transcript of the conversation.)

> Americans: *Please divert your course 15 degrees to the north to avoid a collision.*
> Canadians: *Recommend you divert your course 15 degrees to the south to avoid a collision.*
> Americans: *This is the captain of a US Navy ship. I say again, divert your course.*
> Canadians: *No. I say again, you divert your course.*
> Americans: *This is the aircraft carrier USS Lincoln, the second largest ship in the United States' Atlantic Fleet. We are accompanied by three destroyers, three cruisers and numerous support vessels. I demand you change your course 15 degrees to the north. That's one-five degrees to the north—or countermeasures will be undertaken to ensure the safety of this ship.*
> Canadians: *This is a lighthouse. Your call.*

Imagine the relief, and then the laughter, that must have erupted among the crew of the USS *Lincoln*. How embarrassing—and funny—to discover that you were puffing up your chest to stubbornly threaten a lighthouse! After learning the truth I can also imagine the captain feeling silly, stupid, exposed—and vulnerable. Getting hotter under his starched collar by the minute.

How many men can relate to that feeling of humiliation? I know I can. Becoming the butt of a joke, even an innocent one, leaves a sting that can raise our hackles. We're not supposed to feel betrayed; we're "supposed" to be in control.

As men become increasingly willing to struggle with our stubbornness—admitting we've made mistakes or bad decisions—we are accepting a rare gift, acknowledging personal responsibility. I know in my family—as a son, brother, father, and husband—I have come up against my stubbornness more times than I'd like to remember. That's probably why I could so easily conjure up the image of the red-faced captain. I wonder: Would he ever be able to join in with the laughter? It is precisely *there*, in that place of taking responsibility for his actions, that his growth—and yours and mine—as a man is most palpable, ready to burst forth. His is a story worth remembering.

Meanwhile, a world away, the other scene on the split screen portrays a Western spiritual seeker visiting a Calcutta orphanage operated by Mother Teresa. Because cultural taboos strongly discourage men from working with very young children, there is a buzz of excitement as he enters a large common area. "Uncle! Uncle!" the orphans cry, hungry for contact with a man. He looks at them, hundreds of dark eyes glistening, and feels his heart stir. As he walks through a room nearly the size of a gymnasium, he sees dozens and dozens of children—and an even a larger number of babies lined up in row after row of cribs. Now it's *his* eyes that are glistening, soon followed by salty tears running down his cheeks. His heart beating fast, a thought comes to him: "I could spend my whole life in this room and I'd be fulfilled." He walks over to the cribs and begins picking up the babies, one after another after another, holding them to his chest, cooing into their ears. He keeps this up for quite a while before it is time for visitors to leave. As he reluctantly does so, a quote from Mother Teresa comes back to him: "We cannot expect to do great things," she said. "We can only expect to do small things with great love."

The Navy captain and the spiritual seeker seem so different from each other. Is there a bridge to connect their lives? By paying attention to both men's stubbornness and men's tenderness we can see the arc of possibility men are capable of traveling. In a world where the United States commander in chief refuses to ask for directions—as in, "Can you show me the road out of Iraq?"—we are thirsting for the voices of men who are humbly moving from stubbornness to tenderness. Only when the number of men holding babies exceeds the number refusing to yield the right of way will men be more tender than stubborn, more openhearted than hardheaded.

What Kind of Man Am I?

By Jason Sperber
Spring 2012

The following is a list of stereotypical traits, interests, preoccupations, aptitudes, abilities, and roles, both silly and serious, trivial and not, historically associated and correlated with masculinity, manhood, and maleness via both societal mores and popular culture, which I, in my 37 years of life as a straight male, have totally and utterly failed to adopt, incorporate into myself, and live up to:

I do not enjoy playing, either physically or via virtual statistics-based fantasy league, or watching, via televised broadcast or in person, sports, including but not limited to football, basketball, golf, wrestling, boxing, hockey, bowling, NASCAR, tennis, bull riding, ultimate Frisbee, curling, street luge, competitive rowing, and squash.

I am not, and have never been, a "handy" or DIY-type person. I did not do my own kitchen remodel or snake my own sewer line to unblock the tree roots that used to cause my toilet to overflow every winter. So as to avoid nail punctures and self-electrocution, I will not be building my kids a handmade playhouse or wiring my own surround-sound system. The last time I worked with tools to craft something with my own hands was my Pinewood Derby car when I was a Boy Scout, and even that was with my dad's help. (Did I mention that he has a garage full of tools and table saws and whatnot and that he built my childhood home's deck? And that he played high school football?)

I am not what you would call a "car person." I have not memorized the features and statistical details of my fantasy sports car or truck or SUV, because I do not *have* a fantasy sports car or truck or SUV. I do not know how the car that I *do* drive works, and I do not know how to fix it if it stops working. (See the item above about not being a do-it-yourselfer.)

I do not drink or like beer. Any beer. I am not a teetotaler by any means, but I'd rather have a cold hard cider or a rum and Coke or a chilled glass of Riesling (yeah, not a big red wine drinker, either) than a pint of trendy microbrew or a can of commercial swill. And if all you have is beer, then, yeah, sorry, I'll go non-alc, but thanks for offering.

I don't hunt. I don't like guns. I can't shoot a bow or wield a knife or take someone down with a move gleaned from a UFC cage match. Sorry, but rifle class at Boy Scout camp (and yeah, I'm an Eagle Scout) didn't help much. Not so much with the roughhousing either.

I've had two brief careers as a high school social studies teacher and as an online journalist and community manager. In neither of those jobs did the salaries even approach the expected earnings of my wife, who is a physician, and we knew that would be the case going in, when we got engaged as college students and she was on the road to becoming a doctor and I thought I'd be a teacher for the rest of my life.

Even before kids, I did most of the cooking and laundry in our household, and since we became parents, I do almost all the cooking and laundry. (Growing up, my father the teacher did all the cooking while my mother, who stopped teaching for health reasons, did the laundry.)

I am the stay-at-home-father of two amazing daughters. I am an at-home-parent by choice, and I know that my family is lucky, economically, to have that be a choice, rather than a financial impossibility or a forced situation.

Now, I know, and have already preemptively acknowledged above, that these are all stereotypes, some of them cruder than others. Before people start freaking out, I know that "football + cars + beer = masculinity" is a vast over-simplification veering on a bad joke. I know that. I'm not being totally serious here. And I'm not even saying that I don't regret some of the above—sure, I'd love to be the kind of person (not guy, but person) who can fix stuff around the house without calling in the professionals. And yet...

And yet... Every single one of the examples above has been used, implicitly and explicitly, in seriousness and in jest, interpersonally and via mass media generalization, to question and cast doubt on my masculinity, my manhood, my maleness, my de facto membership in a real or imagined brotherhood of men. And taken all together, well... Why am I bringing this up? I certainly had no intention of plunging either headlong or reluctantly sideways in to the Internet debate over redefining manhood and the "plight" of modern men. Then again, I'm already in the middle of it, aren't I, just by self-consciously calling myself a "dad blogger" and writing about stuff like "involved father-hood" and being a SAHD.

And then, not long ago, I was reading a blogpost, like most blogposts I read, by a fellow parent blogger (in this case, a mom blogger). It was a list of lessons she wanted to teach her sons. It's innocuous and heartwarming enough, full of things like love and learning and responsibility. But it starts with this: 1) *Decide who you want to be.* Decide what kind of man you want to become. Every day behave like that man. You will fail often; keep going."

Number 8 is what stopped me up short: *It's OK to be a man.* If you want, you can be loud, you can play sports, you can hunt and be rough. You don't have to act like women no matter what is politically correct at the moment. In fact, try to always be politically incorrect. Political correctness kills truth and the ability to think for oneself."

And I know she was just talking to her own kids, from her own experiences and her own beliefs, and not necessarily trying to tell anyone else what to do or think or be or feel, but... I couldn't let this go, couldn't get it out of my head. If we are empowered to decide what kind of men we want to be, then why does it feel like we're still being told there's a definition, out there, of what a man *is* that we're supposed to measure up to? Or even further, that there's a (good old, traditional) definition of a man that we can and should be in opposition to *because of* newer, different, less masculine, more feminized versions of "man" somebody is forcing upon us?

Again, I'm not saying the writer is saying any of this, only that this was my reaction, coming from my life experiences. It's okay to be a man. But what does that mean? It's okay to be loud, and play sports, and be rough—echoes of the traditional image of what a man is supposed to be—but what about the opposite? Is it okay to be quiet, and hate sports, and be gentle? Is that still being a man? If that's the kind of man one chooses to be, is that okay? Does that still count? (I'm not even going to get into other thornier issues like belief and sexuality vis-a-vis definitions of manhood, though you can probably guess where I stand.) Even among the diverse community of dad bloggers there's a feeling of, "Yeah, look at us, we change diapers and cook and we parent-not-babysit-dammit, but we still hang out and watch the game with the guys tipping back a cold one." Well, what about those of us who are into the former but not the latter? Or is it just me?

I am not a father of boys. But I was a boy, once upon a time, not too long ago, or at least I like to think so. And I've already told you what kind of boy I was, and what kind of man I grew to be. And I taught plenty of teenage boys, hurtling toward their own definitions of adult manhood, when I was a high school teacher last decade. And even now, when I volunteer at my oldest daughter's elementary school or just observe as I walk across campus, I don't see some entrenched PC culture war being waged, successfully or not, to turn boys into, well, me. I still see those traditional roles and ideas normalized, reinforced, lionized, on the playground, on the sidewalk, in the classroom, by their peers and adults alike. And for boys whose definitions of young manhood are different, who don't play ball on the field or blacktop or act in "boy" ways and do "boy" things, well, I don't see them. I'm not saying they're not there, but just like me at that age, in that situation, maybe they're off somewhere else, doing their own thing, not calling attention to themselves, because everything they've imbibed about what it means to be a man tells them to avoid that attention or suffer the consequences.

The day after I saw that list, I read an article that argued that the opposite of man is not woman but boy. In the piece, about gender as performance, it described men nostalgic for an all-male world not really understanding what masculinity is. Such men believe the opposite of "man" is "woman" and that in order to demonstrate their manliness they must accomplish things woman can't. The better antonym for "man" is "boy." To accomplish masculinity is not about doing things that women don't; it's about doing what boys lack the resolve or maturity to do.

Obviously, it's not just men who conceive of acting like or being a man as the opposite of acting like or being a woman. And it's a false dichotomy, one that serves only to perpetuate stereotypes and unnecessary gender roles and to make outcast and abnormal those who stray from those tropes. And it's a falsehood that I don't want to teach to my daughters.

So who am I? And what does it mean, then, for me, to be a man? It means that I'm a feminist. And an antiracist. I'm an activist and an educator and a father and a partner and a person of color, standing for change, working for justice. And I know that my definitions of all of those labels may be different from yours, and hell, they may be different from mine in a year or two. And that's okay, because identity is process.

Ultimately, I am who I need to be for my children, my partner, myself, and our communities. And all of *that* is what makes me a man.

Beyond Definitions of Manhood
By Carl Erikson
Summer 2002

What does it mean to "be a man?" The men's movement asks this question all the time and gets many different answers. It is a self-defeating question.

Self-defeating because it locks me into "Man"—a stereotype. It locks me into the dichotomy of male and female—both stereotypes, either/or, no ands. It locks me up in prescribed boxes and delivers me into the control of others to be *man*ipulated, bribed, and punished. It denies my freedom of choice, my self, my individual expression, my dignity.

The goal of a "new definition of masculinity" is likewise a self-defeating one. Inherently, a definition sets a single standard for what it defines. A new definition of masculinity is just a new and different stereotype. Males aren't just one thing. They are many different human beings. Even having male genitalia does not guarantee that we are "male," as transgender individuals will attest.

"A more sensitive male" is an oxymoron, impossible to create. By many social definitions, a "male" is insensitive and incapable of expressing feelings. Make him sensitive and then society declares, "He's a fag, a wimp, a sissy, a girl"—anything but male. If a more sensitive male were possible, it would be just another stereotype for men to get locked into by others, another role someone else is telling us to play. Of course, we could define masculinity, maleness, as "open" or anything else. But how can there be a definition if there are no limits or specifics? And why this insistence that there be a definition of "male" anyway? Any definition becomes a box.

The better question, it seems to me, is: Who am I—me, myself? No stereotypes here. No boxes. No either/or. No rules, expectations, direction by society or family for their benefit. The answer to this question satisfies me, instead of putting me into a panic or depression. It puts firm ground under my feet to withstand the ever-growing demands and expectations of others—media, family, institutions, and "common sense." It gives me a direction and purpose from which to confidently judge and choose from among what life puts in front of me.

Like all freedoms, however, this question demands that I consciously discover my self—that I take full responsibility for the consequences of my choices and my expressions of who I am. Society, my boss, the times, fate, and my family are no longer available as excuses for what I choose to do. It's my choice, and I'd better be sure I like the reasons for my choice.

Answering the better question, "Who am I?" is pointless, however, unless I also take responsibility to express who I am. An answer without expression is just a wish. When I express who I am in feelings, words, and actions, my wish comes true, my life changes. In all honesty, though, choosing to express who I am doesn't make my life any easier. It just makes it a lot more meaningful and satisfying.

When you ask the question of who you are and find your own answers, people may well initially oppose your answers and will almost certainly oppose you for expressing them. This opposition can often be strong, ongoing, and sometimes even vicious. However, the certainty of your answer—which you will feel—and the surprising allies who will appear, will help you to withstand the forces opposing you. On the other hand, you may be one of the lucky men who finds the process of change smooth and filled with unexpected cooperation and pleasure.

Whatever the response you get, the better question is not an easy one to answer, particularly if you've spent some time ruminating over "what does it mean to be a man?" The answer to the better question lies within you, where it has lain for years. When you find it, you will likely feel more of a sense of "Aha!" than "Oh my." Your answer will likely entail the rejection of many notions you once held sacred, immutable, even cosmic, and that can be very upsetting. Whatever your feelings, take a deep breath. You'll find your answer will be very personal. Once you come to it, you'll feel like you just hit a game-winning home run, or sang the highest note in the aria, or found the perfect link for your computer program. And you will have no doubt that it is absolutely true, truer than any limiting "definition" of masculinity.

VOICE MALE

Divine Secrets of the Ya-Ya Brotherhood
By Rob Okun
Fall 2002

"Most men don't have a clue how to build and maintain the rich friendships that women take for granted." So wrote *Boston Globe* columnist Sam Allis in a rumination on *Divine Secrets of the Ya-Ya Sisterhood*, the novel and film celebrating the power of friendship among women. Like a wide-eyed kid looking in a candy store window, Allis saw how sweet and deep connection among women is and essentially said, "I want that, too."

Who can blame him—or any man—who notes with sadness or resignation that his friendships with men don't go as deep or feel as connected as those he observes among women? Men bonding on the basketball court or the golf course, kibitzing about the Red Sox, or condemning the latest tale of corporate greed aren't cultivating lifelong bonds where fears are shared, help is sought, souls are bared. What's preventing us as men from getting close to one another? How can we understand our ongoing case of friendship envy?

The answer lies in solving a riddle. Ask the Oracle of Masculinity: "What do you call a man who shares his fears with another man, seeks help from another man, and bares his soul to another man?" And it answers, "A fag." The Oracle of Masculinity has always known this simple, frightening truth. Accordingly, men's "divine secret" to enjoying deep connection and meaningful friendships with other men is overcoming homophobia—working through our unadulterated, red-blooded fear of men who love other men.

Men's views of being *intimate* with another person have been so tightly wrapped into our views of being *sexual* with another person that for most of us the distinction has blurred. We're afraid if we hug another man, cry with another man, admit to another man we sometimes feel scared, because he might get the "wrong" idea and label us gay. (As if that were a bad thing.) Now, consider this riddle: If a woman hugs another woman, cries with another woman, and acknowledges her fears to another woman, what is it called? Healthy!

The culture of conventional masculinity—the one that tells men to go to war and (if you survive) to come home and not talk about what happened—has *always* expected men to keep our feelings in the closet. "We don't want a bunch of blubbering firemen and policemen shedding tears and hugging one another after a hard day's work—that's not manly," society tells men. Of course, that is *exactly* what the firefighters and police officers (along with other rescue workers, women among them) did at the end of a day wading through the rubble of the World Trade Center after September 11. Progress may be slow, but *this* divine secret is out: more and more men are challenging conventional ideas about manhood.

Changing Men

Men are discovering secrets of the ya-ya brotherhood in men's groups and fathers' gatherings in small towns and big cities—and not just across the US but in scores of communities in countries around the world. That's to be celebrated. But there's a long way to go. Just as men have a responsibility to work on preventing violence against women, we have another challenge: overcoming homophobia. It is the civil rights issue of our time. Regardless of our sexual orientation, men of all stripes—husbands and fathers, brothers and sons, workers and thinkers, movers and shakers—are invited to join the struggle. Attempting to free ourselves from a lifelong prejudice is liberating; it offers rewards that may be among the greatest we've ever known: the deep abiding affection, the strong connection, and new-found love of other men.

Hanna Rosin and The End of (Middle-Class Straight White) Men
By Michael Kimmel
Fall 2012

You'd have to have been napping—as those legions of stay-at-home dads often do—to have missed the hoopla over Hanna Rosin's cover story in *The Atlantic* two years ago, provocatively headlined "The End of Men."

Well, now it's a new book that, I believe, will be misread. Rosin's been called a radical feminist for celebrating men's demise, and an antifeminist for suggesting that women have already "won" and that discrimination is a thing of the past. I think some of this misreading is deliberate —people read with agendas, after all. And I think some part of it has to do with the way the book is framed by Rosin and her marketers. Consider that the central thesis of the book is contained not in the big, bold headline "**THE END OF MEN**," but in the smaller print subtitle, "*and the rise of women.*"

I believe that the subtitle—and the subtext—of her work is entirely right, and the title is just as surely wrong. I'll explain in a moment. But first, a story.

I've been teaching gender studies courses at large public universities for 25 years. Being a sociologist, and teaching large classes of 300–450, I often do little surveys in class. When I started, 25 years ago, I asked my women students what they thought it meant to be a woman. Be nice, pretty, smile, cooperate—these were the typical responses I got. When I'd ask the men, they'd say—remember, this was 25 years ago—John Wayne.

When I ask them now, the women say "Huh? What does it mean to be a woman? I don't know. I can be anything I want. I can be an astronaut, a surgeon, Mia Hamm, or Lady Gaga." And, when I ask the men? "Ah-nold."

Okay, so maybe not Arnold anymore. Maybe some other, as Rosin says, "cardboard" cut-out action figure. The women believe that the feminist revolution is over—and they won. They believe they can have it all: they can do anything they want, sleep with anyone they want, pursue any dream they want. And the men are still locked into the same ideology of masculinity that defined my era, that defined my father's era.

In a sense, this change is what Hanna Rosin is writing about—the dramatic change in *women's* lives over the past half century. The question is, what has been the impact on *men* of these enormous changes in women's lives over the past half century?

To try to answer that, I want to tease out some assumptions in Rosin's argument, and then point to a couple of areas in which I think a different framing might lead to a more accurate understanding of the state of American masculinity.

One assumption is causal. The relationship of title to subtitle makes it appear that men ended first, and women have arisen to take their place. Surely this is backwards history. If men are ending, it is attendant upon, and a consequence of, the rise of women. They are women, we hear them roar and we shrivel right up.

The second assumption is logical. Rosin's title and subtitle—indeed, the entire book until the conclusion—assume that gender is a zero sum game, that one rises and one falls, that neither can they neither rise together nor can they fall together. Even if she does not share the interplanetary theory of gender—that women and men are from different planets—Rosin does believe that there is a battle of the sexes, a war between the sexes, and that, at present, as one of her male informants puts it, "our team is losing" (p. 61).

This is what I also call the "either/or" assumption. Either women are winning or losing; either men are winning or losing. Either things are getting better or they are getting worse. Either we're all bowling alone or we're Facebooking everyone we've ever known in a virtual friending frenzy, creating the densest social networks the world has ever known. Either hooking up is his wet dream (and her nightmare) or her sexual empowerment is at his expense.

We sociologists see things differently. We see things as "both/and." Both statements are true. It is understanding the relationship between the two sides is that is our analytic tofu.

The third assumption is sociological: Rosin treats men—or as she calls her two-dimensional cartoon version, "cardboard man"—as some antediluvian dinosaur, unwilling or unable to adapt, slouching toward extinction.

But this assumption raises two questions. First which men is she talking about? When she writes that "men's hold on the pinnacles of power is loosening" (p. 199), is she speaking of gay men, black men, Latino men, working-class men, upper-class men, Asian men, trans men, older men, boys?

Assuredly not. Actually, even if it were the "end of men," it's really the end of middle-class straight white men. And it's not really the end of them, of course. It's the end of their unquestioned entitlement.

Second, if men are ending, what is driving them toward this cliff of oblivion? Is it the rise of women? I don't think so. I think it's the archaic definitions of masculinity that are—and this is key—enforced and policed pretty relentlessly by other men. Rosin omits the central dynamic of masculinity—its homosociality.

In fact, Rosin thinks that the rise of women not only spells men's doom, but also that women are responsible for holding themselves back. As she puts it, "the internal barriers are likely to be the harder fight" (p. 230).

Hanna Rosin does, I believe, focus the conversation on the right issues. Interestingly, in the book's conclusion, she changes course. This isn't the "end of men" at all! Men, she writes, "*will* learn to expand the range of options for what it means to be a man" [emphasis added, p. 263]. Cardboard man is becoming more plastic. And, adds Rosin: "I want to teach them to bend." She can help, but basically nowadays the brothers are doing it for themselves.

The Coming Masculinity

Brendan Tapley
Winter 2010

In late 2008, a different "surge" emerged in the headlines than the military one in Iraq. The FBI released its statistics for hate crimes in a good news-bad news report. Good news: overall, hate crimes declined from the previous year; bad news: there was a 6 percent surge in incidents against homosexuals—the only category that increased—the majority of which targeted gay men (59.2 percent versus 12.6 percent for gay women). What was unclear was the reason. The FBI was quick to say its report never assigns causes for fluctuations, but it seems worth proposing one.

Most men will admit that publicly demonstrating affection toward another man—even platonic affection—can incite from fellow men "the look." Often enough, that look precedes threats or much worse, as in the cases of Jose Sucuzhanay (murdered for walking arm-in-arm with his biological brother), Lawrence King (shot in the head for giving an eighth-grade classmate a Valentine card), or any of 2008's 1,460 hate crime victims.

So far, I've been fortunate not to confront anything "statistical," but the looks and slurs that I've received make me a guy who alternates between showing affection for my male friends and someone who worries about the implications. Whenever I've experienced this disapproval, I've resented those who generate it, which is why it was interesting when I became the "looker."

I was walking in Rome when, for the third time that day, I noticed two men acting affectionately toward one another. I only realized my eyes had narrowed because, when I passed the third pair, arm-in-arm, they returned my gaze with irritation. Taken aback by the expression I'd made and the one it elicited, I became more astonished by the cause I knew I could assign to it. My problem wasn't prejudice. It was envy.

From an early age, men in the US are trained to go without love or loving gestures from fellow men. When that principle of manhood becomes clear, our longing for such love does a paradoxical thing: it both intensifies and goes underground. Men cannot help but feel an increased desire to fill this void; at the same time, we rarely act on it because, by seeming gay, such a desire still contradicts our modern definition of masculinity.

Enter the "danger" of gay men. These men pursue and act on male intimacy as though it should be a given, even a right. Should a man find himself in the presence of loving gestures from or between such men, he is likely to feel, as I did, a psychic split: regarding such overtures as tempting and incriminating. This internal clash between a man's long-held desire and his self-denial can turn a passing disapproval into problematic envy and that envy into resentment, even rage.

I didn't want to hurt the Italians; on the contrary, they had what I wanted: an open fraternity that was so unassailably appropriate its expression was blasé. But no sooner had I felt that longing than it mutated into an instinctive hostility. However absurd this reaction was, I also saw its logic.

As is often true of men, anger conceals our real feelings—in this case, my sorrow. The scorn I'd felt for the Italians allowed me to ignore the disappointing ways I daily surrendered to the masculine tragedy of forgoing true male connection. Such a judgment also excused me from being a braver man who would fight against this fate by risking my own gestures. Indeed, the knee-jerk allegiance I had to what a "real man" was prevented me from actually being one, clarifying for me the real root of homophobia.

The aversion to male love—whether it remains internal or becomes criminal—is not about prejudice. Prejudice is a "palatable" alibi that denies a darker truth. Homophobia is a common reaction to love between men because admitting such love is possible forces men to reevaluate the male "contract." And that presents men with their own good news-bad news situation.

Witnessing real male connection—becoming aware of our longing for it—threatens masculinity, not just because it brings up in men our uneasiness in feeling gay, but more because it exposes masculinity for the raw deal it is: an existential cheat that has defrauded men of a full 50 percent of human connection. Unlike women, who create rich ties within the sisterhood, this forfeiture has lodged an unspoken complaint within our psyches, a primal disenfranchisement that prevents our wholeness. But while an unapologetic conviction by men that male love is part of masculinity would free us from an inherent and stunting bondage (good), it would also sacrifice male privilege (a loss that, at first glance, seems bad).

For instance, would demanding love from our fathers be worthwhile if it meant our accountability as fathers became more rigorous? If love between men were more common than exceptional, would we have to meet a standard of brotherhood that exceeded the frat house and was honored beyond the battlefield? If this subconscious grievance in maleness disappeared, would we have to get on with the business of being fully present, intimate, and responsible to the women in our midst? If male love were no longer taboo, would we have no one to oppress to feel better about ourselves?

Indeed the reinvention of masculinity ends with what some might see as a Pyrrhic victory— the extinction of masculinity's excuses, its low expectations. Because renegotiating the male contract will strip from us the straitjacket whose limitations we men may uncomfortably but willingly wear.

This is the real reason men fight demonstrations of male love. Or in the case of gay hate crimes, why we increasingly attack the messengers of what is a new and coming masculinity. Those who get out of masculinity's raw deal by no longer accepting privation enrage those who abide by it still. Our closeted envy of gay men, rather than letting it transform us or the rules of masculinity, makes pariahs out of the pioneers. We turn their example into a grave offense for the worst reason: to preserve a self-destructive privilege.

Is it any coincidence that in the bluest states in America—where homosexuality is presumably more explicit—the FBI counted most of the hate crimes? Massachusetts (80) and California (263) versus Alabama (1) and Louisiana (2). In the case of hate crimes against gays, perhaps it is not a matter of irrational hate at all, but of rational love that men just don't want in evidence. Because even more explosive than a man confronting a perception of homosexuality and exercising his prejudice is the man who admits his crimes have always been against himself, and he has become his own jailer.

Refusing to "BE A MAN!"
By Steven Botkin
Winter 1999

"Be a man!"

The effects of those three words continue to echo through our lives long after we've realized the lies behind them. Listen to the inflection, the emotional message we can hear so clearly in this simple phrase, carrying equal parts promise and threat.

Be a man! If we can achieve this goal we are promised a sense of power, pride, confidence, mastery, control, and invulnerability. If we do not "cut the mustard," or "make the grade," and "step up to the plate," and "box our corner," we are threatened with isolation, shame, abuse, and violence.

But what does it mean to "be a man?" For years I have regularly asked groups of people what comes to mind when they hear that expression. The responses, from men and women of all ages, are frighteningly consistent. And everyone knows what happens to boys or men who do not fit inside this "box." Matthew Shepard, beaten and left to die tied to a fencepost in Wyoming this October because he was gay, is the ultimate, tragic example.

Most of us who are men know some (usually less lethal, but still pro-foundly traumatic) variation of this story quite well. We remember schoolyards and street corners, and often homes, with our own or our friends' families, where proving that we had an "acceptable" degree of masculinity was an ongoing theme of our daily lives. We learned that any nonconformity to the rules of this masculinity risked making one the target of brutality and ridicule. And we learned that we could have prestige and privilege, power and control, to the extent that we were able to "be a man."

And yet, especially as children, we knew we really did not and could not meet this impossible and inhuman standard. Sometimes we did get sad, scared, and hurt. We did, at times, want to cry and be comforted. If we had enough safety as children we might respond to the command "be a man" with the truth: "I'm not a man."

But it wasn't always safe to tell the truth. So, in subtle and not-so-subtle ways, we practiced hiding or minimizing our gender nonconformities, be-cause we were told that's not how men are. How we dressed, walked, talked, used our hands, expressed our emotions, related with other males, and talked about and behaved toward females was all carefully scrutinized so that we would not betray any deviance from the prescribed rules for being a man. We did not want to be standing alone feeling shame about our difference. So we denied parts of ourselves in order to feel safe and accepted within a dominant culture that demanded of us: "*Be a man!*"

What would it mean now if we were to create a culture in which men join together to reclaim these parts of ourselves that we once hid and denied? If we discovered that, as we peek out from behind our fear, we find the shy and smiling face of another, reflecting our own remembered wholeness. What would it mean if together we found the courage to stand and face the dominant culture, saying with determination and pride, "We do not want to 'be a man'"? We refuse the rigid box of gender conformity. What if we created a community where we could feel safe and accepted in the infinite variety of our gender nonconformities?

It would mean the end of the system of patriarchy, wherein the promise of power is leveraged by the threat of violence. Homophobia, violence against women, and war—the ultimate weapons of gender conformity—would disappear, no longer needed to prove and protect our "manhood." Men would show up in the full rainbow of our expressions. We would inhabit our homes and families, remembering the delights of nurturing relationships. And we would seek out the close, loving companionship of other men and other women. It would mean hope for the world in places where we have long felt only hopelessness.

I believe this is all happening now. Yes, it can often seem agonizingly slow and painful, and there is certainly plenty of overt and covert resistance; however, there is a tremendous wave of liberation moving through our world. Men breaking free from the individual and cultural demand to "be a man" is one key ingredient in this movement.

It's time for us now to assert that we will not be boxed into masculinity by seductive promises of power or intimidating threats of violence. It's time for us now to break through our fear and isolation and come out as gender nonconformists who do not fit or accept prescribed rules of manhood. It's time for us now to call each other out of the shadows of the box with a welcome of acceptance and safety. In this way we are creating a new culture where being a man is an open-ended, ever-expanding expression of possibilities.

Men Come in the Room
By Sean Casey LeClaire
Spring 2004

Men come in the room. Mad men. Glad men. Been had men. Many men. Honest Men. Drunk men. "Barely holding on, man!" Men come in the room. Men whose lives have been ravaged and wives have been raped. Men who have raped men come in the room. Pill popping. No stopping. Pussy hunting. Mushy men. Men come in the room. Barrel-chested hairy men. Scary men. Old men. Young men. Movie-going middle-aged men. Men come in the room. Bald Buddha-loving men. Fast talking. Bullshit walking. Still drinking. Coffee-pouring men.

Men come in the room. Men shoveling shit from their lives. Men without wives. Men who won't listen to their wives. "Gotta get that bitch back!" Men come in the room. Men without men in their lives. Gay men. Straight men. Horny men. Hungry men. Men who were once men. Men with cocks come in the room. Angry men. Anal men. "What's with that attitude man." Men come in the room. Guitar men. Gotta get the hell out of here men. Broken token—just a shadow of a man. Men come in the room. Barely men.

Men come in the room. Doctor men. Lawyer men. Ladies' men. "Who the fuck do you think you are, man!" Woodworking wild men come in the room. Poor men. Poet men. Porno men. Pot-spinning men. Men who have spent more time with the devil than most men—real men. Men come in the room. Money men. Toy-loving men. Men who act like boys. Chain-smoking wheelchair-rolling sober men. Soldier men. Saint men. Sinning men. Only men.

Men come in the room. Crying. Lying. Dying men. Men whose mothers were like men. Fatherless men. Men come in the room. Big men. Soft men. Fast men. Lucky and loose men. Troubled men. Hard-driving finger-flicking never gonna stop pushing the river men. "See you cock-suckers later, man!" Men come in the room. Kick-ass and kiss-ass men. Bleeding in your bones men. Liver-bloated heavy men. Skinny men. Men who can say to other men, "Bigger trees have fallen at my feet, man."

Men come in the room. Men dragged across their front lawns by men-in-blue men. Drinking, fucking, fighting men come in the room. Raging, rocking, no-stopping, truck-driving, boiler-making, metal-shaping, saxophone-playing men. Skull-cracking men come in the room. Badass guns in the car men. Men come in the room. Messy men. Married men. Sacred men. "I can't breathe in here, man!" Forgotten men. Forgiving men. Men with bowl-like bellies, arms, and hands. Men with tree-trunk legs and feet. Laughing men with big balls enter the room.

Men come in the room. Love you till you get better men. Deep men. Men who love their women. Nondrinking men. Jesus-loving men. Men-helping men come in the room. Gotta go back to school men. Tree-climbing, true blue men. Men trusting men. Men come in the room. Trudging the foothills of God men. Mercy men. Word-loving men. "Heard it first here, man!" Circle-praying men. Kid-loving men. Men come in the room and the soft innocence of men with men in a room comes in the room.

"Rooms Change When We Argue"

Russell Bradbury-Carlin
Winter 2003

The doorknobs were
    tarnished and smoky.

Sunlight in the room
    shuffled into corners.

We were debating adult things,
while my teeth strained to sieve out simple words,
and you focused on the farness of the wall.

The pine trim
    clenched out new knots.

The swinging arm lamp thought
    of life with a lower wattage.

Knives, pens, scissors
    quivered and sharpened.

My dead father had slipped into the room and plucked
my seized voice like a violin string with his ghost fingers,
as your parents played you, too, from a distance.

The wall clock strained
    to push its hands.

The windows gripped tightly
    to their frames.

"The After Hours Crowd"
By Patrick D. Higgins
Winter 2009

American boys walk in packs
playing dress up in
small towns, boulevard
walking along panels
illuminated of glass.

American boys get violent
scared straight
sending vibes like
small atom bombs
fallout smells of
musk, fear, Old Spice,
Boy Scouts.

American boys and mall-metal podcast
haircuts get the better
of me, an American boy,
hapless in fashion's prison
culturebound to ignoramus
brethren, fatuous
fumbling for cigarette
taunting nervous girl
as she walks by alone.

American boys atomic and atomizing
walk strong in tough
group same shirt
bent brim hat to
Señor Frog shooter
night for to make
get drunk, get pussy,
get real stupid drunk
like television drunk.

We too Americans, boys
caught somewhere
nomadic in packs

snapping fingers
giggling in 7/4
rearrangers of names
becoming sounds blasts
of rhythm without
territory or time,

We too are America(n), boys,
despite it all,
laugh it out
have it out
have a drink
have a smoke
have a conversation
interrupted
by cell phone
new conversation
text message
on virtual
co-planar getting
co-planar getting
sick.

Let's start a fire, America.

Let's do away with
Boys Who Will Be Boys.

Let's become something else.

In ColorLines, men of color voice their experiences of masculinity and their thoughts on white privilege. Subjects range from health issues to fathering children to working with white allies in the fight against race oppression. Women also offer their perspectives on race and racism. Some men critique the men's movement for not being inclusive enough of men of color, indeed for being actively racist at times. Woven together with many differing strands of thought, this section begins a vital dialogue around the complex intersection of racism and patriarchal masculinity.

A New Future for Black Masculinity
By Byron Hurt
Winter 2009

Even though Barack Obama was decisively elected as the first black male president of the United States, black men continue to be easy scapegoats, mistrusted, dehumanized, controlled, assailed, and stereotyped.

Before and since the election, a series of events have taken place that demonstrate how far we still must travel if we are ever to reach a postracial America. A notice was posted in a general store in Maine for an "Obama Osama" contest, encouraging customers to bet on the day the new president would be killed. An African American voter in New York received a threatening note the morning after the election implying his safety was in jeopardy for voting for Obama. Days before the election, a young woman named Ashley Todd blamed a black man for her own self-mutilation. Troy Davis, a black man whom many believe is deserving of a new trial, has been on death row and may be executed if ongoing intervention efforts are not maintained. New York City police officers shot Kayshawn Forde and his brother Dwayne David in the back, killing both. The Secret Service has acknowledged that John McCain's surrogates and supporters who spewed death threats at the new president put candidate Obama at increased risk of harm. Right-wing media and conservative political pundits employed last-ditch scare tactics to try and reduce Obama to a radical anti-American "socialist" with "dangerous" terrorist connections in an attempt to make voters fearful and uncertain about voting for a black man for president.

But black men—from the politician to the athlete, from the rap artist to the average black man in America—are varied, complex, and far more human than we are ever given credit for being.

As the face of American presidential masculinity has changed, there are other opportunities to sustain interest and nurture new thinking about black manhood. What follows are five books and five films (including my own) that I recommend to people in order to better appreciate the full range of masculinity. They include:

Books

Be a Father to Your Child: Real Talk from Black Men on Family, Love, and Fatherhood, an anthology edited by April R. Silver, Soft Skull Press, 2008)

Men Speak Out: Views on Gender, Sex, and Power, edited by Shira Tarrant, Routledge (2008, 2013)

New Black Man: Rethinking Black Masculinity by Mark Anthony Neal (Routledge, 2006)

The Black Male Handbook: *A Blueprint for Life* by Kevin Powell (Atria, division of Simon & Schuster, 2008)

The Will to Change: *Men, Masculinity, and Love* by bell hooks (Washington Square Press, 2004)

Films

Generation M: Misogyny in Media Culture by Thomas Keith (Media Education Foundation, 2008)

Hip-Hop: Beyond Beats and Rhymes by Byron Hurt (God Bless the Child Productions, 2006; distributed by Media Education Foundation)

I Am A Man: Black Masculinity in America by Byron Hurt (God Bless the Child Productions, 1998; distributed by Media Education Foundation)

Tongues Untied: *Black Men Loving Black Men*, by Marlon Riggs (Signifyin' Works/Vivian Kleiman, 1989)

Tough Guise: Violence, Media, & The Crisis of Violent Masculinity by Jackson Katz and Sut Jhally, (Media Education Foundation, 1999)

A Precious Paradox

By Imani Perry

Spring 2010

These are strange days indeed. We are firmly into the twenty-first century, and yet the 1980s are haunting us. For African Americans it is yet again a decade of dream and deferral.

Back in the eighties, for the young, black, and college educated, the doors of corporate America and other professions opened up and broadened the spectrum of the black middle class like never before. But also, back in the eighties, crack cocaine and the aftermath of deindustrialization crippled areas of concentrated blackness in major urban centers.

Now in the twenty-first century, a new black elite floods the popular imagination as Capitol Hill, the president, and his administration become more and more colorful. But also now, in the twenty-first century, the recession hits black communities hardest, and at the intersection of devastating rates of imprisonment, joblessness, and inadequate education lie a critical, hurting, mass of black Americans.

Then came *Precious*.

The film, released in the fall of 2009, elicited a flurry of responses. The debates over the film were complex, nuanced, impassioned. In fact, among the black intelligentsia there seemed to be more discussion about *Precious* than there was about President Obama's education agenda, the stimulus package, or rising unemployment and imprisonment. That was troubling. But then again, it is easier to fire off a blog post or provide a commentary about a movie than it is to write a concise response to a complicated web of policy, law, and economics. However, I believe the film elicited so much engaged response precisely because it highlighted the challenge of this moment when it comes to race in America.

The film tells an individual story, a poignant one, about an abused young woman in Harlem in the 1980s. If we attend to the individual story, fictional though it may be, our hearts go out to Precious. We see in her story personal resilience, possibility, healing. Those are good things. The film also tells a collective story. The story it tells is about the devastation that the 1980s wrought on black communities, and the failure of the public school system to provide a path out for "the underclass."

In both the collective story and the individual story, there is truth. There is a real Precious out there. The story is fictional, but it is human. The problem is that fictional stories, especially ones on film, don't just stand as individual stories, but they do "representative work." They become part of the way we make sense of the world in which we live. The story of one novelist or filmmaker's imagination becomes the story of entire groups of people or "types" of people. This is especially true when the kind of social location depicted in the story is remote from the experience of the majority of the viewers.

On the one hand, many of us who are familiar with the way the story of Black America in the eighties was told, and the way the story of the rise of imprisonment in contemporary black America is being told, are frustrated with the spectacle of black violence, deviance, and dysfunction that appears over and over again. We are tired of this story of pathology that we see yet again in *Precious*. Instead we want a story that reveals the laws and policies and economic conditions that produce concentrated poverty and its violence. We also yearn for the stories of those who sustain humanity and decency in the face of devastating poverty and marginalization. We would prefer for those stories to be told because they are, after all, far more representative of black life than the wreck that is Precious's life.

And so we balk at a film like *Precious,* rhetorically asking: Doesn't it just recycle those old images of black pathology? And isn't it reviving those stories just when we are beginning to suffer so much again, just when we don't need a convenient explanation of "they are pathological" to facilitate the nation turning its back on the responsibility to provide conditions for all citizens to lead productive lives as participants in the democracy and economy?

On the other hand, some of us want to embrace a film like *Precious* because it highlights a kind of suffering that our society fails to respond to. Children who are poor and of color are inadequately protected in our society. They are more vulnerable to predators, more likely to be victimized on the street and in school, and less likely to have families that are able to marshal resources to deal with trauma, mental illness, and addiction. At the same time, poor, emotionally scarred parents who become abusers have virtually no resources to repair themselves. So when we see a movie like *Precious*, we applaud it for encouraging sympathy and investment in young women like Precious. We think, "Yes, the reality of her life deserves to be depicted, maybe it will inspire action." The film does both kinds of work on the audience at once. Strange indeed.

When it comes to race, the challenge of this moment is for critically thinking members of this society to consider the implications of symbolism (like the black president, or the Oscar-worthy performance by Mo'nique of a dysfunctional, sexual abusing welfare mother) at the same time as we consider the messy, complicated, content of our society, without assuming that these things have a clear or consistent relationship to one another.

Precious demands we bring more to the table than just an analysis of it as a piece of art. If the film stands alone, it gets deployed and interpreted every which way. But if we use the film to open the door to conversations about society, ones that are filled with knowledge, data, and careful analysis, rather than mere anecdote and fiction, then it can do some useful work in our social and political lives. Perhaps it can inspire solutions to problems of representation and policy challenges.

Barack Obama and the Mythology of Black Men

By Dr. Charles Johnson

Fall 2011

Did the election of Barack Obama force Americans to look at blackness in new ways? Do white men have a problem with a black man with power? How do we explain the rudeness shown Obama? Is it simply politics, or is race a factor? Is the attempt to define Obama as an alien linked to his blackness or the "sound" of his name? Would black women embrace Obama the same way if his wife were white? If Obama is defeated in 2012, how might this alter the American narrative? Will we jump to the conclusion that "Reconstruction failed again?"

In the 1980s, my friend Dr. Joseph Scott, then director of ethnic studies at the University of Washington (where I also taught), expressed his belief that black women had done a very good job of publicly defining themselves since the 1970s—creating an image (or meaning) for themselves and their lives that was positive and widespread in popular culture. And then he said, "When it comes to black men, people don't know who we are." In that same decade, writer John McCluskey Jr. and I published *Black Men Speaking,* which begins with Joe's powerful and moving memoir of his life growing up in Detroit in the 1930s, titled *Making a Way Out of No Way.*

I've never forgotten Joe's observation. *People don't know who we are.* A library of books could be devoted to examining that remark. In fact, for a time I was on the editorial board of the *Journal of African American Men*, an academic publication devoted to studies of the situation of black males. Naturally, when McCluskey and I worked on *Black Men Speaking,* we discussed this matter—Who are black men in America?—and he, like Joe, made a memorable remark. He said: Since the beginning of this republic, and probably starting during the time of the colonies, black men have always been a "problem" for white men. In just Darwinian terms, the black man was the white man's competitor—for power, the means of survival, prestige, and, of course, women. The power white men enjoyed during slavery meant, to put it bluntly—they could pass their genetic information along to white women *and* rape black women with impunity.

Black males had to be prevented from any and all sexual dealings with white women. One of the most powerful tropes—or mythologies—in American pop culture is that of the black man during either the eras of segregation or slavery being hunted, killed, lynched, or burned for making overtures that were interpreted to be of a sexual nature toward a white female. (Ah, yes, remember Bigger Thomas's rooftop run across a building in Chicago after he kills Mary Dalton in *Native Son*?) The groundbreaking, classic film *Birth of a Nation* was popular for a reason—it depicted black men (actually white men in blackface) during Reconstruction rampaging and raping across the South until the "knights" of the KKK suppressed their "bestial" and uncivilized behavior. Black women, then as now, obviously did *not* pose the same threat to white male power, and perhaps this is one reason why they have done so much better than black males in terms of integrating into American mainstream society—that is, gaining advanced academic degrees and jobs in greater numbers than black males, many of whom feel (or so August Wilson once told me) that passage through the white man's institutions is basically a form of cultural (and racial) indoctrination, and this is something August said young black males rejected. Indeed, many literary works by black women since the 1970s reinforced the popular—and, I would add, *dominant*—image of black males being violent, animal-like, stupid, and dangerous.

Whole libraries have been written about the American practice of emasculating the black male. Remember how sexually neutered the film roles were in the 1950s for Sidney Poitier prior to his appearing in *Guess Who's Coming to Dinner*? (And during the Black Exploitation film period of the 1970s that sexual neutering was reversed with a vengeance; that did little to improve the imagery associated with black men). In the iconography of black men in America, there were several carefully reiterated images. Black men are often granted by whites the status of being physically superior—as animals are. That meaning is dwelled upon in sports (football, basketball, boxing), and such a meaning leaves in place the racial propaganda of the intellectual as well as creative superiority of white men (except in an area like jazz or black music, where excellence is reluctantly acknowledged). There is a territory the majority of white males categorically refuse to relinquish—that of the mind. (By the way, I seldom talk about being a lifelong martial artist because, back in the 1990s, I noticed that white interviewers seemed way too interested in that dimension of my life—because it suggests violence—and not at all interested in my equally lifelong passion for philosophy. I've always noticed with equal amusement how in the book world my Ph.D. in philosophy, represented by "Dr." before my name, is frequently dropped, as if the work required to earn a doctorate in a field dominated by white males for 2,500 years never took place.)

I was recently conversing via e-mail with filmmaker Brian McDonald about how in popular culture we simply *never* see a black man who is a visual artist, who can *draw*, who has that natural talent (there are many such images of white males). Similarly, we seldom if ever see portrayed in the popular imagination black men who are geniuses—scientists, inventors, authoritative scholars. After six decades of living and studying American culture, I understand full well that the very *idea* of a black man who is intellectually or artistically superior brings tremendous discomfort to the white racist mind, even to the liberal white mind. (Ishmael Reed once called this "liberal racism.") For 15 years, August Wilson and I discussed this matter long into the night. He was a two-time Pulitzer Prize-winning playwright, a man who dominated the American stage for two decades, but the incidents of disrespect he received and told me about were—well, endless. (He always noted each year how many plays by white playwrights became motion pictures while his 10 plays, year after year for two decades, remained unadapted for that medium.) And I, of course, had countless examples of my own since childhood to share with him.

This is what we live with, as black American males. (Just for the record, let me add that black females in the popular imagination today are granted moral superiority and professional competence, but, like black males, not unquestioned intellectual or artistic excellence.) We have lived with being demonized, our talents and gifts ignored or denied, since the time of slavery. The evidence for this in the historical record is overwhelming so I don't need to repeat any of that. And it is what Barack Obama must live with, too. He has an I.Q. of 147. (There are white people who will say that is because he had a white mother.) For some white Americans, his very existence is threatening. And they feel they must try to understand and interpret him in terms of a 300-year-old mythology about black men. That's blunted a bit because he chose a black wife rather than a white one (i.e., he chose not to compete with white men for their women). But—and this is quite amusing to me— columnist Peggy Noonan, who writes for the *Wall Street Journal,* has, since Obama's election, been returning again and again to her feeling that Americans don't "know" Obama, that he doesn't fit any previous cultural molds for a president. She's right. He doesn't. And lately, she and others have been chipping away (since the debt ceiling deal) at both his intelligence and competence.

Americans don't know or understand a black man like Barack Obama. What he culturally represents—a black male who is brilliant, not bestial; eloquent not inarticulate; confident, comfortable in his own skin and even at times arrogant, not humble; cool and rational, not emotional or "angry"— is the annihilation of every cherished, bigoted notion about what black men are or should be in a Eurocentric culture. That image is well understood to be a threat to white supremacy. Many white Americans want him to fail so that the mythology of black male inferiority can be maintained.

Long ago, Ethelbert Miller came to believe that this situation that I've described for black American males will not change in our lifetimes. We can only do, one day at a time, what the ancestors we revere did, and what Obama seems to try to do: take care of business—the duties and responsibilities given to us in this life—step over racism as if it were a puddle at his feet, strive for personal and professional excellence, and take some small comfort in the fact that we, like the predecessors who inspire us, fought the good fight.

Black Men, AIDS, and Community

By Vernon McClean

Spring 2001

Except for slavery, nothing in our history has killed so many black men in such a short time as AIDS. In New York City, 33 percent of black gay men are infected, versus two percent of white men. AIDS kills more of us in the prime of life (between the ages of 25 and 44) than any other cause. Nationally, we are 10 times more likely than white men to be infected, and 10 times more likely to die from AIDS. (Among black women, the death rate from AIDS, tragically, is six times greater than that for white women, and 46 percent greater than for Latino women. This is higher than the death toll taken by breast cancer, hypertension, heart disease, and auto accidents combined.)

AIDS also takes a devastating toll among our children—those the mainstream press calls "the innocent victims of AIDS." However, I believe that all people with AIDS are innocent victims. No one deserves this plague. No child. No adult. No drug abuser. No gay. No straight person.

Unfortunately, because people living with AIDS are usually thought to be ethnic minorities, homosexuals, or drug users, they often get very little sympathy, even from those who are themselves infected with HIV and AIDS.

A few years back, the department secretary at the university where I teach, overheard me agree to address a group of black men in Newark, New Jersey, who were living with HIV and AIDS. As a black woman, she was quick to berate me for associating with "those people" and said she hoped I would not bring the disease back to the office.

Sadly, her attitude is typical of many in the black community. Many resent HIV-infected men because they see them all as drug abusers. Some of them undoubtedly are. But people such as my secretary may not realize that one reason many black men become drug abusers is because we are trying to escape the pain of our daily life in the United States—a life that involves discrimination, stereotyping, racial profiling by police, and violence.

In New York State, blacks and Latinos make up nearly 85 percent of new AIDS cases but receive only 30 percent of state funds. According to Kevin McGruder, executive director of Gay Men of African Descent, Inc., "There is a history of valuing the lives of people of color differently than the lives of white people."

In the infamous "Tuskegee Study," treatment for syphilis was intentionally withheld from more than 400 black men. In my native Caribbean region (Haiti, Puerto Rico), women of color were used as guinea pigs to perfect birth control pills for white women. The same use was made of gay people in

Greenwich Village, New York, in the quest to perfect a pill for treating hepatitis B. I still remember listening to a radio interview in the 1970s in which a white gay leader defended this experiment because he felt that it would show that gays are "good citizens."

These examples should suffice to show that the pressures of life are harsh for black men. The wonder is that *more* of us do not turn to heroin, crack, alcohol, and other drugs in an effort to alleviate the pain of our daily lives.

Yet the question remains: given the devastating effects of AIDS in the black male community, why aren't blacks more concerned about this plague? Perhaps another reason is homophobia—the fear and dislike of gays and lesbians. As the black anti-AIDS activist and renowned choreographer and dancer Bill T. Jones has said, "The black community is the most virulently homophobic. I want to be loved by my folks, but I've spent a good part of my life being disappointed."

Black students often become enraged when I dare to compare the discrimination against us as black men—which, of course, they vehemently condemn—with the murder and oppression of gay men. It is almost as if some black students feel that gays (black or white) *deserve* to be victims of an AIDS-like genocide.

I have an African colleague who remarked to me some years ago that he would not mind if all the "fags" at our university were taken to the middle of the campus and set afire. Evidently, it has never occurred to him that the same people who hate "fags" often hate "niggers," too. Moreover, my colleague evidently does not realize that 90 percent of the children worldwide with AIDS are in his native Africa. In South Africa alone, according to Nelson Mandela, one-quarter of pregnant women are HIV-positive; this sad situation is a result of the sexist attitudes of our African brothers, many of whom refuse to use condoms and frequently have multiple sexual partners of both sexes.

However, in all fairness, homophobia is not peculiar to the black community. Some Jewish students resent the fact that I (as a professor) would compare the AIDS-caused genocide of homosexuals with the Nazi genocide of Jews—even though gays (not Jews) were the first group to be imprisoned in Nazi detention centers. In fact, gay survivors of concentration camps requested a monument in Washington, DC—only to be rebuffed by their fellow Jewish survivors.

So what can we do about the AIDS Holocaust, this plague on all our houses?

First, profeminist men's organizations need to be at the forefront of the struggle against racism and homophobia in the men's movement, and against HIV and AIDS as well. Second, as black men, we need to realize that there is no hierarchy of oppression in which oppressed groups should be debating each other over which group is "more oppressed." This recognition would do much to decrease the tension between, for example, blacks and Jews that exists on many college campuses around the country.

In his "Letter from Birmingham Jail" Martin Luther King said, "Injustice anywhere is a threat to justice everywhere. We are caught in an inescapable network of mutuality, tied in a single garment of destiny. Whatever affects one directly, affects all indirectly."

Healing Rites for Fathers and Sons

By Haji Shearer

Winter 2005

I went to a funeral for a 17-year-old today. He was shot to death a week ago. He lived in a part of Boston where rival groups of young men are adept at killing one another.

JR was popular. There were nearly 250 people at his "going home" service. I'll never forget the beautiful young woman sobbing in the back of the church. Neither will I forget the 25 or 30 hard young men radiating enough hatred that if looks could kill, I'm sure JR's murderers would already be dead. And since looks don't kill, I suspect that many of them had, in their waistbands, more effective means of dispatching the enemy.

As I stood on the sidewalk outside the church, I prayed that the young men milling about the hearse might find a way to transform their hatred before another black teen gets killed. But prayer must be rooted in follow-up action to be effective, and I knew this crisis of young black males killing one another would not be solved by wishful thinking.

My mind was drawn to the afternoon exactly three weeks before, when I joined with 15 other black men to take our sons on a Boys to Men Rites of Passage retreat. For the second year in a row, I participated in an experience for fathers (or men acting in the father/mentor role for sons whose fathers are absent) and sons to explore their relationship with one another and themselves.

An important aspect of all initiation ceremonies is a removal from the familiar.

So we held our retreat at the Starseed Retreat Center in a secluded spot in western Massachusetts. That we took our sons away from TVs, radios, and Gameboys for a weekend in the woods was dramatic enough. Yet the first night we arrived, when our jaded urban and suburban teens displayed youthful wonder at the sight of *so many* stars, we knew we were on to something. Many of the dads looked up wistfully as well.

In fact, the older men were even more visibly moved throughout the weekend. With our teens, we hoped we were planting seeds for the future in their fertile adolescent consciousness, but as men we were already ripe to appreciate the beauty and power of the initiation process. After all, these traditions are embedded in folklore and our ancestral mind, yet none of us men was given an experience like this as we entered manhood. Offering our sons this gift was healing for both generations.

As African American men, we created a rite of passage that reflected our heritage, while also incorporating elements that reinterpreted traditional African ceremonies. We have a strong tradition of oral communication, so we designed dialogues between the older and younger men that encouraged each to share his thoughts and feelings on a particular theme. If you have a teen in your house, you know getting them to talk or listen is no easy task. This part of the ritual gave the young men a chance to be listened to by their elders. And hearing stories of manhood from men other than their father may have helped them listen better themselves.

We used the sweat lodge ceremony to physically and emotionally push our limits. This is a purification ritual found in various Native American cultures where, in simplest terms, participants meditatively build a sauna in the woods. The group enters one by one with the intent of being transformed by the heat and darkness. It is a deeply spiritual experience that connects one with the Earth, with one's own self, and with one's co-participants. Prayers and songs are chanted and sung in the lodge, and many people feel reborn upon exiting. The preparation and execution of this activity took most of one day, and that evening we used the talk circle to process the changes each person felt.

The second day we hiked around a beautiful waterfall. One of the men took a dip in a cold pool below the waterfall. Since this was a Christian group experience, his immersion in the cold water looked like another rebirth, and several men followed him in a spontaneous baptism, which left all who took part feeling clean inside and out.

The bonds created during the weekend will live forever. The boys saw core values of positive masculinity in action: seeking adventure, working together for a common goal, challenging our bodies, sharing our feelings, and using our voices to roar. I hope this inspires other men to create conscious, uplifting rites of passage for their own sons.

I've heard arguments to the effect that such ceremonies are an unnecessary anachronism in modern American culture. A friend recently tried to persuade me that we shouldn't "insert alien rituals" in an attempt to re-create ceremonies that were an intrinsic part of other societies. Eli Newberger makes a similar argument in his 1999 book about the nature and nurture of male character, *The Men They Will Become*. "Rigorous rites of passage don't make much sense when adolescence is expected to last close to a decade for most boys," he writes, "even longer for those who elect careers requiring extensive post-graduate education."

These types of retreats are not meant to replace such key life experiences as going to high school, getting a driver's license, or leaving home for college. What critics of rites of passage ceremonies fail to recognize is that it is not a question of *whether* our sons will have rituals, but of *what kind* of rituals will predominate. Funerals have become a modern rite of passage for young men in my community. The murder rate in Boston has skyrocketed; most of the victims are young men of color. It's difficult to live in my community and not be personally touched by the epidemic of young black males killing one another.

Yet male violence is not just a problem in urban, African American communities. Black folks in America are like the canary in the coal mine. Our fraternal violence bred from despair is highly dramatic and well publicized, but consider the behaviors prevalent in many men and one can see that heartless violence is a cross-cultural phenomenon. Suburban families quick to dismiss violence as something that happens elsewhere need only remember Columbine and other suburban school shootings. Intimate partner violence is widespread across ethnic and class boundaries. The media regularly report that men of varying socioeconomic and racial groups are charged with (and convicted of) the beating or murder of their wives or girlfriends.

Growing up in this atmosphere of violence, our sons—all of them—are at risk. The serious problem of teen violence will require a multipronged solution. Standing outside JR's funeral, I wondered what would happen if all fathers and sons could have the opportunity that I had just weeks before. Would it prevent even one teen murder? Certainly, the re-creation of rites of passage for our young adolescent males is not a panacea. But when fathers and other responsible elders come together to once again initiate our boys into the wisdom of healthy masculinity, it can only help. While we're at it, we may learn something ourselves.

Tears of a Black Father
By Vernon McClean
Winter 2001

The stereotype of a black father is of an individual who is strong, silent, and oftentimes violent. This is only a stereotype. But, as is often true with stereotypes, there is some truth to it.

Having time to spare before attending a concert at the Beacon Theatre in New York City, I entered the five-and-dime store on 72nd Street and browsed through the discount products. I noted that the black Caribbean guard was staring. However, because of my gigantic ego, I thought he considered me a role model, an academic-looking brother who enjoys browsing in discount stores—a pastime not engaged in by most black men (a stereotype).

I then discovered a bargain: a blue chenille bathrobe for only twenty dollars. (I get cold easily; I, too, am from the Caribbean.) I proceeded to drape the bulky robe over my arm. Now, a bulky robe is rather impossible to conceal. Again, I noticed the guard's repeated staring. No longer was I flattered by his attention. I was starting to get annoyed, because the guard not only stared but followed me from the main floor to the alcove, where I continued to browse before paying for the robe.

In the alcove, I angrily confronted him. Did he think I was a thief? Why didn't he follow the white people in the store? He mumbled that I must understand that it was his job to follow me.

Next incident. I was awaiting the opening of a South African concert at a theater called Symphony Space on New York's Broadway. I decided to go to a nearby greenmarket to purchase a soda while waiting. After browsing a bit, I saw no brands of soda that interested me and proceeded to walk out. While exiting, I was confronted by the Asian owner who demanded I open my book bag. When I asked why, he said he saw me put something in it. A white woman who saw the entire incident told me not to open my bag and said she would call a police officer to protect me. But I was weary after a long day of teaching, so I sadly opened my bag and left.

Third incident. A few years ago, I went to the famed Joseph Papp Theatre in New York. In the lobby a young black guard eyed me. Despite past negative history, I was still quite naïve and thought I was being marveled at. Foolishly, I mistook his suspicious stare for veneration. He then approached me and asked why I was sitting in the lobby with the rest of the patrons who were awaiting the opening of the theater. I told him that I was also awaiting the performance. He demanded to see my ticket. I refused and, in turn, demanded to see his superior. Again, another white woman (she and I are now close friends and attend social functions together) came to my defense and told his superior that I was not doing anything to deserve harassment from this guard. (He still works at this theater.)

I remembered these annoying incidents when I recalled Deborah Mathis's term "Blackmotheritis," which she defined as "a nervous disorder afflicting millions of black women with adolescent children, particularly mothers of boys" (*Liberal Week*, September 1, 1997). Unfortunately, this disease is not confined to black mothers. Black fathers also suffer from their own peculiar strain.

Now you can understand the title of this article, "The Tears of a Black Father." I am in pain. I am a nag. This does not fit the traditional image of a black man, who is supposed to be silent and strong. But I am this way because I want my teenage son, Macheo, to stay alive, and because I love him.

From a very early age Macheo would go with me to rallies in New York against police brutality and for civil rights in Harlem and neighboring communities. And, like Deborah Mathis, I have to tell him:

"Keep your hands out of your pockets."

"Don't reach under your shirt. If there's an itch, just live with it."

"Even if it is below zero, keep your jacket open."

"Do not stay out after nine at night, even when visiting your running buddy across the street from the house." (Too many cops have shot black boys in the back at night.)

"Do not wear baggy jeans. You might be mistaken for Tupac Shakur." "Always have the clerk bag your purchase, with the receipt inside the bag."

Macheo (a Swahili name) rolls his eyes but says respectfully, "Yeah, Dad. I know. I'll remember."

He loves me, but he does not always remember.

There have been times at a Kmart when I have had to tell him not to touch the merchandise. "Macheo!" I have gasped. My son's name falls hard from my mouth, alarmingly. "Get your hand..."

"Okay, Dad," he says impatiently, muttering something that seems mad and sad all at the same time.

"I just don't want—"

"I know, Dad, I know. I'm sorry."

I pay for the merchandise and we leave Kmart.

My son. He thinks he's sorry. A black boy who thinks that it is his "duty" to make me laugh after a hard day's work at the university. (He usually succeeds.)

Like Deborah Mathis, I consider it "an infuriating condition," this "black-fatheritis." There are times when I want to defy this disease: "Go ahead, son, scratch that itch, zip your coat; put your hands wherever you want."

But before I speak, I remember my own incidences of racial harassment, and I know that my beloved Macheo will have to encounter this kind of thing all his life. When he and his older brother (Maliki) are not permitted into a store in the shopping mall "because an adult is not with them," he *must* learn to deal with it. To accept it as a penalty for being a black male in North America. Of course, he must keep his anger locked inside him. Of course, this repressed anger will vastly increase the likelihood that he will die from hypertension and stroke many years before his white playmates. As I write, I rough up his shaved head and wrestle with him for a few minutes. He understands my gestures, and laughs. I laugh, too, because I do not want him to see me cry.

An Immigrant Speaks Out After September 11

By Juan Carlos Areán
Winter 2002

Like so many millions of people in this country, I am an immigrant. I was born and grew up in Mexico and have lived in the United States for the last

20 years. I love this country and I'm grateful for the opportunities it has afforded me. I have devoted my adult life to its enrichment and now I consider it my home. However, I have never become a US citizen. I am a so-called resident alien. And, boy, have I been feeling like an alien these days.

Since September 11, I have been trying to figure out how to react, what to think, what to say or not say. And every day, often more than once a day, I have been changing my mind about it all. It is a good reflection of how I'm feeling: I am confused and my emotions are like a roller coaster—constantly changing, sometimes not allowing me to think clearly.

On the other hand, there are three things that I have known all along:

• I cannot just remain quiet. Even though it is very scary for me to voice dissent in this beloved foreign land, it is even scarier to consider censoring myself.

• I stand in total solidarity with the victims and survivors of the attacks, and also with the targets of hate crimes, especially Arabs and Muslims in the United States and abroad.

• I want the cycle of violence to stop right now. I don't believe this war will end terrorism, and it might not even bring justice to the perpetrators of the attacks.

Aside from that, I don't have any great wisdom. What I do have are my feelings and my perspective as an immigrant, which some people have found helpful. This is what I would like to share with you today.

First of all, I have been feeling isolated. After 20 years of living in this country, never have I felt a stronger sense of not belonging.

I have felt left out of the national grieving process. It turned so quickly into things that I don't identify with: the patriotic anger, the rhetoric of supremacy, the sea of United States flags, and "God Bless America" everywhere you turn.

Never mind that hundreds of victims and survivors were not from the United States. Never mind that thousands of grieving relatives don't even live within our shores. We have forgotten to fly *their* flags.

I mean no offense to anyone, but never mind that *America* is not the name of this country, but of the whole continent. Never mind that the United States flag means so many different things to different people. Never mind that, in my humble opinion, God doesn't check the nationality or religion of a person before he or she is blessed.

Clearly I'm moving from isolation to anger. Yes, I'm very angry. I feel angry at the terrorists for causing the horrible carnage and for violating my sense of safety. I am also angry at the arrogant reaction of this government and many of its citizens, and at the racism, xenophobia, and hate crimes that have shown their ugly faces. I'm angry at the ignorance that seems to abound and at the patriotic environment that is attempting to censor dissent. I'm angry when I hear our leaders saying: "This is a war of good against evil" and "You are either with the United States or you are with the terrorists."

Of course, behind the anger there is fear, a lot of fear. I am terrified about the war and about the inevitable retaliations that we're inviting. I am afraid about the future of my children. I am afraid they will be targeted because they are living in the United States. I am afraid they will be targeted because they are not mainstream US citizens. I'm afraid about the possible reinstatement of the draft. For the first time in my 20 years here, I am feeling scared to speak out, and I find myself censoring my convictions, even in front of good friends.

Occasionally I have been feeling powerless. Powerless to stop the war machine that has been put into motion. Powerless to stop the indiscriminate slaughter. Powerless to protect my children from bacteriological and chemical terrorism.

But behind all of these feelings there is great sadness. Enormous grief for the families of the victims of the attacks. Sadness for the people of Afghanistan who, for 20 years, have known nothing but war. Sadness for the people of Iraq, who have been forced to face a catastrophe like ours every month for the last 10 years. I feel sad for the young United States men and women who enlisted in the armed services to try to find the elusive "American dream" and will now have to live a nightmare. I'm so sad that it had to take a tragedy of this magnitude for many of us to wake up, to start asking questions, to take action.

At the Men's Resource Center we have been working for 12 years with men who are violent in their intimate relationships. And we have learned that, in many cases, behind the violence, behind the rage and the anger, there are many other feelings. There is a lot of fear, a perception of powerlessness, a sense of isolation and probably great sadness. We have seen what happens to these feelings when they go unchecked, when they are not processed and understood. They can turn into self-destruction and the destruction of others.

So, above all, I'm feeling this is a time to look in the mirror, to ask hard questions, to understand our feelings. We need a national day of atonement and self-reflection. We need to extend our hands to our adversaries and build bridges. And I'm not only referring to our government and to our "enemies." I'm also talking about the antiwar and antiracism activists. I'm talking about me.

This is a time to move beyond our anger and hatred to cultivate love. A time to work with our fear and depression to be able to shine our light. We need to stop the cycle of reaction and find our wisdom and balance in order to act in an effective and fair way.

Finally, I would like to say without one bit of sarcasm: God bless America. Yes, the United States and also all of America, the whole continent. God bless

Afghanistan and Japan, Israel and Iraq and all of Asia. God bless Egypt, Sudan, Nigeria, and Libya and all of Africa. God bless Britain and Russia, Bosnia and Serbia and all of Europe and Australia. May God bless all the people of the world and help us come together in understanding, compassion, and peace.

A "Good" White Man
By Robert Jensen
Winter 2005

I stepped onto the speakers' platform at the Virginia Festival of Books in Charlottesville with *Newsday* editor Les Payne to discuss our chapters in his book *When Race Becomes Real*. Bernestine Singley, the other panelist, had coedited the book.

As I walked to my seat, I was well aware of Payne's impressive record. Of the two of us, Payne is the more experienced journalist, has won more prizes, has written more important books, has traveled widely and reported on more complex subjects, is older and has done more in his life, and is a more commanding speaker.

So as I sat down, I did what came naturally: I felt superior to Les Payne. If it seems odd that I would feel superior to someone I knew to be more talented and accomplished than I am, then here is another relevant fact: Les Payne is African American, and I am white.

I didn't recognize that feeling of superiority as I sat down. It wasn't until Payne started speaking that my feeling became so painfully clear to me.

Payne talked about how, as a teenager born in the segregated South who attended high school in the North, he had struggled to overcome the internalized sense of inferiority that grew from the environment in which he had been raised. He talked about how deep that sense of inherent inferiority can be for African Americans.

Eventually, I made the obvious connection: part of the reason the struggle Payne described is so hard for African Americans is because white behavior is a constant expression of that feeling of superiority, both subtle and overt.

I recalled my feeling of superiority as we had taken our seats. I had assumed, despite all I knew about Les Payne, his record, and his speaking ability, that I would be the highlight of the panel.

Why?

It might be because I'm an egotistical white boy. Maybe I'm a white boy with delusions of grandeur. But whatever my own personal weaknesses are, one factor is obvious: I am white and Payne is African American, and that was the basis of my feeling.

The moment that particular feeling hit me, I was left literally speechless, fighting back tears, with a profound sense of sadness. I struggled to focus, but it was difficult. Payne finished, and Singley started her reading. When the speaking period ended, I did my best to answer questions. But I remained shaken.

Deep sadness, deeply embedded

Why all of this drama? It was because I fancied myself one of the "good" white people, one of the antiracist white people.

But in that moment, I had to confront that which I had not yet relinquished: the basic psychological features of racism. As Payne talked honestly of struggling with a sense of inferiority, I had to face that I had never really shaken a sense of my superiority.

As I write these words, the feeling of that moment of sadness returns. Do not mistake this for superficial shame or guilt. Do not describe me as a self-indulgent white liberal. The sadness I feel is not for me. The sadness is about how deeply embedded in me is that fundamental reality of racism—the assumption that white people are superior.

That doesn't mean I'm a racist. It doesn't mean my political work or efforts in the classroom don't matter. Instead, it means that what I say to my students about race—that the dynamics of domination and subordination run deep, affecting us in ways we don't always see clearly—is true not only in theory. It is also true in my own psyche.

Payne's words forced me to feel what I had long known. That wasn't his intention; he was speaking to the audience—which was primarily African American—not to me.

Whatever the intent, he did me that service. But I am most grateful to Payne not for that, but for something that happened later.

After the event, I was planning to drive to Washington, DC. When I mentioned that to Payne, he asked if he could ride with me and catch a flight from DC back to New York. I jumped at the chance, in part because I wanted to hear more about his research for his forthcoming book on Malcolm X, but also because I wanted to talk to him about what had happened to me on stage.

Les Payne is a gracious man; he listened to my story, nodding throughout.

After I had finished Payne did something for which I will always be grateful: He didn't forgive me. He made no attempt to make me feel better. He didn't reassure me that I was, in fact, one of the "good" white people. He simply acknowledged what I had told him, said he understood, and continued our discussion about the politics of race in the United States.

During the panel, without knowing it, Payne had given me the gift of feeling uncomfortable. In the car, perhaps with full knowledge of what he was doing, he gave me the gift of not letting me off the hook.

When I dropped him at the airport, I had no illusions. The day had meant much more to me than to him. He had been willing to teach me something, and then he went on to other things. His personal struggle with internalized inferiority was largely over; his chapter in *When Race Becomes Real* made that clear, as did his interaction with me.

But I was left with the unfinished project of dealing with my internalized sense of superiority. And it was clear to both of us that such a project was my responsibility, not his.

"Good" white men

The story doesn't end there.

On the platform with us was Bernestine Singley, who is every bit as black as Les Payne, and every bit as accomplished a lawyer and writer. Why am I focusing on him and not her? Why did he spark this realization in me and she did not?

In part it was because of what Payne talked about on stage; his words had pushed my buttons. Also, I have known Singley longer and have a more established relationship with her. We live in different cities and are not friends in a conventional sense, but I consider her (and I hope she considers me) a trustworthy ally and comrade in the struggle, and a friend in that context. Singley and I also have very different styles, and when we appear on panels together we clearly are not competing.

With all that said, it's also difficult to miss the fact that Singley is a woman and Payne is a man. There was not only a race dynamic on stage, but also a gender dynamic. It's likely that I was, in classic male fashion, focusing on the struggle for dominance with the other man on the panel.

This perception also is hard to face: In addition to being a good white person, you see, I'm also a "good man." I'm one of the men on the "right side." But I also am one of the men who, whatever side he is on, struggles with the reality of living in a male-supremacist society.

Introspection on these matters is difficult; those of us in privileged positions often are not in the best position to evaluate our own behavior. But looking back on that day, it appears to me I walked onto that platform with an assumption of my inherent superiority—so deeply woven into me that I could not in the moment see it—that had something to do with race and gender.

From those assumptions, it is hard to reach a conclusion, other than: *I was a fool.*

I use that term consciously, because throughout history white people have often cast blacks as the fool to shore up our sense of superiority. But in that game, it is white people who are the fools, and it is difficult and painful to confront that.

Somehow, I had allowed myself to believe the story that a racist and sexist society still tells. Yes, I know that Jim Crow segregation is gone and the overt ideology that supported it is mostly gone. But in the struggle to change the world, what matters is not only what the law says, or what "polite" people say in public. What matters just as much, if not more, is what we really are, deep down.

Playing for keeps

All this matters not just because white people should learn to be better or nicer, but because as long as we whites *believe* we are better—deep down, in places most of us have learned to hide—we will not feel compelled to change a society in which black unemployment is twice the white rate. And in which, as a recent study has found, a white man with a criminal record is more likely to be called back for a job interview than a black man with no record.

In the United States, the typical black family has 58 percent of the income of a typical white family. And at the slow rate the black-white poverty gap has been narrowing since 1968, it will take 150 years to close. At the current rate, blacks and whites won't reach high school graduation parity until 2013—nearly 60 years after *Brown v. Board of Education*.

That is an ugly society.

The first step for white people is to face that ugliness, to tell the truth about the system we live in and tell the truth about ourselves. But that means nothing if we do not commit to change—not just to change ourselves, but to change the system. We have to face the ways in which white supremacy makes white people foolish but forces others to pay a much greater price.

We have to stop playing the fool and start playing for keeps.

"Macho" Mongo, and the Men's Movement
By Martín Espada
Winter 1999

Inevitably, we try to envision the next century. Will there be a "men's movement" in twenty years, when my son, Clemente, is an adult? Will it someday alienate and exclude Clemente, the way it has alienated and excluded me? The counterculture can be as exclusive and elitist as the mainstream; to be kept out of both is a supreme frustration. I do not expect the men's movement to address its own racism in depth. The self-congratulatory tone of that movement drowns out any significant self-criticism. I only wish that the men's movement wouldn't be so proud of its own ignorance. The blatant expropriation of Native American symbols and rituals by certain factions of the movement leaves me with a twitch in my face. What should Puerto Rican men do in response to this colonizing definition of maleness, particularly considering the presence of our indigenous Taino blood?

I remember watching one such men's movement ritual, on public television I believe, and becoming infuriated because the lead drummer couldn't keep a beat. I imagined myself cloistered in a tent with some Anglo accountant from the suburbs of New Jersey who was stripped to the waist and whacking a drum with no regard for rhythm, the difference being that I could hear Mongo Santamaría in my head, and he couldn't. I am torn between hoping that the men's movement reforms itself by the time my son reaches adulthood, or that it assimilates, its language going the way of Esperanto.

Another habit of language which I hope is extinct by the time Clemente reaches adulthood is the Anglo use of the word "macho." Before this term came into use to define sexism and violence, no particular ethnic or racial group was implicated by language itself. "Macho," especially as employed by Anglos, is a Spanish word that particularly seems to identify Latino male behavior as the very standard of sexism and violence. This connection, made by Anglos, both intuitively and explicitly, then justifies a host of repressive measures against Latino males, as our presence on the honor roll of many a jail and prison will attest. Sometimes, of course, the perception of macho volatility turns deadly. I remember, at age fifteen, hearing about a friend of my father's, Martín "Tito" Pérez, who was "suicided" in a New York City jail cell. A grand jury determined that it is possible for a man to hang himself with his hands cuffed behind him.

While Latino male behavior is, indeed, all too often sexist and violent, Latino males in this country are in fact no worse in this regard than their Anglo counterparts. Arguably, European and European-American males have set the world standard for violence in the twentieth century, from the Holocaust to Hiroshima to Vietnam.

Yet, any assertiveness on the part of Latino males, especially any form of resistance to Anglo authority, is labeled "macho" and instantly discredited. I recall one occasion, working for an "alternative" radio station in Wisconsin, when I became involved in a protest over the station's refusal to air a Spanish-language program for the local Chicano community. When a meeting was held to debate the issue, the protestors, myself included, became frustrated and staged a walkout. The meeting went on without us, and we later learned that we were defended, ironically enough, by someone who saw us as acting "macho." "It's their culture," this person explained apologetically to the gathered liberal intelligentsia. We got the program on the air.

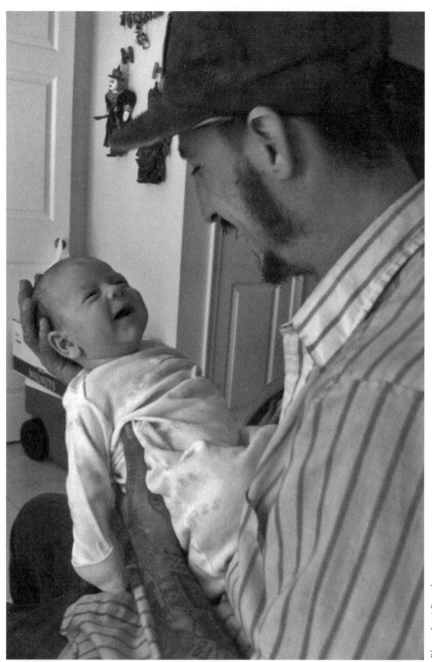

FATHERING

Every man has a father, whether present in his life or not, and many men become fathers themselves. Still, society often undervalues the father-child relationship, despite it being so obviously central to men's lives. In this section, fatherhood emerges as its own category of thought as men articulate the challenges and victories they face throughout the process of parenting. Adult children honestly describe their relationships with their fathers and grandfathers, creating an intergenerational conversation around fathering. For sons, there is also an exploration of how they and their fathers experience masculinity within their relationship.

Apple Pie, Love of Country, and—Fatherhood?
By Rob Okun
Summer 2005

"Being a father is one of the greatest joys I've ever known." "Too many fathers are totally absent from their kids' lives." "I know so many dads who are loving and caring." "Fathers can't be counted on." "Fathers sacrifice so much for their families." "Dads are deadbeats."

What do you think about fathers? Opinions vary: from loathed to loved, reviled to respected. Nowadays, society is holding fathers to a higher standard than ever, expecting male parents to regularly "do the right thing"—to be accountable, to follow through responsibly as fully involved dads raising their children. But for many men such a high standard comes with a cost.

While feelings about mothers and motherhood have evolved in recent years to reflect women's important roles outside of the home, female parents still maintain a respected place in society, right up there with apple pie and love of country. Fathers, however, are more vulnerable. Many feel an underlying tension, a sense of being questioned: *"Are you going to come through, be reliable, or are you going to flake out on your family?"*

This past Father's Day, *Voice Male*'s publisher, the Men's Resource Center for Change, coordinated a newspaper signature ad published in the Springfield *Republican,* a Massachusetts daily with a circulation approaching 100,000. More than 150 men and women endorsed its message, under the headline "Celebrating Fathers and Father Figures."

As admirable as the ad's message is, some who considered endorsing it told me they felt it put too much pressure on fathers, suggesting dads might read it not as a goal to strive for but as a job description impossible to fill. I understand. At times, who hasn't felt fathering *is* too challenging a role, one for which we've never had adequate training. I remember when one of my daughters was turning 13 and her emotional growing pains were excruciating—and not just for her. She became uncommunicative, and I remember feeling lost as she withdrew for a while. It meant a lot then to know I had the nonjudgmental support and counsel of other men, fathers all.

Beyond those difficult fatherhood passages, I know there are countless fathers—and other men—walking around all the time feeling judged, bracing themselves for criticism, expecting to be called on the carpet for falling short as a parent, son, husband, partner, brother, mentor, friend. And not enough of us talk about the pressure and the aloneness that explicit or implicit questioning evokes in us. I know my experience with a daughter becoming a teenager would have been that much more difficult if it hadn't been for the group of men to whom I turned.

The bitter truth is that the "expecting the worst" dread that hovers over a big part of contemporary fatherhood often overshadows our hopes and dreams, our sense of possibility and potential. Whether the road many of us traveled with our own fathers was rocky or smooth, a sense of loss or abandonment often looms just around the bend. It's part of the uneasy sadness many fathers feel. And it is also what clouds our thoughts and actions when the going gets tough. Too many of us carry that burden alone. I can't underscore enough the suggestion that fathers find other dads to talk to. We don't connect the same way mothers do, and, for the most part, society doesn't assist us to create conditions that work for men. But that doesn't let us off the hook of trying to figure out how to find—or create—a circle of support. Imagine the possibilities for contact, insight, affirmation, and a strengthened self-esteem if we did.

Fathering *is* one of the most life-altering experiences a man can know. Many of us felt a frozen part of our hearts begin to melt when we first held our babies. Or when we cared for them solo for the first time. Or first took them to the playground. In other words, when we got in touch with that natural part of being human that finds meaning and fulfillment through nurturing another being.

There is more. Spending alone time with our children. We have so much to learn from being with them. As they grow older, young adults now, I realize I can learn more about myself from witnessing our relationship evolve.

Earlier this summer, I spent a long weekend with the daughter who struggled at 13. She's 20 now, working outside of Baltimore where she goes to college. Our weekend together was special, including a perfect morning hike. Stopping on a trail in the woods to observe a family of deer, I put my arm around her and she put hers around me. We stood together watching, breathing as one, no words exchanged in the stillness of the July morning. I could sense something familiar in the moment. It was the same feeling I had when I held her in the crook of my arm 20 summers ago. Easy. Natural. When the deer family finally bounded off into the woods, instead of feeling as if our special moment broken, I felt our bond as father and daughter had been strengthened. Just as fathers often can't find the words for the powerful emotions that overcome us at our children's birth, I couldn't explain the heightened sense of connection I felt. Happily, I didn't need to. Father's Day came in July this year—as it comes on many other days when I least expect it.

CELEBRATING FATHERS AND FATHER FIGURES

We celebrate fathers, stepdads, and all father figures who work hard and strive to promote respect and harmony in their families and demonstrate great love for their children.

We celebrate fathers who actively engage in raising their children and do their share of family chores, showing that it takes *everybody's* hard work to make a home.

We celebrate fathers who love and respect their partners and strive to work honestly to maintain equality in their relationships.

We celebrate fathers who make the difficult choices involved in balancing family and career, ensuring they make time for their children.

We celebrate fathers who encourage their children to feel good about themselves, promoting understanding and respect between boys and girls.

We celebrate fathers who challenge prejudice that demeans not just their sons and daughters but everyone else's, too.

We celebrate fathers who advance the idea that peace and harmony in the home are preconditions for peace and harmony in the world.

We celebrate fathers who place their children's need for love, safety, and support first, whether they see them each day or some days.

Children thrive when they are cared for by devoted, involved parents— it's love that makes a family. Let's celebrate that fact, not just on Father's or Mother's Day but every day.

—Text of a Father's Day ad that ran in the Springfield (Mass.) Republican, June 17, 2005.

VOICE MALE

Men and Baby Showers

By Tom Weiner

Winter 1994

Men and baby showers. Are the two as incompatible as fish and bicycles? Was the presence of men at their baby's shower at best a trend among New Agers whose heyday has now passed? I was told as much at a recent shower attended by an expectant father and five other men.

What are the consequences for both new families and society as a whole when baby showers are women's domain? Certainly women have done a marvelous job organizing and conducting showers for one another. None of what follows is intended to discredit their efforts. But when men remain uninvolved, how does it affect what occurs? There are several levels to this question. On the surface the absence of men serves to deepen the gulf between men's and women's worlds. If women sponsor showers for one another and men do not attend, then the message is that, even prenatally, children are women's responsibility and that men need not concern themselves about infant clothing, accoutrements, or amusements. For the women in attendance, men are not expected to think about such nest-building pursuits. For the men not there, the expectant father as well as his friends and acquaintances, accepting not being involved or invested goes unquestioned.

When two friends participated equally in a recent shower, many different messages were imparted between them and among their friends. Mark's presence told Carol he wanted to be part of everything that had to do with their baby. Watching him pretend to hold their imaginary baby on his shoulder in one of the outfits they received was a clear indication that he was getting ready and feeling excited about their imminent adventure. Seeing the glances they stole when some of the more dramatic and impressive gifts were unwrapped, as well as the shared appreciation they expressed, served to deepen their connection to one another and their baby. Carol got to feel Mark's support and partnership. His evident good cheer and enthusiasm were perceptible to all assembled. He now will be able to make associations between people and gifts that will heighten his awareness of how his baby and family have been celebrated. Being an equal partner in the shower lets him know that his role is pivotal. His presence lets the men and women in attendance know how involved he wants to be from before the outset. Those men not yet fathers can feel inspired. They can see his joy.

But how does one buck tradition and move toward equality? It is critical to be able to envision the kind of partnership spouses desire. If the commitment to coparenting is a powerful, motivating factor, then opportunities to establish such an approach need to be taken. Just as having men be labor coaches heightens the mutuality of the birth experience, so, too, can having them be part of their baby's shower. There are still too few models for such actions. I remember being disheartened when I was watching a video on infant care within 48 hours of the birth of my daughter, Madeline, in June of 1988. Virtually all care-providers in several of the presentations ranging from tips on diapering to advice about sleep habits were women. Even when the assumption being made was that men were participating in the labor process, the videos fell back on stereotypes of absent, disengaged fathers and super-functioning earth mothers who neither need nor ask for their husband's assistance.

You've got to find your own models and—with friends perhaps, but occasionally in isolation—come up with creative ways to get there. It's all too easy and far too acceptable to opt for society's way of separate, unequal domains. To break out of the constricting roles requires courage and conviction. The payoffs are enormous, however, as your baby reaps dividends from having two equally caring, attentive, involved parents. And, of course, the rewards for both the man and woman are fundamental. As former Massachusetts Sen. Paul Tsongas was heard to say during the keynote address at the Wellesley College "Fatherhood Forum" in 1985, "I never heard of a man who, on his deathbed said, 'I wish I'd spent less time with my family.'" Your baby's shower is a golden opportunity to start spending time with your family.

Raising Boys as an Adoptive Father
By Jacob Stevenson
Fall 1998

My sons were three and five when we adopted them. Since they weren't newborns, they came into our family and our lives already with their own history and experiences—independent of me as a father or my wife as a mother. Consequently, the boys compared me to whatever prior experience they had with fathers, or father figures.

It turned out my sons had derived almost all their opinions about "what a father should be" from television shows! I had never expected that, as a dad, I'd be involved in a sort of Nielsen ratings race with guys like Ozzie Nelson, Robert Young (who was actually cast against type in *Father Knows Best*—in real life he was an alcoholic, suffered from depression, and once tried to commit suicide), and Ralph Waite (the father on *The Waltons*), but so I was, at first. Also, because my boys had had virtually no exposure to an adult male before me, they watched me like a hawk. They'd never before seen a man make breakfast, take a shower, go to work, play with them, fix dinner, or fall asleep.

In short, the whole business of what men do and are was completely foreign and amazing to them, and they made it quite clear that they were absolutely going to find out all about this odd creature: me. I was pretty unaware of this for the first six months, until my wife burst out laughing one evening after we'd tucked the little guys in for the night. "Didn't you notice how at dinner tonight they were both practicing holding their forks *exactly like you do?*" I hadn't, but I quickly became concerned about my silverware etiquette. Many nonadoptive parents—and children—can be insensitive in their comments to adoptive parents. I cannot count the times when many well-meaning, decent people have said things to me like, "Oh, you're the adoptive father. Who's the *real* father?"

This question always offends me, but I try to explain, as cheerfully as possible, that I *am* my sons' real father, though not their biological one. So, too, the boys themselves—not as much now as at the beginning of our family—have been hurt at times by similar inquiries. People do not seem to understand that successfully adopted children are nonetheless in a very conflicted position: they are joyful and thankful to finally belong to a family, naturally, but they also tend to wonder why they were stranded in the first place. Almost uniformly, such children assume it was "their fault," that something must be "wrong" or "bad" about them.

That's a staggeringly heavy burden for any child to bear, and when others make well-meaning remarks like, "You're such a lucky little boy to have a new family," I fear they are completely unaware of how those words burn and sting. It was so important to my older son to be seen as a "normal" boy when he entered kindergarten that he insisted his teacher call him "Mr. Jacobsen" for the first month. He wanted to make darn sure that everybody knew he was my son, I was his dad, and this was our family. (He succeeded, too.)

As a new adoptive father, it's common to go through a "honeymoon" period, generally lasting about six months. Your son will amaze you with his unrelenting goodness during this time. He's testing you. He needs to know that you will be equally good to him in turn. When he becomes convinced that you will, the honeymoon's over, and he'll begin throwing tantrums, telling you that not only does he not like broccoli, he actively hates it, and furthermore broccoli is, as everybody knows, just plain stupid. And Dad, he might add, if you like broccoli, then you're probably stupid, too. In short, he's acting just like little boys act—when they're not scared.

I remember well the day my older son told me I was stupid because I liked broccoli. It was one of the happiest days of my life, because I knew that he and I had arrived— together—at a place where he felt safe and secure enough to understand that he didn't need to be perfect in order to "earn" my love. He had finally arrived at a point when he not only knew he deserved my love, but knew he already had it, unconditionally, then and for the rest of his life. And, for me, that's what being a real father and a real son is all about.

A Teen Father's Adult Life

By Mark Jimerson

Spring 2003

Take a walk down High Street in Holyoke, Massachusetts, on a spring afternoon, and you probably won't have to walk far before you see a young girl pushing a baby stroller. She may look too young to be a mother, but don't be too sure. Holyoke, like many other small cities in Massachusetts and elsewhere, is home to a surprisingly large number of mothers who are very young and very visible, girls who get pregnant and don't hide themselves away, and don't often have abortions. Getting pregnant while in high school, or even in middle school, can actually elevate a girl's status within certain peer groups in this small city.

But what about the fathers of these kids: where are they? Turn a corner off High Street and push open the door to a local barbershop, and you'll find one of them. J.R. Maldonado is sixteen years old and the father of two. Ask him, and he'll show you pictures of his kids. Erised is two years old and Zaphiel is seven months. J.R. isn't waiting for a haircut. He's a barber waiting for his next customer. His girlfriend, Desiree, just flew down to Puerto Rico with their kids, and as soon as he has the money for his own ticket, he'll pack his things and move down there with them. This will be the third time in three years that they've moved to Puerto Rico, planning each time to stay for good. They have a little house of their own down in Guayama. It's all fixed up now, not like last year, when they had to live with her family while J.R. worked on the house. Things got crazy last time, after they found out her birth control hadn't worked and she was pregnant again. And then her brother flipped out one day and came after Desiree with a stick, and J.R., in defending her, got her scorn instead of thanks. It was a family matter, she said, it was none of his business. So J.R. found himself on the outside, and the next thing he knew he was on a plane back to the mainland without her.

Their relationship has often been turbulent, but somehow they have always gotten back together. They started seeing each other three years ago. The first time they had sex was at a party. He was thirteen, but everyone said he looked older. She was fifteen. They were drinking, like everyone else. Birth control was never discussed; not that night, or the other times after that. Then two months later, when she went to the school nurse with headaches and dizziness, they gave her a pregnancy test. It came back positive.

The news made him happy at first, but scared too. He told his mother the day he found out, and she took it fairly well. At forty-one, she already had eight grandchildren, so this was a disappointment, but not a shock. Desiree's mother didn't take it so well. She remembered getting pregnant at sixteen and dropping out of school, and she didn't want that fate for her daughter.

Days and then weeks went by, and J.R. started to panic. He never thought of leaving Desiree or saying the baby wasn't his, like some guys might. But still. "I had my head spinning," he says. "I didn't know what I was going to do, I was so worried about so many things. Especially about money and supporting the baby." He had turned fourteen, but he still wasn't old enough to get a real job. He made a little money cutting hair at home, but not nearly enough. He went through a stage where he was so scared he just kind of freaked out and would start yelling if anyone asked him about the baby that was coming.

J.R. entered high school that fall, and as a freshman he was a starting running back on the football team. But with the baby on his mind, he ended up quitting school in November and doing odd jobs with his stepfather. His girlfriend moved in with him at his mother's apartment, and they managed to get a double bed and a crib into his bedroom. When his daughter was born, he was there to cut the umbilical cord. "The first thing I thought was, 'Look what I created. Look what came out, that I'm going to love so much. That'll always be with me.' I had so many emotions inside that I broke out crying."

Two months later, instead of returning to school, he and Desiree moved to Puerto Rico and stayed with her family, thinking they would have a better chance of making it there. "I was real happy then," he said. "I was incredibly happy." But work was hard to come by and they moved back to Holyoke six months later. The following year they tried it again, and that's when they found out she was pregnant again and there was the thing with her brother and the stick. Back in Holyoke without his daughter or his pregnant girlfriend, J.R. became depressed. "I was like blank for a month or two, or three." He barely had any money, bringing in maybe a hundred dollars every two weeks cutting hair at home, in his mother's apartment. He didn't want to do anything, had no ambition at all, and felt like a failure.

Then Desiree came back from Puerto Rico with their daughter in May, and Zaphiel was born a few weeks later. "I went to the hospital when he was born, and everything was good. I was working and I was happy because I was working. I had my job, I had my kids over here, and my girl. I had everything over here. And everything was going good."

Until they started arguing again. She wanted to go out to the teen dances at the church by McDonald's and he didn't want to go out. She wanted to be with her friends and go to parties, and he wanted her there with the kids when he got home from his new job at the barbershop. When fall came, he enrolled in school, but it was hard being a freshman again after two years away, and anyway, he needed to make money for his kids. His boss at the barbershop was cool—he let J.R. leave when his kids had appointments; he even bought him diapers in bulk and took it out of his pay. So he quit school again, and did his best to support his family.

When Desiree left him the next time, he got so low he couldn't sleep and couldn't eat, and he got real skinny. His mother would hear him late at night in his room, crying. It got so bad they had to call the police one day to keep him from jumping off the balcony of their apartment building. Counseling didn't help, but when Desiree got worried and came back to him, things got better.

Always up and down, their relationship. Always stress in his life. Being a young father isn't easy, not if you're trying to do right by your kids. At least now his friends have kids too, and he knows they'll be there for him. "My best friend, he's always after my kids. He's like, 'I'm gonna get your daughter that jersey right there.' He loves my kids. I don't know, he's just always there. He's always mad cool with me. He helps me out. Most of my boys are. They come by and they're like, 'Oh, you gotta give me a picture of your kids.'"

Still, it's no fun when you're sixteen and you have to buy diapers and formula instead of new clothes for yourself. When you have to work instead of hanging out. When his daughter was born, J.R. admits he relied too much on his mother and others, and didn't do as much as he could have. But he's older now, and he wants to do it right. He has plans to join Desiree and the kids in Puerto Rico and open his own barbershop as soon as he can, to be responsible and independent, and really make it this time. He and Desiree still argue, but they're doing better about talking things out—"like we're supposed to." For his children, he wants what so many parents want: a better life. His advice for them is already prepared: "Go to school. Don't have kids. Wait until you're 30."

His mother doesn't want him to go down there again. She says the kids need a stable home. But now the house is finished and it's time to go back and cut the lawn and get some furniture and get settled in.

"Men's Rights"—or What's Right for Men?
By Joe Kelly
Fall 2000

Advice for a single mom: "*Ensure the man does walk away. Believe it or not, a woman's attitude is 99.9 percent of the problem.*"
How to address family violence: "*We have to stop denying the fact that 65 percent of domestic violence victims are men.*"
The purpose of the women's movement: "*Feminists have more power than they admit, and [we must] expose the lies and hypocrisy of their anti-male message.*"
Solutions to child-support system problems: "*The American Coalition for Fathers and Children (ACFC) is calling for peaceful protests*

due to the abhorrent practices of child support agencies. ACFC does not condone violence as a means of protest. ACFC hereby states it is neither responsible nor liable for the actions of the individuals or independent organizations participating in these protests."

Had enough? I have. And this is just a mild taste of the vitriol fueling much of the so-called men's rights movement. Sadly, reactionary "men's rights" resources are the most widespread and readily available to partners, fathers, and husbands going through the fire of a family breakup. As a father, I am amazed and shocked by the attention these groups direct toward a woman-blaming, "we got screwed," score-keeping attitude as opposed to working for the well being of their children and the deepening of child-father relationships after a breakup.

As a father named Andrew put it in an e-mail, "I thought bad attitudes were 99.9 percent of most problems (male *or* female). I would suggest a book for the author of the comments excerpted above. It's pretty readily available; it's called the Holy Bible. One of the most important themes of this book is the line of removing the large obstruction from one's *own* eyes before trying to remove something from someone else's."

Andrew identifies the key element that fathers' rights groups miss and that pro-gender-justice men have failed to adequately address on a broad scale: *the only attitude we can truly change is our own.* Examining one's own attitudes and behaviors and then doing whatever possible to strengthen and deepen the relationship with one's children is the best way to help both them and us. Such a path is, in many cases (and not exclusively postdivorce), the most difficult one for fathers to travel. However, it is also just as clear that knee-jerk blaming of women, feeling victimized, and remaining stuck in anger and bitterness are pretty much guaranteed to undermine any relationship a father has with his kids as well as to hinder those children's best development as people. And, by the way, such a posture pretty much guarantees that a man's own emotional and spiritual growth will be crippled.

That's not to say men should never be angry, or that they should blindly accept the culture's too-often-dismissive attitude toward fathers. But we have to remember: *we are* this culture. We help create and influence it. And remember that these are *our* children, born of both mother and father. They are no one's property; they are (to paraphrase Kahlil Gibran) on loan from a higher power who places them in our care.

Some men may get a short-lived satisfaction from blaming women for most family problems, and/or the family court system for screwing them, or "radical feminists" for ruining society. But all that those attitudes leave behind is a trail of bitterness. What are the benefits from this kind of attitude and this kind of thinking? There are none.

It's time those of us with a vision of reconciliation between men and women (instead of combativeness between them) start offering our embittered and wounded brothers a rich alternative—the heritage of gender justice and the opportunities it offers, regardless of the personal, familial, or social circumstances one is in. Through sustained and courageous efforts toward gender justice, women have created many more (though still not fully equal) opportunities for themselves in the world of work and community. But not enough men have yet stepped forward to grasp the opportunities in family life that the women's movement has offered us. I think fathers should be leading the way—especially fathers who are in or who have experienced family crises, such as separation or a child's misfortune.

These fathers are prime candidates for recognizing the ways in which our culture fails fathers and men to the degree that it fails to attain gender justice for mothers and women, daughters and sons, fathers and men.

Unless men of heart and their allies open their eyes to the wonderful opportunity such awareness affords them, then the angry, scared, vulnerable men passing through their personal fires will understandably turn to voices raised loud enough for them to hear. The voices of bitter, hateful fathers, men so angered by loss of gender "privilege" that they would blindly lash out seeking revenge. Revenge, vitriol, and an embittered commitment to "scorekeeping" will not improve men's lives or bring them closer to their children. What will? Honestly acknowledging the hurt, anger, grief, and confusion. From that place, motivated by love for their children and themselves, they can begin to heal and move toward a deeper relationship with their sons and daughters, as well as deepening their commitment to obtaining gender justice for all.

I've Got Big Shoes to Fill
By Byron Hurt
Winter 2009

"I knew the second you were born that I was committed to you," my father said to me, standing in a driving rainstorm on Cone Avenue, a block away from our Acorn Avenue home on Long Island. It was a Sunday evening, and with nighttime quickly falling, I sat in the driver's seat of my stalled car, humbled by my father's grace. My teammate Chad, a defensive lineman and my road dog for the weekend, sat on the passenger's side and observed a father unconditionally loving his son.

One week earlier, my pops, who for nearly 30 years worked two jobs—one as a contractor, the other, the night shift at a nearby mental hospital—bought me a red 1988 Ford Mustang. He bought it because I convinced him that I needed a car to commute 30-minutes each way to my new job as a student beat reporter for the *Patriot Ledger*, a Quincy, Massachusetts, newspaper. With no hesitation, he searched for a used car his young, ambitious son could drive.

At $500, the Mustang was a bargain. But on this windy, chilly, rainy evening, as my father dug into his toolbox looking for a screwdriver to fix the stalled car, it was his calming presence in the midst of a torrential downpour that, to me, was priceless.

Dressed in an army green raincoat and a rain hat to match, my father, Jackie Hurt, pulled out his trusty screwdriver from his silver steel toolbox, stuck it into the car's carburetor, and told me to turn the ignition. The car started with ease.

Just like that, he fixed the flooded engine.

Earlier that weekend, my pops implored me to test-drive the car at least once before heading back up I-95 to Boston's Northeastern University. His solid advice fell on deaf ears. I was too busy hanging out and partying in New York City to try the car out for size, or to even look under the hood. Besides, I trusted that my father had bought nothing less than a road-worthy vehicle for my trip back to Beantown. So, as I had done many times before, I played my father's forewarnings to the left, and waited to the very last minute to take the car for a spin.

My pops quietly watched his son run the streets of New York all weekend—coming home periodically to eat, sleep, and change clothes. He saw that I was not heeding his advice; spending little to no time getting to know the used car he had bought at my request. But fathers know best. And he knew that experience, by far, was the best teacher.

The flooded engine, which led me to shamefully call him for assistance that Sunday evening as I was on my way back to Boston, was evidence that he indeed was the old wise one, and that I was still young and immature. I thought about the many times he had been right before. The time when, too small to carry the Sunday newspaper all by myself, he told me to carry it one section at a time, and I, too stubborn and ambitious for my own good at age four, tried to carry it all, spilling pages all over the driveway. The time, at fourteen, when teaching me how to paint a customer's room, he warned me to cover every square inch of the carpet with drop-cloth because the square inch that I didn't cover would be the very square inch that I would inevitably spill paint on—which, of course, I did. There was also the time when he told me never to drive a car on empty, only to come rescue me on the shoulder of the road when I was stranded with no gas. And all the times he told me to pay myself first every payday, by putting money into my savings account before buying sneakers and clothes, yet I'd still find myself short by the next payday.

As my intrepid father walked around the corner in the rain, toolbox in hand, all of those long forgotten moments flashed through my mind. My father has always given me his best advice. Only I didn't always listen.

Full of shame and embarrassment, I revved up the Mustang's engine. I rolled down the window and asked my pops how he could be so patient with me, especially in this horrible weather, and in light of the fact that I did not listen to his advice.

"I knew the second that you were born that I was committed to you—through the good times and the bad," he said. "Have a safe trip to Boston, and call me if you need anything."

Father Hunger
By Mumia Abu-Jamal
Winter 1999

It has been over three decades since I have looked into his face, but I find him now, sometimes hidden, in the glimpse of a mirror. He was short of stature, shorter than I at ten years, fully, smoothly bald, with a face the color of walnuts. He walked with a slight limp, and smoked cigars, usually Phillies. Although short, he wasn't slight, but powerfully built with a thick, though not fat, form. His voice was deep, with the accents of the South wrapped around each word, sweet and sticky like molasses.

Often his words tickled his sons, and they tossed them among themselves like prizes found in the depths of a Crackerjack box, words wondrous in their newness, their rarity, their difference from all others.

"Boys! Cut out that tusslin', heah me?" And the boys would stop their rasslin', their bellies near bursting with swallowed, swollen laughter, the word vibrating sotto voce in their throats: "Tusslin'—tusslin'—tusslin'—tusslin'! Tusslin'!" For days—for weeks—these silly little boys had a new toy and, with this one word, reduced each other to teary-eyed fits of fall-on-the-floor laughter. "Tusslin'!"

He was a relatively old man when he seeded these sons, over fifty, and because of his age, he was openly affectionate in a way unusual for a man of his time. He kissed them, dressed them, and taught them, by example, that he loved them. He talked with them. And walked and walked and walked with them.

"Daaad! I wanna riiide!," I whined.

"It ain't good for you to ride so much, boy. Walkin' is good for ya. It's good exercise for ya."

Decades later, I would hear that same whine from one of my sons, and my reply would echo my father's.

His eyes were the eyes of age, so discolored by time they seemed blueish, but there was a perpetual twinkle of joy in them, of love and living. He lived just over a decade into this son's life, and his untimely death from illness left holes in the soul.

Without a father, I sought and found father-figures like Black Panther Captain Reggie Schell, Party Defense Minister Huey P. Newton, and indeed, the party itself, which, in a period of utter void, taught me, fed me, and made me part of a vast and militant family of revolutionaries. Many good men and women became my teachers, my mentors, and my examples of a revolutionary ideal—Zayd Malik Shakur, murdered by police when Assata was wounded and taken, and Geronimo ji jaga (a.k.a. Pratt) who commanded the party's L.A. chapter with distinction and defended it from deadly state attacks until his imprisonment as a victim of frame-up and judicial repression—Geronimo, torn from his family and children and separated from them for a quarter of a century.

Here in death row, in the confined substratum of a society where every father is childless, and every man fatherless, those of us who have known the bond of father-son love may at least relive it in our minds, perhaps even draw strength from it. Those who have not—the unloved—find it virtually impossible to love. They live alienated from everyone around them, at war even with their own families.

Here in this manmade hell, there are countless young men bubbling with bitter hatreds and roiling resentments against their absent fathers. Several have taken to the odd habit of calling me "Papa," an endearment whose irony escapes them.

It has never escaped me. I realize that I live amidst a generation of young men drunk not only with general loneliness but with the particular, gnawing anguish of father-hunger. I had my own father; later I had the party, and Geronimo; Delbert, Chuck, Mike, Ed, and Phil; Sundiata, Mutulu, and other oldheads like myself. Who have they had?

Yet for a long time I resisted the nickname. I resented being "Papa" to young men I didn't know, while being denied—by decree of state banishment—the opportunity to be a father to the children of my own flesh and heart. My sons were babies when I was cast into this hell, and no number of letters, cards, or phone calls can ever heal the wounds that they and their sisters have suffered over the long, lonely years of separation.

I was also in denial. For who was the oldhead they were calling? Certainly not me? It took a trip, a trek to the shiny, burnished steel mirror on the wall, where I found my father's face staring back at me, to recognize reality.

I am he . . . and they are me.

Hoop Dreams

By Michael Burke

Fall 2003

The sound of the basketball bouncing on the driveway. The clunk as it hits the backboard, then the rim. The swish as it goes through the net, then the bouncing resumes.

When I first heard it again—after twenty-some years of silence—I shouldn't have been surprised, but I came out to witness the miracle: my eight-year-old son out front in the driveway, dribbling and shooting, lining up the shot, giving a little jump and firing it up. He had a new ball, a hoop we'd just put up for him, and a week of basketball camp under his belt, and he was polishing his newfound skills. It was a glorious sight and sound.

And it carried me back—way back, to my childhood in Southern California, and the backboard my father put up above our garage so that I could play. My friend Gary and I spent whole afternoons out there, playing one-on-one or H-O-R-S-E. Sometimes after work my dad would come out and shoot with us, lofting up that push shot he'd learned sometime back in the Cretaceous. Sometimes other friends joined in. But often it was just me, shooting and shooting until the sun went down and well beyond, until my mom called me in for dinner.

It was my therapy, and my escape: whenever school and homework, peer pressure and hormones grew too much to bear, whenever what was going on in the house built up to the point where I had to get out—and before I could escape by just getting in a car and driving off—I had the hoop, and the driveway, the bouncing of the ball, the arc of the shot and the singing twine of the net.

There's a rhythm to it: bounce, bounce, gather, jump, shoot. And I shot and shot: the "paint spot hook," and the other unlikely shots from various grease stains and cracks in the concrete. The layup drills, and the attempts to master Kareem Abdul-Jabbar's famous skyhook. I shattered floodlights after dark, cracked car taillights, ruined innumerable flowers growing innocent in their beds. But for some reason my father—normally precise about order, cleanliness, and keeping things in good repair, and a flower enthusiast to boot—never yelled.

Like other kids, I had my hoop dreams. I wanted to be Wilt Chamberlain or Kareem, tall and imposing, dominant and cool. Or maybe, more likely, a pale white guy like Jerry West, shooting the game-winning shot from half-court as if he worked on it every day in practice, or smoothly driving the lane and laying it in off his fingertips. Or I might be Bill Walton, another tall SoCal redhead who could pass and shoot and play the game.

To *play the game:* to be part of it. That's what I wanted. I hoped to be at least six foot eight, muscular and fast, but had to settle for six-one and slow. I wanted to go to the famous John Wooden basketball camp, but my parents said if I made the junior high team they'd think about it. John Wooden, the Wizard of Westwood, was a basketball god in Southern California; he coached several UCLA teams to the NCAA championship, all the while looking like the quiet, buttoned-down midwestern English teacher he was. He didn't throw chairs, didn't yell at his players or even argue with the refs much. He didn't have to; he was God.

But I never got to Coach Wooden's camp; I was cut from the seventh-grade team after the first tryouts, and it became apparent that athletics was not really my forte. My hoop dreams thereafter were confined largely to the driveway and the blacktop. In high school I got involved in theater and the school newspaper, majored in history in college and began writing poetry. My dreams began to diverge into the areas of literature and book publishing. But I still played—on intramural teams in college, in Riverside Park in New York, in a three-on-three tournament in grad school, and for a few years in a regular pickup game at Amherst College. My dreams had changed, their edges shaved down by the sharp plane of reality, but I didn't love the game any less.

My son's dreams are still new, still fresh. He believes he can be a pro basketball player—or a baseball or soccer star. Of course he also might fly in the first spacecraft to Mars, or appear in the seventh Harry Potter movie (once he masters that English accent). He might do stand-up comedy, argue a case before the Supreme Court, or design a solar car. He might, on the other hand, do none of these things—but for him the sun is always rising, like the ball rising into the air and arcing toward the rim.

I know, but haven't told him yet, how hard it is to become a pro athlete— it's a long shot. I haven't told him what else I know: that the sun goes down eventually, settling toward the horizon like a ball on its downward arc, and you don't know if it will slide cleanly through the net or rim out. The future's unknown.

But this afternoon the rain has stopped, and I look up from whatever's been worrying me—the calls I have to make, the work yet to be done, the lawn unmowed, the laundry piling up—and I see him practicing his moves: the crossover dribble, the double crossover, the in crossover, the in-and-out. I hear the ball bouncing, and see the shot go up: I see the ball rising toward the basket, I see my son watching it go, I see and hear the *thunk* as it hits the backboard, then slides through the net. The bouncing begins again. I think I'll go out and join him. The sun has come out, there's a place to play, and dreams, whatever they are, look beautiful in this light.

Choreographing the Father-Son Dance
By Rob Okun
Summer 2012

Rain was gently falling overhead; clouds obscured the stars. I was safe and dry in my son Jonah's tent. I turned off the flashlight and dozed. I was sleeping a parent's weekend sleep—one ear open waiting for his safe return. Old habits die hard; I needn't have been so vigilant. He had only gone in search of cell service to call his girlfriend to say goodnight; he was years past high school curfews.

Jonah is our youngest and had recently finished college. As a graduation present we were spending the weekend at a writing workshop at a conference center and camp we both have a long history with and deeply love. We hadn't done something like this for some time—just the two of us going away for a few days—so the gift was as much for me as for him.

Fathers and mothers benefit from one-on-one time with their progeny, regardless of their age. Parenting adult children (Jonah has three older sisters in their late twenties and early thirties) isn't as straightforward as raising younger kids. Hopefully, after a few decades on the job, we've learned to shift from the spread-the-peanut-butter-on-the-bread Mother/Father role to TC (trusted consultant) available 24/7. It's a practice, though, learning to balance offering support with keeping hands off. I don't always get it right. The weekend Jonah and I spent together afforded me plenty of opportunities to practice. I had to pay attention, knowing when it was time to lead and when it was time to follow in the beautiful, complicated father-son dance we'd been choreographing for more than two decades.

When he returned to the tent, unzipping the flap slowly so as not to wake me, I whispered a greeting. "Everything okay?" "Yeah, Dad. Everything's great."

Once he'd settled into his sleeping bag, we lay in the dark for a long time talking, my heart brimming over with happiness. It was not about the content—rich and varied—it was about how comfortable we were, how relaxed, how intimate. For me, the weekend had been a success before it had barely begun. I slept deeply until a hard rain fell at first light.

As private and personal as these moments are, isn't it better for men to talk about them with one another than bury them under the cloak of men's silence? How else can we break free of our legacy of isolation, of too rarely sharing our feelings? How can we hope to transform our lives if we are stuck in our silos of individual invulnerability? How can fathers help raise sons to access their emotional lives if we aren't willing to access ours?

Becoming a father, of course, isn't necessary for every man to become a full adult, to find his way as a man. But even for those who aren't fathers, there are plenty of occasions to mentor, to "uncle"—to access that part of ourselves that innately knows how to nurture.

There's a tenderness to fathering that gets lost in popular culture's stick figure sketch—dad as good-natured bumbler. Happily, change is afoot; it's time to quicken the pace.

As more men step forward to honor their roles as fathers, there's an opportunity for even more of us to take the initiative to balance our private personal approach to fathering with a more public, political one. Our underrepresented voices in the ongoing war against women, for example, is a case in point. It is an apt moment for fathers to organize *as fathers* on behalf of our wives, daughters, and sisters—biological and otherwise. It's a powerful time for fathers to embrace that enduring insight from the women's movement: the personal is political. Rather than stand mute when old-school men seek to impose their will on decisions that rightly belong to women, I imagine campaigns that begin with "As a father, I…" The Fatherhood Brigade remains an underdeveloped force for social change.

After the weekend, Jonah went back to his house and garden and I returned to mine. If previous patterns prevailed, some days would pass before I'd hear from him. As difficult as it is going from total contact to no contact at all, it gave me a chance to reflect on our time together. In quite moments throughout the weekend, whether attending the same workshop or sitting together at meals, I'd look over at him engaged in conversation and marvel at the man he has become—considerably more emotionally intelligent than I was in my early twenties. What I realized was this: In the father-son dance we've been practicing since he was a baby, we had learned more than just how to avoid stepping on each other's toes. Now we were learning how to balance the space between leading and following. That lesson, I realized, applies to all the other parts of my life—from my work with men to my relationships at home. In the space between leading and following is everything I need to know.

Remembering the Loneliness of Fatherhood
By E. Ethelbert Miller
Summer 2009

On Father's Day I was hundreds of miles away from my son and daughter. They are twenty-two and twenty-seven and living in two different cities. I'm not a missing dad. I've never been missing. Neither was my father. I come from the tradition of quiet and silent men. The tradition of fathers who never left their wives and children, but instead "disappeared" into basements, backrooms, back porches, and bedroom corners. The tradition of men who could always be found asleep in front of a television set or sitting in the dark, mumbling at walls.

I come from the tradition of fathers who were watchers and providers; men who were ignored or unable to help during emergencies. My fatherhood has been defined by such things as my inability to drive, master the tools in a toolbox, or place a star at the top of a Christmas tree. How many times during a family crisis did my wife just pick up the phone and call her brother in Iowa or a friend living down the street?

Within his own home, my father was never viewed as "the smart one." He bestowed this title on my brother Richard, his first born and later my sister as a result of her becoming a nurse. Every family should have someone in the medical profession. It's like having a second key or a smoke detector that works.

I grew up watching my father pushed into the corners of rooms at family gatherings in Brooklyn. No one ever looked to him for an opinion. I never heard him having any major political agreement or disagreement with someone. My father was invisible until someone died. That was when he became a man of comfort for relatives that he always considered distant.

When I think about my father, I am reminded of the loneliness that comes with fatherhood. I am reminded of the intimacy that never raised its hand. Stoic is a word I can't use to describe him. Sadness seems like the proper sweater he could have worn.

My father, Egberto Miller, coming home late from work, night after night. My mother always up and ready to fix him something to eat. Yet how often did she join him at the table? Where was the intimacy? Was it the darkness outside the kitchen window? Did my parents just simply speak a common language?

The shadow of my father continues to fall over my fatherhood, as the period of my life moves toward fall. My children are grown. They are perhaps a few years from becoming parents. I picked up the newspaper today and read where President Obama wants to begin a national conversation on fatherhood. A conversation, maybe that's what was missing during all my days of fatherhood. A conversation, not a lecture or an explanation. A conversation where one talks and listens, and where one is listened to. How many of us live quiet lives of desperation? We live without partners, within and outside marriage.

We talk about fathers and fatherhood but we often lip-synch. We say those things we want others to hear. My father never really said much to me. My conversation was always with my mother, as I find my own children are with theirs.

What we never seem to talk about is how the men who stayed with their families suffered from the absence of intimacy in their lives. We never talk about the quiet death of their hearts. We fail to record these stories because we prefer myths and fairy tales. We want to believe in happy endings, especially on Father's Day. I remember my father at Father's Day because he was a good man. Was he happy? No. I overheard my father praying one day to God. I was little at the time. I was surprised to see my father on his knees in the bedroom. I was even more surprised when God didn't answer.

Fathering Your Father
By John Badalament
Spring 2010

At the age of twenty-five, not yet a dad myself, I walked into my father's office to reconcile our past; he thought we were going out for lunch. Up until that point I had not yet discovered the courage to speak honestly and directly with my father about the past. All that would change in just ten short minutes. I told my father that we weren't actually going to lunch, that he should stay seated and not respond to anything he was about to hear. He had been given plenty of time to speak over the years; now it was my turn to talk. Barely able to breathe, I said, "You've done a lot of great things for me as a dad." After describing a few, such as how he had supported my love of baseball and patiently taught me how to drive, I said, "And. . . I want you to know that growing up with you was also very, very difficult. You were irresponsible, alcoholic, and abusive. As a consequence, I have struggled, and still struggle to this day, to feel good about myself. I don't want you to do anything. I'm an adult, and these are my issues to deal with now."

He opened his mouth to speak, and for the first time ever, I raised my hand and without a word, motioned for him to stop. I knew that if I allowed him to talk, he would almost certainly try to explain, minimize, or deny what I was saying, and like most loyal sons, I would back down from speaking the truth of my experience.

Confronting my father at the age of twenty-five was the single most difficult, emotionally raw moment of my life. As a kid, I was taught that vulnerability got you nothing but trouble and thus learned to hate it. The currency of my upper-middle-class boyhood was as follows: being tough, "getting" the girls, and holding your own in sports. If you had no currency, you were at risk of verbal or physical reprisals. I spent a great deal of time and energy avoiding situations in which I could be taken advantage of, proved wrong, or made to look like a "wimp." Implicitly, discussing feelings and relationships with or around other boys was forbidden.

When I left my dad's office that day, I assumed my departure would mark the end of our relationship, that he would want nothing more to do with me. Paradoxically, once I found my voice and spoke up—as uncomfortable and frightening as it was—our relationship actually grew stronger. While we didn't necessarily spend more time together, speak more often, or agree on everything (past or present), a more honest dialogue developed between us. There was no longer one voice, one truth, or one authority. We became two adults, not a father and a child. Don't get me wrong; my dad didn't enjoy the experience of being confronted with his past, but the effect of that one conversation was deep and long-lasting. Four years ago my father became ill from years of neglecting his diabetes. As his condition worsened, it became clear he wouldn't be leaving the hospital. I remember looking him in the eye one afternoon and saying, "You can go now, Dad. There's nothing left to do here." He looked back at me, smiled, teared up, and nodded. Our peace was made. A few days later he quietly passed away.

I feel fortunate for having had the chance to reconcile with him—by holding my father lovingly accountable, as each new generation must do—but sad that so much of his story was shrouded in mystery. I knew very little about his life as a husband and a dad: What did he love about being a husband and a father? What did he worry about as a father? What brought him joy? When did he feel like he was doing a great job as a father? What did marriage and fatherhood mean to him?

It's never too late for the truth. This is why I remind dads—myself, included—of that all-too-common movie scene in which the dad is on his deathbed and finally tries to talk to his adult child (usually a son) to admit his mistakes, to reveal his humanity, thereby giving the purest possible expression of love. Finally, in the fading light, his vulnerability opens the door for the child to have a voice, to reconcile a lifetime of distance, conflict, absence, or emotional silence. As modern dads, we must rewrite this scene for our children. They need not wait so long.

In my educational consulting work, I do an activity with students in which they anonymously write down two questions they've always wanted to ask their dad. No matter what their ethnic, cultural, racial, or socioeconomic background is, the students' two most common questions are almost always: "What was your relationship like with your father?" and "What was your childhood like?"—sometimes worded as, "What were you like at my age?" Though they may not ask, children want and need their dad's stories, even if they never knew who their dad was. I call it the elephant in the living room of child development: the missing stories of men's lives, particularly men's emotional lives.

Like many dads, growing up I did not have the kind of close, emotionally connected relationship with my father that I want with my children today. Are there aspects of his legacy I want to keep or pass on to my children? Yes. Are there mistakes I'm determined not to repeat? Of course. This is not, however, a matter of intention only—what dad doesn't *want* to be close with his children? The question is *how*: How can I give what I didn't get?

In my workshops for parents, I often ask dads to describe the kind of relationship they are trying to build with their children. Whether I'm at an elite private school, a prison, or a public library, the responses are similar. Most dads and dad figures want to have a strong, close bond with their children, to always be a trustworthy and vital presence, and to be someone to turn to for advice, support, or just to talk with. Most dads want their sons and daughters to feel secure in knowing that they can always come to them and share what's going on in their lives, good and bad.

In the past decade of working with dads of all backgrounds, I have heard this chorus grow louder: modern dads want connection, closeness, and intimacy. Unlike fathers of generations past, whose lives were so often cloaked in silence and mystery, dads today are increasingly vocal about this vision. Modern dads want to be the competent, caring, and supportive parents and partners that deep down we know we are capable of becoming. This is my cause for hope. It starts with modern dads speaking the truth about what fatherhood means to us—how it challenges our beliefs about manhood, raises fears about repeating mistakes of the past, and ultimately reveals our capacity to love another human being unconditionally. It starts with also making space in our relationships to truly listen to our loved ones. Our children and families not only want but need us to deliver on this new vision of fatherhood.

When Fathers *Mother*
By Donald N.S. Unger
Summer 2000

"It's not easy being a mother, is it?" the librarian says, smiling over my shoulder, as I change my then six-month-old daughter's diaper on a desk in the back room.

I close my eyes very briefly, try not to grit my teeth, remember to breathe.

"I'm not *being* a mother," I tell her, as softly as I can manage. "I'm *being* a *parent*."

"You're doing what mothers usually *do*," she tells me. And I think it best to let the conversation die there. I don't have the time, the energy, or the tact. In situations like that, almost a daily occurrence when I'm out with my daughter, it's as though I lose my voice.

I had been "invited" to work, to score entrance exams for the freshman writing course that I was teaching; I was taking care of my daughter, Rebecca, four days per week that term, but, in a fit of the kind of flexibility that I realize is rarely extended to working mothers, my department chair had simply suggested that I bring the baby with me for the morning, rather than miss all the fun.

Fathering

So I came in early, folding playpen in tow, took my daughter into the back offices in the library, where we were going to be working, stripped her, fed her, cleaned her up, changed her, and got her dressed again, while the librarians buzzed in and out, doing their work. But there's always commentary.

Does it sound lighthearted, a slightly cynical, but essentially harmless, observation about statistical reality? Does complaining about this make me seem thin skinned? Try this if you're a working woman, particularly in one of these once male dominated professions, a doctor, a lawyer: Someone observes you at work and says, "It's not easy being a man, is it?"

All in good fun? In today's atmosphere, a statement like that is close to actionable.

I don't want to get into issues of "oppression envy" here. For the record: it would be silly to argue that men have suffered, or suffer now, discrimination on anything like the scale that women have had to deal with throughout history. Still, as is becoming increasingly obvious to both social critics and economists, we've had *half* a revolution in the last 30 years, made great strides toward opening up a broad range of jobs to women, certainly made a good start toward leveling the playing field in outside-the-home employment; on the domestic side, increasingly, no one's home.

A good piece of this is due to economics. The same 30 years that have marked professional progress for women have seen a stagnation in middle-class wages that all but requires both partners in the household to work. But, as first-wave feminists were quick to point out, the language that we use also has a profound impact on how we see ourselves and each other, how we interpret the world and our roles in it, what we see as possible, and what we even lack the words to effectively describe.

We've had an incomplete, somewhat one-sided, linguistic revolution: we've done a great deal to truly neuter the neuter pronouns and other terms that, in English, have traditionally been male. If these changes have not yet completely suffused our society, the battle is still essentially over: college writing programs routinely require nonsexist usage, as do the style books of all the major publishing houses; when you call a department head a "chair" rather than "chairman," people don't scold you anymore that you've referred to the person as a piece of furniture.

And on the other side, the language of domestic work, the words we use to describe the roles usually ascribed to women? That hasn't changed, nor does there seem to be any movement afoot to work toward or facilitate that change: "to mother" is to care for and to nurture; "to father" essentially means to inseminate. The somewhat antiseptic phrase "to parent" has some currency, but reflexively, as with my librarian friend, what people fall back on is female-centered language. This leaves men out, makes us invisible, takes away our voice, in a care-giving role that, cultural critics on both the left and the right agree, is being dangerously neglected.

I don't say this because I want "points." I haven't been active in caring for my daughter because I'm looking to earn a merit badge of some kind. I would like my gender to be as invisible and unworthy of commentary as is increasingly the case for women who do a broad variety of jobs, from physicians to carpenters. But I do want my existence as a parent to be acknowledged, and not just as an oddity. And I do want linguistic parity.

Writing more than 20 years ago in *Language and Woman's Place*, Robin Lakoff observed that to call a man a "professional" identifies him as a doctor or a lawyer or someone else in a respected occupation; to call a woman the same thing implies that she is a prostitute. Similarly, to be a "master" is to have power over something; to be a "mistress" is to have an illicit sexual relationship. She identifies this "lack of linguistic equivalence" as one of the keystones of inequality. She was right. And it cuts both ways.

Some people understand this intuitively, and it is in them that I find hope. Several summers ago, I took Rebecca, then two years old, on her first subway ride; my mother and I took her to the Museum of the American Indian. The train was crowded when we got on in Brooklyn, standing room only. I held her against my chest with one arm, her legs wrapped around my waist, the fingers of my other hand light on one of the support poles—but this didn't last long. A middle-aged Jamaican woman, sitting across the aisle from where I was standing, got up and gestured me into her seat.

"It takes two to tango," she said to my mother, over the din of the train, nodding approvingly in my direction. "It takes a mother *and* a father." A simple statement, and a small sacrifice on her part, but one that touched me very deeply because it's so rare. My wife and I have been impressed to discover, in the last couple of years that, in our generally unfortunate cultural context, parenthood is one of the few things that trumps race—by which we mean, parenthood is one of the few bridges over the chasm of race. It creates, we have found, more, and easier, interracial interaction, more real and perceived common ground, than almost anything else. But what this woman was doing, in addition to reaching across that divide was ignoring gender as well. She read me as a parent with a child, and in spite of the fact that it is traditionally men who give up seats to women, younger people who give up seats to older, her respect for parenthood propelled her toward a different kind of etiquette.

The *language* the woman on the train used, moreover, was perfect; two simple sentences, the second of which contained a quiet but clear, straight equivalence between "mother" and "father," no italics, no sarcasm, no lifted eyebrow. For a brief moment, I existed; she gave me space and, in *her* choice of words, because we exist not just in other people's eyes but reflected in the words with which they gift us, with which they choose to describe us, she gave me voice.

An Infertile Father's Abundant Life
By Jeff Kelly Lowenstein
Summer 2002

I cannot have children.

I discovered this unwelcome fact in November of 2000, when in the course of routine prepregnancy testing for my wife, Dunreith, I learned that the sperm sample I had produced contained no sperm. In the months that followed, I "parked" at the local reproductive laboratory, and generated two more samples that confirmed the initial results. When I had testicular sperm extraction surgery, doctors searched for just four sperm to use in a procedure in which a single sperm is injected into a single egg. They found none.

Since ancient times, in cultures across the globe, the ability to father children has been one of the most fundamental ways one's manhood has been evaluated; an infertile man is considered to be "dead" by some branches of my Jewish religion. Here in the United States, infertility rarely generates open discussion. If mentioned at all, it is generally cast as a woman's problem, even though one out of four couples that confront the issue do so exclusively because of the male partner's sperm count. From the time that I became a young man, I had imagined myself playing with the three children that I would help bring into the world. Realizing that these dreams would never materialize shocked me. My disappointment turned into shame, and shame transformed into a feeling of inadequacy.

Yet I am a father. Two Labor Days ago, at a beautiful park, Dunreith, her seven-and-a-half-year-old son, Aidan, and I stood under a tree with three roots that joined at the base. The three of us held hands in a circle as Dunreith and I stated our commitment to be together forever, and a justice of the peace declared us husband and wife.

Adjusting to fatherhood and accepting my infertility challenged me. Becoming a dad to a boy who had not had one often felt like I had jumped on a treadmill going 9 miles per hour. Aidan wanted my time, but not my limits on his behavior, and he resented the loss of his mother's exclusive attention. After fourteen years as a classroom teacher, I struggled with parenting's more fluid nature. Dual absences—of Aidan's Israeli biological father, whom he has never met in person, and of the child I will never be able to conceive—haunted me, too.

But both identities have eventually become more comfortable, like a pair of new shoes that initially pinched my toes and then molded to my feet. Dunreith's continual encouragement and time's passage have helped. So have driving Aidan to and from school, playing dodgeball with him in our backyard in the afternoons, and coaching his third-grade soccer team. I have shared many stories of my youth with Aidan that were sparked by his passage through the same age. The three of us have established sacred rituals of Thursday night pizza and Friday night movies. Throughout this time, Aidan's presence has served as a balm for the pain my barrenness has caused. Each time he calls me "Dad," even in moments of conflict, my wounds have healed ever so slightly.

Eighteen months later, I have developed greater compassion for, and a deeper connection with, my own father, with whom I had previously had a distant relationship. My own bouts with temper and my struggles with balancing commitments to family and to work have helped me understand many of Dad's actions when I was a boy in a different light. More broadly, I have come to understand the ways in which the intent behind a parent's decisions and a child's interpretation of them are rarely identical.

I have also comprehended that our choices and our identities are both inextricably linked and continually changing. While the larger society and our traditions influence the way we initially understand our essential roles—parent, spouse, worker—it is our circle of intimates that truly confers membership in, then teaches us how to inhabit, these timeless positions.

But mostly I have learned about what happens when one's most deeply held assumptions become explicit because they turn out to be unreachable. After mourning the loss of experiences I had always thought I would, but never will, have—going to the hospital with Dunreith for the birth of our child, holding that baby in my arms, all the firsts—I have discovered that true parenthood comes in raising, not siring, a child. Whatever mistakes I make, and they are many, I rest secure in the knowledge that I committed to being Aidan's dad the day that Dunreith and I wed, not three months later when I discovered that I could not father my own son or daughter.

On Father's Day I will call my father to exchange greetings. Dunreith, Aidan, and I will eat breakfast together, and will go to the park where we were wed. As we stroll by the same spot where I became a father, I will marvel at my good fortune, my appreciation greater, not less, because of my unanticipated journey to entry in this treasured club.

The Last Hunt
By Michael Messner
Spring 2011

Mr. Roosevelt, when are you going to get beyond the boyishness of killing things?

—John Muir, to Teddy Roosevelt, 1903

Fathering

For it is not in giving life but in risking life that man is raised above the animal; that is why superiority has been accorded in humanity not to the sex that brings forth but to that which kills.

—Simone de Beauvoir, 1949

The last time I went hunting with my dad, I didn't carry a rifle. A few years earlier, I'd realized that I hated killing animals. Now in college and living away from home, I'd come to associate deer hunting with the Vietnam War culture that I'd turned so virulently against. The Beatles seemed to speak to me when they sang, "Hey Bungalow Bill, What did you kill, Bungalow Bill?" But on some other plane of consciousness, somewhere deeper than my political views, I still knew that neither Dad nor Gramps was the crass, trophy-hunting "All American bullet-headed Saxon Mother's son" mocked by John Lennon's dripping sarcasm. I'd hunted with Dad and Gramps since I was a seven-year-old boy. I knew they approached the activity safely and with an ethical reverence for the animals they hunted. And I knew that hunting was the main way Gramps connected, father-to-son, with Dad; and they, eventually, with me.

But this was 1973, and I had now denounced hunting—at least to my friends at college—as a violent proto-military activity through which men bonded with each other, excluded women, and subjugated nature. Hunting was part of everything wrong with the world, everything I was fighting to change.

Nevertheless, here I was, a twenty-one-year-old commie peacenik, my long hair tied back with a paisley headband, coaxing my beat-up powder blue Corolla with the "Question Authority" bumper sticker 200 miles south in the scorching August sun of the Sacramento Valley, to hang out with a bunch of short-haired, middle-aged, Nixon-loving, gun-toting men.

Dad had phoned a couple of weeks earlier to invite me to join him at his new hunting club near Los Banos. His voice sounded thin, uncharacteristically tentative on the other end of the line.

"I figure it's been what, three or four years, Mike? Why don't you drive down for the weekend? I can bring your rifle."

I wasn't so sure about this. "Will Gramps be there?"

"No, Gramps had to give it up a couple of years ago. He's 77 now."

That was the kicker, picturing Dad hunting without Gramps. "Okay," I said, my voice likely conveying my mixed feelings.

As soon as I hung up, I decided I would go, but I would honor the secret promise I had made eight years earlier never again to shoot a deer. And this time, I would not hold to this vow through subterfuge. This time I would do it straight up, publicly, by not carrying a gun.

This had seemed a noble idea in the comfortable privacy of my college apartment the night I hung up the phone with my dad. But now, as I shot down the arrow-straight stretch of I-5, my cassette player blasting Derek and the Dominos, Clapton's guitar lacerating the hot air buffeting through my open windows, a knot of worry swelled in my stomach. How would Dad react to my decision to join the hunt with no rifle? This would be awkward, at the very least. I didn't expect Dad to be pissed at me; worse, I feared I'd embarrass him in front of his longtime hunting friend Bob Shackelford, not to mention the guys I'd never met in his new hunting club. I doubted that anybody had ever walked a hunt unarmed with those guys. As my car tires ground to a halt on the rocky dirt road of the campsite, I dropped the volume on my stereo. Through my bug-splattered windshield I spied Dad and Bob laughing with two burly men as they unloaded sleeping bags, coolers, and rifles from their jeeps and pickup trucks. And I wondered, not for the last time: What in the hell am I doing here?

Over the past four decades, starting in my college years, I have been preoccupied with the question, "What is manhood?" Inspired by feminism, I have interrogated my own life and the broader social world around me, wondering how it is that men commit so many horrible acts of violence against women, against other men, against ourselves, and indeed, against the natural world. In my teaching, public lectures, and books about boys and men, I have rejected the simplistic but popular idea that males are naturally hard-wired to dominate others—that "all that testosterone" predisposes us, like the positive ends of two magnets, to repel away from human intimacy and to be drawn instead to guns and violence. Instead, I ask different questions about boys and men: How does our immersion in cultures of domination and violence distort our humanity? How do we nevertheless manage to connect with one another, to find and express love and intimacy with others?

A boy's developing sense of masculinity is insecure and tentative, and most of us learn early on to hide our self-doubts beneath a veneer of bravado. I know I did. As a young boy, I was very aware of the daily risks to my fragile sense of self, as I watched other boys and men routinely suffer humiliation—or worse—for showing any sign of vulnerability or weakness. I learned from the adult men around me, and through a succession of popular culture images of male heroism—Davy Crockett, John Wayne, John Glenn, and Willie Mays among them—that the world promised to heap status, glory, and love upon me if I grew up to be tough, if I suppressed my empathy for others, and especially if I became a winner. I swallowed this idea of male heroism hook, line, and sinker.

When boys like me buy into the myth of male heroism, what happens to our very human needs for connection, intimacy, and love? After we shut boys down emotionally, after we scare the crap out of them with the knowledge that it is grown-up boys who fight and die in wars, after we convince them they will be viewed as failures if they lose in the competitive marketplace of manly success, what kinds of ways do we offer these boys to connect with others? What situations do we put them in, and what kinds of opportunities do those situations offer them to experience closeness with others? For Gramps and Dad, hunting provided this means of connection.

When Dad was a boy, Gramps took him hunting several times a year to Lake County, in northern California. These and imagined future hunting trips became the foundation of their relationship, and a major subject of the letters they exchanged when Dad was in the South Pacific during World War II. During the decades following the war, Dad returned the favor by taking Gramps hunting, until Gramps was too old to continue. These hunts made them the best of pals for life. By the time I was seven, Gramps and Dad had placed a rifle in my hands and had begun to initiate me into a men-only world of hunting for quail, pheasant, and especially deer. Hunting worked well for Gramps and Dad; ultimately, it did not work so well for me. By the end of my teen years, I had decided to lay down my rifle, and had taken a path to manhood that I saw as very different from the roads taken by Gramps and Dad. But in rejecting hunting, I was letting go of an emotionally salient lifeline that had been extended to me, from my grandfather through my father. Years after Dad's and Gramps' deaths, I continue to poke at the scars left by this self-imposed wound. And I wonder: what kind of a father am I? I have offered my two sons a different model of manhood. Is it better?

The day of the hunt, I tromped loudly down the bottom of the ravine, flanked on the left and right ridges by several armed men. With no rifle in my hands, my usefulness on this hunt was essentially to play the role of a dog, fighting blindly through thick shrubs and brush, hoping to flush out a buck for the men. We didn't see a single deer that day, and as we returned to camp and started preparing dinner, I wondered again if I'd embarrassed Dad, showing up from college with my long hair and my bizarre insistence on walking a hunt unarmed. Maybe I shouldn't have come at all. Dad, who would die four years later, walked up and handed me a can of Burgie, still dripping chips of ice from the cooler. We each took a welcome slug of the cold beer. And he said, "Thanks for coming, Pal."

After the group polished off a dinner that included an industrial-sized vat of delicious rigatoni, Dad passed a bota bag to me, and showed me how to extend my arms fully as red wine streamed directly into my mouth. Later that evening under stars made opaque by hissing Coleman lanterns, one of the guys took up his accordion and played an upbeat Italian tune. Dad, clad only in his white boxers, tucked-in white T-shirt, and a smile, climbed on top of his cot and performed a graceful tango as all of us exploded into laughter and cheered him on.

My Children, June 1993
Bruce MacMillan
Winter 2002

I hear seventeen-year-old Daniel, tall,
shaving now, the water in the bathroom
turning on and off, on and off, as
I lie in bed this morning: high school
finals this week, college visits this summer.
Fourteen-year-old Thomas, once near, now
determinedly disheveled and unruly, roaming
with friends, asking questions—zen, anarchism—
slipping easily into grumpiness and pimply self-
consciousness. Both bright and inquisitive, maybe
too adventurous for their own good. I watch
them both with fingers crossed, touching them as
often as I can.

After the Funeral

Richard Jeffrey Newman
Summer 2011

That night, again, I dreamed you were leaving,
but this time I was older, and when I walked you
through the marketplace, and you put down
your suitcase to embrace me, I drew
the silence of all the years *you'd* been dead to me
around my right to grief. I wished you gone
and you were. In photographs, I see you
feeding me, your face younger than mine now.
In one, I'm a small bundle on your shoulder,
and the flat of your palm is the world against my back,
teaching me to let go of what is useless. You
have been useless to me. You never knew
the red shepherd I threw my Frisbee for.
In my mind, I matched him stride for stride,
and when he leapt to snatch the floating disc from air,
he called to me and we sailed off, a boy
who could run with the wolves, a dog with language
and the gift of flight. I named him Larry,
after you, but true names are secrets,
so I called him Joe.

MALE SURVIVORS

In a dream you saw a way to survive and you were full of joy.

—Jenny Holzer

Courageous men speak out about incidents of abuse in their pasts and presents, as well as chronicle their healing process as survivors. Offering indispensable resources, insights, and personal testimonies, the men speaking throughout this section bravely tackle their own traumas in an effort to create a dialogue and a support network for male survivors. From advice for supportive family and friends to messages of encouragement for other survivors, this section sheds light on the experiences of an (unfortunately) oft-overlooked group: male abuse survivors.

Finding the Child Within
By Mike Lew
Summer 2004

One of my clients carries in his briefcase a framed photograph taken when he was a child. He treats the picture with respect, keeping it wrapped in a soft cloth and handling it gently. Sometimes we look at the photograph together, while he tells me about himself as a boy.

Another client will sometimes prop up an early boyhood photograph on the sofa during his session, as a reminder of a time before the abuse.

Thom Harrigan, codirector of The Next Step Counseling, asked each member of a men's recovery group to bring in a childhood picture. He reported to me that most group members showed up with several pictures of themselves and sometimes snapshots of their families. They all knew that it was important to them to make these connections.

Part of your recovery work needs to focus on your childhood. That is, after all, when the abuse took place. The boy you were is an important source of information about the man you have become. You carry him with you in the form of memories, feelings, reactions, attitudes, personality, and physical characteristics. There are a number of reasons to get to know him.

At times you still feel like a scared, lonely, abused child. Part of your self-concept was frozen at the time that you were abused. Emotionally, you don't recognize that you have gotten through the ordeal. The world still feels like a risky place. When you are confronted with a difficult or frightening situation, try to ask yourself, "How old do I feel?" Chances are that you feel young, small, and weak. Returning your attention to childhood helps you to get a better picture of who you were—and who you are.

Initially, you may have some difficulty finding something positive to say about your younger self. Many survivors have carried their negative self-images from childhood. They blame themselves rather than the abuse for their unhappiness, shyness, fear, confusion, and isolation. Nothing could be further from the truth.

The fact that you survived into adulthood is proof that, as a child, you were resourceful, creative, and strong. (Yes, I'm talking about you!) You owe a debt to that little boy. It is because of his courage and determination that you are moving on your recovery today. And it is a debt that you are able to pay. He deserves your respect and friendship. You are an adult he can count on absolutely. You are living evidence that he will make it through his difficult, lonely childhood. Recognize that he was working by himself with limited resources, and he overcame tremendous odds. What a terrific little guy! If he could do all that without help and support, imagine what he could have accomplished with the right kind of care, love, and encouragement.

Getting in touch with the reality of yourself as a child will help you turn around your equally inaccurate picture of your adult self. There are many ways to reconnect with the child within you. Here are some suggestions:

• *Make use of photographs.* If you can, take a look at pictures taken before you were abused as well as afterward. Notice how they are different.

• *Write a letter to yourself as a child.* Tell him how wonderful he is and that he never deserved to be hurt. Reassure him that he will survive, and that the abuse will not go on forever.

• With the help of friends, or in a workshop or group, *create a drama or fantasy about your childhood:*

• You can have someone else take the role of you as a child while you reassure him that he is fine and everything will be OK.

• You can play out returning to the scene of the abuse as your adult self, protecting the child by standing up to the perpetrator. Take along allies or reinforcements if you like, but be your own hero.

• You can set up a scene of yourself as a child the way it always should have been. Imagine a safe childhood, peopled with kind, loving, protective adults.

• *Learn new ways to play.* Don't worry about appearing foolish or feeling silly. That's what it's all about. There's nothing like playfulness to bring out the child within you.

I recently saw a lapel button that said, "It's never too late to have a happy childhood." While you can't change the past, you can forge a new perspective on it that will allow you to have a happier adulthood. Befriending and reassuring the child within strongly reinforces adult recovery by creating new insight into past experiences.

Resources

Organizations for Survivors

Malesurvivor: Committed to Eliminating Sexual Victimization of Boys and Men (formerly NOMSV, the National Organization on Male Sexual Victimization)
www.malesurvivor.org
(800) 738-4181

Sexually Abused Males Surviving (SAMS, Canada)
www.nsnet.org/sams
(902) 678-2913

Incest Resources, Inc.
46 Pleasant St., Cambridge, MA 02139

National Coalition Against Sexual Assault (NCASA)
www.dreamingdesigns.com/other/indexncasa.html
(717) 728-9764

National Organization for Victim Assistance (NOVA)
www.try-nova.org/index.html
(800) try-nova

One Voice: The National Alliance for Abuse Awareness and American Coalition for Abuse Awareness (ACAA)
e-mail acaadc@aol.com or Ovoicedc@aol.com
(202) 462-4688

The Safer Society Foundation (Vermont)
www.safersociety.org
(802) 247-3132

Survivors and Victims Empowered (SAVE)
www.s-a-v-e.org
(717) 291-1940

Voices in Action, Inc. (Victims of Incest Can Emerge Survivors)
www.voices-action.org
(800) 7-VOICE-8

12-Step Programs
Incest Survivors Anonymous (ISA)
www.lafn.org/medical/isa/home.html
(562) 428-5599

Sexual Abuse Anonymous (SAA)
P.O. Box 9665, Berkeley, CA 94709

Sexual Assault Recovery Anonymous Society (SARA; Canada)
(604) 584-2626

Survivors of Incest Anonymous (SIA)
www.siawso.org
(410) 893-3322

Clergy Abuse Organizations
The Linkup (national organization of survivors of clergy abuse)
www.thelinkup.com
(773) 334-2296

Survivor Connections, Inc.—The True Memory Foundation
(Rhode Island)
www.angelfire.com/ri/survivorconnections
(401) 941-2548

Survivors Network of Those Abused by Priests (SNAP)
www.survivorsnetwork.org
(312) 409-2720

Partners of Survivors
Partners of Adults Sexually Abused as Children (PASAC)
www.PASAC.net

Memory Has No Statute of Limitations
By Paul Ehmann
Summer 2003

Coffee and the paper. My morning ritual. I scan the national news and the local stuff. Today I notice there are no articles about children being molested. I breathe a denying sigh of relief and wonder if normal people think with the caution flag out like I do.

I've done all I could to forget: piles of drugs, barrels of alcohol, promiscuous sex, and now food for my comfort. Therapists have told me, "It's a miracle that you're even alive." How do you reconcile that?

Fifteen years of therapy have not unleashed a complete and deserved self-forgiveness. It's been 35 years since I was sexually trespassed, but it seems like yesterday. It always comes back. Shame exacts an unyielding grip. It's sadly ironic that even the notion of simply noticing no articles about sexual abuse can set me up to remember my own. This day my memories are vague and easily shaken off. Tomorrow's newspaper may bring on another reason why recall lives on. In perpetuity. Another day shot full of memories. Today I'll hear and read more how the Catholic Church is hiding the perpetrators while defending and "monitoring" itself. No wonder kids still keep the secret.

The more powerful the trauma, the longer it takes to fully acknowledge it. Where we come from, we learn not to pay attention to details. So we carry the secret along with the empty sentences that cannot describe our hurt. There are no words for this type of shame, no words for the unfounded guilt, no words for a child's newfound lack of expression, no words for the secrets kept, no words for the stolen dignity, no words for the love lost, no words for the shattered trust, no words for the imperceptible injury, no words for the coldly dispatched spirit, no words for lingering memories. There is only anger and frustration. Again today I'm forced to remember. The respite went unnoticed. It's good to leave memories unopened for a while. They can return with a fury.

The light was red and I was idling. Out of the corner of my right eye I saw the silhouette. I'd seen it from the other side too many times. I have the displeasure of running into him on occasion (we still live in the same town and at one time lived on the same street) and the degree of emotional strain I feel is different each time. This time the air is sucked out of me, momentarily asthmatic with disbelief. Won't he ever go away?

He was staring straight ahead, profiled inside the safety of his car, but I could see his face clearly. (In my mind's eye the safety glass shatters as I fly through the unopened window, grab his beefy neck, and twist the life out of him. I weep at the realization that even his death gives life to memory.) I turn left and, pulling away, know that once again he hasn't seen me. I instinctively know that I'll keep this incident to myself, and, once again, the secret is hidden.

So here it is. A despicable man makes a decision to abandon all social responsibility; he snatches the unquestionable innocence of a kid and soils forever the never-to-be-known dreams of an unstained child. He drops his baggage on the short-legged table of a boy barely twelve and walks away from the experience drunk with sexual relief while stuffing the spirit of a boy into his pocket like a matchbook.

Two days have gone by and I've barked at my wife, kicked the cat, begun sleeping late and, worst of all, gone silent. I don't have a spare word. Searching my soul with brutal introspection, trying to wrap my arms around hope, I squeeze the empty air and shrug with expected disappointment at another hopeless moment. This is the real crime. It's one of time. Time after frustrating time, the memory comes back. And with it the unanswerable questions. Could I have done something different? What if I'd…? Jesus, I wish…

Secrecy is the common thread among survivors of sexual abuse. There is never anyone to tell. Under threat of violence comes the inherent knowledge that you won't be believed, so you keep it to yourself. Don't share this, you tell yourself, and a child relies on his now distorted intuition for answers. If you expose him, he'll deny it (he said so), and you'll be branded a faggot or a liar. The confusion is unbearable. The cycle of shame cannot be broken by a child, not without the support of an adult.

This one moment of his selfish sexual gratification, endured by a child 35 years ago, will steal three or four days from my present. It sneaks up on me like a night shadow, and in an instant I become the trembling, confused, secretive child who withstood the abuse. I am affected and carry a profoundly unnatural sorrow, like my heart is attached to a lead sinker. I do not wallow. A survivor's will to live uncannily floats to the surface while the persistent resentment of having this uninvited emotional attachment to a pedophile loiters in an unsafe harbor.

Memory has no statute of limitations.

Still Healing After All These Years
By Les Wright
Fall 2002

I am nearly fifty. I have survived alcoholism and drug addiction. I have survived nervous breakdowns. I have survived homelessness and destitution, multiple suicide attempts, posttraumatic stress disorder, and living on SSI. I live with anxious-depressive disorder. I have lived with HIV for 22 years. In order to survive these adulthood traumas, I first had to survive a childhood of sexual abuse, incest, and rape; of parental perpetration, denial, and rejection. I have survived in a sexually predatory society that has literally beaten into me that "real men" do not get raped or sexually violated, and that gay men in particular deserve every rape, attack, or other sexual violation perpetrated against us.

Childhood sexual trauma robbed me of self-confidence, self-trust, self-esteem, and the ability to feel safe in the world and trust other people. It miseducated me to best succeed in self-destruction. I live within a psyche I can neither trust nor escape, and a body that, after decades of abuse, now refuses me physical intimacy. Nonetheless, after all these years, I am still here—alive, sane, sober, healthy, socially functional, stabilized by a battery of medications and decades of therapy, having acquired the skills to advocate for myself and the courage to fight back.

I was six years old the first time I was raped, by my then-17-year-old cousin Jake (a pseudonym). I grew up in a tenement, surrounded by a dozen cousins, all but two of them male. Jake made me his sex slave—he tortured me sexually, taunted me, showed me off to his friends, and occasionally had me sexually service his buddies, just to show off his total control over me.

My parents looked the other way. My mother admonished me to take my beatings like a man and to "get used to" what kind of life "that sort of person" could expect in adulthood. My father, who ignored me, except to belittle me as a "little pansy" by day, used me for his sexual pleasure by night. I believed I was unworthy of love; I felt profound guilt and shame because I believed everything that happened to me was somehow my own fault. (Even today, I cannot quite shake the feeling that I am doing penance for unspeakable crimes I must have committed in past lives.) By age ten, I was desperately seeking love and approval, offering my still prepubescent body to every man whose love or approval I sought. At seventeen, I made my first suicide attempt.

Leonard Shengold calls this experience "soul murder." Other professionals have called it "the shattered psyche." I call it "living with emotional AIDS." To this day I do not understand how I have survived even a fraction of this. Fear and rage have been my constant companions, as well as a sense of utter bafflement over what "correct" reality is—my reality has often had little or nothing in common with the reality other people seem to live in.

Somehow the life force within me has always overpowered the doomsday machine within my psyche. Over time I began to heal myself. I learned to advocate for myself, and eventually mustered enough courage to challenge, and "fire," clueless, ill-informed, or wrong-headed therapists, psychiatrists, doctors, and support groups. I still rarely trust institutional treatment systems or bureaucracies, as in my experience they tend to re-traumatize the patient-victim in the name of helping us.

To my astonishment, in 1993 a job opportunity in Boston fell out of the sky and into my lap. I left San Francisco, life on SSI and MediCal, and a threadbare but trustworthy support network. But the support I sought in Boston either did not exist or proved useless. Over time I came to Fitchburg and, since 1997, have established a new, tiny, carefully handpicked support network of professionals at Burbank Hospital and UMass-Worcester. I found an MD, an RN, and a psychopharmacologist who *understand*—who are dedicated to healing, and *not* to the wealth and power trappings of their professions.

Within the past twelve months I found my way to the Men's Resource Center in Amherst. This is the only place where I have felt safe since coming to New England. The MRC is a model program—under-recognized, underfunded, and still "too scary" for many men who are in desperate need of the support it can offer.

I continue to heal from my wounds by serving as a peer facilitator, especially in service to the adult male survivor support group and by slowly building trust and bonds with other men I have met here—gay, straight, bi, and transgender—many of whom are also healing from sexual wounding. We share a commitment to healing ourselves and each other, and by extension, to help begin healing society as a whole—a society which has essentially thrown us all away for not being "real men." Many of us are sensitive, nurturing, vulnerable individuals who have been duly victimized by society for our "gender betrayal." Some of us are victims-turned-victimizers (which is often the flip side reaction to childhood assault and abuse) who have found their way to the MRC's Men Overcoming Violence program, where they are actively seeking to unlearn their reactive violent behaviors.

I will continue to heal, but I will never be free of the ever-present pain, rage, and self-doubt caused by childhood sexual assault, abuse, and willful neglect. The consequences of sexual trauma are akin to a chronic illness, which can, in many cases, be successfully managed, but for which there is still no "cure."

A Different Response to Touchy Feely
By Jacob Stevenson
Fall 2000

And the hands kept touching me and
touching me, all over me and
over and over
the hands kept touching me and wouldn't stop
even though I said no

—L.K., male survivor, age 37

While it is somewhat misleading to speak generically of a "men's movement"—there is far too much diversity among the various camps of opinion—it is important to consider certain shared imperatives which seem to be sacrosanct across cultural lines. It is especially worthwhile to consider how one such imperative may affect male survivors, in terms of both our personal recovery and our eventual reintegration into the mainstream of society. In particular, attention needs to be paid to the portion of male society committed to redefining along feminist lines the "role(s)" of men in our culture.

What I'm referring to is the nearly ubiquitous tendency among many men's groups to encourage, promote, or passively demand both interpersonal hugging and group embraces. While it is easy enough to understand how and why contemporary men have wanted to shift the expression of their brotherhood in more tactile directions (a change stemming, perhaps, both from the feminist movement and from many women's comfort with same-gender touch), it also presents puzzling questions for the male survivor. Physical touch for most survivors is, after all, charged with far more significance than it is for the male population at large, and in fact can be an invasive and threatening gesture—especially when the survivor feels compelled to conform to the wishes and rituals of any group with whom he is associated.

Since safety is essential to any survivor's growth and health, it stands to reason that a good rule is to ensure that any and all physical contact is obtained by permission, and that an agreement to hug is fully reciprocal and nonthreatening. Sounds simple enough, but it's not. It is almost as though participants in the men's movement are so eager to prove their evolution away from sexism that they wear their hugs on their chests like Boy Scout badges.

While the inherent intent of freeing men to enjoy and share genuine physical contact with one another is admirable—and a significant reversal of many inbred cultural taboos and other such nonsense—many men see that freedom as an indication of an elite, rather than egalitarian, status. The importance and beauty of becoming a New Man carries within its charm the danger of a most immature kind of seduction: I'm better than Old Culture Men, and I can prove it to you by hugging you, whether you want to be hugged or not. Try to imagine what might be the response, should hug-happy New Men begin hugging women in the identical fashion. It wouldn't be pretty. You can be sure most women would inform the overzealous New Man that her body belongs solely to her, thank you very much, and he'd better ask permission first next time.

What appears to have sifted through the cracks of some portions of men's-movement consciousness is that conferring the right to say *no* to anything is not at all a negative stance. When a survivor, or any man or woman for that matter, reclaims his or her undeniable right to say *no*, in the same breath he or she is lending credence and power to his or her right and capacity to say *yes*. When we recognize that others possess this crucial power of saying yes or no with equal validity, we also automatically infuse them—and ourselves—with the full respect each deserves.

Nevertheless, it is not always easy. Why do men (and women) have such difficulties grasping a concept as simple as ownership of our bodies? How is it that even men who publicly identify as survivors feel forced into a position of *demanding* the respect and safety that permission to touch confers? Why can't we just *ask* for it? Male survivors intuitively recognize the threatening quality of nonpermissive touch. Our histories have given us at least that much wisdom and humility. We also recognize the richness and honesty of mutuality, where two men, both willing, join arm in arm. Survivors thrive when we work shoulder-to-shoulder; but not in dark rooms, not with the assumption that you can rub shoulders with us any time you please. You can't. Believe it or not, the phrase *you can't* is a completely positive statement. May the day come when all men fully understand that. Maybe then we will truly be new men.

Spouses, Friends, and Family: Cosurvivors or Secondary Victims?

By a Recovering Survivor
Winter 1998

One of the great frustrations I've experienced in my recovery has been the recognition that there seems to be no existing support system expressly for spouses and friends of survivors. I call them cosurvivors. Yet there is clearly an overwhelming need for support groups directly designed for cosurvivors. The pain, frustration, and confusion they experience is no less powerful than that felt by survivors. In some ways their position is even more difficult and perplexing, because it is hard to imagine that their loved one, now in a safe and happy environment, still lives with fear, pain, and injury.

I cannot count the number of times survivors have reported their spouses saying to them, "Why don't you get over it? It happened—(what? 20, 30, 40 years ago, take your pick)—just forget it and get on with your life." Of course, what we survivors in treatment are doing *requires* us to remember, so we *can* get on with our lives.

Many adult survivors of abuse and trauma experience a type of "reliving" of aspects of the original injury, in part because the survivor needs to reprocess that experience in a healthier, safer way. This reprocessing can be expressed over a wide gradient of degrees, ranging from vivid memories, chronic nightmares, and flashbacks to full-fledged abreactions. Most people have had flashback memories from time to time, and those recollections can be extremely compelling. Still, these are certainly recognized as a memory, rather than a current reality. Abreactions are experienced as a current reality, rather than a memory.

All of the above requires a survivor to do "memory work" with his/her therapist. Though ideally I might wish to confine this sort of memory work to the safe warmth of my therapist's office, it hasn't been an entirely controllable option for me, or any other survivor I've met. The harsh reality, and a source of great guilt and shame for many survivors, is that our recovery necessarily occurs out in the big, bad world as well as on the therapist's couch. Our healing process directly impacts those around us—our spouses, friends, families, and coworkers. Simply put, the world becomes witness to our original victimization.

Let me give you an example of how difficult it can be for a spouse living with a survivor. One evening my wife—I'll call her Greta—came home from a brief trip to the grocery store to buy milk. Prior to that, the night had been pleasant and uneventful; over supper the children had happily giggled telling about the games they'd played at recess. Greta was pleased with the progress on the grant proposal she was writing, and everyone raved about the spaghetti I'd made for dinner. It was a beautiful, crisp spring evening, squirrels vying with the chickadees and titmice at the birdfeeder outside the bay window. We watched a little television with our sons and read to them at bedtime.

By the time Greta had left to fetch the milk, the children were long asleep and I was nested cozily in my favorite chair, reading. When Greta returned, I was no longer in the living room. Hardly cause for alarm, she no doubt thought; I might have gone to bed, or taken a bath, or simply moved to another room. After a few minutes she quite naturally began looking for me, not out of worry but because that's what spouses generally do.

After searching most of the house, she eventually found me, cowering in a corner of the basement, covered with a blanket and shaking in fear.

"You kept saying 'Trouble!' over and over again," she told me later. "I tried to talk to you, but you couldn't hear me. You didn't sound like you," she continued. "And you couldn't even see me."

"What did I sound like?" I asked. "You sounded...you sounded and looked like a little boy, maybe four or five years old," she said. "And the little boy was in trouble." "Yes," I said, "he was." She began to cry. "Look at your right arm." I raised my arm, and there was a long slash from the elbow halfway down toward my wrist. It was still bleeding. I didn't feel a thing. "Must've scratched myself somehow," I muttered. "You wouldn't let me touch you," she said. "You cut yourself again. I can't handle this. I don't know what to do. What do I do?" she asked, her voice breaking. But she got no answer. I had none to give.

While the above example may seem extreme, it is a relatively common experience for many survivors and, of course, for all those exhibiting multiple personalities. It is also pretty common for cosurvivors to witness these sorts of episodes. In this particular instance, I had undergone a switch from my adult self to one of my younger alters.

What Greta was obliged to see was a four-year-old boy being terrorized and physically punished in a horrible fashion. She saw, heard, and recognized this boy, even though at the time he happened to be clothed in a 42 year-old man's body. And there was nothing she could say to him, because he couldn't hear her. There was nothing she could do for him, because he couldn't see her.

Greta became a secondary victim of my old, original perpetrator because witnessing abuse is itself inherently traumatic. Imagine yourself, tied to a chair and gagged, completely powerless, and being forced by a thug to watch him/her brutalize your partner, wife, husband, or child—and being powerless to protect them.

In the anecdote I've recounted I *was* powerless to protect her. And that is why many survivors like me carry deep guilt with us so much of the time. Having moved from victims to survivors, the last thing we want to do is abuse anyone else; certainly we don't want to subject them to the traumas we've endured. But a key part of our tortuous journey back to health requires breaking silence, shattering the secrets. The four-year-old in the basement didn't have the patience to wait for his next therapy appointment. He needed to try to come out of hiding *now*, not tomorrow. He did the best he could, and no doubt it took a lot of courage on his part. But he didn't have the tools then to recognize that he was in a new, safer world.

The way I've learned to stop cutting myself in the present required me to go back to 1956, to bandage and heal a certain four-year-old. In a sense, I am "raising" him anew—until he and I are both 45, and quite contemporary.

Still, there must be a forceful recognition by survivors that our partners need and deserve support, too. Because though the abuse our loved ones suffer from us may be passive, unintentional, and abhorrent to us, it is nonetheless completely real. That is the starting point, I think—as survivors to acknowledge that trauma has a way of traveling from person to person, and trying to contain its expansion is not only impossible but counter-productive to all. I cannot break free of my secrets by learning new ways to hide.

There is no way I can prevent Greta from being a cosurvivor, though I know her status as such stems directly from her relationship with me. Nor can I say that she actually "chose" that role, because neither she nor I were aware of my personal history until many years after we fell in love. What I can do is work as responsibly as possible to ensure that she does not slip from being a cosurvivor into being a secondary victim of my perpetrators.

How? Our personal insights have been helpful for us but are not necessarily of use to others. And, though these insights have been helpful, it would be totally dishonest of me to imply that it has made matters easy. It is not easy. It is difficult, sometimes painful. Because as my wounds heal, Greta inevitably becomes increasingly aware of them. A cast and a sling are poor camouflage for a broken arm, after all. We experience difficulty and stress in our relationship—but it is fair to say there would *be* no relationship if we didn't utilize the following tools. Here are some suggestions I offer as a patient, not a professional.

1. Recognize that your spouse is not your therapist, but be honest and direct in explaining how at times being a survivor colors your behavior and attitude.

2. Encourage your partner to describe his/her experiences with you, as *he/she* perceives it.

3. Offer suggestions toward alternative approaches to flashbacks, switches, etc. For example, though the boy in the basement didn't recognize Greta, he probably would have recognized a teddy bear or a cup of cocoa. Had he felt safer, and comforted, he might have described to Greta the trouble he was in.

4. Set limits. In my experience, the worst time for me to discuss my recovery with Greta is after therapy or a group session. My mind is too full, my body always feels strange, and my emotions are ping-ponging all over the place. This isn't just my response; many survivors feel exactly the same. We know our spouses are being loving and supportive when they ask, "How was the meeting tonight?" as soon as we get home, but the truth is that we've likely done as much talking as we can for the evening. We may need quiet. Our partners need patience. Ask us tomorrow. We'll answer as well as we can.

5. Designate a "safe place" in the home, a place where the survivor can go during upsetting incidents. This is especially valuable in dealing with issues of anger or rage, when the survivor is reacting to the enormity of his/her oppression. For me, anger is such a new and novel emotion that I realize it utterly confuses me. I was never allowed to show anger, so I am just learning how to feel it, let alone express and manage it. But my partner needs to be safe, too—and, as with trauma, safety tends to travel from person to person. If I feel I'm doing what I can to keep Greta safe, I feel safer, too.

6. Negotiate. As a survivor, I have a lot more questions than answers. As a cosurvivor, Greta also has more questions than answers. When we share our questions and areas of concern, we can at least determine what we want to focus on as an area for improvement.

7. Don't make surviving your lifestyle, or your partner's. I readily admit that during the first year I was in professional treatment, I was utterly consumed by the subject of my abuse and diagnoses. Lord knows how many books and articles I read, how many doctors and therapists I contacted, how many hotlines I called. I now know that my response was hardly unusual, but it took a while for me to understand what my first therapist meant when she once said, "Take a day off, man!" I was pretty much obsessed with recovering as quickly as possible. But try as I might, I couldn't force the issue. And while I thought I was "working hard," (and I was), I was also quite literally putting the screws to myself and Greta. By the end of that first year she needed a break as much—or more—than I did.

8. Talk about your recovery, but not all the time. Take your partner out to a movie and devour lots of popcorn. Talk, for a change, about *anything* unrelated to survivor work. Rent a cheap motel room and have fun.

9. Support your partner. Recognize and appreciate that he/she is doing hard work right alongside you.

10. Rest. All this hard work is tiring on everyone. Buy a new couch so you and your partner can potato together on it.

11. Should your partner be lucky enough to know another cosurvivor, encourage him/her to pursue a supportive relationship with that person. Because there are no support groups expressly designed for cosurvivors, their sense of isolation can be just as acute as the loneliness felt by survivors.

12. Professional help can be good for cosurvivors, too. This sometimes creates anxiety in survivors: Will he/she be talking about—gasp—us? Yes. Let's not pussyfoot around it—your partner *needs* to talk to others about you. Just like you need to talk about your perpetrator, your partner needs to discuss meeting that same perpetrator, through you.

Writing this column was very difficult for me. I recoil in horror at the thought that my response to abuse, even in healing, can be hurtful to others. But I recognize it as an unavoidable reality. I can't change that. What I can change is how I deal with this ugly fact—I can stop recoiling, and start addressing the problem head-on, as well as I can, calling upon all of my resources, and the input of Greta, my therapist, my family, my friends, my co-workers, and every other survivor I know.

We can only defeat the genie by destroying the lamp in which it hides.

Ten Thousand Children: A Turning Point
By Richard Hoffman
Summer 2002

In every struggle there is a moment that is afterward recognized as the point when the tide began to turn, when success became sure. Those who have struggled, over the past two decades especially, to bring the reality of children's widespread sexual exploitation to light can only hope that the present attention to the assault on children by Catholic priests may serve as such a tipping point.

Until now, the spotlight (quite literally, the *Boston Globe* Spotlight Team) has been on the Archdiocese of Boston and its protection of serial child rapists. Perhaps this is as it should be; after all, the only thing worse than a wolf in sheep's clothing is a wolf in shepherd's robes. However, in the discussions that have followed, the focus has been on the church, on the nature of the priesthood, on the psychology of the perpetrators of this recurrent atrocity, and on who knew what and when. But the most important thing to understand is the real scope of this tragedy, and the number of children who were harmed.

For years we have been hearing that incidents of child sexual abuse are few, that wild-eyed fanatics have created social hysteria, that most children pass into adulthood without encountering such psychopaths. But let's do some simple arithmetic.

As of this writing, the Archdiocese of Boston has turned over the names of 100 priests to district attorneys. Does this mean that 100 children were sexually assaulted? Not at all. Therapists who treat sex offenders, law enforcement people, and forensic psychologists all know that most men who violate children are serial offenders. The coach who raped me when I was 10, for example, turned out to have had more than 400 victims over a 40-year period. Christopher Reardon, who like most predators kept records of his many victims, had a list describing the private parts of 250 boys. Reardon had not reached the age of 30 when he was arrested. Many of the priests named, on the other hand, are quite old.

Let's err on the safe side, though, and say, oh, 10 boys per year for 10 years, or five boys per year for 20 years; in other words, 100 victims each. That's 10,000 children! Oh, and then there are John Geoghan's 118. And James Porter's 70. Let's not forget Reardon's 250. That's 10,438 victims of those predators *whom we know of.*

We have not even begun to hear about those priests who belong to religious orders and run schools, orphanages, and youth programs, orders such as the Xaverians, Salesians, Franciscans, Marists, Paulists, Vincentians, Jesuits, and others who do not work for the archdiocese.

And we have not even begun to look at the scope of the sexual abuse of boys *outside* the church. The Roman Catholic Church, venerable blueprint for patriarchy, itself the very genome of empire, oldest and most practiced of all secretive, misogynist hierarchies on earth, is not the only powerful institution hiding those who exploit the innocent. What is visible—now that the benign mask of paternalism has fallen—is the terrible toll that patriarchy takes on boys.

"Where is the lamb for the sacrifice?" asked Isaac atop the mountain, his father Abraham's hand on the knife.

The abuse of a child is a lesson in power. It defines power for the child: it says that power is making others do your will. For men, this message is congruent with many other lessons we receive from our culture. Real power, however, is what was taken from us, not only by acts of violence and violation, but by lies about the nature of, the meaning of, and the responsibility for those acts, lies about who we are.

Often when we talk about recovering from the trauma of childhood sexual abuse, we talk about healing. The metaphor of healing a wound is only so useful, however—the truth is even simpler and more terrible: the sexual violation of a child is a violation of the child's history, not merely the child's psyche. It is a lie told to the child about his or her worth, a lie that disrupts the story as it had been unfolding and establishes new premises that engender a different narrative, or make a coherent individual story not congruent with the master narrative—the story of power over others—nearly impossible. The psyche, with its grief and outrage, is exiled, and there is no spirit left, no authentic power, to withstand the proffered false narrative telling you who you are and what you must become. This is the story of childhood in patriarchal culture. This is the sacrifice of Isaac, complete with his initiation and induction into the bloody warrior's covenant with the god of conquest, a covenant sealed by means of a genital wound (which, compared to what *almost* happened, and to what happened to that hapless ram, by now looks like a good deal). This is also the story of Iphigenia, daughter of Agamemnon, sacrificed to the gods in return for winds to sail warships to Troy.

In the case of boys, this toxic proto-narrative inscribed, tattooed as it were, on Isaac's psyche, seems to say that the whole of the world is an arena in which one strives, and in which there are necessarily winners and losers, and that all the others one encounters there are either adversaries or allies against one's adversaries. This is the *über*-ideology of "manhood."

For a boy, a so-called young man, to be victimized is to have lost in a world of contention and aggression. To have lost is to invite further violence. To have been victimized is to be a "loser." Boys, and the shamed and silent men they become, do not keep their victimization secret to protect those who have abused them but to protect themselves from further abuse. Those who prey upon children know this. Silence is logical in this context. Denial is the anesthetic required to go on, to "play hurt," even to survive and grow up at all. Later, other painkillers are offered to us, and most of us, to our eventual peril, liberally avail ourselves of their help. In a world of winners and losers, the simple act of telling the truth becomes outlandish, terrifying, and forbidden.

When a man chooses to break his silence about boyhood sexual abuse, he becomes a kind of defector from an ideology that sees the world as an arena in which other men are all competitors and each new circumstance yields only victims and victors. It is my belief that only those men with the courage to refuse this conceptual imprisonment and instead choose wholeness can begin to lead us out of the nightmare of patriarchy. This liberation, this difficult extrication from lies, shame, and silence, this grief, anger, hope, and truth, has the potential to restore not only the souls of those of us who have suffered abuse and betrayal but also our common life. The violation of a child, after all, is an offense against the community. It is a crime against the future. Through the cumulative effect of many separate acts of truth telling and encouraging others to follow suit, we help to regenerate in our communities a respect for truthfulness, for honesty as a primary value. And *that* will make the world a safer place for children.

Betrayed as Boys
By Richard B. Gartner
Winter 2002

In 1988, I started treating the first man I specifically conceptualized as having been sexually abused in boyhood. I had been in practice for more than 15 years, as a dynamically oriented psychotherapist, as a systems-oriented family therapist, and finally as an interpersonal psychoanalyst. In retrospect, I realized that "Patrick" was certainly not the first man I treated who had a history of childhood sexual betrayal. He was not even the first to tell me about inappropriate or unwanted premature sexual experiences with older friends, relatives, or caretakers. I was, however, a product of my own training and a prevailing conventional wisdom among clinicians that such stories should be treated cautiously because of the likelihood that they emerged from parents' fantasy lives and wish fulfillments. So, while I had not doubted my patients' stories, I also had not encoded them as descriptions of sexual abuse. Nor had I thought about patterns of behavior common in men with histories of childhood sexual betrayal.

My work with Patrick proved to be a watershed for me. As he slowly began to recall horrifying stories of sexual abuse in early childhood, I was forced to rethink how to understand them. If they were entirely fantasies, then Patrick was floridly psychotic, which I did not believe. But if his stories were even partly true, then he had been the victim of grievous crimes perpetuated by his father and brother. As time went on, the picture became fuller as his sister confirmed that she too had been sexually abused by their father. My doubts about Patrick's stories dissipated. Instead, I began to think about how his adult symptoms of recurrent depression, night terrors about a stranger breaking into his room, obsessive but impersonal sexual fantasies, long-term isolation, and difficulties in interpersonal relationships all made sense in the context of chronic sexual abuse in early childhood.

I began to educate myself about the literature on childhood sexual abuse, which focuses mainly on women. As I sought help from colleagues, my interest in sexually abused men grew, and I began to get referrals of other men (and women) with similar histories. More referrals came when I started a group for these men after I could not find one in New York City for Patrick.

Once I began to work with men who defined themselves as having been sexually abused, I started to think about other patients differently. I was more likely to inquire into their early sexual histories. Interestingly, more patients told me about inappropriately sexual childhood histories without my ever asking. My receptivity about the subject had in some way been communicated to them.

When a patient I had treated for several years during and after my psychoanalytic training returned to see me after an absence of some five years, I was especially struck by how much my thinking had been transformed. He reminded me that just before he stopped treatment he had asked whether I thought he might have had a history of boyhood sexual abuse, even though he had no actual memories of it. I was confused about how to explore this possibility in the absence of memories, so I gave an equivocal response. He now told me that shortly thereafter he stopped the treatment "in despair."

I now realize how limited my thinking had been. This man's symptom picture—which included obsessive and compulsive sexuality, masochism, cross-dressing, and severe interpersonal isolation and distrust—was certainly consonant with a history of childhood sexual abuse. Nevertheless, I had never thought in such terms during his earlier treatment.

Incest and the sexual abuse of children have long been taboo and misunderstood subjects in popular culture and the clinical literature. Sexual victimization of all children has chronically been denied in our society; the sexual victimization of boys, however, is even more universally minimized, underestimated, and ridiculed than the abuse of girls.

Perhaps these social views of male sexual victimization have started to change as stories about boys' sexual victimization gain greater currency in the popular press. Scandals have been widely reported about victimization of boys by men in church, scouting, childcare, sports venues, and on the Internet.

Interestingly, in each of these stories the victimizer came from outside the family, reflecting some research findings that most abused boys suffer from extrafamilial victimization. Incestuous abuse of boys is virtually never reported to the press, however, even though its prevalence is also well documented. Indeed, denial of the extent of childhood incest has been almost universal in our society: to believe in the widespread incidence of incest is to question the sanctity of the family, where children are thought to be protected from harm.

The pervasiveness of the denial of childhood sexual betrayal, especially the sexual abuse of boys, was illuminated for me several years ago. I was invited to an international conference to give a paper about the treatment of sexually abused men. Just as I was hosting the meeting, the conference program came. My paper was not listed in it. Surprised, I called the program chair when I arrived. He did not remember me or my paper. At that moment, I felt the sense of unreality that patients have told me they experience in the face of their family's denial of ongoing sexual abuse.

Flustered and confused after a daylong flight, I momentarily wondered if I was mistaken about the initial request to read my paper. I grounded myself when I realized that the conference chair's letter of invitation was in my hand as I spoke to him. He apologized and found a place for me on a panel at the meeting, albeit one on which none of the other papers related to mine. The addition of my paper to the program was announced at the conference opening, but was not listed on any of the notices posted around the meeting rooms until I insisted. At the panel itself, the moderator, an American scholar and psychoanalyst, permitted the speaker before me to continue for fifteen minutes beyond his allotted twenty-five. Seven minutes after I began to talk about the experiences of sexually abused men, this moderator handed me a note that read, "Can you wrap this up? We're supposed to be having a coffee break now." Luckily, several colleagues in the audience protested that they wanted to hear my paper.

At another conference, this one specifically concerned with male sexual victimization, I met several people who helped me to focus my own writing about this subject and to find my voice. One was an experienced, psychoanalytically trained therapist from a southeastern community. Of retirement age, he said he had come to the conference for help in writing an article about treating patients with trauma histories.

At first, his comments at presentations focused on the intellectual and didactic components of what was being addressed. He seemed to be trying to minimize or deflect others from the wells of feeling that were being tapped by the material. After listening to both therapists and nonclinicians express their emotional responses to what they were hearing, he rigidified his approach until another member of a workshop he took confronted him about this. He grew silent, then, astonishingly, began to weep. He poured out the story of his own sexual abuse. In the 50 or more years since these experiences, he had never hinted about them to another soul except his analyst, and even then he apparently had minimized their impact. By the end of the conference, he found several kindred spirits, seemed looser and far more open, and also achieved his initial goal of learning more about the psychological impact of trauma.

My writing and therapeutic practice are deeply influenced by my belief that most sexually abused men want and need much more than "symptom removal"; rather, they seek to develop a more nearly consolidated sense of self, a greater attunement to their emotional lives, and increased ability to develop and maintain a tie with an intimate other. I believe this is most likely to happen in a therapeutic experience that carefully examines the relational aspects of all a man's actions and internal psychological events. When I work with a sexually abused man, the intricacies of his specific situation, history, and character become the foreground of our work; no one is fully defined by an "abuse history."

I am deeply grateful to those who gave me permission to describe our work. My relationships with all the men I have worked with and written about have moved me and changed how I look at human interaction. These men have courageously faced terrifying pasts. Their stories have stirred me; their resolution in the face of their histories has astonished me. I have learned from them more than I can say.

Breaking the Silence on Sexual Abuse

By Randy Ellison
Spring 2012

Child sex abuse is the ultimate elephant in the room. Statistics and experts in the field report one in six boys and one in three or four girls are sexually abused before they turn eighteen. That means that approximately 20 million men and 30-plus million women—roughly 20 percent of the adult population of the United States—were sexually abused as children.

Even as we view sexual abuse of children as a heinous and horrific crime, we prefer to not picture it happening and definitely don't want to imagine someone we know committing these violations. Perpetrators are not strangers dressed in dark clothes, hanging around schools and ice cream shops. More than 90 percent of perpetrators are known to the victim. If that weren't enough, 40 percent are family members. What would you say if someone accused your brother, father, uncle, minister, or teacher of abuse? Human nature typically denies the possibility and usually sides with the accused.

Likewise, when institutions get a report of suspected abuse by a long-time employee, they use any rationale to dismiss it. *"It probably didn't happen and even if it did we'll just believe him (or her) when they say it won't ever happen again. Okay, now we can move on and get back to a more acceptable reality."*

Mathematically we are prosecuting at most 2 to 3 percent of sexual assaults on children. Remember society's unspoken code of silence: "innocent until proven guilty, and we really don't want to believe anyone could do that." To that collective sense of denial, add another dangerous ingredient: most pedophiles are master con artists. They not only groom their victims, they are very good at making people like them, especially showing how much they care about children.

If you have any business that deals with kids, pedophiles will be drawn to you for easy access to victims. All organizations working with young people need to screen very carefully. They also need a *written* policy on what they do to protect children, including a proviso that no adult will ever be in a private one-on-one environment with kids. The policy should be posted where it can easily be seen, and every parent and child should have it explained to them and be given a copy.

Simply put, we need to be much more vigilant about protecting our children. Notice if someone is paying undo attention to one child in particular. Someone who offers to take a child out for a treat, offers to give him or her a ride home or small gifts should set off red flags. This is especially true if it is a child who doesn't get much attention socially or displays needy behaviors. It is better to question and report suspicions than not to address nagging concerns and instead turn away. It is not about *them* (victims and perpetrators)—it's about *us*. We need to reprogram ourselves to keep children safe.

How do perpetrators undermine children's safety? Part of the grooming process is to get the victim to bond with and feel a loyalty toward the perpetrator. This is one reason survivors have difficulty reporting the abuse. For me, I just dissociated the abuse behavior from the rest of my relationship with the perpetrator (in my case a trusted minister). I never thought about it. It would happen, and I would put it away and live the more acceptable parts of life that made sense to me.

Loyalty definitely is part of the reason people don't tell. I know of several cases where pedophile ministers or priests die, and their victims actually come to honor them at their memorials.

Another major factor is fear and shame. Some victims are threatened into silence or feel the abuse was their fault. This is especially true for boys, who often experience physical arousal and an inexplicable satisfaction from the abuse; they feel shame from those feelings and become confused about right and wrong. Remember, in the developing mind of a child, being sexually abused by a trusted adult or loved one is like two trains in a head-on collision. The abuse is in direct conflict with everything the child has been taught about relationships. Every line is crossed or destroyed.

The results are devastating. A lot of survivors, myself included, feel as though our souls were stolen. My abuse threw me off the track of my life. I thought I would be a minister, but not only did I not do pursue that path, I dropped out of college and drifted, both through several careers and life in general. I never let anyone get close to me. To try and deal with what I was carrying, I became an alcoholic and a drug addict. To compound matters, we moved a lot. It was as though I was running from something and doing my best to forget what it was.

Did you know it is estimated that as many as 80 percent of people in residential alcohol and drug treatment programs were victims of abuse? It's the same figure, 80 percent, for those being treated for schizophrenia. More than half of all women in prison report they were abused as children. Of the 200 men on a special program on *Oprah* about male abuse (of which I was one), four-fifths of us reported contemplating suicide and 30 percent of us had tried to take our own lives.

If a person becomes a victim of child sexual abuse, his emotional maturation stops. We do not develop into the adults we were meant to be. In addition, we lose the rest of our childhoods, locking the child away. Once a survivor gets to a point of safety and is ready to deal with the abuse, some amazing changes can happen. It is an important and joyful experience to go back and honor the lost child within, to learn to play again.

As I faced my fears and shame I simultaneously began to mature and develop again. My addictions no longer ruled my life. I found myself in new, meaningful relationships and making friends. I am no longer alone, and I am able to give and receive love freely without fear.

If you have never spoken about or dealt openly with your abuse, I encourage you to start with someone you trust—open the door with a friend. Counseling and therapy is a must. You cannot unpack all you have locked away by yourself. That process will require learning to put yourself first. You have value, and you are not responsible for what happened to you. It is a difficult process, but the payoff is life changing and life affirming. You will find you can replace fear and shame with joy and satisfaction. I wish you strength on your journey.

Resources

Male Survivor (malesurvivor.org)

Male Survivors is committed to preventing, healing, and eliminating all forms of sexual victimization of boys and men through support, treatment, research, education, advocacy, and activism.

RAINN (rainn.org)

The Rape, Abuse & Incest National Network is the nation's largest antisexual violence organization. RAINN operates the National Sexual Assault Hotline at 1.800.656.HOPE and the National Sexual Assault Online Hotline at - online.rainn.org, and publicizes the hotline's free, confidential services; educates the public about sexual violence; and leads national efforts to prevent sexual violence, improve services to victims, and ensure that rapists are brought to justice.

NSVRC (nsvrc.org)

The National Sexual Violence Resource Center is an information and resource hub nationwide addressing all aspects of sexual violence. The NSVRC staff collects and disseminates a wide range of resources on sexual violence including statistics, research, position statements, statutes, training curricula, prevention initiatives, and program information. With these resources, the NSVRC assists coalitions, advocates, and others interested in understanding and eliminating sexual violence.

Information about Abusers
Association for the Treatment of Sexual Abusers (atsa.com)

This international, multidisciplinary organization is dedicated to preventing sexual abuse. Through research, education, and shared learning, ATSA promotes evidence-based practice, public policy, and community strategies that lead to the effective assessment, treatment, and management of individuals who have sexually abused or are at risk to abuse.

Center for Sex Offender Management (csom.org)

The Center for Sex Offender Management (CSOM) is a national clearinghouse and technical assistance center that supports state and local jurisdictions in the effective management of sex offenders. CSOM aims to provide those responsible for managing sex offenders with ready access to the most current knowledge by synthesizing and disseminating research and effective practices to the field and by offering specialized training and technical assistance on a wide variety of issues related to sex offender management.

Publications

Engaging Bystanders in Sexual Violence Prevention by Joan Tabachnick
www.nsvrc.org/publications/nsvrc-publications/engaging-bystanders-sexual-violence-prevention
This free book presents a compelling orientation to the importance of engaging bystanders in sexual violence prevention. An excellent training resource, it provides activities and trainer instructions throughout that make

it a useful educational guide on bystander engagement in sexual violence prevention.

Preventing Child Sexual Abuse in Youth Serving Organizations
CDC www.cdc.gov/violenceprevention/pub/preventingchildabuse.html (the Centers for Disease Control and Prevention) has developed Preventing Child Sexual Abuse Within Youth-serving Organizations: Getting Started on Policies and Procedures [PDF 4.5MB] to assist youth-serving organizations as they begin to adopt prevention strategies for child sexual abuse.

Evicting the Perpetrator: A Male Survivor's Guide to Recovery From Childhood Sexual Abuse by Ken Singer
bookstore.nearipress.org/index.php/books/featured-products/evicting-the-perpetrator.html. Includes exercises and assignments. Useful for professionals working with survivors, their families, even perpetrators who were sexually abused.

Joining Forces: Empowering Male Survivors to Thrive by Dr. Howard Fradkin, based on the experiences of 750 survivors who have participated in MaleSurvivor Weekends of Recovery

Outing Yourself as a Survivor
By Jacob Stevenson
Summer 2000

> *I used to think I'd had a nervous breakdown. I don't call it a breakdown anymore. I call it a breakthrough.*
>
> —R.U., female survivor and multiple, age 38

In the course of my eight years of recovery, healing, and treatment, I have been in one-on-one therapy with fourteen different practitioners, attended countless groups of varying sorts, and been hospitalized five times. Sadly, this frenetic itinerary is hardly an unusual journey for many male survivors, or for most multiples, regardless of gender. But one advantage to having juggled so many disconnected pieces of this professionally endorsed jigsaw puzzle is that it has allowed me to observe a number of commonalities between caregivers. Otherwise separated by philosophy, personality, and approach, certain techniques and mind-sets appear quite ubiquitous. It is my opinion that some of those shared threads of approach and attitude are at best counterproductive for the survivor—and at worst, harmful and abusive in and of themselves.

In the seminal book *Victims No Longer*, Mike Lew speaks of the "survivor's voice." Using Lew's general description, I think it might better be called the "victim's voice," and will so name it here. He accurately describes it as soft, monotonous, betraying little or no emotion. And so it tends to be, at first: survivors are apt to mirror the gentle, near-hypnotic murmurs often associated with a perpetrator's seductive utterances. Indeed, the survivor's spoken voice can be a form of self-hypnosis for the victim, a kind of lulling into calmer, safer waters of consciousness. (It is, of course, equally true that the shrill, uncontrollable, and sometimes violent emotional outbursts survivors might experience readily mirror the rage-filled assaults perpetrators confront their victims with at times, but that is a subject for a different essay.)

The functions of the perpetrator's voice and the victim's voice are virtually identical at bedrock: to deny that which is. The perpetrator seeks to deny the nature of his/her action, the damage it causes, and his/her own responsibility in the commission of such an assault. Ultimately, a perpetrator wishes to deny the reality of the trauma: it didn't really happen, and even if it did, it was *your* fault, and it certainly didn't happen the way *you* remember it.

Denial performs a very similar job for the victim. After all, if it didn't *really* happen, it can't possibly hurt, can it? Or if it happened to some other part of me—the existence of which I may or may not have some awareness of—then someone else got stuck holding the bag stuffed with angry cats, right?

Slightly right but mostly wrong. The beauty of any dissociative response by a victim is that it protects us very well, often for very lengthy periods of time. The ugliness of dissociation is that it is a masterfully constructed web of deceit and denial, oftentimes a complete refabrication of histories that never existed, and never will exist within the boundaries of fact and circumstance. As my first therapist originally described my "breakdown," I had simply arrived at a time in my life where I was safe enough to confront the pain and danger successfully. Up until that time, though, I had very much needed to be wrapped up in my snug, warm, and muffling voice of numbness and noninvolvement. How exciting and frightening it was to finally drop those hindering blankets and dare the coldness of bright daylight!

But while I intuitively sought to move in one direction—to a new place where my voice could be loud and vibrant and unconcealed—I began to notice that all the therapists, social workers, shrinks, and doctors I encountered were speaking *in my old voice*. They, too, uniformly spoke so softly I needed to strain my ears to catch their words. Their drone, their cadence was so interchangeable that, were I to close my eyes, it's quite unlikely I could have distinguished one from another. Their voices were warm, slow, and seductive.

They were talking in the voices of perpetrators and victims. And what they were saying were old, too-familiar words to me. "Everything we share here is confidential; no one else will know." "It's OK to tell your secrets to me; I'll protect you." "This might very well be scary, but it *won't hurt you*." "This process will take a long, long time." "I'd like to see you at least twice a week." "There is nothing you cannot tell me. I'll keep you safe." And these words were spoken in dimly lit rooms, crammed with overstuffed furniture upholstered in pastels. Everything was neutral, because neutral is safe, right?

The stated rationale for the above trappings of treatment typically suggests that they are designed to create an ambience of trust, comfort, and accessibility. But such therapists seem to have little or no awareness of how intricate a re-creation they have achieved of the mood, the set, and the vocal tone of past assaults. Far from establishing a comfort zone for the survivor, such an environment only beguiles the client back into a hush-hush, let's-share-special-secrets world that further isolates and excludes him from the bright, brassy reality so readily available to others. We are told we are no longer freaks, true. We are, rather, "special cases," thus deserving of "special treatment."

And there are many, many others, just like you, we are told and promised by our caregivers. But when we are delighted by this hopeful information, and ask the obvious question—Where *are* the other men like me? And how can I meet them?—the silence is thick as choking smoke, and the caregiver's warnings are ominous and unforgiving. Yes, we are told, there are occasionally such groups of male survivors. But there is usually a six-month waiting list. Why? Because there are so many male survivors, and so few therapists qualified to run such groups. Participants must be carefully screened, after all. As a survivor, you must be *very careful* whom you tell, you know.

Why? Why must male survivors be carefully screened? Because it could be dangerous if you get triggered. Why must I be careful in choosing whom I out myself to? Because you are vulnerable to attack, and being a male survivor, unfortunately, still carries with it a great deal of stigma.

All of which is nothing more or less than a perpetrator's ideology and technique. I cannot re-form a sense of society when I am denied contact with my peers, and I cannot de-stigmatize the facts surrounding victimization in the silent dark. Yet that prescribed and recommended isolation and denial confirms the worst fears of many male survivors.

It is exactly the opposite of what we need as human beings, and what we need to do as advocates and activists. A case in point: I cannot count the number of male survivors who hold an odd but understandable hostility toward women, particularly toward women survivors. They are angry and resentful because they feel the women get the attention; they get the ink in the papers. "Why don't the newspapers tell *our story*?" these men ask.

My own question to such men is simple but devastating: "Why don't you write a letter to the paper and tell *your story*?"

Because, they respond, "*I'd have to sign my name to it. People would know.*

Because I'd be too stigmatized. I might lose my job. My friends might think I'm a queer. My wife might stop sleeping with me. What will my children think of me? And my therapist tells me I must be careful whom I tell." And on and on.

Bullshit. Far from there being any disgrace in being a survivor, there is courage and strength to spare. Survivors, by definition, are more than worthy of respect and admiration. We've already made it, folks. We are done with the old secrets; why should we replace them with new ones? Even if those new secrets are "therapist-approved," they remain deadly to us as individuals, and passively continue the cultural dismissal of abuse in all forms. Secrets render all survivors terrified and impotent—not a healthy situation for anyone.

To me, the healthier approach is to bring the subject out in the open and to deal with issues of abuse and trauma within a group format, where everyone can speak freely, ask any and all questions, without fear of reprisal or ostracism. Destroy the secrets and you destroy the stigma.

But we are largely not doing this, whether as male survivors, therapists, or the community as a whole. Because abuse and trauma are scary and painful, we apparently conclude that *knowing* survivors must also be threatening and, possibly, dangerous.

More bullshit. Allow me to describe these people to you, these people I know who call themselves survivors.

They own or manage restaurants. Some of are dishwashers, hosts, or hostesses. They are truck drivers and real estate agents. They are medical doctors and pro athletes. They are movie stars and the homeless. They are men and women. Some are children, or teenagers, or middle-aged, or elders. Some have black hair or red hair or brown hair or blond hair or white hair. Survivors are straight or gay or bisexual or transgender or transsexual or multisexual. Some will actually vote for the Republicans, others for the Democrats. Some are independents.

In short, they are us. I have met them, because I no longer choose to hide either my identity or my history. Because I make no bones about that, other survivors are free to identify themselves to me safely, should they so choose. And then we all begin to take one step out of the darkness, beyond the artificial quiet and calm, and into the windy, noisy daylight.

And when these men who are taxi cab drivers and college professors and ditch diggers all step forward—under the bright lights—as survivors, then we will begin to see our stories in the newspapers. Then we will begin replacing denial and soft voices with truth and confidence. Then men angry with female survivors will instead join hands with our sisters, learning from their wisdom and understanding how our shared pains might easily translate into the most profound sort of beautiful reciprocity.

Then we will be able to solve the problems of abuse and trauma, because we will be ready to stare them down with honest, unflinching eyes and the support and compassion of a sparkling new society, a world remade.

"The Taste of a Little Boy's Trust"
Richard Jeffrey Newman
Summer 2013

Snow still falling this late,
when each house framed
by the window above my desk

is dark, and even my wife's breathing
has grown indistinguishable
from the quiet, snow still falling

as a truck rolls by, big-cat-svelte
on eighteen wheels, orange
running lights spreading

up and down my block
a Halloween glow
in mid-December,

like a space vessel landing,
bringing me the boy I was
standing in the courtyard, searching

the descending whiteness
for the shapes of ships
I longed to fly away on,

snow still falling this late
when I could be sleeping,
the way I should have been

the night I saw my mother nude,
and her friend on his back, and them both
too slow to hide what they were doing,

and I told my brother and we tried it,

and we tried to understand
why grown-ups did it—*how could you let someone*

pee in your mouth?—snow still falling this late
is the whisper we tried to laugh in, breath
the old man dropped, syllable—

when—by syllable—*will I*
see you?—into my ear, and I
couldn't move, wouldn't,

and so it wasn't me
who followed him upstairs, who listened
to the lock click shut in the door, and it wasn't me

whose belt he unbuckled, and when
his pants joined mine on the floor, it wasn't
me he pled with, whose head he used

both hands to pull toward him
when I balked, whose mind
at this moment always whites out

until it wasn't me
who unlocked the door and walked
to where the snow is still falling,

as if even now he waited
in the apartment above mine,
and no matter how many times

my brother asks, I won't go out,
not even to be first sled down
a virgin hill of the season's new snow.

In 1992 Gloria Steinem met with the staff of the Oakland Men's Project. OMP cofounder, the late Allen Creighton, is standing, on right.

Feminism is the radical notion that women are human beings.

—Cheris Kramarae, historian and activist

In homage to the women's movements that have contributed so much to the profeminist men's movement, men voice their support for and affinity with feminism and the women in their lives. Women, in turn, negotiate their relationship with profeminist men and offer advice to such men on how to be effective feminist allies. Together, men and women articulate how they might work together for the cause of gender justice and to sculpt an egalitarian world.

Feminism for Men... in 1914
By Floyd Dell
Summer 2013

Floyd Dell was an American novelist, playwright, poet, and literary critic born a century and a quarter ago in 1887. His influence was felt in the literature of major American writers working in the first half of the 20th century including Theodore Dreiser, Sherwood Anderson, and Carl Sandburg. In 1913 Dell became managing editor of The Masses, *a socialist magazine founded in New York City. Dell was considered one of the leaders of the bohemian community in Greenwich Village before the outbreak of World War I. Despite his literary acclaim, including penning a Broadway hit in 1928, today he is remembered mainly for his fierce support of feminism. He details his beliefs in the article below, first published a century ago in* The Masses, *in July 1914—six years before women got the right to vote. Although some of his depictions of marriage and family life fail to anticipate gay rights, his tongue-in-cheek portrayal of men's options reveals a prescient insight into the evolution of the profeminist men's movement that emerged six decades after Dell's article was first read.*

The Emancipation of Man

Feminism is going to make it possible for the first time for men to be free.

At present the ordinary man has the choice between being a slave and a scoundrel.

For the ordinary man is prone to fall in love and marry and have children. Also the ordinary man frequently has a mother. He wants to see them all taken

VOICE MALE

care of, since they are unable to take care of themselves. Yet, if he has them to think about, he is not free.

A free man is a man who is ready to throw up his job whenever he feels like it. Whether he is a bricklayer who wants to go out on a sympathetic strike, or a poet who wants to quit writing drivel for the magazines, in any case if he doesn't do what he wants to do, he is not free.

To disregard the claims of dependent women, to risk their comfort in the interest of self or of society at large, takes a good deal of heroism—and some scoundrelism, too.

Some of the finest natures to be found among men are the least free. It is the most sensitive who hesitate—and are lost to the world and their own souls.

And this will be true so long as women as a sex are dependent on men for support. It is too much to ask of a man to be brave, when his bravery means taking the food out of the mouth of a woman who cannot get food except from him. The bravest things will not be done in the world until women do not have to look to men for support.

The change is already under way. Irresistible economic forces are taking more and more women every year out of the economic shelter of the home into the great world, making them workers and earners along with men. And every conquest of theirs, from an education which will make them fit for the world of earning, to "equal pay for equal work," is a setting free of men. The last achievement will be a social insurance for motherhood, which will enable women to have children without taking away a man's freedom from him. Then a man will be able to tell his employer that "he and his job can go bark at one another," without being a hero and a scoundrel at the same time.

Capitalism will not like that. Capitalism does not want free men. It wants men with wives and children who are dependent on them for support. Mothers' pensions will be hard fought for before they are ever gained. And that is not the worst.

Men don't want the freedom that women are thrusting upon them. They don't want a chance to be brave. They want a chance to be generous. They want to give food and clothes and a little home with lace curtains to some woman.

Men want the sense of power more than they want the sense of freedom. They want the feeling that comes to them as providers for women more than they want the feeling that comes to them as free men. They want someone dependent on them more than they want a comrade. As long as they can be lords in a thirty-dollar flat, they are willing enough to be slaves in the great world outside.

They are afraid that women will cease to ask them to do things, will cease to say "Thank you!" They are afraid women will lose the timidity and weakness which make them turn to men for help. They are afraid that

212

woman will emancipate her legs with trousers. (And so she will; only they will not be so ugly as the garments at present worn by men, if Paul Poiret has anything to say about it!)

In short, they are afraid that they will cease to be sultans in little monogamic harems. But the world doesn't want sultans. It wants men who can call their souls their own. And that is what feminism is going to do for men—give them back their souls, so that they can risk them fearlessly in the adventure of life.

The fact is that this Occidental harem with its petty lordship over one woman, and its inefficient voluptuosities after the day's work, is not a fit place for a man. Woman has long since discovered that it is not a fit place for her.

The fit place for men and women is the world. That is their real home. The women are going there. The men are already there in one sense, but not in another. They own it, but do not inhabit it. They do not quite dare. The world is a home only for the free:

> "For there's blood on the field and blood on the foam,
> And blood on the body when man goes home.
> And a Voice valedictory: Who is for Victory?
> Who is for Liberty? Who goes Home?"

Sweethearts and Wives

It is a time-honored masculine generalization that sweethearts are more fun than wives. This proposition really implies another, that wives and sweethearts are two distinct and different things. If we admit the validity of the latter proposition, the former stands unquestionably true.

This is, as somebody once pointedly remarked, a man-made world. Certainly the distinction in theory and practice between a wife and a sweetheart is a masculine creation. No woman, it may be affirmed, having once been a sweetheart, would ever of her own free will and accord cease to be one.

For observe what it means to be a sweetheart. In the first place, there is the setting, the *milieu*, the scene of action. This is definite by virtue of its remarkable diversity. One is a sweetheart in the park, in the theatre, in the elevated train, on the front steps, on the fire escape, at soda fountains, at baseball games, in teashops, in restaurants, in the parlor, in the kitchen, anywhere, everywhere—that is to say, in the world at large. When two people are being sweethearts, they inhabit the world.

And they inhabit it together—that is the next thing. It is one of the conditions of being a sweetheart that you are always "along" whenever possible—and it is generally found possible. It seems to be the proper thing for one of a pair of sweethearts to be always where the other is. There is never any reason, or any excuse, for a sweetheart staying at home. The fact that a man cannot take his sweetheart to work with him is universally held to justify him in neglecting his work. But when he plays, he can take her with him, and he does. He takes her to the theatre, he takes her to the baseball park, he takes her out to Duck Creek and teaches her how to fish.

That is the third thing about being a sweetheart. She is not shut out from his society by reason of differences in habits or tastes. The assumption is that their habits and tastes ought to be alike. If she doesn't understand baseball, he explains it to her. If he likes golf, he teaches her how to play. If he loves poetry, he sits up and reads her his favorite poets. He doesn't permit any trivial differences to come between them. If she has been brought up with the idea that it is wicked to drink, he will cultivate her taste in cocktails. He will give her lessons in Socialism, poetry, and poker, all with infinite tact and patience. And he will do all of these things very humbly, with no pride in his own superiority. He will bring his most cherished ideas anxiously to her for her approval, and listen with the most genuine respect to her criticisms. They plan their future with the solid democratic equality of partners in the business of life.

Which is all very delightful. But in the course of time they are married, and very shortly after that the sweetheart becomes a wife. She is still the same person—she hasn't changed. But the conditions have changed... There was once a man—I don't pretend to approve of him—who had a wife and also a sweetheart, and he liked the sweetheart so much better than the wife that he persuaded his wife to divorce him, and then married the sweetheart; whereupon he simply had to get another sweetheart, because it was just the same as it had been before. The poor fellow never could figure it out. He thought there must be some mysterious and baneful magic in the marriage ceremony that spoiled things. But that superstition need not detain us. Proceed we to an inquiry as to where the difference really is. There is the matter of rendezvous. The whole spirit of meeting a sweetheart is that one is never quite certain whether she will really be there. Usually, as a matter of fact, she is late. One is anxious or angry, but one is never complacent about her coming. She may have misunderstood or misremembered the street corner. She may be waiting somewhere else. Or she may have changed her mind—a devastating thought.

But with a wife it is quite different. It is impossible for her to forget the place, for there is only one place. It is neither at the elevated station nor in the park nor on the library steps. It is a place quite out of the world. And she will always be there. Or, at least, if she isn't there, she ought to be. "A woman's place is in the home."

This saying applies only to wives. It does not apply to sweethearts. No man ever thought his sweetheart belonged at home. He regards her home with hostility and suspicion, and keeps her away from it as much as possible. It is only when she is a wife that he begins to think he has a right to expect her to be there. When he thinks of her, it is always in that setting. He thinks of her in that setting complacently. When he goes there to meet her he does not go anxiously, with a beating heart. The home is not a rendezvous. It is not one of the delightful corners of the world where two companions can meet for an adventure. It is a place out of the world where one keeps one's wife.

Home is a place quite different from the rest of the world. It is different by virtue of the things that are not done there. Out in the world, anything is likely to happen. Any restaurant may hatch a business deal. Any barbershop may be a polling place. But business and politics do not belong in the home. They are as out of place in that atmosphere as a "jag" or a display of fireworks. And from not being done in the home, they come not to be thought about there. Cooking, clothes, children—these are the topics of interest for the inmate of a home. These things are interesting. They are quite as important as baseball or politics. But they lack a certain imaginative appeal. They are not Homeric enough. A new dress is an achievement, but not the same kind of achievement as a home run. A new kind of salad is an interesting experiment, but one does not stand around offering to bet money on the results. In a word, the home is a little dull.

When you have got a woman in a box, and you pay rent on the box, her relationship to you insensibly changes character. It loses the fine excitement of democracy. It ceases to be companionship, for companionship is only possible in a democracy. It is no longer a sharing of life together—it is a breaking of life apart. Half a life—cooking, clothes, and children; half a life—business, politics, and baseball. It doesn't make much difference which is the poorer half. Either half, when it comes to life, is very near to none at all.

Of course, this artificial distinction does not strictly obtain in any particular marriage. There is an attempt to break it down. It is an honorable attempt. But our civilization is nevertheless built on that distinction. In order to break down that distinction utterly, it will be necessary to break down all the codes and restrictions and prejudices that keep women out of the great world. It is in the great world that a man finds his sweetheart, and in that narrow little box outside of the world that he loses her. When she has left that box and gone back into the great world, a citizen and a worker, then with surprise and delight he will discover her again, and never let her go.

A Question of Privilege

If the cult of masculine superiority is to be maintained, there must be some things that women are not allowed to do.

From the Polynesians with their sacred mysteries which women are not permitted to witness, to modern gentlemen in their exclusively masculine clubs, there has always been the instinct to dignify the male sex by forbidding certain of its privileges to women.

Counteracting this instinct is the instinct of comradeship. Man as a comrade of woman violates gleefully the taboos established by man as a male.

As a male, man has reserved for himself the ceremonial vices of drinking and smoking. As a comrade of woman, he finds it fun to initiate her into these mysteries.

A long as men were comrades only with special classes of women, excluding their wives, smoking and drinking tended to be restricted to actresses, dancers, and courtesans. But now their wives have appropriated these habits, partly to the delight and partly to the scandalization of men. There is a lingering resentment at this infringement of a manly custom.

It is the same way with games. There is no reason why women should not have their competitive athletic exercises just like men. They do, and the men let them, expressing their half-conscious resentment only in their patronizing attitude. But they do resent it.

It is the same with clothes. They pass ordinances to keep women off the streets when they venture to wear the new trouser-like skirts. They gather in crowds and hoot at the shameless female who cannot even let a man keep his pants to himself.

Swearing—yes, it is the same way with swearing.

And it is the same way, precisely, with the vote. All the reasons that men give for not wanting women to vote are disingenuous. Their real reason is a deep annoyance at the profanation of a masculine mystery. The vote is all we have left. The women have taken everything else that we could call ours, and now this—it is too much!

"Can't we be allowed to do *anything* by ourselves?"

Why Are Some Men Still Afraid of Feminism?
By Michael Kaufman
Spring 2012

I'm a strong believer that men gain a huge amount from feminism. It's been a theme of my writing and public speaking for thirty years. But, let's face it, you don't make omelets without cracking a few eggs. In this case, the eggs are the forms of power and privilege men have traditionally enjoyed:

• In the past, we men only had to compete with half of humanity for most jobs. Now, we have to compete with all of humanity.

• At night, men got to relax, go out with friends, or pursue our careers, sports, or hobbies while our wives (even if they worked outside the home) did most child care and domestic work. Now, we're expected to do our fare share.

• Some workplaces were straight out of locker rooms. Now, with sexist behavior challenged, for some men, work just isn't as much fun.

• No matter our personal abilities, society automatically valued us. Some religions said we were closer to God. We were automatically seen as stronger, more rational, and leaders.

• In relationships we got cooked for, shopped for, cleaned up after, and emotionally stroked.

• We could (if we so chose) have power in getting sex. Now, we can get put in jail for things that not long ago were seen as men's rights.

• In some families and relationships, we were the ultimate decision-makers. Now, we have to share power and decision-making.

In other words, some men are afraid of feminism because it challenges forms of men's power and privilege that one-half of our species foisted on the other about 8,000 years ago. Giving up is hard to do.

Being a Man is Hard to Do

Here's the strange thing: many men also fear feminism because they fear they're not "real men." I've written a lot about this, what I call "men's contradictory experiences of power." What this means is that the ways we set up our male-dominated societies not only bring men power and privilege but, paradoxically, is the source of pain for men.

One source of this pain is that we set up impossible ideals of manhood. You know: always strong, fearless, in control, etc. Of course no man can live up to these ideals. But so long as we had uncontested male-dominated societies, we could pretend to ourselves and one another that we did. Why? Because we could contrast ourselves to the other half that clearly did not.

Now that women are asserting their strength, power, smarts, and sexuality, now that women are saying that anything a man can do, they can do as well, it takes the wind out of the sails of many men. If deep down they didn't feel like real men before, now those feelings are unconsciously multiplied.

Changing Ideas Is Hard to Do

In spite of amazing changes that are benefitting most women and most men, the ideas associated with male domination still cling hard:

- Religions and traditional beliefs have a life of their own and a deep staying power. Especially in a time of economic, political, and social upheavals when the future seems tenuous, some men (and women) cling to old ideas.

- Old ideas continue to morph and adapt. You might think that right-wingers are against women's equality. But actually, many of their current ideas would have been seen as crazy feminist ideas forty years ago: A woman can be president or prime minister? Women are as smart and capable as men? Women have as much right as men to pursue careers and education? ... In other words, feminism has actually had a big impact even when it seems there is still huge opposition by some men and women to it.

- Parts of the media have continued to do a remarkable hatchet job on feminism. Ask people in many countries about the specific issues associated with gender equality or violence against women. Many (and in some countries, most) will take a feminist stance. But ask if they agree with feminism and they'll bring out their stereotype of who or what a feminist is and say "No!"

Finally, feminist women and profeminist men haven't done a good enough job of transforming the mainstream. If we truly believe our ideas are just and right, then everyone should subscribe to them! We should not be afraid of working in the mainstream. We should not be afraid of differences among us, but rather we should find ways to work with those who we don't see as natural allies, and agree to disagree on specific issues. We should not be afraid to make mistakes or to not be perfect.

A Feminist Wife Embracing Men's Work

By Willow Brocke

Fall 2001

As a feminist, I can talk for hours about the living, breathing reality of women's economic, social, and sexual oppression. However, when I first heard about the men's movement I was highly suspicious. "Why do *they* need a movement?" I thought. "They already own and control everything—what's their problem?" The whole thing smelled of backlash to me.

Then I met my husband and started learning to love a man—close up. Slowly I began to understand what some of the issues might be. I know that as a woman, I will always remain an outsider to the men's movement, and would never attempt to define the nature of men's struggles.

I also know that my husband's struggle to reevaluate what it means to be a man has not been undertaken in a vacuum. When you share the same bed, bathroom, kitchen table, and bank account with someone, you feel the bumps and stretches of their personal growth. I had two choices: resist the changes or grow with him. So, like any normal marriage partner, I did both.

Laundry Rights

I'm sure my early feminist friends would tell me that falling in love with the "enemy" clouds one's political judgment. Perhaps they're right, but when the dating fire died down and we began to have those "future of our relationship" discussions, I'm sure it was the feminist in me who decided she'd better hold on to this one. We were having an argument in my apartment one afternoon when it suddenly dawned on me that during the whole irritated dialogue, he had been washing, drying, and folding my laundry! He wasn't doing it to impress me. In fact he was frustrated as heck with me—he was doing it because it was there.

At that moment, the lightbulb came on over my heart—along with the words: *I can work with this.* The point is that my husband "gets it." He is one of those men who honestly do *half* of the housework and childcare. He is fair; and he's been that way for ten years now. So when he began to challenge me about *my* sexist behavior, I had to admit he had earned the right.

Defensive Driving

"I really hate it when you do that," he said one evening on the way home from a dinner party.

"What?" I asked, already defensive as I pulled out onto the highway.

"Make sweeping generalizations about men."

I rewound the party in my head. "You mean when Larry called the guys downstairs to play pool?"

"Yes," he said. "I heard you say something about 'the boys and their toys,' and then you laughed."

I was caught; it *was* a sweeping generalization. But wasn't it true? Didn't men generally seem to avoid meaningful conversation with one another by distracting themselves with some kind of game, gadget, or activity?

"Why play pool then?" I asked, confident of my observation, "Why not just talk to each other?" This was when he really started to sound exasperated—I realized this was going to be more than a friendly debate.

"If you'd been paying attention," he declared, "you might have noticed that for the hour before we went downstairs we were *trying* to talk—but the women were dominating the conversation. Not just in terms of sheer verbiage but also reinterpreting, redefining, and re-directing what the men said."

"We did not!" I denied. "Give me an example!" I always ask for examples when I know I'm losing an argument.

"Remember when Doug was trying to talk about how much he enjoyed taking his son Jamie on a fishing trip last month?" he asked.

I did. He continued, "Before he could even get the story out, his wife started telling everyone the trip had been a kind of 'initiation' for Jamie?"

"Yeah, so?" I asked defiantly.

"The point," he concluded, "is that this is his wife's interpretation of what was important about the trip. We never got to hear the rest of Doug's story because the women started talking about the whole 'male initiation' thing—Doug gave up."

"Oh," I said, starting to see that he might have a fledgling point. After a couple more equally good examples, I was beginning to understand the retreat to the pool table in a different light and realized why my sweeping generalization had sunk the eight ball on the first shot.

Holding Back the Flood

Over the next few weeks, with my husband's help, I began to see a pattern of interaction I had not been aware of. My words were defining the emotional, moral, and relational aspects of our life together. Words like "appropriate," "assertive," "compassionate," "fair," "compromise," and "consultative" were all helpful terms for negotiating our relationship—but they were all coming out of my mouth—and they were flooding the place.

Why was this happening? It was happening because I was good at it. I'd been practicing since the day I'd read the sign on the kindergarten wall that stated in no uncertain terms that girls were made of "sugar and spice and everything nice."

Before the year was out, my kinder-girl friends and I had already started a club to save the bugs that the "mean" boys had wounded. It was our job to understand how the bugs felt—we were the girls. Practicing the language of emotion, compassion, and connection was not only expected of us, it was our responsibility; we were in training to hold families together. While the boys were doing the bug squashing that was expected of *them*, we were busy squishing our substantial power into the language of relationships.

Apparently, now that kindergarten was over, my husband was trying to let me know that my rapid-fire ability to define and shape our emotional landscape with words was interfering with his ability to define it for himself.

As much as I hated to admit it, if my husband was calling me sexist, it was probably a fair call.

Now For the Hard Part

Nothing is true for everyone all the time. Some women are terrible at expressing their feelings and some men are wonderful at it. However, if there *is* a general pattern of men and women "squishing" our power into gender-acceptable "inner" and "outer" domains—what will help us find a better balance?

It's a tough question. If we want to shift the balance of gender power, not only do men have to loosen their grip on the political and economic world—including definitions of the terms—women have to be willing to loosen our grip on verbally exploring and mapping the emotional landscape between people. How can we do this? Well, these days my husband attends a men's group where he talks about his experiences and builds close relationships—on his own terms. What does he say there? Is he finding the best words? I have no idea. That's why it's so important that he goes—and I don't.

Things are also different at home now. And since my husband and I are both family counselors, we have a habit of offering our experience to others. Here are a few triple-tested suggestions for learning to share the emotional word-space in your relationship.

If you tend to dominate in the emotional arena:

• Ask how your partner is feeling—but don't rush the response. Recognize your partner may need time to "dig down" and find the right words.

• Keep breathing, be patient, and remember how much you love this person.

• Resist all urges to "fill in the blanks" or tell your partner how *you* think they feel, no matter how sure you are of being right.

• When your partner does express feelings, listen to what is *actually said* and "check it out" to see if you got it right. Then be quiet again— there might be more.

• If you're aware that your partner is going through a difficult experience, make sure your partner is talking *to you* about it more than you are talking to your partner about it.

• When taking a walk through the neighborhood after dinner, let there be silence. We all need quiet reflection to allow feelings to surface.

If you are learning to name and express your feelings:

• Ask for the time you need. Try: "I'm not sure how I feel about that—let me think about it and tell you tomorrow." Then make sure you do.

• Choose a good time. No one is a good listener when feeling exhausted or overwhelmed.

• If you notice your partner "feeding" you the words to define your experience, ask him or her to stop. Tell your partner it's important for you to name your own experience, even if it takes a little longer.

• Remember that while anger often feels "less vulnerable" to express, it is only useful for determining what the problem is—never for solving it.

• Be patient with yourself. Many forces have probably conspired to keep you disconnected from your feeling self. Start naming them.

• Look for a group where you can share the truth about your life with other people who struggle with the same issues.

• Question the notion that you shouldn't *need* anyone—it's dangerous to your health, the health of your family, and the health of your community.

Following these suggestions may prove to have a powerful effect on the terms of your relationship. What I notice is that my definitions of relationship issues no longer cancel my husband's out—he's got his own words for what's going on and he's not afraid to use them. You might think this creates more conflict in our relationship but it doesn't.

Just like women who "make it" in business often bring a fresh perspective to the male-dominated world of commerce, men who learn to speak the language of the heart have a lot to teach us about how to love the people we love—without losing ourselves.

Taking the time to listen and value my husband's experience of the relational world has not weakened my perspective as a feminist—only expanded it. I may be a lone voice on the way to the feminist forum, but I suspect that women will never really be free to express their collective power in the world until men are free to express the collective contents of their hearts—and vice versa. So take a load off, feminist sisters. Sharing the power of the emotional domain is a lot like getting help with the dirty laundry—it frees you up to do other things.

An Open Letter to Gentle Men
By Erica Little-Herron
Spring 2007

Dear Gentle Men,

It has come to our attention that you harbor some misconceptions about us and our intentions, ones which we most fervently hope to dissuade you of, because these misunderstandings and falsehoods are preventing us from working together toward a more balanced society. Allow us to reassure you:

1. We do not wish to castrate you. We have no desire to have your testicles in jars of formaldehyde on our nightstands.

2. You may rest easy. We are not asking for a complete role reversal in which we put you in the positions we have occupied these many thousands of years; we do not want to confine you to home, cooking and cleaning, caring for the children, and bringing us a beer while we watch the game after a long, hard day at the Senate. We admit to sometimes having playful revenge fantasies about it, but not really.

3. Some of us are lesbians, but most of us aren't. Many of us are adamantly checking out your hindquarters as you walk by. Most of us can, in fact, "get a man" if we so wish.

4. A lot of us like lipstick and the occasional short skirt. It's just that we don't like to be expected to wear these items.

5. We want you to think we're hot, just as you want us to find you physically attractive; it's fine that you like our breasts. It's just that we want you to realize there is a fully functional brain behind our long-lashed eyes, and a human heart beating beneath those jugs.

6. We like sex. No, really. We do.

7. Most of us appreciate that you've been opening doors for us. That's very nice of you. But (contrary to some of the things we've heard you muttering) that really doesn't make you the gender that is being oppressed and subordinated. We're sorry, but opening an occasional

door or even picking up the tab at Red Lobster does not "even the score," and if you think that it does then you have not been paying attention. For example, we would gladly trade your chivalrous portal-opening skills and the $23.45 you just paid for dinner… for equal wages.

8. We're not blaming you for everything (a good bit of it is our bad), and we don't think we're the only ones suffering from the current state of affairs. For example, we imagine it must suck that if you actually want to stay home with the kids instead of climbing the corporate ladder, then you're labeled a big ol' wuss who's been whipped. We are also aware that since sexism is largely an unconscious social construct, only a very small number of you are ever actually consciously trying to "keep women in their place" and an equally small number of you are even aware that there's a problem to be addressed. But we give you kudos when you are willing to allow yourselves to be made aware of the issue and the proposed solutions to it.

9. The dictionary defines feminism as "the doctrine advocating social, political, and all other rights of women equal to those of men." Feminism does not claim the superiority of women, nor does it involve man-hating. Indeed, it is not even an all-girls club. Chicks dig feminist guys.

10. Actually, we are not particularly angry, and we are not perpetually PMSing. We just want change and we're starting to get impatient about it because it's been a really, really long wait for us.

We cannot achieve equality without you. You are the other half of the equation, the other half of humanity, and we regret to assert that you are the ones in power. With power comes responsibility, responsibility that we are happy to share with you. We hope very much that you will consider dropping the baseless fears some of you hold about us, because we think of you as our allies, not our enemies. Ours is not a "war of the sexes." Ours is a war on sexism. We invite you to enlist.

Much Love,
Feminists

P.S. Please put the toilet seat down. Thank you.

No More Mr. Good Guy
By Tal Peretz
Winter 2010

I like being "the good guy." I really enjoy the appreciation and approval I get from women when I tell them that my chosen life work involves ending sexism. I love the sense of connection I feel when they see me as an ally, a confidant, a guy who "gets it," and I get to feel like we share a very big secret: that there are problems with the way our society's gender rules are set. When I volunteer at a local women's shelter, or march in a protest for women's rights, I like to know that my presence is appreciated. Lately, though, I've been troubled by this feeling, especially because I've noticed that I sometimes get more appreciation than the other people there, and the only explanation I can come up with is that I get unearned kudos because I'm a man.

I've been talking with a lot of men who do antisexist work, sometimes in formal interviews for academic research, sometimes among friends. For me, and many of these men, the reason we are against sexism is, at least in part, because of the harm we've seen sexist oppression do to women. The flip side of this is the unfair privilege granted to men just for being men. I worry that this unearned male privilege is still present when men are in anti-sexist spaces, doing antisexist work. This can create situations where, in the very spaces devised to further the concerns of women, men and their concerns take precedence. To be fully honest and complete in our work against sexism and unfair male privilege, we have to be aware of it within our movement as well, not just in the larger society.

The Pedestal Effect
To maintain awareness of this unearned male privilege and excess appreciation of men doing antisexist work, it helps to have a name and some idea of how it happens. I've taken to calling it "the pedestal effect." As one interviewee said, it's "things like praise for showing up—I didn't necessarily do anything, I think it's just … people are just so pleased to see a man who actually takes an interest, and I can see how that's comforting or refreshing. But a lot of times it's just the fact that I'll put in the hours, and there's other people who do as much as I do … it just seems like I get more than my share for doing my part."

Sometimes the pedestal effect is used to intentionally ensure that men know they are welcome and wanted in spaces where they are the minority, and so I don't want to sound ungrateful. Like I said, I like knowing my presence is appreciated as much as the next person. I just want to make sure that the women doing the same work as I am are getting the same appreciation.

Men working against sexism are, sadly, still rare. A friend who has volunteered at a domestic violence and sexual assault shelter for a number of years put it succinctly: "Most of these organizations don't see many men come through, or even bother caring." Sometimes just this rarity brings special attention, leading to premature self-congratulation, to paraphrase Michael Kimmel. Kimmel also encourages us, correctly in my opinion, to recognize and appreciate that men do take risks and make sacrifices in working toward gender justice. But this means that those men who show up seem exceedingly selfless, perhaps even inherently "special." I've experienced this when someone introduces me and says "He gets it," or "He's one of the good guys." Whereas women working against sexism are seen as working in their own self-interest, any effort men make for women's rights is seen as selfless, and thus more virtuous then the same effort by a woman (even if the person judging is also a woman). This is one reason for the pedestal effect.

A second reason is simply that pervasive male supremacy in the rest of society benefits men so much that it carries over. Men come to this work from a society that has trained them from birth to believe in their own superiority, sometimes subtly and sometimes overtly. Although most men never recognize it as privilege, we are accustomed to being listened to, to people automatically assuming we are capable and competent, to being in control of social situations, etc. The effects of this training don't dissipate automatically, and there are very few opportunities for men to make the sustained, in-depth effort necessary for effective consciousness-raising (and of course, male socialization discourages exactly this sort of talking about emotions, deep issues, and personal pain). So, what can be done about it?

Stepping Off the Pedestal

A few years ago, when we both volunteered at the same shelter, a friend—let's call him Mike—and I were talking. I mentioned that I always felt a little awkward and uncomfortable when the volunteer trainer thanked me for coming—I noticed that she didn't thank anyone else nearly as much. Mike not only confirmed my opinion, he told me that she puts him on the pedestal as well. Having been there longer than me, Mike had developed a strategy for dealing with inflated praise, by saying: "If you need to [thank me], let my mother know. I'm sure she'd appreciate it." I thought this was clever, because it redirects the focus of appreciation and the conversation.

Since then, I've noticed other strategies some men use to reduce the effects of unfair privilege and unequal praise. Some, like Mike, pass along the appreciation to women they see doing the same work as them but getting less praise—their mothers, mentors, or other women in the room working alongside them. Others make an explicit point of frequently referencing and recognizing the contributions women have made to the work they do, and some of the particular women whose footsteps they are following. Perhaps the most important thing is just being aware of male privilege, and checking to make sure it isn't contributing to the creation of a pedestal under you.

Checking to make sure you aren't being unfairly privileged can be awkward. It may even mean intentionally stepping back from rewarding positions that bring recognition if the position came to you due to male privilege. I was recently asked to give a talk for Women's Week at a distant university. The organizers offered to cover my travel expenses, something not out of the ordinary in these situations. I accepted.

As the date approached I got more and more uncomfortable, thinking about the fact that I was invited out there to speak because I am a man. What if some woman hadn't been invited, so they could afford to fly me out there? Or, worse yet, what if women were invited but had to cover their own expenses? It might not be intentional, but the scarcity of male voices speaking on the topic might make my presence seem more valuable, thus garnering me special treatment that I hadn't earned.

I spent the better part of an hour composing a very polite and carefully worded e-mail, asking whether that was the case and informing them that if the budget was tight, I'd rather the money be spent on women presenters. I made clear that I greatly appreciated their offer and would gratefully accept any funds they could make available, as long as I could be assured that I wasn't getting special treatment because of my gender. They wrote back and let me know that that wasn't the case, and that they would still very much like to have me. I felt a lot better about going, knowing that my presence was not taking away from the women who are my allies.

Supporting and building alliances between and with marginalized groups is one of the most important things men can do. Simultaneously, though, we need to be holding each other accountable. We need to create spaces and find ways of supporting, coaching, guiding, and encouraging one another in the tricky and emotionally demanding task of working against our own privilege (like Mike did for me). We need to make sure we are being good people, not just "good guys."

Pop Culture and Pornography
By Gail Dines
Spring 2007

As an antiporn feminist, I have read about our death in porn magazines, in *Cosmopolitan*, and of course in a slew of postmodern academic books and articles. The sheer numbers of people who attended our conference in

Boston on pornography and porn culture make clear that our burial was indeed premature. We are fully alive, energized, enraged at the pornography culture, and ready to do what it takes to reclaim that which is indisputably ours—our lives, our bodies, our culture, and our feminist movement.

The conference, Pornography and Pop Culture, brought together women and men who are activists, antiviolence experts, academics, antiracist educators, students, and citizens who feel in their soul that we are living through a major cultural crisis. Everywhere we go we are bombarded with the droppings of the pornography industry. Our lives are overwhelmed by images that scream misogyny. Turn on the TV, surf the Internet, flip through a magazine, pass a billboard, and you are visually assaulted by images that encode male visual entitlement to technologically perfected female bodies. And then as if this isn't bad enough, we are told that these images represent our sexual freedom, and to be angry or enraged is evidence that we are antisex, prudish, and hopelessly old-fashioned. To that I answer that our rage is clear evidence of our refusal to be colonized or commodified by corporate, patriarchal ideology that is reactionary, antifeminist, and harmful to all our lives.

Some reading these words may have been involved in the feminist antiporn movement back at its inception in the late 1970s. Others may have been in diapers during this period, or not yet born. Whatever our age though, we must remember those incredible activists, authors, and academics who helped build the first antipornography movement. Women like Andrea Dworkin, Catherine Mackinnon, Diana Russell, Robin Morgan, Susan Brownmiller, and many more who worked tirelessly but got little name recognition. Women who made it possible for us today to understand pornography as a form of violence against women that degrades, humiliates, and debases.

Looking back over the last couple of decades since this first feminist antipornography movement, it is clear that we now live in a very different world. We developed theories and activism in a time when most pornography was in magazine form and porn stores and porn theaters were the major distributors of pornography. In those days there was a clear economic and discursive distinction between pornography and pop culture. Today the pornography industry is seamlessly folded into the mainstream pop culture industry. Reputable cable channels such as HBO, Showtime, and MTV often carry shows that look like ads for the porn industry. The men who run the porn industry today have traded in their seedy image and mafia connections for Armani suits and economic connections to international banks and media moguls.

We are indeed now living in a new pornographic age, and to be effective organizers, activists, and scholars, we need to rethink our theories and reframe our activism. These new developments— and the ways in which the feminist insights into pornography as misogynist ideology writ large on the female body—suggest our work is more critical than ever before. The analysis, research, and theory building that we focus on today, we apply tomorrow to activism, as our theory is only as good as our activism and our activism only as meaningful as our theory. Our aim is to interrupt the endless flow of pro-pornography messages that spew out from the pop culture.

Feeling overwhelmed by this pornographic culture is why so many people are taking this issue on. In a pop culture increasingly swamped with pornographic imagery and ideology, to be antipornography is to be an outsider. It means being ridiculed, mocked, and derided both in and out of the academy. And increasingly antipornography feminists are finding the feminist movement to be an inhospitable place.

But feminism has transformed the world more than once with its unapologetic, unflinching politics of radical social change. We are now once more about to begin a new chapter in our ongoing struggle for a world where all of us are bathed in dignity, equality, and joy. As feminists, we should strive for nothing more, and accept nothing less.

Men Celebrating Women's Equality Day
By Rob Okun
Summer 2007

Besides celebrating women's advances, Women's Equality Day—celebrated August 26th each year—offers men a chance to think about we can advance our own lives.

If we're willing to honestly examine our long-held fear of powerful women—and the false notion that we lose some of our power as women gain more of theirs—there's much for men to learn from the day. Not the least of which is a direction for leading rewarding lives, including understanding our inner world more profoundly. In this arena, women have long led the way. If that's a problem for some of us guys, well, it's time for us to get over it. Healthy leadership knows no gender.

Nearly 50 years ago, when women began renewing their demand for self-determination and freedom across the board—including the ongoing process of examining all female roles in society—they uncovered a silver lining of independence from which men can benefit too. But first we have to unflinchingly examine our fears. Many of us have felt confused, unsure, angry, and threatened by the gains women have made. In some households, being supplanted as top wage earner triggered men's insecurity; in others, it was women returning to school to finish a long-delayed degree. Some men feel they're paying a steep price for sharing power: not just losing control but also self-respect.

VOICE MALE

What a set-up. For healthy men, sharing power can have such a healing, eye-opening upside: offering us an opportunity to lighten the load of responsibility so many of us still feel we have to carry.

Danger lurks, though. Many unhealthy men, too shut down to examine their own lives, may cross the line, exhibiting controlling, even abusive behaviors. These behaviors must be confronted. Some believe the advances women have made—increased job and career opportunities, improved wages, better child care—have come at men's expense, as if freedom and independence were finite: "If she has it, then I've lost it," the thinking goes. Truth is, liberation is like love: there's an infinite supply.

Instead of men feeling resentful about the gains women have made, we might study women's accomplishments and apply what we learn to our own lives. For instance, many women have been public about their struggle to balance the world of work and career with that of relationship and child rearing. The public conversation about the "mommy track" may be a difficult one for women, but it reminds women they are not alone.

Sadly, men wrestling with those same issues usually do so in private, too often sitting in silence and isolation. In groups I've facilitated and with individual men I've counseled, I've heard the same refrain: "I was always too ashamed to talk about it." Unsympathetic supervisors have frowned upon, or have been outright hostile to, men who tried to organize their work schedule in order to make the game, the recital, the doctor's appointment. As a result, many spoke about the despair they felt, the lack of support. Some described developing physical conditions that seemed to develop out of their inner condition: high blood pressure, depression, even suicidal thinking.

For many men, the idea that sharing with others the stresses they were carrying could actually play a crucial role in shifting their experience had never occurred to them.

The world inhabited by my three daughters—twenty-nine, twenty-six, and twenty-two—and son, nineteen, has been informed by the struggle for equality women have been waging since before they were born. They've all benefited greatly from their mothers' many fierce acts of independence. That one daughter is in Tibet right now working on a film about Buddhist nuns, that another just completed an emergency medical technician certification training in Montana, and that the third is in North Carolina finishing nursing school speaks volumes about what women can achieve.

Does their younger brother, a college sophomore, feel undermined by their stepping into the big, wide world, arms flung open, reaching for the sky? Hardly. He's inspired. Just as I am. He knows there is room for him to think big, too. He freely acknowledges how his sisters' many trips, when he was in elementary, middle school, and high school to Asia, the Middle East, and Central and Latin America, emboldened him to begin his own international travels.

Like many men, I've backed away from admitting the fear and vulnerability I've sometimes felt navigating my life. Long before I began finding strength and hope, wisdom and love, friendship and healing, in the company of men, I found it with women: women in the antiwar movement in Washington, DC, in the late 1960s; strong leaders in the antinuke movement in the 1970s; proponents of feminist political art in the 1980s. Their uncompromising honesty all contributed significantly to my learning how to open up to myself.

I didn't have the language for it at the time, but women were modeling a kind of courage I was hungry for, going for a full life without limits.

It's fitting that men join a celebration of the 19th Amendment that the suffragist movement left to the world in 1920. While we're celebrating, let's include a generous dollop of hope for what's possible for our sons, too.

So thank you, sisters, for being unwilling to accept the restricted lives patriarchal society imposed on you for so long. Thank you for setting no limits for who you could become. Thank you for articulating the link between the civil rights and the women's rights movements. Thank you for expanding that link to include so many other vital causes—from gay and transgender rights to environmental justice and immigrant solidarity, to name just a few. Thank you for your leadership in the antiwar movement, then and now.

As important as Women's Equality Day is in marking what women have accomplished, there is still a long way to go. Yet as a powerful symbol for men to consider, it raises a question: Can men commit to appreciating women's lives and women's leadership on more than just this one day? Absent our fears, jealousies, and unfulfilled longings for connection, can we unabashedly commemorate this holiday and, in the process, open to our own possibility, our own questions? I hope so. For those of us who can, we will be well on our way to celebrating our own Independence Day.

Dancing to a New Maskulinity

By Lacey Byrne
Summer 2012

It was the divine feminine in the movement that first drew me to ballet. That and the striking costumes and the captivating stories. Of course, as a child, I did not see through the veneer of a woman being lifted high above a man's head, never thought to challenge the patriarchal stories of romance. I grew up wanting to be a ballerina. I wanted to soar through the sky and be spun around endlessly.

When I discovered feminism in college, I came down to earth. I put my love of ballet in the closet since it no longer fit in with my feminist sensibility. I didn't give up on movement though, discovering Modern and African dance, and yoga. Still, whenever I encountered ballet I felt conflicted, suspending my feminist ideals of equality and gendered physical strength to watch women search for true love—witnessing a dramatic display of scorn acted out on the stage.

These days, I am faced again with where to turn when I reach the corner of love of dance and feminism—not far from the busy intersection of femininity, masculinity, and gendered movement. I decided to try and negotiate these windy roads through a new work, *Maskulinty: Unfolding Codes of Gender.* I wanted to bring my feminist beliefs and perspectives—along with my background as a producer, dancer, and choreographer—into the studio, both to look at the mask behind masculinity and, more broadly, to analyze gender and movement.

Contemporary sociology (and women's and men's studies courses at universities and colleges) tells us everything is gendered; sports, music, food, fashion, even colors—not to mention our roles at home and at work. The way women and men walk, sit, stand, and greet one another are all steeped in gender conformity. And yet there are places we can go to ask questions about hips swaying, legs kicking, arms reaching, and who supports who on the dance floor. It's the world of dance.

Maskulinity examines what it means to be a man and how our culture defines manhood, masculinity(ies), and conventional notions of manliness. The performance reflects my interest in using movement to explore the consequences for individual men and women—and the implications for younger people (male, female, transgender)—of unmasking masculinity.

In dance, movement between a male and female dancer begins with audience members presuming a sense of sensuality; it is "normal"—usually seen in the context of a story of heterosexual passion. The same movement, however, executed by two men, is often seen through a gay story line if done rhythmically, or as hetero competition if done aggressively, at a faster tempo.

In rehearsals for *Maskulinity*, when two male dancers move slowly and with passion, I simultaneously found myself feeling uncomfortable and satisfied. I suspect the discomfort comes from my socialization—how I've been trained to think about men being intimate with one another. The discomfort surprised me because I am a passionate supporter of gay rights and believe I have never felt homophobic, intellectually or emotionally. Obviously, though, I am not immune to the culture's messages about men being intimate with one another. Sexualized pop culture rarely shows us two men embracing or, Goddess forbid, dancing together.

As I probe deeper into my feelings, I find myself deriving satisfaction in the knowledge that when we are uncomfortable, society (me included) is taking a giant step forward. (I don't know about you, but I could feel society straining—like children with growing pains—when President Obama and Vice-President Biden made public their support for gay marriage equality.)

The same movement performed between two women makes me uncomfortable in a different way. It is beautiful and sensual, pleasing to the eye, but I struggle not to accept the culture's insistence on sexualizing the interactions of the women. Too often work is produced with men in mind as consumers—*their* fantasies about two women being together. But, if the women's actual sexual orientation is revealed and they are, in fact, lovers, male viewers are angry; the performance is no longer for them.

Despite the stereotype of the dance world being a gay-friendly environment, it isn't immune to homophobia. When boys decide to dance, their peers sometimes ridicule them, label them gay—whether they are or not. Still the dance world is way ahead of much of the rest of the culture in being comfortable with gay people. Among the next steps in ending discrimination against gay people is celebrating, not questioning, boys and men who dance. Now is a perfect moment for proclaiming that dance is actually manly. Society accepts male nurses—as well as female doctors; it's time we stop stigmatizing men who dance.

Who Has the Market on Hips?

Working on *Maskulinity*, I found myself asking the question, "Who has the market on hips?" There is a lot to think about in those two protruding bones that swivel the backside and the pelvis in multiple patterns. Shakira sings that her hips "don't lie," and the late Patrick Swayze's swiveling hips in *Dirty Dancing* are forever imprinted in our collective memory. But what about how women and men swivel? Men tend to thrust hips back and forth, suggesting intercourse. Women usually circulate the hips and tilt the pelvis back, lifting the backside in invitation. In *Maskulinity*, we reversed the roles: inviting the male dancers to swivel their hips and women to thrust theirs back and forth. It was a powerful contradiction of gender stereotypes.

Race and gender intersected in *Maskulinity* through the collaboration between me, a white female, and Ras Mikey C, an African American male and principal choreographer. We approached the social and political markers that serve as the foundation for *Maskulinity* differently. Ras doesn't claim to be a feminist, and that allowed for illuminating debates from our differing perspectives—a real asset to the project. In the research phase of creating *Maskulinity*, we viewed several social issue documentaries produced by Media Education Foundation founder, Sut Jhally, including *Dreamworlds 3: Desire, Sex & Power in Music Video*; *Codes of Gender: Identity and Performance in Popular Culture*; and *Tough Guise: Violence, Media and the Crisis in Masculinity* (featuring the work of Jackson Katz); and Tom Keith's 2011 film

The Bro Code: How Contemporary Cultures Creates Sexist Men; (all films produced and/or distributed by www.mediaed.org.) I paid attention to the objectification of women and the propensity for and the proliferation of violence. Ras approached the stories from the perspective of a dehumanized culture. He was stunned witnessing a cascade of images of sexualized bodies selling entertainment and commercial products, contextualized by voice-over analysis of a society run amok. On a spiritual level, he said, he felt assaulted. Together, we brought our angles and ideas from the screening room to the studio; the dancers could contend with them in rehearsal.

Part of *Maskulinity* involves men competing for the attention of a woman, but it evolves into being more about the men's relationship with one another than about her. Eventually the men become angry by her disinterest in them and they use her body as a way to express their anger—and their aggression toward one another. One of the dancers is the "bystander"— frustrated and helpless, and unable to locate his moral compass, lacking the courage to intervene. The inspiration for the story came from the chapter "Party Rape" in Michael Kimmel's important 2008 book, *Guyland: The Perilous World Where Boys Become Men.*

Without context, the audience would mostly likely believe a romantic connection exists between the man and the woman. But the duet, both moving and passionate, tells a different story. Because it follows a violent depiction, it can be read on a level deeper than heterosexual romance. Perhaps the bystander finally has the courage to act and is personally vindicated; or the male "rescues" the female from the violent act; or we see a striking juxtaposition of tender sensuality between a man and a woman rather than witnessing a woman's body being violently flung around. Ras, who created the duet, and I see it differently. Inspired by the tenderness between the two dancers, he sees a story about healing; I see a man contending with his complicity, powerlessness, and urgency to finally intervene. What will audiences see?

We can't control how audiences will react to *Maskulinity*. As *Voice Male*—and men like Sut Jhally, Jackson Katz, and Michael Kimmel, among others—has been long examining, removing the mask from contemporary masculinity is an ongoing undertaking. By creating a work about masculinity and locating it inside a dance world steeped in femininity, the vignettes about manhood, relationships, and violence, among other topics, hopefully will serve as a springboard for audiences to enlarge their thinking not just about masculinity(ies) but about the pressing issue of gender in contemporary culture. I still may have my childhood yearning to soar through the sky and twirl endlessly, but now I just might want to be the twirler, the one to lift a man high above my head.

Beyond South Dakota: Time for Men to Champion Reproductive Rights

By Rob Okun
Winter 2007

"I have a son, eighteen, and three daughters, all in their twenties. Imagine if even *one* parent in South Dakota had a daughter who'd been raped and became pregnant. Must that family follow a state law that *forbade* the young woman from aborting the rapist's child? That *compelled* her to bear her assailant's baby as the state's way of responding to her assault? That was a law I knew I had to challenge."

I shared those sentiments, if not those exact words, numerous times last fall on the front steps of South Dakotans' homes, where I spent several days before the November midterm elections. I was one of the hundreds of activist-volunteers criss-crossing the state, working to overturn the most restrictive abortion ban in the nation. Happily, "our side" won—55 percent to 45 percent. Even in a conservative, antichoice state, South Dakota voters decided "enough is enough."

Now the celebrations are over and much work remains, in South Dakota and beyond. Those who favor upholding the protections the Supreme Court afforded women in *Roe v. Wade* nearly three and a half decades ago would be well advised to pay close attention to the strategic and well-organized state-by-state battle currently being waged to restrict women's reproductive rights and freedoms. The campaign is being coordinated and financed by a coalition of far-right political and religious institutions with close ties to the Republican Party and the Bush administration. To thwart the opposition's efforts—currently being organized in a dozen states—many organizers are considering ways to better engage men in the struggle.

Beyond the size of the victory, what was heartening about it was the energy the scores of volunteers from around the country brought to the Campaign for Healthy Families, the statewide organizers. Arriving by plane, bus, van, and car, volunteers fanned out across key South Dakota cities and towns to help get out the vote to repeal the law. College students—many able to attend thanks to the generosity of the American Civil Liberties Union—outnumbered middle-aged veteran activists, but everyone felt a spirit of enthusiasm and energy. Savvy, gritty, native South Dakotan men and women in their late twenties and early thirties were in key leadership positions, orienting out-of-state volunteers to the conservative political opinions of many of the state's residents while underscoring that those very residents also had a strong aversion to governmental meddling in their personal lives.

On my first day, another volunteer and I hopped into one of a legion of rental cars organizers provided and split up to canvas a well-to-do neighborhood in Sioux Falls, the state's largest city (pop. 130,000). We had lists of houses to visit, urging residents to vote to repeal the ban the Republican-controlled state legislature had passed last winter and Republican governor Mike Rounds had signed into law in March. Proponents of the law's signs outnumbered opponents by four or five to one, I estimated, raising concerns about our chances for success. I soon learned why the final vote and the public show of support would be so out of alignment. I spoke with a doctor in his fifties, an arthritis specialist, who was initially wary when he opened his wide, ornate front door. After determining which side I represented, he shared some disturbing observations: he was afraid to display a lawn sign announcing his opposition to the restrictive abortion law—his neighbors would do more than ostracize him, he said; he feared they would threaten him personally or vandalize his property. From the pulpit of his church, he said, he was being told to vote to uphold the ban; leaflets were handed out *in church,* he went on, *and* were being mailed from the church through the US Postal Service (all violations of the law). He said he felt afraid to complain since he couldn't be assured of his anonymity. He felt encouraged, he said, that the Campaign for Healthy Families had people out canvassing, but then stopped short; we'd spoken long enough. He didn't want to draw any undo attention from his neighbors for chatting too long.

A couple of days later I was walking through neighborhoods in Watertown, about 100 miles from Sioux Falls. It was late afternoon, I'd been out for more than four hours, the temperature was dropping; I was tired. A man who resembled a scary character from a children's story—wart on a knobby, misshapen nose, shiny bald head, dark hair sprouting from large ears, lines creasing his forehead—opened the door to his brick corner house. I was wearing a colorful Campaign for Healthy Families T-shirt that made plain where I stood on the state's abortion ban. I felt tense as he sized me up, reading the T-shirt, studying my face. *Should I turn on my heel before he blasts me?* I asked myself. Before I could answer my own question, he thrust out a calloused, meaty hand and began pumping mine up and down. Parting his lips wide to reveal a mouthful of misshapen teeth, he gripped my hand even tighter, leaned into my face, and bellowed, *"I'M WITH YA!! I'M WITH YA!!"* I jumped back and would have lost my balance had he not been squeezing my hand so tightly. Before I could fully recover he let go, gave me thumbs-up and said, "Good for you."

In Madison, a day later, a woman in her thirties was chatting with a neighbor, leaning against an old sedan, smoking. She was on the other side of the debate and wanted me to know I was in the wrong. Even though we had been advised not to debate those whose votes we were unlikely to receive, it was difficult not to hear her out, or to share a thought or two of my own. Had she considered, I asked in a quiet voice, the psychological and emotional ramifications for a teenage girl who became pregnant after being the victim of incest from a relative (in addition to rape, there was no exception in the law for incest or the physical health of the mother). "God will take care of her" was her simple reply. "God will give her whatever strength she needs to bear the baby and to love the child." While some young women might be able to do so, I allowed, what about those whose emotional or physical states were too fragile? "The Lord will take care of everything, and everyone," she answered, extinguishing her cigarette in the driveway by the old car. Case closed. I knew it was time to move on.

The journey the other volunteers and I took into the heartland of our country underscored the deep divisions that exist in the United States, but also connected a network of allies ready to expand the movement for reproductive justice. I was impressed that among the South Dakotan volunteers—and staff—were a number of younger men. Men who shared with me how their parents had impressed upon them the importance of responsible sexual behavior and, in some cases, had imbued in them a genuine concern for the cause of reproductive rights. I was grateful for these conversations and felt encouraged by them.

Tired and hungry after a weekend of canvassing, 120 of us crammed into one of the Campaign for Healthy Families offices for hot food and a debriefing. In the past two days, organizers told us, we had collectively visited nearly 14,000 households! A roar of astonished approval rang out; people put down their food to whoop and cheer. We felt a kinship in that moment, a shared sense of accomplishment. We felt what we had done had really mattered.

The South Dakota abortion rights story is just one of many human rights stories I hope more men will pay attention to. Abortion is a highly personal decision that women must freely make, without governmental interference. Still, men's voices—as allies, as partners, as brothers, as fathers—can be a great asset in the chorus of support.

Back home I felt buoyed, witnessing men's capacity to do the right thing, especially when the stakes are high. For the daughters of South Dakota, the stakes couldn't be higher. In the days ahead, when similar abortion bans in Arkansas, Mississippi, Ohio, and elsewhere are being debated, men will have increased opportunities to engage in the conversation. Will we see a growing number who feel the same way as the men who volunteered in South Dakota? Men in other states across the country—fathers and sons, brothers and uncles, cousins and neighbors— have an opportunity to stand up, not just for their own wives, partners, and daughters, but for all women and girls. If they do, it will demonstrate a kind of courage that until now only a small number of men have offered to women: that the reproductive rights movement is our movement, too.

VOICE MALE

Canadian Feminists' Uneasy Alliance with Men Challenging Violence
By Michele Landsberg
Spring 2000

The chandeliers glitter, the silver coffee pots sparkle, the ice tinkles musically in the goblets, and the Royal York's Canadian ballroom is packed as the good people tuck into pancakes and scrambled eggs—and all this in the name of men striving to end male violence against women.

It would have been unimaginable nine years ago, when a few stalwarts braved the suspicion of feminists and the sneers of macho guys to begin the White Ribbon campaign against male violence. Indeed, attendance at Toronto's White Ribbon breakfast last Thursday vaulted in one year from 300 people to an impressive 1,100. The occasion was upbeat. Toronto mayor Mel Lastman jovially proclaimed November 25 to December 6, 1999, as official White Ribbon Days. Noeleen Heyzer, director of UNIFEM, the United Nations women's agency, came from New York to deliver an affecting keynote speech, praising the history of women's activism, saluting the men for their efforts, and declaring that day—November 25—as the first UN International Day to End Violence Against Women and Girls.

Most poignant was Therese Daviau, mother of one of the young women slain ten years ago at Montréal's École Polytechnique, who implored the audience to educate their children against violence, and said, "Our girls must not have died for nothing."

The coffee came around again. Jack Layton, cochair of the White Ribbon Campaign, reminded us that every man who pins on a white ribbon is pledging "never to commit, condone, or remain silent about violence against women."

All the money raised at the breakfast goes to local front-line agencies: Toronto Rape Crisis Centre, Assaulted Women's Helpline, Education Wife Assault, the December 6 Fund, Family Abuse Crisis Exchange, Dressing for Success, Native Women's Resource Centre, Woman Abuse Council of Toronto, and Riverdale Immigrant Women's Centre.

And White Ribbon suffers no shortage of money. Of its $250,000 annual budget, it gives $50,000 a year to the Canadian Women's Foundation. White Ribbon has a downtown office, four full-time staff members, and a new education bureau to distribute an anti-violence education kit to thousands of schools. Shoppers Drug Mart celebrated the breakfast by presenting a check for $20,000. Without a doubt, White Ribbon is one of the more dramatically successful advocacy campaigns on "women's issues" that I've ever seen.

Men and Feminism

So. . . with all this goodwill flowing, why did so many feminists in the crowd choke a little on their pancakes? What made so many of the front-line women from agencies that will benefit from White Ribbon's largesse feel guiltily, just a little, furtively, as though they'd like to—well, not exactly bite—but maybe just take one small nip at the hand that feeds them?

These are, after all, the allies that women have needed. We know that all the defiant Take Back the Night marches or candlelight vigils in the world will not actually stop rape, battering, or murder. Every shelter worker, rape counselor, and worn-out female fundraiser in that ballroom had to feel intense relief that these men were taking up the battle.

Relief, too, that these guys got the message and were ready to acknowledge and share with the sisters in the cause.

So why that little edge of unease?

I can answer that question. Gazing around the ballroom, listening to the news that White Ribbon groups have sprung up on every continent, I was stunned by the sheer, graceful, effortless display of male power. In 25 years of the women's movement, not a single antiviolence women's organization could ever have filled a ballroom with so much money and influence. Education Wife Assault, for example, has worked tirelessly for two decades, in a church basement, with just $70,000 in core funding from the United Way—and it probably could have slaved away for another 20 years without getting so much as a sandwich lunch from corporate coffers.

Corporations don't give to feminists; they give to guys. White Ribbon's success, in fact, is built on the same male entitlement and pride of place that makes lesser men think they have a right to pound out their fury on their wife's body, the same male privilege that lets men rape their date and get away with claiming it was "consensual."

What's wonderful is that, at long last, so many men are trying to use that male privilege positively, to stop the steady, underlying thrum of aggression and brutality.

Oh sure, I know that some men who pin on a White Ribbon are reluctant to confront even minor abuses of male power. They wouldn't dream of challenging a buddy's sexist joke or speaking up against a harassing colleague.

Still, in the history of the world, it's a minor miracle that a group entitled to power would take the radical step of beginning to shift the balance. Feminists are grateful. A little grumpy, but grateful, and intensely glad to have some brotherly help in changing the world.

VOICE MALE

Desire
By George Bilgere
Summer 2012

The slim, suntanned legs
of the woman in front of me in the checkout line
fill me with yearning
to provide her with health insurance
and a sporty little car with personalized plates.

The way her dark hair falls
straight to her slender waist
makes me ache
to pay for a washer/dryer combo
and yearly ski trips to Aspen, not to mention
her weekly visits to the spa
and nail salon.

And the delicate rise of her breasts
under her thin blouse
kindles my desire
to purchase a blue minivan with a car seat,
and soon another car seat, and eventually
piano lessons and braces
for two teenage girls who will hate me.

Finally, her full, pouting lips
make me long to take out a second mortgage
in order to put both kids through college
at first- or second-tier institutions,
then cover their wedding expenses
and help out financially with the grandchildren
as generously as possible before I die
and leave them everything.

But now the cashier rings her up
and she walks out of my life forever,
leaving me alone
with my beer and toilet paper and frozen pizzas.

Men and Feminism

A Feminist Responds to Desire
By Maia Mares
Summer 2012

Reading George Bilgere's poem set the feminist neurons in my brain firing. Something about it didn't sit right with me. Perhaps it was the theme of man-as-provider with its explicit descriptions of what he'd "pay" for, what he'd "purchase" for her. The narrator expresses dedication to the family he dreams of, surprising me by tempering his objectification of the woman's body with a longing for the domestic. Like many lonely, single men, he is not able to access whatever emotional ties he might feel for his children or wife and cannot envision himself explicitly saying how much he cares. Instead, he hides behind his material and financial contributions to their welfare.

Though the sight of the woman's legs arouses a refreshing fantasy of family, not sex, it's the poem's representation of the woman that's troubling. Her "slender" and "delicate" body, along with her "straight" hair, call up an image of the tired-out beauty ideal of a thin white woman dominant for far too long. (Not to say thin white women cannot be beautiful—they are—but by repetitively equating a single body type with what constitutes beauty and perfection deprives readers of a rainbow of other possibilities.)

Despite the narrator's descriptions of old-school domestic femininity and gender roles, I found myself empathizing with him, glimpsing a snapshot of his interior life. He appears to be a man whose own conceptions of his masculinity are in transition. Even as he objectifies her, his desire seems to suggest a steering away from traditional masculinity. One day, perhaps, he'll be able to leave his lonely life of beer and frozen pizza and cocreate with a partner a life that's rich, whole, and equal.

The Egalitarian Dialogues
By Rob Okun
Spring 2004

Will men ever recognize that the days of trying to limit women's freedom of expression are over? Those thoughts were on my mind after I learned that an Amherst, Massachusetts, businessman had spearheaded a drive to try and stop female students from performing *The Vagina Monologues* at the town's high school the night before Valentine's Day.

But those supporting both women's empowerment and men redefining masculinity owe the play's critic a thank-you for illuminating the need to bring more men into the crucial conversation about women's truth. Eve

Ensler's provocative play is certainly about women's lives. But it's also about men waking up to women's reality.

The businessman, Larry Kelley, said he was uncomfortable with the "C-word"—"I can't say it out loud," he told a meeting of the school committee. His queasiness symbolizes many men's discomfort with admitting how little we know about the dangerous world our mothers and daughters, wives and partners, sisters and nieces live in: a world where sexual harassment and sexual assault are commonplace. A world where personal security means checking the backseat of your car before getting in it. A world where going out at night means carrying a whistle, or a can of Mace. A world most men, myself included, find it hard to personally feel. It's not easy for men to acknowledge how widespread violence against women is, nor how much further we have to go to create a safe, egalitarian society. Hardest of all is to admit that getting there means giving up some of the privilege we enjoy.

Kelly grabbed a few headlines nationally with his complaint, alleging that *The Vagina Monologues* is inappropriate for high school students. He neglected to say student attendance was voluntary, that the evening performance was scheduled when school had recessed for vacation, and that the play culminated a week of in-school workshops (also voluntary) spotlighting issues the play raises, namely: promoting greater awareness of, and actions to prevent, violence against women.

It is understandable that men feel vulnerable and confused about male and female roles nowadays. And it's natural that some of us are going to stumble crossing this new, unfamiliar landscape. I certainly have. But such vulnerability is no excuse for trying to censor women, including female students willing to meet life's challenges head-on—even if those challenges are appearing years earlier than either they or the adults in their lives would like.

Given the highly sexualized nature of so much of popular culture—from song lyrics to computer games, from MTV to Hollywood—that *The Vagina Monologues* was performed at a high school was a refreshing educational strategy.

Males owe a debt of gratitude to brave young women like those who discovered in *The Vagina Monologues* an artistic and educational forum to draw attention to women's plight. Perhaps the support the young women showed one another will inspire their male counterparts to find their own collective voice to challenge the box of conventional masculinity most of us are trapped in. As the father of a son at the high school under discussion, I hope so.

I'm glad my son and his peers could discuss such sensitive issues at school-sponsored workshops. Those gatherings served as antidotes to the nonstop misogynist assault pop culture directs at all of us, particularly the young. Still, like a growing number of men worldwide, I know we must redouble our efforts. For women's sake. For men's sake. For our children's sake. I hope the day is coming where men will leave the cast of *The Patriarchy Monologues* to instead join women and men in an ensemble production called *The Egalitarian Dialogues*. There's a play whose script is still being written.

What Do Women Have to Do With Men's Healing? A Lot
By Rus Ervin Funk and Lundy Bancroft
Summer 2012

There is frequent discussion, at times an open debate, as to the role of women in men's healing. Many men regularly make the argument that men need and deserve healing time and that this healing requires men to be in male-only spaces. (A number of men's organizations subscribe to the belief that it is only in male-only spaces that we, as men, can be "one hundred percent honest and take the risks we need to take to in order to heal ourselves and each other.")

Like most men, we agree that men focusing on our own healing is an essential element of our own liberation and well being. However, we take strong offense to the notion that women can't be, shouldn't be, or are somehow detrimental to men's healing efforts. What follows is our response to some of the more common arguments to men's healing in men-only spaces.

What man wouldn't agree that it is valuable for men to focus on our own healing? Yet it doesn't necessarily follow that men can only heal in male-only spaces. To us, such a notion is erroneous at best, and dangerous at worst—for both men and women. Both women and men have strong and powerful relationships with one another. Most men need, deserve, and experience relationships with both women *and* men to best heal from our wounds.

Male-space-only arguments often contain elements that suggest that men not only know better than women what is best for men but also what is best for women. Within these arguments often are statements of how women need men to go and heal ourselves—"It is better for women if men are healthy and in touch with a healthy masculinity" is an example of the kinds of arguments used to encourage women to support men taking part in healing circles or related activities. Of course we agree that women benefit from men who are healthy. Still, what healthy man would consciously choose *not* to take advantage of women's voices and women's perspectives? Men defining healthy manhood in isolation from women reinforces the gender binary that is actually healthy for no one. Indeed, it can lead to some pretty awful outcomes for both men and women.

We support developing a healthy *humanity* more than narrow gender definitions. A healthy humanity involves all of us having more access to connect with and express all of our qualities—those labeled "masculine" and those described as "feminine." Doing so, it seems to us, means having women and men (and trans folks for that matter) actively involved in all aspects of our lives to provide us examples and support for accessing and expressing those qualities which we have difficulty accessing and expressing. As such, men being in male-only spaces for small periods of time really only makes sense if it is balanced with men being in all or mostly women spaces as well.

We wonder if those who support male-only healing space would argue the same, say, for white only healing spaces with a parallel lack of transparency and accountability. The same arguments could easily be said about white people—that we, as white folks, need to heal from the harms we've experienced by being white and take full responsibility for our whiteness and become healthier white people. Having white people gather together in white-only spaces to achieve these goals has traditionally and consistently resulted in much different outcomes.

Women have long been subjected to core sexist beliefs held by men: that women are filled with irrational fears; that they do not know what is best for them; and that they don't recognize when men are actually acting in women's best interests. These same arguments are often used when women raise concerns or express some critical perspective of men's healing circles, activities, or efforts.

There Are Good Reasons for Women to Question Some Men's Healing Work

Many women—and some men—are suspicious of men's claims that when we spend time by ourselves freeing ourselves from the straitjacket of traditional masculinity, women always benefit. In our decades of antiviolence men's work, we have heard from many women who recounted experiences of their male partners' involvement in the "male liberation" movement. Some recurring themes include:

> • His participation in men's weekends—or other personal growth activities—often leaves her burdened with family responsibilities, including caring for small children. If she questions him about his plans, some men irritably respond, "You want me to be more the kind of man you are looking for, so why are you complaining when I try to work on myself?!" In that act, her feelings and needs are discounted.

> • His process of becoming more aware of and "in touch with his feelings"—along with developing a better understanding of a "deeper masculinity" and an increased sense of bonding and connection with other men—doesn't necessarily result in his treating her any better than he did before, for example, being more patient, respectful, caring, understanding, empathic.

• His bonding with other men, sometimes through gripe sessions about women (including the complaint that women don't really understand "men's healing work") results in men being more impatient with women's questions about what they are doing. He may be gaining "evidence" for his point of view—blaming his partner in particular—and women in general—for his unhappiness.

• Men don't get to tell women what is in their best interests; only women get to decide that. And, if women are expressing mistrust about the process at some men's retreats, then it is our responsibility as male allies to look closely at the source of that mistrust rather than (re)actively dismiss it. Doing so would be much more productive than disparaging women—at times openly—for their concerns.

• The fact that there are many men who argue in support of male-only healing efforts (even in the face of women's criticism), offers strong evidence for why women have good reason to doubt that men's personal liberation work includes—as part of men's healing—facing, challenging, and changing belittling attitudes toward women.

Consider another assertion we have heard, which goes something like this:

A wise woman always understands when a man needs to get out of the house to spend time with other men. He may be acting uptight with her and the kids or he's stopped listening or worse, he's begun to be aggressive. When that's happening, a wise woman will strongly urge her man to "take space" then and there.

This statement suggests that when men behave badly it is *women's* responsibility to figure out what he needs and urge him to get the support he deserves. Where is the equality in that? Such a standard is one of the pillars of sexism—that women should cast aside their needs and put men's needs first.

Here's another approach: If a man is getting short with his partner and his kids, and has stopped listening, he needs to first and foremost take responsibility for his behavior and start paying attention. Second, he needs people in his life challenging him to respect women and children *and* to treat them kindly. And, if he's beginning to "act out aggressively," what he could probably best benefit from, according to research, is at the very least counseling from a practitioner experienced working with men acting abusively, or, if called for, to be removed from the house. Some have argued that a "healing response" from the person to whom he acted aggressively/threateningly toward would be for him to "take space." That strikes us as rewarding his aggressive behavior by sending him off (maybe to spend time with other men) rather than being held accountable for his behavior. Among the results are leaving his wife to bear the consequences of his absence. How liberating is that—and where is the equality in it—when women are left to do all the childcare and housework while men are off thinking deep thoughts? Don't get us wrong. We applaud and encourage men to look deeply inside; we just won't endorse doing so at the expense of women's capacity to live fully emancipated and safe lives.

There are men in favor of male-only healing who suggest most women believe that, "If it's good for men, it must be bad for women." Most men who have worked alongside women understand that often women *do* have concerns about men's undertakings. Still, overwhelmingly they support our endeavors to be good to ourselves, just as long as it's not at the expense of them or children. Historically, it is men who have considered the advances women have made as having negative consequences for men. Imagine this argument coming from a white person explaining the mistakes people of color are making in failing to trust white people; or if a straight person wrote about the supposed thinking errors of gay men and lesbians—such arguments would rightly be considered highly offensive. We don't see any difference when men are the objectifiers and women are the objects.

One critical aspect of men's healing must include preparing men to become more involved in their communities, more active as mentors and supporters of younger men and/or women, more engaged in combating violence against women, and/or other forms of oppression. We can best integrate men's healing with developing men as allies with women and girls in the healing of our communities and world. Men's healing, in and of itself, is not enough; it needs to be part of a greater mosaic of *everyone's* healing.

A significant part of men's healing involves learning how to support and be true partners with women—as well as compassionate mentors to girls—while also working for a world promoting justice and respect. Studies suggest that men who live in environments of relative gender equality have much better health and better relationships (among a range of other outcomes) than do men who live in environments of gender inequality. What that suggests to us is that, rather than going off by ourselves to heal in the absence of women, men actually may be better served by working—and healing—alongside women while working to create a world that respects and values everyone.

Another common argument is that men need to be taught by other men how to be men. Lacking any clarification, that contention suggests that single women raising sons cannot succeed, are ineffective, or worse. Countless women, particularly African Americans, would question such a position, as would the many men who have had highly successful lives that they attribute to their mothers' guidance and leadership (again, African American men in particular). Our own lived experiences as men, supported by a wide range of readily available evidence, suggest that when men are taught to be men in the absence of women, men are more unhealthy, and women, children, and communities suffer.

Of course men can and do provide good guidance to other men—compassionate, caring, challenging—and such guidance certainly is an important contributor to our well being. But the ability to listen well to women, to learn from them, and to take guidance from women in forming our identities, is every bit as important. We believe the survival of the planet depends on men's efforts at listening to women.

Building Successful Alliances

We each have been involved in the struggle for gender justice for more than thirty years. During the early years of our involvement, there was widespread mistrust of males who presented themselves as women's allies. Some men chose to disparage women for not welcoming men. Others of us chose to respect women's concerns and listen carefully to their experiences. And what they described to us was multiple experiences of having been betrayed by men who claimed to be profeminist allies. Some, they reported, disparaged women's opinions, pressured them for dates, or advised battered women that the man they were with was really serious about changing and that she should give him another chance. In a few cases we learned of men in the movement who were perpetrating physical or sexual violence against women. By taking the women's sources of mistrust seriously, we were able to work on developing systems of accountability for men, making it harder for men who were not genuine allies to hide out. The result? Men are increasingly welcomed as allies in the struggle to end violence against women, and the level of mistrust is far lower. Still, women do get burned sometimes.

The lesson, then, is that women will trust us when we prove ourselves trustworthy. And so far there are a lot of women who have concluded that many men in the "male healing work movement" haven't yet earned their trust. One choice is to blame women for not trusting the movement. An alternative we hope men will choose—in the name of solidarity with women in their battle for liberation—is to make the changes we need to make in order to deserve women's trust.

A Guy's Guide to Becoming a Profeminist Ally
By Maia Mares
Summer 2012

As coleader of the feminist group on my college campus, I'm always initially skeptical of men who approach us as allies and identify as feminists. I don't feel this way because I hate men; on the contrary, some of the people I love most in my life are men. Neither do I believe that men can't do feminist work or be effective profeminist allies to the movement. It's just that the pattern so far has been that very few male allies have impressed me, and very many male allies have disappointed me.

But I'm not ready to give up on men, especially not after my three months as an intern at *Voice Male*. Reading the words of more than a hundred profeminist men—as well as working with many others—has made me reevaluate the ways I think men can be profeminist. My experience at *Voice Male* has also helped me develop my own set of suggestions for men embarking on profeminist personal development and social justice work.

I remember the start of my own process of becoming a feminist and the harsh realities it forced me to face. Indeed, being a feminist continues to challenge me as an advocate for social justice and as a human being. It's hard work and there's a lot to understand. Being a feminist sometimes makes me feel like crap; it's not all sisterhood and womanly bonding and solidarity. Feminist theory constantly seems to be blowing apart everything I think I know and makes me question whether I can even know anything at all. Confronting my own privileges as a white, educated, middle-class, able-bodied, cisgender woman often makes me feel highly uncomfortable, frustrated, guilty, and disappointed in myself.

My point is that being a feminist isn't easy, not even for women. It isn't a label you can simply affix to yourself on a whim. First, there's the movement's history to be grappled with. Identifying as a feminist requires a certain amount of privilege and thus comes with a lot of responsibility to acknowledge that privilege and to do your best to undo the very systems of inequality that grant you it. As a man, it is likely you may have more privilege than most feminist women. It is also possible that on some axes, certain feminist women may have more privilege than you do, but that does not mean that you are not still privileged as a man in a system that largely benefits men. You can be privileged in one way and underprivileged in another. Understanding the complexities of oppression and how different oppressions intersect is key to being a feminist or a profeminist. And yes, that can be very difficult to navigate.

So what do I think men can do to be effective profeminist allies? I don't profess to have all the answers, but I do have some tips for men who wish to be pro-feminist allies on a college campus.

> • **Listen and collaborate.** *Really* listen. I mean, sit down, be quiet, and just listen. It may sound harsh, but feminist spaces often function as safe spaces, and a man intruding into that space can cause discomfort or even destroy the feeling of safety altogether. Understand this possibility and make an effort to cause as little disruption as possible. If you're attending a meeting of a feminist club

or discussion group, ask the members beforehand if it is okay for you to be there. If they say yes, ask what you can do to make your presence as discreet as possible. It may be uncomfortable at first, but the more you listen, the more you learn. The only way to be an effective feminist or profeminist ally is to listen to the people you want to help and help them however they ask you to help. It is not okay for you to come into a feminist space having previously decided exactly what you are going to do to help. Trust the women you are working with to know what they need from you. Ask them directly what you can do and listen to what they say. This goes for men's profeminist groups as well. Work together with women; they know what's up.

• **Don't derail discussions.** Derailing can happen in several different ways, but the most common that I have experienced are 1) moving the focus away from women (usually to men) and 2) asking for explanations of very basic feminist concepts. Switching the focus back to men is frustrating because one of the very basic tenets of feminism is the idea that women's experiences should be brought to the fore, since they rarely are in any other spheres. While many feminist issues can and do involve men, before you bring up men or men's experiences, consider whether you might end up removing the focus of the discussion from women. Ask yourself whether this is an appropriate time to switch the focus. What is the purpose of the discussion? What would the discussion gain from your comment? What would it lose?

The second way derailing often occurs is when men who wish to be allies do not have a sufficient understanding of basic tenets of feminism and end up interrupting and sidetracking a discussion by asking about very basic ideas. Do some research beforehand. Google "Feminism 101" and do some reading. Feminist women will often be more than willing to help you understand something if you ask for help in a tactful and respectful way, but when you ask for help in the middle of a discussion that clearly hopes to advance past feminist basics, you are interrupting and focusing the discussion on you, as well as expecting that the women around you should drop what they are doing and instead devote their time to educating you right then and there. Instead, if there is something you do not understand, ask someone. If it is not possible to ask during the discussion, wait until the discussion is over. Ask if there are any resources available to help you understand. Most feminists would be happy to point you toward a book, website, or blog that contains the information you need. (If you don't subscribe to *Voice Male*, consider taking out a subscription and using it as the basis of a men's discussion group.)

• **Debate respectfully**. Realize that women are authorities on their own experiences and do not appreciate you telling them that you know better. If a woman says she experienced a sexist event in a certain way and you contradict her, you are in effect telling her she is not the authority on her own life and experience. If she is willing to answer questions, feel free to ask, but don't disrespect her by telling her you know better. Always entertain the idea that you may be wrong. Furthermore, recognize that many feminist issues hit home pretty hard for many women. These aren't abstract concepts that we discuss for fun. Rape, domestic violence, catcalling and street harassment, wage gaps, lack of day care, and other institutionalized support for parenting, housework, the pressure of beauty standards—from major to minor, these issues can and do make women's lives miserable, or at the very least difficult. Understand that these are not abstractions. These are not lofty philosophical ideas that you can debate without getting personal or emotional. When you debate feminist issues, you are debating the substance of women's lives. Doing so requires respect, sensitivity, and consideration. If a woman is getting angry or upset, by all means, let her feel those emotions. Do not tell her she is crazy or irrational, and above all do not ask if she is PMSing. Understand that women's emotions are justified. Instead of blaming her for feeling the way she feels, reflect on the tone and content of the discussion and ask yourself what it was that could have upset her. Was it something you said? Was it how you said something? Could the discussion have touched upon something highly personal for her? Think about it. If an apology is required, apologize promptly and sincerely.

• **Step up and step back**. This is a phrase I first heard within the environmental movement and I think it applies to all social justice work. Learn to balance. Learn when it is appropriate to take the lead and when to follow. Learn when to take the initiative and when to simply do what is asked of you and no more. Communicate. Ask the women you are working with about what you should be doing. Striking the right balance between stepping up and stepping back takes practice. Eventually, you will get a feel for it, though you should always ask yourself and those you're working with if what you're doing is appropriate and helpful.

It's difficult to be either a feminist or a profeminist ally, and if you feel discouraged sometimes, you're not alone. A lot of what's necessary comes with practice and you *will* mess up. We all mess up, but when we do, we need to take responsibility for our mistakes, apologize without making excuses, and do our best to make amends. But difficulty should not turn you away from working toward equality on all axes. It's important work, and we're up against some seriously nefarious social forces. But it's not all doom and gloom either. I personally find immense comfort in the fact that working toward gender justice (and, more broadly, social justice) can lead to a better world for people regardless of gender. It sounds idealistic and a bit cheesy, but that certainty keeps me dedicated to and passionate about social justice. We're dealing with issues that can make or break a person's quality of life, if not his or her life itself, and that makes this work vitally important.

Reports of the Demise of Feminism Are Premature
By Rob Okun
Fall 2013

> *I don't know why people are so reluctant to say they're feminists. Maybe some women just don't care. But how could it be any more obvious that we still live in a patriarchal world when feminism is a bad word?*
>
> —Ellen Page, actor

> *If the word 'feminist' has negative connotations, running away from the word won't fix that. Whatever new word you come up with will eventually take on the same negative connotations. Because the problem isn't with feminists; it's with those who demonize feminism.*
>
> —Rebecca Cohen, cartoonist

With such an onslaught of pressing issues facing those concerned about gender justice today (for starters consider the recent actions to severely restrict women's reproductive rights by the legislatures in the US states of North Carolina, Ohio, and Texas, and by Clear Channel in Kansas), the current debate about whether it's still appropriate to call oneself a "feminist"—or a "profeminist"—seems to me to be a huge, politically divisive distraction.

In our 24/7/365 online culture there's a tendency to overlook history, if not an outright attempt by some to rewrite it. The current debate about the usefulness of the word centers around concerns that feminism has been poorly "branded," including having been irreparably smeared by conservative commentators. (What else is new? The effectiveness of a movement can in part be judged by the actions of those trying to squelch it.) It is disconcerting to think some would abandon the word at a moment when rape, both in military and civilian culture, the sex-trafficking pandemic, and the mainstream "pornification" of sexuality are such an ongoing threat. If ever there was a time calling for an explicitly feminist response, it is now.

The fact that some longtime proponents of the ideas embodied in feminism are now shying away from identifying themselves as actual "feminists" is disappointing and contributes, perhaps inadvertently, to erasing the history of the feminist movement (including men's supportive role in it)—a history that stretches at least as far back as the struggle for suffrage. For someone to proclaim to be articulating a vision of "gender equality" (the term some prefer), while distancing themselves from the "F-word" by name seems to me both nearsighted and shortsighted. It obscures the legacy of male privilege and helps erase one of feminism's greatest contributions to social justice: creating and sustaining a space for ongoing dialogue and questions, self-critique, and internal conflict in the service of a more nuanced understanding of all systemic oppressions. It also ignores, undermines—or both—the rich gender justice history that's been at the forefront of much profound social change, the impact of which is still being felt today with gains from Middle America to the Middle East.

On the wall in my office is a copy of a handbill announcing a meeting, "What is Feminism?" scheduled for the People's Institute at Cooper Union in New York City. Nothing unusual about it, except, perhaps, the date—*February 17, 1914*. Among the dozen scheduled female and male speakers was Frances Perkins, first woman to serve in a presidential cabinet, appointed secretary of labor in 1933; and the novelist, playwright, poet, literary critic, and editor of *The Masses*, Floyd Dell. His July 1914 article begins with these words: "Feminism is going to make it possible for the first time for men to be free." That was a century ago and it's just as true today as it was then.

From my vantage point in the profeminist men's movement—a movement active on every continent (see menengage.org)—a steadily growing number of men recognize the truth in Dell's century-old observation. Our lives *are* better since embracing feminism—as sons and brothers, partners and husbands, fathers, and coworkers. Encouraged to leave the constraints of the "man box," which seek to impose a rigid definition of manhood, more of us have begun to access a range of feelings—from finding our tears to accessing our hearts. I am particularly heartened to see how many younger men are identifying as profeminists on college and university campuses. (I'm fortunate to have three serving as summer interns.)

As I went to return the old handbill to my wall, I noticed more text describing a second feminist meeting scheduled as a follow-up to the initial "What is Feminism" gathering. It featured seven women speakers addressing a range of issues, including "The Right to Work"; "The Right of the Mother to Her Profession"; "The Right to Her Convictions"; "The Right to Her Name"; "The Right to Organize"; "The Right to Ignore Fashion"; and "The Right to Specialize in Home Industries." And the name they bestowed on *that* meeting? "Breaking into the Human Race." It's a hundred years later and women still recognize its truth—from the state house in Austin, Texas, to the Democratic Republic of Congo. It's not a branding problem that needs addressing; it's sexism.

Perhaps some of the people who profess to be more comfortable with the term "gender equality" than the word *feminism* will rethink their position and step forward to recommit themselves to the cause. Imagine them joining a crowd filling a cobblestone square at dusk as the town crier calls out into the darkening sky not about the passing of a monarch but instead about an egalitarian movement growing stronger and stronger. "Hear ye, hear ye," the crier intones. "The Feminists Are Alive. Long Live the Feminists!"

MEN'S HEALTH

The tough guy image of traditional masculinity can prove very damaging to men's health, as many men within this section can attest. From being out of touch with one's emotions to feeling ashamed of contracting a "women's disease," the trappings of masculinity can cause men to feel discouraged about taking care of themselves. In this section, men voice their concerns, offer advice to other men, and share their experiences as they attempt to live healthy lives.

Healthy Men: A Contradiction in Terms?

By Joe Zoske
Summer 1998

I'm worried. The diagnosis of American men's health is serious, and the prognosis is guarded. Indeed it has reached a public health crisis. Men lead in most of the top 15 causes of death and consistently die earlier than women, and too little is being done about it.

The numbers are revealing and scary. Compared with women, we suffer 90 percent more occupational injuries and deaths, visit doctors one-fourth as often, delay treatment until symptoms are extreme, live more reckless lives, own more guns, drink and smoke more, become disabled by contact sports, resist using seat belts and safety helmets, have worse diets, are more overweight and sedentary, and are more medically illiterate—to name only some of the negative indicators. And, if we are gay, old, or poor, our risk factors increase two to ten times! That's a harsh statistic, yet it's true, and it's been true for decades.

So, what do we do? Often the response is to blame or shame men as being stupid or lazy about caring for themselves, or to trivialize men's bodies as unimportant, or to manipulate us with slick, vanity-based marketing. However, what men really need is the understanding, information, and support to act more responsibly toward our physical well being.

Unfortunately, what men do that harms us is often what we do to define ourselves. That's the trap of conventional constructions of masculinity, which mold a "hard body/tough attitude" model of manhood. We grow into an adversarial relationship with our bodies, dominating their inherent wonder and wisdom as we continue what Deepak Chopra calls our "joyless striving." Even as a specialist in men's health, I see it in my male family and friends, and I struggle with their resistance in attending to medical warning signs.

Men generally perceive their health in two ways: from the outside in, and from a performance point of view. That's why their concerns usually center on things like baldness, the ability to keep working, muscle definition, erectile function, and sports. Most have relatively little understanding of male anatomy and display poor self-care skills. It's not surprising, then, in workshops that discuss prostate disease or genital health, that most men still reveal a lack of basic understanding of how erections physiologically occur, or even where their prostate is. We have spent so much of our lives relating to our bodies as machines that we've developed "somatic deafness"—an inability to hear our bodies' warning signals of pain, discomfort, and breakdown.

Remember the old joke, "Real men don't eat quiche?" Newer versions related to health might read, "Real men don't wear sissy safety equipment" or "Real men don't have flabby abs." This fits the current media image of the masculine body: the rugged, 30-something stud with a washboard stomach, a butt of steel, a good head of hair, and a negative HIV test, heading off to become a winner at work and play. However, men's bodies, like men's lives, are more diverse than that false standard. They can be old or young, fit or disabled, energetic or tired, graceful or pain-ridden, living in clean or harmful environments, with unique genetic predispositions.

The Road to Manhood and the Road to Wellness need not diverge. Indeed, they are interdependent. It is only those outmoded messages of masculinity that separate our bodies from our minds and cast us into harm's way. As we befriend our bodies, learn about them, listen to them, and take better care of them, they will give us the vitality to thrive as men.

While AIDS activism has done much to politicize the health-care debate, raise consciousness, increase research, and educate and organize men, fundamental initiatives are necessary for the general male population and their broad health-compromising lifestyles. Efforts within the health-care system are in their infancy, but change has begun. The first men's health center was started near Dallas in 1989 (the first well-men clinic appeared in the United Kingdom in 1984). Congress passed a National Men's Health Week proclamation in 1994 in response to public health recognition of men's mortality and morbidity (the week in June ending with Father's Day). There has been a slow increase in research on the gendered health needs of men (prostate cancer, impotence, fertility, etc.),with a few hospitals developing specialized men's services (most commonly, urological), and professional organizations are beginning to give men's health some attention.

It will take a great deal more individual and collective action, however. Only we live inside our bodies, and only we can stop harming them. We are also our brothers' keepers, as we are in this life together. There is much that professionals, friends, organizations, and the health-care system can do better.

In support of our efforts to become "Real Men," I offer the following prescription:

Read—Learn about male anatomy, how your body functions, and the latest medical information.

Examine yourself—Men have a growing rate of skin cancer, and needlessly suffer testicular cancer (highly curable upon early detection) and other scrotal problems. A monthly TSE (testicular self-exam) and whole-body scan with your eyes and hands can save your life.

Act—Machismo kills. If something looks or feels wrong, don't wait. Get an opinion. You'll still be in control of what to do and can keep the information private, but becoming informed will be empowering.

Link up—Shop around for a practitioner, now, before you're sick or hurt. Find someone who understands men's special medical needs—someone you trust. Start building a relationship, one that you may depend upon someday to save your life.

Manage stress—Too much work pressure, alcohol, and anger are serious warning signs. Learn how to widen your options for dealing with responsibilities and hassles, and don't forget to laugh and dance once in a while.

Exercise—Follow the sensible advice about moderate regular fitness training. It's good for the body, mind, and soul. It builds resistance, gives strength and energy, and dissipates tension. Avoid workout-a-holism.

Nutrition—Learning to plan nutritious meals, shop wisely, and enjoy the process of cooking healthy food is not rocket science. Good nutrition is the best medicine you can take.

Men Overcoming Depression
By Michael Burke
Spring 2003

African Americans called it the blues. Winston Churchill referred to it as the Black Dog. One man I know described it as "walking through a black cloud, like a dream in which I could not speak." For me, depression has always felt like various shades of gray: an opaque filter placed between me and the world, blotting out its vibrant colors.

Whether blue or black or gray, depression is debilitating. It robs us of energy and enthusiasm for life. It takes away appetite, sleep, sex drive, decisiveness, and the will to get up in the morning. It can lead to thoughts of suicide, feelings of worthlessness and self-loathing, and a sense of hopelessness: "Things are always going to be bleak. It's never going to get any better."

How do I know? Because I've felt it—all of the above and more. I've talked and corresponded with a number of other men who've struggled with depression, and as a men's support-group facilitator I've seen many men who are depressed. Some of them know it; many of them don't. But by now I recognize some of the signs: lack of affect and monotonous speech delivery; slouching in the chair or covering the face with the hands; lack of engagement with what's happening in the group; short, uncommunicative responses to expressions of concern: "Oh, it's all right, I guess… " "Not much is going on, really… "

Men who are depressed also may act it out in socially inappropriate and destructive ways, as therapist and author Terrence Real points out. They may be drinking, using drugs, being violent, having affairs, or acting recklessly, discharging their anger or neediness on others. They may not be seen as "men who are depressed," but rather as alcoholics, abusers, controllers, womanizers, boys who never grew up. Yet their actions, Real maintains, are essentially defenses against depression. (His 1997 book about male depression, *I Don't Want to Talk About It,* is considered a classic in the field.)

Depressed men's destructive behaviors may cause them to be fired or incarcerated, injured or killed, served with a restraining order, ostracized or isolated. If we as men don't seek help ourselves we may be called on our actions—if we're lucky—by someone who cares enough to push us to get help, at least with the symptoms. We may be dragged into a therapist's office by our spouse or partner or other family member—someone who loves us but who has had it with our behavior and has given us the ultimatum: "Come to counseling or it's over."

When we're depressed, it has an effect on those around us. More specifically, according to Michael D. Yapko, clinical psychologist, family therapist, and author of *Hand-Me-Down Blues,* those of us who are fathers may be passing along our depression to our children, and possibly their children—not so much genetically but because *we are modeling depressed behavior.* Depression is the face we show the world, so depression is what our children see every day when they see "Dad." "All behavior has message value," writes Yapko, and our children hear us loud and clear. As they grow older they may internalize the depressive mode, learning lessons we didn't intend to teach.

Depression distorts the outlook, coloring our thoughts and interactions with pessimism and self-doubt. We see the cloud behind every silver lining;

we immediately jump to put a negative spin on events; we blame ourselves first when things go wrong; and we look at any potential change in our lives with an eye toward the worst possible outcome. What's more, we believe we'll always feel this way, that there's no hope of better times.

Recent studies have shown that depressed people are more "realistic" than nondepressed people. Pessimists—I reluctantly include myself—take a dim view of life, as a protection against the wounds it can inflict. We may pride ourselves on our hardheadedness—yet this "realism" doesn't improve our mood, doesn't lead us to contentment.

Optimistic people are happier. Optimists greet the day with hope—like a friend of mine who met me one morning with a sunny smile and "Well, it's a beautiful day, and we have our lives." To which I thought, *What kind of pop-psych bullshit is that?*

But you know—he's right. Much as it pains a dyed-in-the-black-wool pessimist to admit, my friend's mantra is a huge improvement over the one that's often come up for me first thing in the morning: "I wonder how I'll get through today… " And one of the things I've started to learn, slowly and painfully over the last few years, is that we may not always have control over how we feel, but we can empower ourselves to create affirmations—new, more positive thoughts—that shed a happier, more optimistic light on what we're doing. Because if there's a choice—and I have to believe that in my mind, at least, there usually is—isn't it better to start from a point of "It's a beautiful day, and I have my life" rather than "It's a shitty (or potentially shitty) day, and what good is my worthless existence"?

Don't get me wrong. I'm not auditioning for Up with People, or setting myself up as a prophet of a You Create Your Own Reality school. I'm just suggesting that if we start to shift our thinking into a more positive key, it does begin to color our outlook for the better, and can also have an impact on what happens around us. It can affect our relations with other people, for example, as well as improving our own mental and physical health. This creates a sort of chain reaction, whereby some of those "good vibrations" flowing out of us come back in the form of the reflected care and concern—and love—we get from others.

But just changing our thinking is not enough. We need strategies to overcome depression and keep it away. What else can we do to begin to move out of our depression and isolation and into fulfillment, connection, and joy? There are no easy answers, but from my own experience, and from reading about depression and talking with other men about what has worked for them, here are some suggestions:

• **Get help**. Take action—today—to begin your healing. Start with a thought: *I will do something to help myself. I deserve to feel better.*

See a therapist, or a physician you trust, and tell him or her what you've been experiencing. Therapy can help, and medication might make a difference.

• **Talk with others**. Check out a support group, such as those offered by men's centers, or others you feel comfortable with. You'll meet other men who've dealt with depression, and they can help. Get out and see friends—real friends you can be honest with; you may be surprised at the offers of support you receive and at how good it feels just to be heard. If friends are in short supply, plan activities you enjoy that will put you in contact with other people: join a hiking or biking group, volunteer with a charity, attend a house of worship or meditation group, or just hang out downtown having coffee and chatting. Interaction with others helps reduce the isolation factor, so harmful to men.

• **Move your body**. Exercise and physical activity can dispel depression and keep it at bay. Find an exercise routine or activity you like and make it part of your weekly schedule. Go to the gym, swim, find a pickup basketball game, call a friend to play tennis or racquetball. Get outdoors and walk or bike or ski—just being outside in the fresh air, moving your body, can improve your mood immeasurably.

• **Develop your spiritual side**. This could mean something organized, such as a particular religion or spiritual path, or it could mean meditation, poetry, journal writing, painting, being in nature, playing music, or any activity that calms the mind and brings a sense of fulfillment and peace. Are there things you used to enjoy that you don't do anymore? Chances are they're connected to your spiritual self, and doing them again will feel amazingly good.

• **Work on your relationships**. If you're in a committed relationship, you might explore couples counseling or cocounseling—both to check out how the relationship is doing (how your partner feels about it and how you feel) and to learn how your depression is affecting your life with your partner. You can also try to find more time together—going out, resurrecting your romance and sex life, and doing some of the fun things you used to do. If you have children, spending more time with them—whether playing games, taking them places, being outdoors, or just doing homework, dishes, or gardening together—can be a real solace and a boost.

• **Read**. If you're a reader, reading is itself a joy and a comfort. I list some books on depression below—but just as important is to read something that captures your interest, gets you jazzed. It might be a novel, poetry, or a biography of some inspiring person. It might be medieval history or quantum physics for all I know. Whatever; just choose something engaging and uplifting (and non-depressing!).

• **Be honest—and compassionate—with yourself**. Don't try to do everything at once, or think you're going to be on top of the world tomorrow. And don't punish yourself when you're not—don't bludgeon yourself for the day you missed the gym, the morning you stayed in bed, the times you let the machine answer the phone. Don't fool yourself that you can or must be perfect, that the work will be easy, or that at some point you'll absolutely have it licked. But do start loving and caring for yourself, be compassionate about your weaknesses—while acknowledging them honestly—and as a bonus you'll become more understanding, and less judgmental, with other people.

Once you get started on this healing journey you'll think of other things to do along the way. The important thing is to begin: to start building structures into your life that will make you happier over time, to create new relationships and mend existing ones so that you have a network of support. This is extremely important for men, as most of us were never taught to be intimate with others, many of us were taught that it wasn't okay to be honest and open or to have emotions (other than anger), and all of us have probably suffered from the damaging effects of our isolation. But we can learn how to be connected, and we can teach ourselves to appreciate and enjoy the life that opens up before us.

Living with Suicide
By Paul Ehmann
Summer 2005

Depression sinks in on a cloud of distraction. Suddenly I'm under the dull throb of a personal suicide watch. Never saw it coming. The doctor, my GP, fidgets on the metal stool in the exam room.

"Do you have a plan?" he asks, looking not at me, but at the chart.

With a laugh, I reply, "Of course not. Just a thought." I know my practiced, pat answer will keep me off the flight deck. I play with this disease like a kid with a yo-yo, sometimes wrapped tight around the axle, sometimes spinning lazily at the end of a walk-the-dog. Always going around the world. On March 29 of this year the backslide toward my childhood is complete: I'm twelve again, and Coach, that foul bastard, has got my dick in his mouth.

History has dictated my emotionality and the absence of it. Never able to relieve myself of my past, I've tried therapy, group counseling, even a week away at an intensive program. Memory is persistent. Silence is deadly. Abuse lasts.

Ten years ago, on the sixth anniversary of my sobriety, I sat across the desk from my newest therapist. The four-hour intake included a physical and mental observation. He could have, but didn't, caress my spirit, which lay gray and wilted on my sleeve. I leaned back in my chair and thought I aced the exam. Again. Honesty is a precious concealed commodity on the personal suicide watch. You can't give up too much.

He was writing. Then he passed the note over the cluttered mahogany desk. It was written on a prescription pad.

"What's this?" I asked.

"A script for Buspar (antianxiety) and Serzone (antidepressant)."

"What for?" I said.

"You have major depression, Paul, and I fear for your life. This will help."

No one ever feared for my life. Even in the darkest days, the days I made lighter with alcohol and cocaine, the days that swept into nights and binges a week long. The constant refrain, "You'd better slow down, you're killing yourself," from my brother, my parents, and my wives, did not register as concern. More like nagging.

Suicide thoughts are a constant with me, a thread in my spiritual tapestry since the first time I was sexually abused at age six or seven. The notion returned the other day without fanfare on my son's twenty-sixth birthday. That's a long time. I'll be fifty soon. Notice the hope? That's the confusing thing. Makes me believe I'd never actually do it. Off myself, that is. There have been attempts, I'm told. Unconscious efforts to overdose or to wreck the car. A progressive march toward death by alcohol and drugs. A death wish. I minimize the ticker tape thoughts of running into bridge abutments or off the cliffs or into the trees. Normal thinking for me. What's the harm?

I was in my mid-twenties when I made the decision to die. A weeklong drunk full of promises to stop drinking crept up on me while I slept. She was gone. Work, I supposed, or anywhere but next to me. I was asleep on the floor next to our bed. The car, full of scratches from an off-road excursion, was hidden from view in the garage. The loneliness and despair of a remorseful drunk can sometimes be overwhelming. This morning or afternoon, I couldn't be sure, was particularly bad. *This is it,* I thought. *Don't make it messy.*

I was glad we didn't have guns in the house. An intoxicated person really stands less of a chance in a logical world. Pulling the trigger could be an inexcusable mistake. An act of drunken despondence and no one would know you weren't really ready. You were just weary. Momentarily empty of hope. So my "weapon" was a pile of coke. I made the embarrassing phone calls to my sister-in-law and my wife. "I don't know what's going to happen." I cried. There was no overt threat. The implication lost on the ears of the knowing. I paced the house like a father waiting for the delivery of a stillborn. *I don't want to die*, I thought, and the pacing grew more frantic, *but I've already made the phone calls…*

In an instant I emptied the bag on the table. Maybe half an ounce. I just sat there looking at it. All that life ahead and no way to live it. I put on my clothes and my sneakers. I took a pull of vodka and rolled up a bill and snorted the pile as fast as I could. Gagging dry heaves were no deterrent. Then I went for a run. I was not a jogger. My intention was to fulfill the prophecy of a drug overdose, have a simple heart attack and make it neat. The suicide hat trick. A wake filled with "It's so sad," "What was he thinking," and "I told ya so."

Surviving a suicide attempt is about as embarrassing a predicament as has been invented. A thundering failure. And if you're fortunate enough, the ultimate grace.

So the doctor, convinced that I don't have a plan, suggests I go back to therapy again. I know that the absence of alcohol and drugs in my life is the reason I still have one. The therapist will want me to rehash my past, and then put me on antidepressants. I will resist, insisting on toughing it out. The death wish will whirl and eventually cease. Thought and deed are now rarely contiguous, and I'll pull out of this depression wondering, *What was I thinking?*

Mostly I'll keep it to myself. Secrets are still warm and comfortable. I am triggered to relive the crime of sexual abuse with the abruptness of the evening news. Lately it's been the 24/7 of the Michael Jackson case—and more insidiously, more damaging, the unapologetic, pedophile-shuffling Catholic cardinal from Boston being given the honor of saying high mass for his pope. The lack of compassion glows red, like a grade-school backhand across the face.

The memory of my abuse will move quickly out of the physical and lodge deep in the emotional. It's a crime of time and it lasts a lifetime. Some lifetimes are shorter than others. I'm one of the lucky ones. I just live with the thoughts. The gnawing. Maybe this time I'll take the meds. Or not.

VOICE MALE

I Don't Know What I'm Feeling: Teaching Men to Speak Emotionalese
By David Kundtz
Spring 2004

> *Alexithymia: Difficulty in recognizing, describing and expressing emotions—one's own or those of others.*

Run or Cover

Given the culture in which men have been raised, it's no wonder that many of us are challenged by the feeling part of life. We often can't seem to recognize and talk about the feelings we are having at any given moment.

What we do instead is run away or cover up. As soon as we feel something, or someone else in our presence is feeling something—especially if it's a strong feeling like fear or attraction—we run from it before it has a chance to let us know it's there, much less get expressed. Running means changing the subject, distracting yourself with some other activity, or moving on to something new.

Or we cover it. With TV, music, sports, humor, sex, laughter—anything that covers over and hides the feelings.

So when someone asks us what we're feeling, we can often truthfully say, "Oh, nothing." We're not lying, because we run so quickly from the feeling or cover it so well that we literally don't know it is there.

There's a name for the condition I'm talking about: *Alexithymia*. It's from Greek words meaning "no words for feelings." A few of us guys have it really bad; most of us have at least a light case of it.

Steve's story: "I can't tell you."

Here's a story of a man who is very good at the thinking side. He is a member of Mensa—only very high IQs invited. His name is Steve. He and his wife, Amy, are in their late thirties, with two young kids, their own home, and successful working lives. They have come to see me, a family therapist, because their marriage is troubled.

During our fifth or sixth session, without warning, Amy says she believes their marriage cannot survive and she wants a divorce. Bam! Just like that.

To this sobering announcement Steve reacts with a sad, vacant stare into space. It lasts a long fifteen seconds; no one says a word. I am as surprised as he is. Then, without saying anything, he calmly stands up, picks up his coat and briefcase, and walks out of my office.

Jump ahead two weeks.

After several attempts, I convince Steve to come in on his own "to talk about it." When he comes to my office, I can feel him bristle. He doesn't want to be here. We start talking; or rather, *I* start talking. From him I get nothing but grunts, noises, or shakes of the head. Clearly he is in pain. A couple times he glances at me, silently begging me to end the torture and let him go. He just can't say much of anything.

After one particularly long period of silence, I notice I am really getting annoyed and think to myself, *This must be what his wife feels.* Then I ask, "Well, Steve, what about just telling me, briefly, what you are feeling right now, knowing that your wife intends to divorce you?"

His response begins slowly, then quickly builds force as his eyes snap wide to attention, rise up and rivet me. His face becomes flushed, his body rigid, his fists clenched, and his look enraged.

Then he bolts from his seat, storms across the room, turns back toward me—now fevered and furious—raises his arms high *(to attack? to entreat?)* and screams, "You sound just like my wife! Don't you see?" And then even louder and more anguished, "I don't know what I'm feeling!"

When my heart returns to its normal beat and I take a deep breath or two—he is now slumped in his chair, spent and embarrassed—I say in a quiet voice, "Oh."

After a moment I said it again, "Oh." I could only hope the simple word expressed what I wanted him to know: that I heard him, not just his words—I'm sure half the building heard those—but him.

More important, I wanted him to know that I actually believed him: He did not know what he was feeling, about his marriage, his possible divorce, and even about his wife.

Steve simply did not know his emotional state, and thus could not put it into words. He knew he was in pain, but beyond that he simply didn't know. It wasn't that he didn't want to know. In fact he *did* want to know. It wasn't that he really knew but just wouldn't tell me. No, he really *didn't know.* He truly had no words for his feelings.

Steve was in his late thirties when this happened. He was so used to not knowing his feelings that he didn't know that he didn't know.

Never Too Late

In this situation—not being able to put into words the emotions you are experiencing—many men find we are misjudged as stuck-up or stubborn or even stupid. Sometimes we even judge ourselves with those words. But in the vast majority of situations this is not true. Almost always what we are going through are the effects of our lack of training in the ways of dealing with feelings.

VOICE MALE

Many times, when the feelings finally do come out, they come out in a confusing way or in an explosion, like Steve's did. And often they get us into trouble. At best we're accused of overreacting; at worst we're seen as fearsome or violent. It's a no-win situation

There's a point I want to make with Steve's story: By following the simple Three Steps to Emotional Fitness you can begin now to find ways to attach words—or some other healthy means of expression—to your feelings, and thus you can avoid such a sad situation: (1) Notice the feeling (2) Name the feeling. (3) Express the feeling.

Steve continues his slow but sure journey to emotional fitness. Although he and his wife separated for a few months, they both did four months of counseling and he joined a weekly men's group. They got together again and are now giving the marriage a very hopeful second chance.

It's never too late!

THREE STEPS TO EMOTIONAL FITNESS

What do you actually do with feelings? How do you deal with them? What are the practical steps for a man to take? One answer is the Three Steps to Emotional Fitness. They are:

1. Notice the feeling. Don't run, don't cover; stay with it. Feelings often begin in the body.

2. Name the feeling. Pick a name to identify what you feel. What exactly is it? Is it anger, sadness, fear, confusion, resentment? Try to discover what the feeling is about.

3. Express the feeling. Get the feeling outside you. "Go public" with it (as appropriate!) by talking with a friend, moving your body, writing in your journal, singing, yelling, smiling.

The quick version of the Three Steps to Emotional Fitness can be used any-time—while you're in the car, during a class break, at your computer, as you walk down the street, as you wait in line, on your way home. Just remember: *Notice, Name, Express.*

Healing Emotionally After Testicular Cancer
By Brian Pahl
Summer 2004

When I was 21, I found a lump on my right testicle that turned out to be cancer. During the next three months I would endure the removal of one of my testicles, major exploratory surgery to my abdomen, the discovery that the cancer had spread, weeks in the hospital, and two rounds of chemotherapy. All in all, it was the most painful, terrifying thing I have ever experienced. It took me over four years just to admit that. I thought it would be weak of me to acknowledge my fears, but I realize now that I have never been stronger. The words that follow are a window into my experience with testicular cancer, the anguish I continued to feel after treatment, and what I am doing to heal emotionally from what was the most difficult time in my life.

It was September 1992 and a week after my second and final session of chemotherapy. I packed my things and moved to Los Angeles to live with a friend. I had to get away. Three months of my life had been stolen from me, and I was not about to sit around and waste any more time feeling sorry for myself. I figured it would be best for me to get back to the things I had been doing prior to having cancer. I thought I was doing what was best because my doctors, family, and friends seemed supportive of my decision. It was important to me to prove to myself and everyone else how strong and determined I was. Being a strong patient had helped me fight the physical part of having cancer, and I thought that acting like a strong survivor would help me overcome my emotions.

It worked for a while, because I refused to believe or acknowledge that any negative feelings existed. I simply ignored my emotions, and for four years I continued to reject the notion that I had unresolved feelings, even though they would arise from time to time. I failed to realize that moving away and assuming the state of mind that I did would prevent me from dealing with the emotional turmoil going on inside.

I am now able to admit that I still feel traumatized from having cancer. At times, I still feel like a victim. Occasionally, I break into tears watching a movie or reading a book because memories of what I experienced become vivid in my mind. The fear, the pain, and the uncertainty that were a part of having cancer all become real again—even if only for a few moments. I wake up every day to this enormous scar on the front and side of my torso. It will never allow me to forget what my mind and my body endured; it continues to remind me of the fear I feel today. Yes, I am afraid. I am afraid that all of the effort I put into making myself well might have been for nothing, because the cancer could come back. On the other hand, I feel just fine, aside from the pains left over from two operations. I feel like I did when I was first told I had cancer—and that scares the hell out of me.

In my healing process, I've had to confront the loud voice in my head that says, *"It's time to get over this, Brian. You had cancer four years ago, and you are doing just fine. Stop acting like a baby. Stop being a scared, sensitive fool and move on. Besides, your cancer was nothing compared to the cancer that terrorizes little kids or that takes a woman's breasts. You just lost a little testicle; stop feeling sorry for yourself and being selfish. Get over it, man."*

These thoughts are also the source of a number of "why" questions: "Why do I still feel like this? Why does this still bother me so much? Why can't I just get over it?" To answer the "why" questions and understand how I could "still" feel this way, I had to admit to myself that having cancer definitely was a terrifying and traumatic experience. And, considering what I had endured I had to give myself permission to recognize that my feelings were natural. This was absolutely necessary in order for me to stop criticizing myself and my feelings.

Why was this so traumatic? Right from the beginning, I had it in my head that cancer meant death. I thought of my great-grandmother, who fought cancer for many years. I remembered the pain and suffering she went through and all of the weight she lost, and her slow, agonizing death. I did not think I would endure the same type of struggle, but in my mind cancer symbolized pain, agony, slow, ruthless evil, and death. I was not only fighting a disease in my body; I was fighting for the survival of my entire being.

In *Illness as Metaphor* Susan Sontag writes, "As long as a disease is treated as an evil, invincible predator, not just a disease, most people with cancer will indeed be demoralized by learning what disease they have. The solution is hardly to stop telling cancer patients the truth, but to rectify the conception of the disease, to de-mythicize it." Long before cancer manifested true, real, physical pain within my body, it was real and painful and terrifying in my mind. We associate cancer with painful treatments, suffering, agony, poison, surgery, cutting, wasting away, invasion, tumors, superstition, fear, death. We surround it, coat it, and protect it with these references and labels, which serve as armor and make it increasingly difficult to overcome. If we remove the protective shield, it becomes merely cancer, a disease, and our odds of defeating it become much greater.

At one point I became very angry while reading Sontag's book. I thought of how I viewed cancer: as a sniper sitting in a tree firing upon people, picking them out at random and trying to destroy them. I became enraged and started to cry. I shouted the word "cancer" over and over again. *"Cancer. Cancer. Cancer. Cancer. Cancer! Cancer!! CANCER!"* My anger intensified, and I wept. A few minutes went by, and I started feeling better. I was getting the cancer out of my mind and was letting go of emotions I had been holding on to for years.

The Western medical philosophy believes in ridding the body of disease at all costs, short of ending life. The objective is purely physical. Meanwhile, emotions and the psyche of the patient are ignored. I had two great doctors, and I credit them with my survival. I look back on my treatment and see them doing all they could to get the cancer out of my body. The disease was being cured—but *Brian* was being put through hell, and he needed someone to help him cope with all that he was feeling. One of my doctors attempted to address my emotional concerns by talking with me about them, but (no surprise) my insurance company limited my visits with him.

I am physically healed, but I am not emotionally healed. When I went to the doctor the very first time, I felt fine. I was not ill. I had no aches or pains. The only problem was a lump on my testicle. Then I was told that I had cancer, and they proceeded to do all of these terribly painful things to me to rid my body of something I did not really know was there. They told me this was all needed in order to cure the disease. I was confused in a way, because, since I did not feel sick, it was as if I were being deceived. All of the treatment, all of the agony and pain I went through and continue to go through mentally and emotionally was geared toward something I didn't *really* know was there. My treatment was far worse than any symptoms I was experiencing.

The next step was to explore what I had done with my feelings and seek them out. When I was being treated, I did what I could to show everyone that I could be strong, even though I was screaming and kicking and crying on the inside. I let my emotions show when I couldn't take it anymore, but otherwise I locked them away. The word "strong" continues to appear because I thought I was being strong. My friends, family, and medical staff reinforced this by telling me how well I was hanging in there. My mother and my doctor suggested counseling as a way to deal with the pain and fear, but I refused. *It's not that bad,* I remember telling them. I believed that I was doing okay dealing with this on my own. Counseling or a support group was absolutely out of the question, because either of the two would bring up feelings when I was doing everything in my power to deny their existence.

Another reason I stuffed my feelings inside was because I wanted to *take it like a man.* I learned early on that real men don't cry. Real men don't show their emotions. I learned these things the hard way because I am a guy who does cry. I do show what I am feeling, and I have been mocked, teased, criticized, ridiculed, and beaten up for it. The list in my mind goes on forever as to why I might be less of a man. Losing one of my nuts added to the list. I was so concerned with what other people thought of me, especially now, that I thought the best thing would be to tough it out. This was my chance to stop being a sissy and act like a man. Being strong and fighting my illness the way

I did was an attempt to make people proud of me, to make *me* proud of me. What I learned, though, is that "acting like a man" made my life worse. Acting like a man cut me off from who I really was and made my experience so much more painful than it needed to be. My healing was made harder because I knew the entire time that sooner or later the feelings I had ignored would rise and make me take notice. I postponed this moment as long as I could, in the belief that this was "manly."

Today, I can see that having cancer was a traumatic event in my life. I can see how I suppressed my feelings and refused to give them notice. I am now paying attention to those feelings, so that I may get on with my life. I still struggle with the notion of manhood, but I am trying to focus less on the man society tells me to be and more on the person I want to be.

Once I had a better understanding of my experience, I wanted to talk with other men who also had testicular cancer. I sought men out over the Internet and through my doctors. Most of the men who responded identified with the same feelings I had, but a couple of guys said it was "nothing" to them. One of them said: "I almost don't feel like the word *cancer* even applies to me. And I would *never* refer to myself as a 'cancer survivor,' because I never felt my survival was in question. A guy I work with lost his nine-year-old step-daughter to an *extremely* rare type of cancer. *She* had cancer. *Her* survival was *always* in question. Testicular cancer just does not compare to that, not mine anyway." He makes a valid point.

Sometimes I agree with what he said about other people's cancers being worse than mine, and it makes me feel guilty and selfish that I am still hung up over having a "delicate" type of cancer. I think where we differ is that my cancer had spread, and my survival *was* in question. Regardless, I have learned that I cannot change how I feel. I cannot change the fact that what happened was horrible, and that it affected me the way it did.

Another guy said: "I agree with your sentiment that the psychological effect of suffering cancer in such a 'defining' area is often under-regarded ... I get extremely tense around routine checkup time, because more than anything, I do not want to have chemotherapy again. I was first diagnosed in 1984... 12 years later, I am happy, healthy, and married, but it is still hard to talk about." It meant a great deal to me to hear from these men. It made me feel like less of a freak to know that other people have had the same experience or thoughts as I have had. My biggest fear is getting cancer again. I am getting to a point, though, where I am worrying about that less because I know it is out of my control.

I still have so much work to do. I am at a point now where I am less critical and more accepting of my feelings, but I need to give myself a break when it comes to feeling sad. Most of my life I have listened to the message "Don't be a sissy." I know I cannot erase that message overnight, but I am on my way to replacing it with a new mantra: "Let your feelings be." I plan on continuing to examine gender and identity roles, and men's and women's socialization to better understand how that conditioning may have contributed to my anxiety and the repression of my feelings during and after treatment. I am going to continue talking with cancer survivors and sharing our stories. And I'm going to try and take a little time each day to reflect on and honor my feelings, whatever they may be. And I will continue to be thankful for my life.

Unmanly Conditions
By Joe Zoske
Summer 2000

Nothing threatens a man's sense of masculinity like a physical malady that sneaks up on him, leaving him feeling weak, vulnerable, and helpless. The discomfort, threat, and loss of control are compounded when he comes down with what is commonly known as a "woman's disease." Then physical and emotional pain combine, leaving a growing sense of emasculation and shame in their wake.

Sound strange? Seem like a remote circumstance? Not for the thousands of men who experience such misfortune each year. When headlines speak of ovarian cancer or abortion, we know the subject is women's health. Likewise, stories of prostate disease or testicular cancer are surely about men. But what about breast cancer, osteoporosis, eating disorders, and distorted body image?

Images of women leap immediately to mind: women struggling with the impact of a mastectomy, brittle bones, anorexia, or bulimia. Yet these conditions have no gender boundary. While they affect women at much greater rates, increasing numbers of men are falling victim to them as well, and having to deal with a host of extra challenges related to their gender—including embarrassment, social isolation, fear of being seen as "unmanly," denial and disbelief, and both under- and misdiagnosis.

Take breast cancer. *Fourteen hundred men will be diagnosed with it this year!* Men might prefer to think of this as "chest cancer," but the medical reality is the same. Just ask Richard Roundtree—the 1970s film actor who played the tough-guy hero in the *Shaft* movies. Earlier this year he went public, after carrying a seven-year secret. At the age of 44, he had a modified radical mastectomy for malignant cancer, which removed chest tissue from his nipple to his underarm, followed by six months of chemotherapy. He's a survivor, but 400 times a year men are not. For those facing this devastating diagnosis, the silence surrounding it (imposed by themselves and society) leaves them very much alone, and at greater risk for becoming another fatality.

Then there's osteoporosis—the demineralizing of our bones, weakening our very structure from within. Although it mainly affects women, two million men have the disease, including one-third of men over age 75, and another three million are at risk. Men experience one-third of all hip fractures, have a higher rate of dying from them than women, and also suffer painful and debilitating fractures of the spine, wrist, and other bones. Yet despite the large number of men affected, osteoporosis in men remains underdiagnosed, underreported, and inadequately researched. For decades women were disadvantaged by their risk of heart attacks being overlooked or minimized. The same can be said for men and osteoporosis. Risk factors include smoking, excessive drinking, lack of exercise, inadequate calcium intake, and steroid use.

Of course, exercise is a preventative for bone loss, especially weight-bearing/ strength-building exercises. But even here, men can take things to an extreme. Picture a bulked-up guy, looking more muscular than the rest of us will ever be. Imagine him looking into a mirror and seeing something different, and horrifying—a scrawny weakling who never has enough muscle. This condition—body dysmorphia—is affecting more and more males (younger males, too, especially teens), whose passion for bodybuilding gets out of control.

Body dysmorphia is a serious psychological condition, often coexisting with depression, use of body-enhancer drugs, mood shifts, and other obsessive-compulsive behaviors. This severe preoccupation with body image—muscle as manhood—can lead to complete social withdrawal and, in its most extreme form, suicide. With the arrival of prescription testosterone gel this summer and continuing emphasis on high-stakes athletics, there is concern that the incidence of this condition will grow, as will its many physical and emotional side effects. Numbers of men are hard to estimate, as it is usually not discussed or identified; indeed, the opposite is true—bulking up is idealized and rewarded among men (and even women). However, when men suffer from dysmorphia, there is intense isolation in the face of clear danger, and men are often ill-prepared to deal with it for fear of looking weak (the exact thing they are obsessively trying to avoid).

In the realm of eating disorders (anorexia, bulimia, etc.), men account for 5 to 10 percent of all eating-disorder sufferers. Studies show that men more frequently use excessive and obsessive exercise and bodybuilding prior to and during their eating disorder, and there appears to be a higher rate of eating disorders among gay males.

Furthermore, men are less likely to seek, or be identified as in need of, treatment for an eating disorder, because of the social stigma and bias associated with having a condition that has generally been perceived as a "woman's problem." Again, isolation and inadequate care often occur, and disability, depression, and death can be the result.

It has been proven that social support (family, friends, health professionals, support groups, etc.) is a key factor in successful coping with serious illness. Having a positive attitude, and being armed with up-to-date information, a sense of optimism, and personal empowerment are equally vital. To be better able to handle the above situations, therefore, requires *connection*. In the face of this need, these "unmanly" medical conditions represent yet another opportunity for men to reach out to one another, to build and rally around our community in support of a fellow man—thus aiding him in moving from victim to survivor.

Let's get real: health care for men needs to get beyond penises and prostates. How many of us have been instructed in breast self-examination, let alone testicular self-examination? How often do our medical practitioners bring up our potential risk from so-called women's diseases? Let's start by asking direct questions ourselves, doing our part to keep healthy and alive. It's about time.

My Father's Breast Cancer
By Laura Barron
Fall 2011

I had my first mammogram not long ago. I'm 42 and felt that I had avoided the inevitable breast vice grip long enough. To my knowledge, no one in my family had ever had breast cancer. Somehow I always thought I was immune to this beast—which ravages one in nine women at some time during their lives. I have little stress, love my work, sleep well, eat a high-soy vegetarian diet, exercise, and regularly practice yoga. Of course, one of my favorite childhood teachers boasted this same healthy lifestyle, yet the disease took her at only thirty-seven. So I should have known better. But this is not a story about my own diagnosis. I just got my results and all the tests were normal. One down. However, a recent turn of events has me wondering if the cards won't be stacked in my favor for long.

My parents visited my husband and me in Vancouver for the holidays. They arrived a week before Christmas, just two days after "the news."

Honey, the doctors have found a lump.

Where, Daddy?

Well, I never had big tits before, but, believe it or not, it's in my breast.

Oh, that's weird. But I guess that means it could be anything. Men don't get breast cancer.

That's what I thought. But maybe they haven't called me 'one in a thousand' my whole life for nothing. So, the lab ran a biopsy just to be safe. I won't have the results until we get back to Arizona.

Apparently, his interest in protecting me from the truth, at least until the holidays were over, prevented him from telling me what else the doctors said. I am not one to worry. I reminded myself, *Lots of people find lumps. We Barrons never get cancer.* But then, I faced the facts. Four years ago, my dad's brother went in for a routine colonoscopy on a Friday, only to discover that he had a small, localized tumor. They promptly removed it the following Wednesday. He didn't need chemo or any other therapy. He doesn't even consider himself a cancer survivor. Just a bump—or a lump—in the road. Considering that, I was still sure that my dad's lump would be just fine. At least that's what I was going to tell myself in order to fully enjoy the first ski vacation we'd had together in twelve years. And, of course, there was the Feast of the Seven Fishes to prepare. A decadent six-course meal that had been a treasured Christmas Eve tradition in my mother's Southern Italian family for years.

The holidays passed with the usual overindulging, out-of-tune Christmas carols with Dad at the keyboard, and general good cheer. But as soon as Boxing Day rolled around, I began to notice the pall that hung over my parents usually chipper demeanors. In fact, as former captains of their respective high school football and cheerleading teams, their excessive conviviality normally rivaled that of Kelly Ripa on Ecstasy. But over Saturday brunch, they were both unusually quiet and distracted. We went through with our plans to visit the aquarium. But upon returning home for a leftovers lunch, I finally asked,

So, is one of you finally going to talk about the elephant in the room?

My mom spoke first.

We already know it's a mass, not just a cyst. The sonogram results were immediate.

Sonogram? Neither of you even mentioned that they already ran other tests. But aren't lots of masses still benign?

With more fear than I've ever seen on my invincible father's face, he said,

You should have seen the pessimism in the doctor's face. Who wants to hear, 'I definitely do not like the look of this?'

As a retired dentist, my father puts a lot of stock in professional medical opinions. Now it was my turn to be the cheerleader.

Well, there's no point worrying about it until we know. But, of course, that's all any of us could do for the next four days until the results came.

I took them to the airport on Monday morning and cried the whole way home, releasing the hypothetical grief I was terrified I might have to face. Of course, I knew I would one day lose my parents. But they are both so unusually healthy and youthful. And three of my grandparents lived past 90. That inevitability was still decades away. It shook me to the core imagining that I might be wrong.

As soon as I returned home I googled "male breast cancer." *Never, I repeat, never use the Internet during a health scare.* Within five minutes, my stomach was in knots. My mother had mentioned that Dad's lump was just under his nipple. She even told me I could touch it if I wanted. (I declined, thinking that this was an invasion of my father's privacy.) It turns out that's exactly where all male breast cancer is located. And it most commonly hits men 60–70, due to hormonal changes at that age. My dad was 69 at the time. Strangely, it's even more common among Jews, and my grandparents were Jewish immigrants from Russia. This was not looking good. Then I read the clincher: *Only one percent of lumps found to be masses in men's breasts are benign.*

Holy sh**! There's a 99 percent chance my father has breast cancer!

And that was not the worst statistic that I learned. Unfortunately, 90 *percent* of male breast tumors are already metastasized—because of late detection; that's three times the rate of spreadable cancers in women's breasts. Now, I was totally freaked. But there was a silver lining. The lucky 1 percent had growths that were called fibroadenoma. Though I was never normally one to be superstitious, I typed that word into my computer 64 times (my lucky number) trying to influence the fates. But secretly, I realized the unlikelihood of this fortune. So I prayed at the top of a mountain, in a yoga class, before bed, while driving, anywhere I could, that at least his cancer had not spread. *Ductal carcinoma in situ.* I never thought I'd be memorizing such medical terms. I figured a localized form of breast cancer—that only required surgery and no chemo or radiation—was the best of the worst news we could hope for.

I spoke to my brother every day until the "verdict" came in. He was even more of a wreck than me, since his wife's father had just died of lung cancer only three months earlier. When Wednesday came, I found myself useless until one o'clock, the time I knew my father would be visiting the lab for the results. It took two more hours before he called.

The results? "Suspicious but inconclusive," my parents reported.

My family optimism had apparently rubbed off on me. I chose to take this as good news since I'd never heard of a biopsy unable to detect an actual cancer. If it was truly aggressive, of course it would be obvious. But we wouldn't find out for certain until the following Monday. Not knowing was absolutely the worst.

Finally, our wait was over. My father was in the lucky 10 percent: the marble-sized growth under his nipple was a localized tumor with no signs of having spread!

"I never thought learning I had cancer would feel like winning the lottery," Dad said. "Mom and I already bought the champagne. We're so relieved! But, if you can imagine it, your father is having a mastectomy in a couple of weeks."

That's great! I exclaimed! *Now you have an excuse to go out and buy yourself a chest full of new bras.*

I got my sarcastic sense of humor from him, so I assumed he'd appreciate the joke. And I was feeling elated to think that there were now dozens of years of his dry one-liners ahead of me. That is, until his presurgical appointment. The phone rang at nine o'clock Tuesday night.

They got the biopsy wrong. I do have an invasive cancer. It has spread beyond the nipple into my breast tissue. They think they caught it early, but we won't know if it's in my lymph until the surgery next week. And there's something else. Remember my puffy cheeks I told Mom not to worry about? Well, they informed me I have swollen saliva glands and they're quite concerned. They can't even operate until they rule some things out.

What things?

Well, honey, it could also be cancer, or even HIV. They're running more tests.

Waiting for the verdict, my family endured another week in purgatory. I went to very dark places I didn't even know existed. The dread of previously unimagined possibilities clouded everything. Happily, all Dad's tests came back negative. "It's nothing" the doctors reassured him. But we'd heard that before. Part way through his ordeal, my father admitted he had actually discovered the lump months earlier only to have his family doctor dismiss it as "nothing" at his annual physical. Reader take note: male breast cancer is so rare many of the best physicians are still uninformed. My father's unwavering confidence in the medical system was certainly being tested—as was mine. So, I felt pretty unmoved by this sliver of good news. I needed to hear that the lymph nodes were clear before I could breathe easy.

And then they were.

"They didn't find any cancer in his lymph nodes, and they said they got everything. I can even take him home tonight," my mother reported.

After a month of Academy Award-winning performances acting as his "rock" without ever shedding a tear, Mom sounded exhausted but extremely relieved.

"Your dad's too tired to speak on the phone. But you can call him tomorrow."

When he picked up the next day, I could hear a Scott Joplin recording in the background. His good friend was setting up his keyboard in the den. Mom always made him keep the unsightly thing under their bed between uses. It clashed with their pristine southwestern décor, she said. But now she was going to let him keep it out permanently. Nothing like cancer to get your priorities straight.

The doctors reported that Dad wouldn't even need chemo. "In all likelihood you'll live another 30 years," his oncologist told him. And that news was not even the sweetest: Our already close family was reminded how much love a daughter and a son can have for their father. Our perspective on so much had shifted. This harrowing experience rendered many valuable lessons. Before, I hadn't even known that men could get breast cancer. It's considered such a rarity that when I completed my recent mammogram survey, I was confronted by this question:

Is there any history of breast cancer in your family?

☐ *Mother*
☐ *Sister*
☐ *Grandmother*
☐ *Aunt*

There wasn't even a box for "Father!" Through this experience, I learned I was hardly alone in my ignorance. I encourage *everyone* to let their husbands, brothers, fathers, and sons—all the men in their lives—know that women are not the only ones who should practice regular self-breast exams. We can all benefit from vigilance and early detection.

When he got on the phone, Dad sounded ecstatic. "I was thinking," he said. "How about you fly down here this spring and we hike the Grand Canyon together." The year before, at 68, my dad had accomplished this amazing, 20-mile, round-trip-in-a-day feat *twice*—first with a friend, then with my brother. Before the cancer, I'd tried to convince him to do it once more with me, but he'd sworn, after that second time left him limping for weeks, he would never do it again. It's amazing what a genuine health scare can inspire.

I can't wait.

Living—and Loving—with Erectile Dysfunction
By George Marx
Spring 2012

Twenty-five years ago I sought other "pregnant men" to share our hopes and fears about impending fatherhood. While there may have been some interested dads-to-be out there, I never found them. Fathering wasn't "hot" then. It also wasn't taboo. A decade later, though, when erectile dysfunction (ED) gradually began affecting me, I was totally on my own. I didn't know anyone with the condition, had nowhere to go and no one to ask for help.

In retrospect my ED clues started at age forty-four, though I wasn't sure then that something was wrong. Occasionally, I wondered—but was scared to do anything.

Fortunately, I had learned from feminism—so central to my earlier men's movement activism—to remember that I wasn't ruled by my penis. Sex should be holistic, I believed, not primarily defined by intercourse, or by my genitals. Emotionally, though, it was totally different. I wasn't crushed, but I was seriously hurting. Sadly, I hurt alone.

Lost at 47

I was looking forward to a wonderful, long weekend with my love. We were going to chill out from life's pressures, relax, catch up on things together, and share the magic of our normal extended hours of sweet lovemaking. Then a one hundred percent failure—I couldn't get it up! Maybe, I told myself, I was just tired from the trip.

We relaxed… no pressure, sweetie… no talk about what had just happened. Several hours later—a repeat nonperformance—Groundhog Day. Again, we pretended everything was okay. The next day was déjà vu all over again. On top of my obvious failures, our usual cuddling just didn't feel right to me.

There had always been a relaxed informality to our lovemaking. Intercourse wasn't our main focus. It was part of our unhurried, soothing, incredible times together, but it wasn't "it."

Still, I was really shook! I remembered occasional premature ejaculation decades back, but I had never previously "failed" with my love. I hadn't been drunk or sick, so why couldn't I get it up? Once, sure, a fluke; but five, six, seven repeated failures—what the fuck was going on?!

We lived 2,000 miles apart. A long distance relationship brought its own set of problems. Now I felt a further distance; serious unrelated issues had come up for me that weekend. It was an isolating, lonely time. Despite my love's desires to work through our issues, I decided to break off the relationship.

Over the next several years my ED affected me in limited ways. I had no dramatic failures, but sex was never easy. I was in a long-term relationship, but my partner and I avoided talking about our growing emotional distance. Sexual issues seemed secondary to other concerns.

Although it no doubt would have been a big help, I never talked seriously with my best friend. When I tried to talk about my ED, he seemed uncomfortable. I certainly couldn't talk with coworkers or anyone at the health club!

A Few Years Later

By the time I turned fifty-two my self-esteem had plummeted as my ED symptoms intensified. I didn't hide my ED issues from my new partner. At first we didn't understand how seriously it would affect our relationship.

My penis became a distant "other." Sometimes I thought it was erect when it was totally soft. Sometimes it was almost the opposite. One of us always had to feel it to tell if it was erect enough to consider intercourse.

I was increasingly stung by my partner's words: "You're not hard enough." Though not spoken with malice, her words really stung. I had trouble sharing my feelings. I felt like I owed her what I couldn't give. Despite her reassuring words, I was scared she'd leave me.

At my partner's request, I made an appointment with my physician to get a prescription for Viagra. Although he had previously seemed attuned to my medical needs, he told me he knew very little about ED and seemed bothered by the topic. Maybe I was hypersensitive, but it sure felt like he couldn't wait to get on to his next patient. I was hurting and I left the office feeling like he didn't care. He did, at least, refer me to a urologist.

That doctor could find no clear cause for my ED, a fairly common occurrence. He gave me samples of Levitra, Cialis and Viagra to try. Viagra was the only one that worked that had no serious accompanying side effects. At first I was able to achieve an erection around 30–50 minutes after I took it. Still, my erections felt awkward, different in ways I can't easily describe.

We had to plan times to make love. It couldn't be too soon after meals or when I was exhausted. After waiting for a pill to take effect, a specific routine began: 1) I'd be "tested" for hardness. 2) If my penis was hard enough, we'd rush into prep mode—she would apply a lubricant. 3) We would then immediately attempt intercourse.

There was no more taking care of her desires or needs first. To me, that felt wrong, very wrong. I was always terrified that my erection would disappear. Intercourse became planned, nonpleasurable—a chore for both of us.

Although I thought I needed successful intercourse to feel good about myself, with increasing failures, I was scared to try. Absurd as it may sound, I was nostalgic for my increasingly distant memories of wet dreams and morning piss hard-ons.

About a year after first using Viagra, we gave up on it. By then I nearly always either couldn't get erections or would quickly lose them as soon as we tried to have intercourse.

Lessons I've Learned

Physicians initially seek to "cure" ED so men can have healthy sex lives. We are screened for underlying medical conditions (including undiagnosed, potentially life-threatening ones) and for medications whose side effects might cause our ED. Blood tests and routine exams focus on common causes such as low testosterone or high cholesterol, and/or blood pressure levels. Low testosterone can make us seem like "little boys" who can't achieve erections and have no interest in sex. Antidepressants and other meds, such as those we take to fight cancer, also can cause ED.

My testosterone levels were normal. My cholesterol and blood pressure levels were high normal (possibly, but not conclusively related—lowering them, it turned out, didn't change anything). No doctor ever determined what caused my ED, sadly too common an outcome. You can imagine my frustration. I didn't want a bunch of explanations; I simply wanted my problem fixed.

For many men, sex = intercourse = affection. Feeling that they are no longer "a real man," many escape into work, television, porn, or other distractions. Shame and fear distance us from our emotions. We try to hide them from our partners who often feel rejected. They blame themselves after acting "nicer" or "sexier" fails to help. Men commonly make a bad situation worse by either showing obvious anger or remaining deliberately stoic.

Many, perhaps most, men with ED resist seeking medical help. If our initial medical efforts don't go well, we rarely persist in seeking better, more accepting help. Living with ED can easily result in each partner badly hurting. We want support. Often, both partners are emotionally isolated, not feeling safe to talk with friends, family—or each other.

How we can help ourselves and our lovers? My partner and I have struggled through my ED together. We've learned to listen, to talk honestly, and to share our deepest feelings. We've tried multiple medical options. We both agreed that a "final option"—a penile prosthetic implant (which involves significant surgery)—was not desirable for me or us.

Physical intimacy such as gentle nuzzles, simple hugs, and soft kisses—are all important for both of us. We've learned to sexually explore what works and feels good for each of us. This includes using various parts of our bodies as well as sex toys. Achieving an orgasm without a fully erect penis is more difficult, but is still pleasurable.

My love lives with the reality that we can't have the "quickies" she'd like. We both miss the closeness intercourse can provide. Still, we both appreciate our shared emotional and physical intimacy.

I've written about ED several times on my blog. I've found limited, but important support through an e-mail group: "supportEDpartners" (health.groups.yahoo.com/group/supportEDpartners/) which, though primarily for women, is accepting of men's participation.

Men with ED can improve their lives—and those of their partners—by telling their stories. We can help end the stigma and resulting emotional isolation by reaching out to one another. We can learn a lot from one another.

While my article speaks solely of my experience in heterosexual relationships, I hope the greater men's community will address how ED affects *all* men regardless of orientation.

A First Wave Survivor Speaks Out: The Forgotten Generation of People with AIDS
By Les Wright
Fall 2002

I have been living with HIV infection for twenty-two years. I was labeled as "testing positive for exposure to the HTLV-III virus: test results inconclusive;" "disabling ARC, combined with clinical anxious-depressive disorder and post-traumatic stress disorder;" "AIDS" (based on a T-cell count of 55); "symptomatic HIV disease" (based on an HIV-induced medical condition called ITP, whereby the spleen turns on the immune system and destroys healthy red blood cells, producing a medical condition equivalent to hemophilia; the risk of death from internal bleeding from ITP is far greater than from the progression of AIDS); upon a successful splenectomy, I was upgraded to "asymptomatic HIV infection"; my current status is "HIV-infected non-progressor," and I have not taken a single HIV-related medication for nearly three years.

The year 1981 was the turning point in my life. It was then, in the second of the fifteen years I lived in San Francisco in the gay Castro District, that I got clean and sober, returned to graduate school at UC Berkeley, and became infected with HIV. At the time, rumors were circulating in the Castro about a mysterious "gay cancer" and a "gay pneumonia." One of my roommates, a sales clerk at a Castro liquor store, brought home every day the rumors, gossip, and horror stories his customers were sharing.

The earliest medical professionals took one look at my "highest-risk" profile (urban gay male "lifestyle"—sex, drugs, and rock and roll), threw their hands up in the air and, in their scientific lingo, essentially told me to prepare to meet my maker.

In the first months and years of the AIDS epidemic, individuals in the gay male communities hardest hit—New York, Los Angeles, and my hometown of San Francisco—banded together to deal with AIDS head-on. It meant fighting battles on several fronts simultaneously: caregiving for the terminally ill (AIDS patents were being turned away from hospitals, and medical personnel were refusing to touch PWAs [people with AIDS]); organizing infrastructure to provide communications, information, and support; agitating for political action at the local, state, and national levels (shamefully, it was five years into the epidemic before then-President Reagan even uttered the word AIDS); and educating ourselves about the medical dimensions of HIV infection, the bureaucracies of the health care system, and the politics of funding for medical research and treatment. It was a battle fought mostly by PWAs themselves, their allies among gay men and especially lesbians, and some medical folks. All the while we were fighting the enemy within—the virus. Even as new recruits to the fight stepped into action, the ranks of the activists were decimated, over and over.

My neighborhood became a version of *The Night of the Living Dead*. And the sense of being cut off from the rest of the world made it feel like an episode from *The Twilight Zone*. Grassroots groups sprang up to provide social support services, medical referral services, and whatever else seemed to be direly needed. Meanwhile, society at large would ignore AIDS Ground Zero for another five years.

We lived suspended in the tormenting liminal space of unknowing. We looked after our own, while not understanding what was going on; we beseeched and besieged the medical community to take this epidemic disease seriously; we fought against the irrational demonizing that "it" was a "gay disease" and against the concomitant walls of prejudices—that we deserved it, that it would remain confined to the gay male community, and that as long as society turned a blind eye to us, it and we would magically "go away."

As a long-term survivor I was among the first to "go back to work." I left my safe haven among the living dead in San Francisco, subsisting on $500 a month in SSI payments, the kindness of the few people who didn't turn their backs on me, and the always threadbare AIDS support systems. In 1993 I accepted a teaching position at a college in the Boston area. Relocating to the East, once again, I found myself totally on my own.

When I survey where things are today I feel profoundly demoralized by how little progress we as a society have made—despite decades of AIDS awareness education, safer sex education, the rise of a multinational AIDS drug industry, advances in medical and psychological support, and the relative transformation of HIV infection from a guaranteed death sentence to the illusion of a manageable chronic disease.

In short, gay men are having as much sex as ever, and the sex they are having is growing steadily and increasingly unsafe. And increasingly, gay men are now entering into a tacit agreement to deny reality—as is much of the rest of the population, apparently, particularly younger people. As a college professor, I have observed an increasing rate of cigarette smoking among my undergraduate students, despite all that is now known about nicotine addiction and cigarettes. Recreational drug use and abuse of alcohol is as high as ever, and is disavowed as much as ever. Although not all of my students are gay, of course, they are practicing many risky behaviors reminiscent of my experiences of twenty years ago. When I tease them, as a recovering alcoholic and drug addict, about what goes on in the dorms, typically they put on their best angelic Sunday-morning faces and assure me that the binge drinking, the drug club scene, the dorm-room sex and date rape that are as much a part of their daily student experience as they were in my day, are not happening. And then they light up another cigarette and go on about their business.

Sexuality is a human universal, and sexual appetite a basic human need—either coupled with love, intimacy, and romance or as a vital drive common to all species. How to have sex in an epidemic is still an unsolved problem. And in 2002 we are still just barely at the beginning of the worst medical crisis in recorded human history. But ignoring it or denying it, and not practicing what we preach, have so far not—and never will—make HIV go away.

Ejaculation Control: Why Not to Come Tonight
By Haji Shearer
Summer 2004

I gave away my virginity when I was sixteen. It was a lousy performance. Once I figured out where to enter, the action was over momentarily. My girlfriend was kind and patient—perhaps because I demonstrated other useful skills. Eventually, I improved. Part of that improvement came from paying attention to my partner, part from books. Two years later, by the time we ended the sexual aspect of our relationship, I believed, like many men, that it was a privilege to sleep with me.

Over the years, in contemporary writing culled from ancient Indian and Chinese manuscripts, I learned the theory behind men increasing their sexual pleasure without ejaculating.

As I prepared this essay, I did a quick survey of some of my more enlightened male friends and was surprised that no one was using this technique. The most salient question asked of me was a shocked, "Why would I want to do that?" There are two basic answers. The first is because it can give you, the man, greater pleasure. The second is because it can give the woman more pleasure as well.

Let's look at the first reason first. Too-frequent ejaculations result in both the ejaculatory fluid and the rich orgasmic experience decreasing almost to nonexistence. Any man who has experienced multiple ejaculations with little recovery time knows this. On the other hand, sex without ejaculation requires no recovery time and can produce strong feelings of full-body pleasure different from, and in many ways superior to, the ejaculatory sneeze.

Whenever a man ejaculates—regardless of age, body type, or income—he experiences a temporary loss of energy. A pleasant sensation to be sure, but a depletion nonetheless. That's one explanation for the classic stereotype of men falling asleep after sex. From personal experience, I can attest that there is no male energy loss after sex without ejaculating. "Why bother?" you ask. "Where's the pleasure for me?" Think about the thrusting, squeezing, licking, and kissing. All these aspects of the sexual experience are pleasure-filled, but subordinated because they pale in comparison to ejaculation. Men tend to be more goal-oriented than women when it comes to sex (and, one could argue, other activities as well). Curtailing our obsession with getting to the "finish line" of ejaculation creates the space to enjoy these more subtle pleasures to a higher degree.

In addition, the fact that there is no energy loss is itself another payoff. Instead of being depleted, imagine being energized by sex. When you stop—either because no more time is available or because your lover has had enough—you are still erect and ready. Using visualization and physical movement, you can circulate this retained energy up your spine and along your limbs to energize your entire body. You are still full of stamina. You don't feel tired. You and your partner have enjoyed all the pleasures of sex except your ejaculation, and you are able to jump up to perform any other kind of physical or mental work with added vigor (including more sex!).

The second, more altruistic reason why a man would want to have sex without ejaculating is to increase his partner's pleasure. As we explore this angle, let's define "premature ejaculation" as any ejaculation that occurs before the man desires it and before his partner is fulfilled. Left to my own inclination, five to ten minutes of sex would be fine. My unrestrained tendency is to get the intense pleasure of ejaculation quickly, then move on to something else (and get another quickie later).

My desire to slow down and pace myself is due largely to concern for my wife, who takes longer than I do to become aroused. Without consciously delaying my own sexual gratification, I could not satisfy her. Listening to other women and men has convinced me that my wife and I are not unusual in our patterns of arousal. In American culture, instant gratification—the "wham, bam, thank you ma'am" model—is promoted as the ideal, encouraging selfish sexual attitudes, particularly in young men. I too was indoctrinated with the modern American concept of copulation, so having sex without ejaculating seemed irrational and counterintuitive to me at first. Some men are simply not interested in delaying their sexual satisfaction, and thus some women are left unfulfilled by the premature ejaculation of their mates.

In my experience, women take an undetermined and changeable amount of time, based on many variables, to reach erotic fulfillment. They do, however, generally take more time than a typical man takes to stroke straight to ejaculation. Attempts by a man to set an arbitrary time of 5, 15, or even 45 minutes before ejaculation creates a potentially problematic expectation that the woman must also reach her peak by that time. And if you, as a man, ejaculate before your woman is fulfilled, you have failed and must endure her disappointment. If you are not accosted with your failure immediately, you will suffer it in an indirect form in the future. Some of you know what I'm talking about. I suspect much of the tension that occurs between men and women is traceable to this unfortunate sexual dynamic.

This is a good point for disclaimer. I have not mastered ejaculation control, as my wife can attest. I don't always bring her to satisfaction before I ejaculate. In fact, my understanding of her satisfaction is evolving as I mature. I used to think the goal for her was to have an orgasm every time (as was my goal). As I listen to my wife more, I realize she doesn't need to reach the heights of passion each time we get horizontal. Thus, I begin to understand the famous female fascination with cuddling, which is much easier for me to participate in and enjoy if I am not racing off to ejaculation land.

This is the basic theory of ejaculation-free sex. If you deem it worth a try, you can practice some exercises that are best learned over time and are themselves the topic of full-length articles. Briefly, let me address one crucial aspect of the practice, the physical ability to control ejaculation. In *The Tao of Health, Sex, & Longevity,* Daniel P. Reid explains a simple exercise that teaches a man to "lock the gate" that controls ejaculation: "While urinating, a few seconds before the flow of urine stops, sharply lock the flow, as if you were 'holding it' while looking for a toilet. After a second or two, relax the contraction, let the flow of urine resume, then immediately 'squeeze it off' again. Each squeeze will cause a strong spurt of residual urine as the urethra is contracted. Repeat this three to five times, or until no more urine spurts out when you squeeze, than hold the last contraction for 5-10 seconds while you tuck yourself back in and zip up."

The muscle you develop in this exercise is the same one you use to control ejaculation during sex. Strengthening it will allow you to physically control your ejaculations with less difficulty. Once you locate the muscle you can practice contracting and relaxing it anytime. (Think of the added value to those boring meetings you have to attend!)

The more difficult aspect of the practice will be convincing yourself there is pleasure beyond ejaculation. This can only be known by direct experience. You needn't give up ejaculation entirely. There is obviously pleasure to be found there. However, I am suggesting you sacrifice a percentage of your ejaculations for an even greater prize. If you want to move beyond the ordinary realm of sexual interaction, exploring the deeper pleasures of ejaculation-free sex will open doors of delight for you and your mate. If you can gently bring your old mental habits under control by delaying ejaculation, you may find, as I did, fruits of sexual pleasure that men addicted to ejaculating will never taste.

Vday.org founder Eve Ensler and Congolese gynecologist-obstetrician and activist Dr. Denis Mukwege.

OVERCOMING VIOLENCE

> *What do we think happens to men when they are not allowed to cry? Bullets, I think, are hardened tears.*

> —Eve Ensler

Though occasionally perpetrated by women, domestic violence, sexual assault, and rape remain overwhelmingly within the domain of male violence. What about our culture perpetuates such violence in men? How can men overcome their own violent histories and change for the better? How do aspects of men's lives such as sports, war, and pornography contribute to making such violence permissible? This section asks these questions and others as it explores the culture of violence that permeates men's lives and how it is linked to traditional masculinity.

When Men Do Nothing

Stephen McArthur
Summer 2012

(Inspired by Martin Niemoller's "When they came for me...")

First, he began to tell her what to wear, and I did nothing because, obviously, he cares what she looks like.

Then, he came home from a bad day at work and told her the house looked like crap and said she was a pig, and I did nothing because it is his house, isn't it?

Then, he started calling her bitch and stupid fat whore when he was angry, and I did nothing because I give money to breast cancer research and wear a pink ribbon;

Then, he warned her not to go anywhere with her bitchy best friend, and I did nothing because he was just trying to protect her;

Then, when she did meet her best friend for lunch, he put his fist through the wall a foot from her head, seething with anger and spittle, and I did nothing because he did tell her not to, didn't he?

Then, he told her not to go *anywhere* without him, and I did nothing because it's not really my business;

Then, when she did, he showed her the gun he bought, and I did nothing because I am active in the peace movement;

Then, when she threatened to call the police, he told her they wouldn't believe her, and I did nothing because the cops can handle this type of thing;

Then, when she told him she didn't want to have sex anymore and he forced her, I did nothing because she's his wife, isn't she?

And then, when she said she was leaving him, he said he would commit suicide if she did, and I did nothing because it was just an idle threat;

And then when she did leave, he found her and shot her, and I did nothing because it was too late.

And besides, isn't there some kind of woman's group that could have dealt with this?

The Macho Paradox
By Jackson Katz
Spring 2006

Most people think violence against women is a women's issue. And why wouldn't they? Just about every woman in this society thinks about it every day. If they're not getting harassed on the street, living in an abusive relationship, recovering from a rape, or in therapy to deal with the sexual abuse they suffered as children, they're ordering their daily lives around the *threat* of men's violence.

But it's a mistake to call *men's* violence a *women's* issue. Take the subject of rape. Many people reflexively consider rape to be a women's issue. But let's take a closer look. What percentage of rape do women commit? Is it 10 percent, 5 percent? No. *Women commit less than 1 percent of rape.* Let's state this another way: men perpetrate over 99 percent of rape. Whether the victims are female or male, *men* are overwhelmingly the perpetrators. But we call it a *women's* issue?

It's my premise that the long-running American tragedy of sexual and domestic violence—including rape, battering, sexual harassment, and the sexual exploitation of women and girls—is more revealing about *men* than it is about women. Men, after all, are the ones committing the vast majority of the violence. Men are the ones doing most of the battering and almost all of the raping. Men are the ones paying the prostitutes (and killing them in video games), going to strip clubs, renting sexually degrading pornography, writing and performing misogynistic music.

When men's role in gender violence is discussed—in newspaper articles, sensational TV news coverage, or everyday conversation—the focus is typically on men as perpetrators, or potential perpetrators. These days, you don't have to look far to see evidence of the pain and suffering these men cause. But it's rare to find any in-depth discussion about the culture that's producing these violent men. It's almost as if the perpetrators were aliens who landed here from another planet. It's rarer still to hear thoughtful discussions about the ways our culture defines "manhood," and how that definition might be linked to the endless string of stories about husbands killing wives, or groups of young men raping girls (and sometimes videotaping the rape) that we hear about on a regular basis.

Why isn't there more conversation about the underlying social factors that contribute to the pandemic of violence against women? Why aren't men's attitudes and behaviors toward women the focus of more critical scrutiny and coordinated action? In the early twenty-first century, the 24/7 news cycle brings us a steady stream of gender violence tragedies: serial killers on the loose, men abducting young girls, domestic violence homicides, sexual abuse scandals in powerful institutions like the Catholic Church and the Air Force Academy. You can barely turn on the news these days without coming across another gruesome sex crime—whether it's a group of boys gang-raping a girl in a middle school bathroom, or a young pregnant mother who turns up missing, and a few days later her husband emerges as the primary suspect.

Isn't it about time we had a national conversation about the *male causes* of this violence, instead of endlessly lingering on its consequences in the lives of women? Thanks to the US battered women's and rape crisis movements, it is no longer taboo to discuss women's experience of sexual and domestic violence. This is a significant achievement. To an unprecedented extent, American women today expect to be supported—not condemned—when they disclose what men have done to them (unless the man is popular, wealthy, or well-connected, in which case all bets are off).

This is all to the good. Victims of violence and abuse—whether they're women or men—should be heard and respected. Their needs come first. But let's not confuse concern for victims with the political will to change the conditions that led to their victimization in the first place. On talk shows, in brutally honest memoirs, at Take Back the Night rallies, and even in celebrity interviews, our society now grants many women the platform to discuss the sexual abuse and mistreatment that have sadly been a part of women's lives here and around the world for millennia. But when was the last time you heard someone in public or private life talk about violence against women in a way that went beyond the standard victim fixation and put a sustained spotlight on men—either as perpetrators or as bystanders? It is one thing to focus on the "against women" part of the phrase. But someone's responsible for doing it, and (almost) everyone knows that it's overwhelmingly men. Why aren't people talking about this? Is it realistic to talk about preventing violence against women if no one even wants to say out loud who's responsible for it?

For the past two decades I've been part of a growing movement of men, in North America and around the world, whose aim is to reduce violence against women by focusing on those aspects of male culture—especially male peer culture—that provide active or tacit support for some men's abusive behavior. This movement is racially and ethnically diverse, and it brings together men from both privileged and poor communities, and everyone in between.

This is challenging work on many levels, and no one should expect rapid results. For example, there is no way to gloss over some of the race, class, and sexual orientation divisions between and among the men ourselves. It is also true that it takes time to change social norms that are so deeply rooted in structures of gender and power. Even so, there is room for optimism. We've had our successes: There are arguably more men today who are actively confronting violence against women than at any time in human history.

Make no mistake. Women blazed the trail that we are riding down. Men are in the position to do this work precisely because of the great leadership of women. The battered women's and rape crisis movements and their allies in local, state, and federal government have accomplished a phenomenal amount over the past generation. Public awareness about violence against women is at an all-time high. The level of services available today for female victims and survivors of men's violence is—while not yet adequate—nonetheless historically unprecedented.

But one area where our society still has a very long way to go is in preventing perpetration. We continue to produce in the United States hundreds of thousands of physically and emotionally abusive—and sexually dangerous—boys and men each year. Millions more men participate in sexist behaviors on a continuum that ranges from mildly objectifying women to literally enslaving them in human trafficking syndicates. We can provide services to the female victims of these men until the cows come home. We can toughen enforcement of rape, domestic violence, and stalking laws, arrest and incarcerate even more men than we do currently. But this is all reactive and after the fact. It is essentially an admission of failure.

What I am proposing is that we adopt a much more ambitious approach. If we are going to bring down the rates of violence against women dramatically—not just at the margins—we will need a far-reaching cultural revolution. At its heart this revolution must be about changing the sexist social norms in male culture, from the elementary school playground to the common room in retirement communities—and every locker room, pool hall, and boardroom in between. For us to have any hope of achieving historic reductions in incidents of violence against women, at a minimum we will need to dream big and act boldly. It almost goes without saying that we will need the help of a lot more men—at all levels of power and influence—than are currently involved. Obviously we have our work cut out for us. As a measure of just how far we have to go, consider that in spite of the misogyny and sexist brutality all around us, millions of nonviolent men today fail to see gender violence as their issue. "I'm a good guy," they say. "This isn't my problem."

For years, women of every conceivable ethnic, racial, and religious background have been trying to get men around them—and men in power—to do more about violence against women. They have asked nicely, and they have demanded angrily. Some women have done this on a one-to-one basis with boyfriends and husbands, fathers and sons. They have patiently explained to men they care about how much they—and all women—have been harmed by men's violence. Others have gone public with their grievances. They have written songs and slam poetry. They have produced brilliant academic research. They have made connections between racism and sexism. They have organized speakouts on college campuses and in communities large and small. They have marched. They have advocated for legal and political reform at the state and national level. On both a micro and a macro level, women in this era have successfully broken through their historical silence about violence against women and found their voice—here in the United States and around the world.

Yet even with all of these achievements, women continue to face an uphill struggle in trying to make meaningful inroads into male culture. Their goal has not been simply to get men to listen to women's stories and truly hear them—although that is a critical first step. The truly vexing challenge has been getting men to actually go out and *do* something about the problem, in the form of educating and organizing *other men* in numbers great enough to prompt a real cultural shift. Some activist women—even those who have had great faith in men as allies—have been beating their heads against the wall for a long time, and are frankly burned out on the effort. I know this because I have been working with many of these women for a long time. They are my colleagues and friends.

My work is dedicated to getting more men to take on the issue of violence against women, and thus to build on what women have achieved. The area that I focus on is not law enforcement or offender treatment but the *prevention* of sexual and domestic violence and all their related social pathologies—including violence against children. To do this, I and other men here and around the world have been trying to get our fellow men to see that this problem is not just personal for a small number of men who happen to have been touched by the issue. We try to show them that it is personal for them, too. *For all of us.* We talk about men not only as perpetrators but also as victims. We try to show them that violence by men against one another—from simple assaults to gay bashing—is linked to the same structures of gender and power that produce so much men's violence against women.

But there is no point in being naïve about why women have had such a difficult time convincing men to make violence against women a men's issue. In spite of significant social change in recent decades, men continue to grow up with, and are socialized into, a deeply misogynistic, male-dominated culture where violence against women—from the subtle to the homicidal—is disturbingly common. It's *normal.* And precisely because the mistreatment of women is such a pervasive characteristic of our patriarchal culture, most men, to a greater or lesser extent, have played a role in its perpetuation. This gives us a strong incentive to avert our eyes.

Women, of course, have also been socialized into this misogynistic culture. Some of them resist and fight back. In fact, women's ongoing resistance to their subordinate status is one of the most momentous developments in human civilization over the past two centuries. Just the same, plenty of women show little appetite for delving deeply into the cultural roots of sexist violence. It's much less daunting simply to blame "sick" individuals for the problem. You hear women all the time explaining away men's bad behavior as the result of individual pathology: "Oh, he just had a bad childhood," or "He's an angry drunk. The booze gets to him. He's never been able to handle it."

But regardless of how difficult it can be to show some women that violence against women is a social problem that runs deeper than the abusive behavior of individual men, it is still much easier to convince women—of all races, ethnicities, and religious beliefs—that dramatic change is in their best interest than it is to convince men. In fact, many people would argue that, since men are the dominant sex-class, and violence serves to reinforce this dominance, it is not in men's best interests to reduce violence against women, and that the very attempt to enlist a critical mass of men in this effort amounts to a fool's errand.

For those of us who reject this line of reasoning, the big question, then, is how do we reach men? We know we're not going to transform, overnight or over many decades, certain structures of male power and privilege that have developed over thousands of years. Nevertheless, how are we going to bring more men—many more men—into a conversation about sexism and violence against women? And how are we going to do this without turning them off, without berating them, without blaming them for centuries of sexist oppression? Moreover, how are we going to move beyond talk and get substantial numbers of men to partner *with* women in reducing men's violence, instead of working *against* them in some sort of fruitless and counterproductive gender struggle?

That is the $64,000 question. Esta Soler, executive director of Futures Without Violence (formerly Family Violence Prevention Fund) and an influential leader in the domestic violence movement, says that activating men is "the next frontier" in the women-led movement. "In the end," she says, "we cannot change society unless we put more men at the table, amplify men's voices in the debate, enlist men to help change social norms on the issue, and convince men to teach their children that violence against women is always wrong."

Call me a starry-eyed optimist, but I have long been convinced that there are millions of men in our society who are ready to respond well to a positive message about this subject. If you go to a group of men with your finger pointed ("Stop treating women so badly!") you'll often get a defensive response. But if you approach the same group of men by appealing, in Abraham Lincoln's famous words, to "the better angels of our nature," surprising numbers of them will rise to the occasion.

For me, this is not just an article of faith. Our society has made real progress in confronting the long-standing problem of men's violence against women *in my lifetime*. Take the 1994 Violence Against Women Act (VAWA). It is the most far-reaching piece of legislation ever on the subject. Federal funds have enabled all sorts of new initiatives, including prevention efforts that target men and boys. There have been many other encouraging developments on both the institutional and the individual levels. Not the least of these positive developments is the fact that so many young men today "get" the concept of gender equality and are actively working against men's violence.

A number of studies in the past several years demonstrate that significant numbers of men are uncomfortable with the way some of their male peers talk about and treat women. But since few men in our society have dared to talk publicly about such matters, many men think they are the only ones who feel uncomfortable. Because they feel isolated and alone in their discomfort, they do not say anything. Their silence, in turn, simply reinforces the false perception that few men are uncomfortable with sexist attitudes and behaviors. It is a vicious cycle that keeps a lot of caring men silent.

I meet men all the time who thank me—or my fellow activists and colleagues—for publicly taking on the subject of men's violence. I frequently meet men who are receptive to the paradigm-shifting idea that men's violence against women has to be understood as a men's issue. Their issue. These men come from every demographic and geographic category. They include thousands of men who would not fit neatly into simplistic stereotypes about the kind of man who would be involved in "that touchy-feely stuff."

Still, it is an uphill fight. Truly lasting change is only going to happen as new generations of women come of age and demand equal treatment with men in every realm, and new generations of men work with them to reject the sexist attitudes and behaviors of their predecessors. This will take decades, and the outcome is hardly predetermined. But along with tens of thousands of activist women and men who continue to fight the good fight, I believe that it is possible to achieve something much closer to gender equality and a dramatic reduction in the level of men's violence against women, both here and around the world. And there is a lot at stake. If sexism and violence against women do not subside considerably in the twenty-first century, it will not just be bad news for women. It will also say something truly ugly and tragic about the future of our species.

VOICE MALE

On Being the Partner of a Rape Survivor
By Tom Schiff
Spring 1991

> *Years ago I lived with a rape survivor. Living with a woman who has been raped is a vivid reminder of the effects of men's violence. It is frightening because I know the culture that created such men is deeply rooted in all of us; it is heartbreaking to see the result of anger, violence, and despair. And it is infuriating to know the cycle continues. I wrote this essay more than twenty years ago. Even though we are no longer together, I kept the piece in the present tense as a way to connect with other men who may be experiencing a version of what I went through. I have a great deal for respect for my former partner for many reasons, not the least of which is the courage and fortitude she had—and has—to deal with the violence perpetuated upon her.*

I live with a wonderful woman who was raped on several occasions. She — no, *we* are—nearly ten years later, dealing with the after effects of these heinous acts. It has been one of the greatest challenges of my life. Dealing with the ups and downs of mood swings and flashbacks, processing conversations, finding a balance between being supportive and not being smothered in neediness—as well as finding time for myself—has taken a toll.

One of the hardest parts about being the partner of a rape survivor is dealing with my own anger. There is just so much of it. I am angry at the men who assaulted her. I am angry at a system that perpetuates men thinking of women as objects over which they can exert control. I am angry at a legal system and a media that reinforce those notions. I am so sick of seeing movies in which men are violent to women in relation to sex, with the women accepting or, worse, being portrayed as liking it.

But some of the most difficult anger I have to deal with is the anger I have toward my partner. Why didn't she deal with these issues *before*? Why now? These "events" happened long before we were together. It is little consolation to realize she is going through all this now because she feels safe with me. My anger stems from wanting a partner who was the way she was when we first got together: playful, bold, sexually alive, and confident.

My anger also stems from fear. People tell me our relationship will be so much stronger on the other side of this, having worked together to create intimacy. I don't know if that's true. Judging from my current experience, I can't say what will happen. I fear sex will always be a challenge. I fear there will always be issues we have to discuss because, say, I moved my fork in a way that triggered a flashback, or performed some other simple act precipitating a similar result. I fear we may never have children if she doesn't feel emotionally prepared. I fear she will be a completely different person on the other side of this and I won't know her, and maybe won't want to know her.

I'm never quite sure who is going to be there when I get home. Sometimes she is happy, energetic, and playful, other times timid and frightened. Sometimes we get into arguments and I feel like I'm arguing with someone I don't know, or about things that just aren't part of my life. Invariably, after a while, I figure out what's going on and I'll ask, "Did something happen today?" At that point I will hear about flashbacks, insecurities, fears. These situations happen often.

A while back, my partner and a friend decided to prepare a special dinner for the friend's partner and me because we had both been so "supportive and wonderful" in helping them deal with their recovery. We had a really nice evening. The next morning, while my partner and I were making love I saw the color drain out of her face. We stopped and she curled up and began to cry. Her flashbacks wouldn't stop. After an hour or so, she was able to calm down enough to move, but she was a mess for much of the next two weeks.

My partner and I love each other very much; we continue to be in love. We have learned how to talk about a great many things, and our relationship is getting stronger. She has taught me—among other things—new ways to listen, new ways to look at my masculinity, and new ways to love. Slowly, things really are getting better.

But none of this has been easy for me. I continue to need to talk about this experience and to find support. One of the avenues I have sought for this support is the Men's Resource Center. There was a group forming for partners of women who had been raped. I thought such a group would be huge; after all, rape statistics estimate that approximately one out of every three women will be raped in her lifetime. Much to my dismay, I am often the only one to show up. While I get a lot out of speaking with the facilitator, I would hardly call myself a group.

I hope some of you reading this, who also may be partners of rape survivors, will find support. Find ways to connect with other men who are partners of survivors. There is a lot we can gain from one another. It is a hard process, but it's a lot easier to have a place to talk about it. And it is one way we can work to change the cycle of violence against women.

VOICE MALE

Breaking Out of the Man Box
By Tony Porter
Spring 2009

It's high time for men who are "well-meaning" to begin to acknowledge the role male privilege and male socialization play in domestic violence, sexual assault, and violence against women. It's time for men to claim the collective responsibility we have for ending violence against women. It's time to become part of the solution.

So you are a "good guy," not one of those men who would assault a woman. *You* would never commit a rape or hit your wife or girlfriend—you're not part of the problem. So how can you become part of the solution? You are exactly the kind of man who *can* help to end violence against women. So just what is a good guy? I call him a "well-meaning man." A well-meaning man is a man who believes women should be respected, including his wife or girlfriend and other women in his life. A well-meaning man does not assault a woman. A well-meaning man believes in equality for women, that women should be treated fairly and justly. A well-meaning man, for all practical purposes, is a nice guy, a good man.

My work, my vision, is not to bash well-meaning men. An assault on men is not going to end the assault on women. I seek to help men understand, through a process of re-education and accountability, that, despite all our goodness, we men have been socialized to continue a system of domination, dehumanization, and oppression of women.

I do not come to this work as a man who thinks he knows it all or who "has it all together." I, too, am a "well-meaning man." For twenty years I worked in the field of alcohol and chemical dependency. Early on in that work I began to address the importance of cultural diversity in the field. After about three years I realized I had to go much deeper than a cultural diversity approach permitted. My work then began to focus more on issues related to group oppression, particularly racism. As I went about my business addressing the "ism" of race—racism and its relationship to alcoholism and chemical dependency, women I worked with began to confront me on my own "ism"—sexism.

At first I felt insulted, thinking (and sometimes verbalizing), "I'm a good guy, I'm no sexist." This remained my mind-set for quite some time. Only through a series of events that challenged me did I begin to dismantle my cherished belief.

Over the next five years I immersed myself in learning, owning, and addressing my sexism, as well as the collective sexism of men. I began to understand, to see that what emerged in my consciousness was that domestic violence, sexual assault, and all other forms of violence against women are rooted in a sexist, male-dominated society.

As well-meaning men, through our inaction we have allowed violence against women to be seen as a "women's issue." We spend little, if any, time addressing this epidemic. We look at violence against women through our own lens, a male socialized perspective that leaves little room for any true accountability for men. We don't mean to harm women; many of us have no idea what we're doing. Rather, we are just going with the flow, doing things as we always have. This approach has limited our ability or willingness to be concerned with how we affect women or how women experience us. One of the key things we have not done, and continue not to do, is listen to women.

Deeply imbedded in the socialization of all men, well-meaning men included, is the conscious and unconscious ability (and sometimes desire) to tune women out, to silence them, to take away their voice, to not listen. Many men justify this action by saying that women talk too much, or they nag. We make no connection to the reality that if men would listen, women would not need to repeat themselves or be so detailed. As men, well-meaning men, if we choose to listen to women and take their direction, we could actually end violence against women as we know it here in the United States.

Three key aspects of male socialization create, normalize, and maintain violence against women: men viewing women as "less than"; men treating women as "property"; and men seeing women as "objects." All three are major contributors to violence against women, perpetuated consciously or not by all men, including well-meaning men.

We must begin to examine the ways in which male socialization fosters violence against women. We must begin to examine the ways we separate ourselves from men who assault and abuse women, while simultaneously (through our inaction) giving them permission to do so. We make monsters out of them as a means of supporting our position that we're different from them. We remain focused on fixing *them*, pathologizing *their* violence, blaming family history, chemical dependency, mental illness, or an inability to manage their anger, while for the most part these are not the reasons men abuse women. It makes sense that we would expend the energy to "fix" them in order to maintain and even strengthen our status as "good guys." In doing so, we squeeze out the space needed to understand and acknowledge that violence against women is a manifestation of sexism. Once we can admit that violence against women springs from sexism, we have to acknowledge that all men are part of the problem.

The men we identify as "the bad guys," who assault and abuse women largely do so by choice. Through our silence, these men receive a kind of permission to behave this way from those of us well-meaning men. We give men who abuse and assault permission in several ways: We stay quiet and "mind our own business." We minimize the consequences and have limited means to hold these men accountable. We historically hold the view that violence is actually only physical abuse or sexual assault. Taking this position allows us to leave ourselves out of the equation and puts distance between the abuse and us.

Okay, some of you may be saying, "Slow down, you're throwing too much at me too fast." All right. I will slow down. I'll walk you through what I've learned, step by step. We'll do it together. I will share with you many of my personal experiences. It is critically important to note that what I'm sharing is based on the teachings of women. If there is any contribution that I have to offer, it is that I am finally starting to listen.

What I'm sharing also grew partly out of a series of discussions I have had with men over the last five years: men of all ages, ethnic groups, levels of education, and family backgrounds. What did they all have in common? They were all "well-meaning men." I invite you to join in and examine your own role as a well-meaning man in this society. I invite you to begin to challenge other well-meaning men to join you. Together we can create the social change that will help to create a world that is more respectful of and safer for women. This work is long overdue. It's time to get started.

Man to Man: A Community Letter
By Paul Kivel
Fall 2007

As a longtime activist on issues of male violence, activist-author Paul Kivel, a cofounder of the Oakland (California) Men's Project, regularly receives requests to help intervene in situations "where men have abused their partners, have sexually assaulted someone, or are generally acting disrespectfully and abusively toward women in their lives." It was common that friends and acquaintances would express surprise when they learned a man they knew had been acting abusively. In each of these situations, Kivel says "it felt like having to start from scratch, because there had been no previous discussion of expectations about how ... to live together." Recognizing the need to clearly communicate with men who expressed interest in joining a new kind of men's community—one that fostered an awareness of male violence and that wanted to help build a safer and healthier community—Kivel sat down and wrote the letter below "to address individual men in communities that I live, work, and play in." His motivation? "We still, all too often, assume that "our" men have it together and are safe and nonabusive in their personal interactions."

A Letter to Men Entering Our Community (to everyone who was raised as or who identifies as male):

Welcome to our community. Whether you are entering our neighborhood, our workplace, our school community, our congregation, or other collective spaces, I hope you will be welcomed, safe, respected, and fully able to participate in our activities and life together.

There are many ways in which people's safety and well being are undermined in our society. One of the primary interpersonal ways that people are attacked is rarely talked about directly, therefore I need to talk with you about safety and healing from male violence. No matter how special or different or evolved or progressive we think our community is, male violence is happening among and around us.

Many of my friends, family, neighbors, colleagues, joint travelers, and acquaintances have experienced violence from men. Male violence has had a devastating impact on their lives and on the lives of all of us. The cumulative result is that we cannot come together to rebuild our communities, establish a just society, or create intimate partner and family relationships without dealing with the shadow cast by this violence.

I don't know you. I don't know your past history of relationships, I don't know your intentions, and I don't know, or know that you know, what you will do in various interpersonal situations you may find yourself in. So we need to talk, man to man, as you enter our community.

You need to know that many of the women, men, transsexual and transgender people, and youth in your life have experienced, survived, and are still healing from child sexual and physical abuse, teen dating violence, and many kinds of domestic violence and sexual assault, as well as from various forms of racial and homophobic violence (you may be one of them). The pain of this abuse was compounded by the fact that men like you and me did not respond, did not believe, did not support the survivors, and often even colluded with the perpetrators. You need to know that people seldom lie about the abuse they have experienced and that they seldom talk about it either, for fear of further pain, among other reasons. Therefore you may not even know about the kinds of interpersonal violence that those around you have experienced.

For me, there is only one healthy, safe, and healing way to be in relationship with the people around me, and that is to create relationships built on respect, consent, and mutuality, and even though that may not always be enough. In this context I am referring to every level of interaction, from casual encounters at the bus stop or in a store to the most intimate moments of a sexual relationship.

For me, respect means coming from the place of deepest recognition and valuing of the body, spirit, culture, and individuality of the person I am relating to.

Consent means only engaging in conversation, interaction, acts of physical intimacy, or other forms of contact with the expressed affirmation of the other person. No one can give consent if they are underage, asleep, on drugs, don't speak the language, are physically, emotionally, or financially dependent, intimidated, threatened, harassed, cajoled, or manipulated into saying yes when he or she does not really want to. If you have any indication that your behavior is causing someone else pain or that the individual is engaging in behavior that he or she does not really want to, then your responsibility is to stop and check out the accuracy of your impression.

Mutual means to me that both people in the relationship get to establish the boundaries of the relationship and those boundaries will be honored until mutually changed.

I invite you to consider what these three words mean to you.

Respect, consent, and mutuality are principles, not rules. If you are looking for rules then this may not be the community for you. I encourage you to operate from your deepest place of caring about others, not from a fear of "breaking the rules" or of being incorrect. We live in interdependent communities, accountable to one another. Given the violence in our lives and communities, building relationships is a never-ending process of trying to be loving to ourselves and to act in loving ways toward others. With that in mind, if you have any doubt, at any time, that what you are doing may not be completely respectful, consensual, and mutual, check it out with the person you are with, or with others.

I also encourage you to find other male-identified people to talk with about these issues and other aspects of male socialization and male supremacy. Most of us learned early on to hide our feelings and cover our pain, to take abuse and pass it on, and to expect male privilege and entitlement, including emotional, physical, sexual, and other caretaking services from women. You may be hardworking, well intended, creative, committed, charismatic, well read, and/or working for justice. Yet you may still act abusively toward those around you unless you are doing the personal antisexist work necessary to unlearn abusive patterns.

I also think that each of us has a responsibility to support, and lovingly but firmly challenge, the men around us when we see or hear that they are being abusive, acting in disrespectful ways, taking advantage of male privilege, or acting out of male entitlement. There are many institutional systems that perpetuate male violence. But sexism also continues because men collude with other men in perpetuating it. We not only collude; we often actively bond with other men around the objectification, sexualization, marginalization, and exclusion of others. It is certainly not always easy, but it is absolutely essential that we step up as men to challenge other men. Our intervention not only can stop the abuse; it can also break the collusion that allows male violence to continue.

Women, children, and men will only be safe, healthy, and collectively liberated when all systems of oppression are eliminated. In the meantime, we each have a role to play as allies in the struggle to end male violence in all the many forms it takes.

I invite you to join, or redouble your efforts in that struggle. Again, welcome to our community!

In love and solidarity,

Paul Kivel

Challenging Rape Culture
By Robert Jensen
Winter 2003

It is not surprising that we want to separate ourselves from those who commit hideous crimes, to believe that the abominable things some people do are the result of something evil inside them.

But most of us also struggle with a gnawing feeling that however pathological those brutal criminals are, they are of us—part of our world, shaped by our culture.

Such is the case of Richard Marc Evonitz, a "sexually sadistic psychopath," in the words of one expert, who abducted, raped, and killed girls in Virginia and elsewhere. What are the characteristics of a sexually sadistic psychopath? According to a former FBI profiler who has studied serial killers: "A psychopath has no ability to feel remorse for their crimes. They tend to justify what they do as being OK for them. They have no appreciation for the humanity of their victims. They treat them like objects, not human beings."

Such a person is, without question, cruel and inhuman. But aspects of that description fit not only sexually sadistic psychopaths; slightly modified, it also describes much "normal" sex in our culture.

Look at how women are depicted by the pornography industry, which takes in an estimated $10 billion a year in the United States, primarily through sales to male customers, Routinely women are as sexual objects whose sole function is to sexually satisfy men and whose own welfare is irrelevant as long as men are satisfied.

Consider the $52 billion-a-year worldwide prostitution business: Though illegal in the United States (except in Nevada), that industry is grounded in the presumed right of men to gain sexual satisfaction with no concern for the physical and emotional costs to women and children.

Or, simply listen to what heterosexual women so often say about their male sexual partners: *He only seems interested in his own pleasure. He isn't emotionally engaged with me as a person. He treats me like an object.*

To point all this out is not to argue that all men are brutish animals or sexually sadistic psychopaths. Instead, these observations alert us to how sexual predators are not mere aberrations in an otherwise healthy sexual culture.

In the contemporary United States, men generally are trained in a variety of ways to view sex as the acquisition of pleasure by the taking of women. Sex is a sphere in which men are trained to see themselves as naturally dominant and women as naturally passive. Women are objectified and women's sexuality is turned into a commodity that can be bought and sold. Sex becomes sexy because men are dominant and women are subordinate.

Again, the argument is not that all men believe this or act this way, but that such ideas are prevalent in the culture, transmitted from adult men to boys through direct instruction and modeling, by peer pressure among boys, and in mass media. These were the lessons I learned growing up in the 1960s and '70s, and if anything, such messages are more common and intense today.

The predictable result of this state of affairs is a culture in which sexualized violence, sexual violence, and violence-by-sex are so common that they should be considered normal. Not normal in the sense of healthy or preferred, but an expression of the sexual norms of the culture, not violations of those norms. Rape is illegal, but the sexual ethic that underlies rape is woven into the fabric of the culture.

None of these observations excuse or justify sexual abuse. Although some have argued that men are naturally sexually aggressive, feminists have long held that such behaviors are learned, which is why we need to focus not only on the individual pathologies of those who cross the legal line and abuse, rape, and kill, but on the entire culture.

Those who find this analysis outrageous should consider the results of a study of sexual assault on US college campuses. Researchers found that 47 percent of the men who had raped said they expected to engage in a similar assault in the future, and 88 percent of men who reported an assault that met the legal definition of rape were adamant that they had not raped. That suggests a culture in which many men cannot see forced sex as rape, and many have no moral qualms about engaging in such sexual activity on a regular basis.

The language men use to describe sex, especially when they are outside the company of women, is revealing. In locker rooms one rarely hears men asking about the quality of their emotional and intimate experiences. Instead, the questions are: "Did you get any last night?" "Did you score?" "Did you f—— her?" Men's discussions about sex often use the language of power: control, domination, the taking of pleasure.

When I was a teenager, I remember boys joking that an effective sexual strategy would be to drive a date to a remote area, turn off the car engine, and say, "OK, f—— or fight." I would not be surprised to hear that boys are still regaling each other with that "joke."

So, yes, violent sexual predators are monsters, but not monsters from another planet. What we learn from their cases depends on how willing we are to look not only into the face of men such as Evonitz, but also to look into the mirror, honestly, and examine the ways we are not only different but, to some degree, the same.

Such self-reflection, individually and collectively, does not lead to the conclusion that all men are sexual predators or that nothing can be done about it. Instead, it should lead us to think about how to resist and change the system in which we live. This feminist critique is crucial not only to the liberation of women but for the humanity of men, which is so often deformed by patriarchy.

Solutions lie not in the conservatives' call for returning to some illusory "golden age" of sexual morality, a system that was also built on the subordination of women. The task is to incorporate the insights of feminism into a new sexual ethic that does not impose traditional, restrictive sexual norms on people but helps creates a world based on equality, not dominance, in which men's pleasure does not require women's subordination.

WHY IS RAPE A MEN'S ISSUE?

Because Men Rape. Ninety-nine percent of all reported rapists are men. *(US Department of Justice)*

Because Men Experience Rape. One out of seven men will be sexually assaulted during his lifetime. *(National Coalition Against Sexual Assault)*

Because Rape Hurts All of Us. In a world where three out of four sexual assaults are acquaintance rapes, it's hard for women to trust men. In a world where dominance and sexual predation are celebrated as positive masculinity, it's hard for men to be themselves.

Because Men Know Survivors. Chances are good that you already know survivors of rape. If someone you care about discloses rape to you, you need to know how to help.

Because Men Can Stop Rape. The women's movement has been working against rape for many years, and offers experience and skilled leadership. But men's violence against women will only end when men take responsibility for changing the actions and attitudes that make it possible. **Take Action!**

—Courtesy of Men Can Stop Rape

10 THINGS MEN CAN DO TO STOP RAPE

Know that language is powerful.
Words that dehumanize women, frequently in a sexualized way, are common. When we describe someone as an object to be acted upon, then discarded, it gets easier to treat her that way. Use humane and respectful language. Challenge the people around you to do the same.

Communicate about sex.
We have a cultural myth that "good sex should be intuitive," but the reality is that it is based on communication. Consent can never be assumed. We also have cultural pressures for men to "score," and myths that women really want to be forced. Coercion and force are illegal. Get comfortable talking with, and listening to, your partner. "No" means *no*.

Speak out.
You may never have the opportunity to prevent a rape in progress. However, you will have many, many opportunities to challenge the attitudes and behaviors that are part of the larger rape culture. When you see harassment, intervene. When you hear jokes about violence against women, don't laugh, and explain why it's not funny. Write letters to magazines that promote images of women as dehumanized sex objects. Support laws that protect women from violence and help them successfully prosecute their abusers. Silence = Complicity.

Support Survivors, listen to the women in your life, and *believe* them.
More than 1 million women are raped in America each year. One in three women will be sexually assaulted, 40 percent before the age of 18. Chances are, you already have survivors of rape in your life. Learn how to be supportive, know your local rape crisis center where they can get resources and help, and get support yourself.

Give your time.
Volunteer for organizations working to end violence against women. Get further training on how to be an effective ally. Know that most rape crisis centers and community organizations are funded exclusively through grants and donations. Support their work in whatever ways you can.

Talk with women.
Find out what it feels like to live with the threat of rape every day. Find out how they like to be supported. Ask what they would like you to do to challenge rape. Really listen.

Talk with men.
Find out how rape has impacted their lives. Find out how much men lose by being seen as potential rapists. Find out what other men have to say about how to change that reality. Find out how to support male survivors of rape and sexual abuse. Really listen.

Organize.
Create a men's movement against male violence against women: start a dialogue group to examine cultural attitudes about rape, start a men's antirape group, bring workshops and trainings into your school or workplace. Check in with your local men's center or women's center for resources and support.

Work against all forms of oppression.
Violence against women, sexism, racism, heterosexism, and homophobia—all forms of oppression are linked. We cannot end one without challenging them all. Challenge yourself to grow every day, and know that every prejudice we hold injures others and limits our experience.

Create a new masculinity.
Be brave enough to openly value equality. Use your strength and privilege in the service of justice. Live your potential without harming others. Celebrate the construction of a new masculinity that does not depend on the dehumanization of others. Find others who share your vision. You are not alone.

—Center for Women and Community, University of Massachusetts, Amherst

What's a Nice Feminist Like Me Doing in a Place Like This?
By Sara Elinoff Acker
Winter 1999

In 1985, I got my first job in the movement to end violence against women—answering the hotline at a battered women's shelter in Burlington, Vermont. Our program received hundreds of calls a year from women who were virtual hostages in relationships—being physically and emotionally abused and controlled, economically disempowered and spiritually undermined every single day of their lives.

This was more than a job—it was a profound expression of my commitment and politics as a feminist. I had been a women's studies major in college and had worked after college in a feminist health clinic. The epidemic of male violence against women and children greatly distressed me, and I was grateful for the opportunity to actually do something about it.

Whatever innocence I had I lost at that job. I heard horrible stories of violations women suffered at the hands of their partners. I heard about children who were sexually abused by their fathers, stepfathers, or mothers' boyfriends. My heart ached and raged for these women and their children. Our organization's mandate was clear—to help these women know that they did not deserve to be treated this way by anyone, that it wasn't their fault and that we were here to help them get free.

In my organization, and in the battered women's movement, the prevailing attitude about batterers was cut and dried. These were men who benefited profoundly from their power and control over the women and children in their lives. The prospect that these men would be willing to give up that power, to transform their abuse and enter into more egalitarian relationships with their family members, was extremely unlikely. Why would an abuser, who is getting everything he wants from his ability to dominate his partner through control and fear, ever want to change the power dynamics of his relationship? Batterers had too much to gain from being abusive.

We believed that most abusers wouldn't stop their abuse unless they were incarcerated. We thought batterer intervention programs were a lost cause—a waste of valuable resources that should be going to the battered women's movement instead. We believed these programs gave women false and dangerous hopes about their relationships. We felt it was our responsibility to warn the women we worked with. If they wanted an abuse-free life, they would need to leave their relationships.

Back then, if someone had told me that ten years later I would be working in a batterers' intervention program and that I would be a staunch believer in the ability of some abusive men to profoundly transform themselves into nonviolent men, I probably would have been very insulted. Or maybe I would have laughed. Certainly, I would have met such a prediction with extreme disbelief.

But here I am, in my seventh year as the partner services coordinator for the Men Overcoming Violence program (MOVE) at the Men's Resource Center. And yes, I do believe with all my heart that a man who is willing to take full responsibility for his abuse, leaving no stone unturned, and who is prepared to make a long-term commitment to getting help is capable of changing his attitude, his behavior, his relationships, his entire life. This kind of profound change doesn't happen for the majority of men who walk through our program doors. Some of the men make some changes; some make none at all. But this transformation *does* happen. I have seen it. I have met these men. I have talked to their partners and I know it is possible.

How did I get to this place, this new way of looking at men who are abusive? To arrive here, I had to be willing to reexamine and rework some of the core paradigms that have shaped my analysis of domestic violence. I had to trust that I could hold on to my feminist politics, my understanding of sexism and misogyny and its devastating impact on women and children, and still make room for another truth—the truth of men's distorted development and behavior in a sexist, gendered culture, and the damage that this has created for men. I had to embrace the truth that abusive men (and all men) both simultaneously benefit from *and* are hurt by the ways males are socialized in our society. I had to meet men who had come to realize not only that their abuse was damaging to others but that it was in their best interest to change. They understood that not only their behavior, but also their whole idea about what it means to be a man, needed to change.

Over the years I've been working at MOVE, many of my ideas about batterers and battering have been challenged. One is the idea that batterers only benefit from being able to maintain control in their relationships. Certainly, on many levels, batterers *do* benefit from maintaining the abuse. But how can someone "benefit," on the deepest level, when his children are afraid of him, when his wife has withdrawn completely from him, when his marriage is disintegrating, when his tendency toward violence alienates his coworkers, or gets him arrested, or lands him in jail? How can men "benefit" when their abusiveness has resulted in a higher incidence of heart disease, alcoholism, depression, and suicide? On the most fundamental human level an abuser does not benefit from being abusive. All of the gains received by being abusive come with an enormous price tag for the people he loves and for himself.

Domestic violence literature describes batterers as being all-powerful, manipulative, and entitled. On one level this is true. But something else is going on as well, which has more to do with fear than with power. In order to understand the complexity of the dynamics of battering, we must be willing to maintain a kind of "double vision"—to simultaneously hold two ideas that seem contradictory but ultimately are not.

The abuse, the control, the power-over tactics, and the explosive anger are all part of a programmed repertoire of masculinity that has caused immense damage to women and children. Yet these behaviors also hurt men. It is a mask of behaviors and attitudes that often obscures a very different reality—a reality of someone who may feel so isolated, so locked into a damaging construct of masculinity that the only way he can feel powerful is by overpowering others. As young boys, men in our society are quickly taught lessons about how to cope with fear, vulnerability, and the threat of violence. The solution prescribed by our culture is for them to "get tough"—to dominate others or risk being dominated. There is an essential link between an inner experience of powerlessness and the development of power-over behavior.

Working with batterers requires an ability to maintain this dual perspective. First and foremost, abusive behaviors and attitudes must be strongly challenged and dismantled. The Men Overcoming Violence program vigilantly confronts any and all acts of physical and emotional power and control, as well as sexist attitudes toward women. At the same time, we recognized that abusers are often acting out of a faulty and damaging script, centuries old, in which power is defined as "power over another." MOVE teaches about a different kind of power, a "power from within" that does not need to dominate or terrorize or belittle another human being.

Both Gandhi and Martin Luther King Jr. taught that we must "hate the sin, but not the sinner." Likewise in our work, we hold the men accountable for their behaviors while holding out hope for their fundamental goodness—their ability to evolve into gentle, respectful, peaceful men. We are not naïve. We realize that many men who abuse will never stop abusing. But we still believe that change is possible. I have been shocked by how many people who work in this field are fundamentally cynical about the possibilities of abusive men healing. What I believe instead is that a change in consciousness, an awakening, is always available to any of us who are humble and honest enough to admit how we've been wrong and to commit ourselves to living differently.

In September 1997, a Japanese television news station crew came to our community to film a documentary on domestic violence, featuring the story of Yoko Kato. They filmed a group of MOVE participants talking about their ongoing journeys in overcoming their violence. I stood in the hall and listened as man after man shared his story. With shaking voices, they revealed the depth of their abuse and betrayal of the ones they loved. The pain in the room was palpable. One man tearfully talked about his moment he awakened to the truth of his abusiveness—when he really noticed how frightened his children were of him. He cried, and the tears sprang from my eyes as well. Then he told how he is slowly but steadily gaining back their trust, and the trust of his wife, through his daily practice of staying nonviolent. He had been coming to the MOVE program for more than three years, and he talked about how some of his coworkers now teased him because they sensed he was becoming "different"—no longer a tough guy, but more gentle and vulnerable. He said that in spite of the teasing, in spite of the incessant pressure to "act like a man," his path was clear. He was intent on saving his family and saving himself. The MOVE program was a turning point in his life, and, for the first time ever, he was proud of the man he was becoming.

That night I found myself wishing the advocates for battered women I have worked with over the years could have witnessed this extraordinary group. We often feel so hopeless about ever being able to end the family violence that has plagued our world for centuries. Listening to these men share with absolute sincerity and depth the transformative process they've been engaged in has made me feel hopeful. I know they represent only a minority of the men we work with and that many others go on abusing after they've left the program.

Still, these men help me to believe that the ones who have been violent can break the chain of violence.

Now, when somebody asks me, "What"s a nice feminist like you doing in a men's organization?" I answer that I work at the Men's Resource Center because it is a feminist organization that holds out the vision that men can change. It's an organization that recognizes that to create a nonviolent world, men *must* change. To help that to occur, we must all tirelessly confront men's violence while simultaneously speaking to men's pain. Through this dual approach, transformation happens. I have witnessed it.

We know that the healing of violence has to happen on all levels—from the individual to the family to the culture at large. This is work we must do together as men *and* women. I am thankful to have found a place with my brothers to do just that.

Finding the Peacekeeper Within
By Jan Passion
Winter 2011

I was three years old when I watched the cops take my father. Before they arrived, I watched my parents fight over a gun.

Their own guns drawn, the cops forced my dad into a waiting squad car. I sat beside him in the back while my mother and brother followed in our car. I think Dad was bleeding from a bullet that grazed him during the fight. Somehow, in all the trauma and chaos, it struck me—at age three—that this wasn't right: More violence wasn't the answer.

Seven years later my father killed himself, and that wasn't the answer, either. The legacy he left me is that violence is never the answer. But how else to protect oneself against violence, if not by violence? Thanks to my father, I set course early in life to figure out an answer to that question. My searching would eventually lead me to Nonviolent Peaceforce (www.nonviolentpeaceforce.org).

Before arriving there, I spent a decade working with perpetrators of domestic violence and their victims. I learned a lot about my father, working with men who acted just like him. I learned to more deeply understand the humanity of these men, who caused so much pain to their loved ones. I learned I could hate their actions without hating them. I learned that by listening to them, and by showing them that acting out violently was a choice, that by giving them a safe place to speak of their own injuries, and that by not taking sides against them, these men began to change. They changed not by force but of their own accord. They began to see the power of choosing nonviolence over violence.

Slowly the seed of nonviolence began to grow, and the wall of violence they'd erected to protect themselves began to erode. As they stepped from the rubble of their violent pasts, just like me, these men began to see solutions other than violence to protect their lives.

The work of Nonviolent Peaceforce is a larger-scale version of my work in domestic violence. Both put mending lives and mending relationships first. Civilian protection is the number one mandate carried out by unarmed civilian peacekeepers, and we are rigorously trained to respond nonviolently even when under extreme threat.

I remember when one of our vehicles carrying three peacekeepers was surrounded by a group of violent young men. They smashed all the windows, hit the driver in the head, and flashed a grenade under his face.

Because this driver, a Kenyan peacekeeper, was able to respond nonviolently and was backed by his colleagues' courage to remain calm, the situation de-escalated and the result was a meeting the next day. Once a dialogue opened, the attackers began to understand the mission of Nonviolent Peaceforce, and once they saw that we do not take sides, they apologized for their violent outburst. The incident reminded me how tempting it is to write people off who commit violence. But if we have the courage to hold their humanity in our hearts even as we witness or are harmed by their acts, we can prepare the ground for nonviolent action and thus prepare the way to peace.

I was to learn another lesson in courage from a fifteen-year-old child soldier. I never found out at what age she had been abducted. She came to us seeking help after she escaped her captors and discovered that she was not safe at home in her own village with her family. This was in part because she had short hair, which marked her as a female fighter. Though she wanted more than anything to stay with her family, she knew she risked reabduction and would face a severe penalty for desertion if retaken.

We spent a day accompanying her to another part of the country where she could escape the daily trauma of the life of a child soldier and be safe while her hair grew out. It was only one day out of the lives of the three of us accompanying her, but it made all the difference in her getting to keep hers. She was very quiet on the 10-hour journey, which involved passing through many military checkpoints. She had the stillness of terror about her. She did not make eye contact and answered our questions through the translator in monosyllables. But once we arrived at the safe place, her expression seemed to soften, and in her eyes I read the message, *"I'm going to make it. I am safe."*

This young woman is still in her teens today, and when I think of her, I am reminded why the unarmed civilian peacekeepers of Nonviolent Peaceforce do what we do. We do our work for young girls taken as child soldiers. We do our work for young boys who hold grenades to people's faces. We this work for ourselves. And some of us do it for our fathers.

Breaking the Secret Code of Dudes

By Eve Ensler
Summer 2009

I have been doing a lot of thinking about what it means for women and men to be allies in the struggle to end violence against woman and girls. I know that if we are going to end this violence—and I maintain that it is possible—it will only happen if men join women equally in the struggle. For many years I have wondered why ending rape and brutality was women's work when 95 percent of the violence inflicted on women is done by men. We don't rape ourselves.

How come we have been left to survive the rape, recover from the rape, press charges against the rapist, make everyone aware of the possibility of other women being raped, form networks, NGOs, help lines, shelters—devote our lives to stopping rape? How come rape, something we never asked for, something that violated us and devastated us, then becomes *our* responsibility and consumes our lives?

I do not hate men. On the contrary, I have a son who is the center of my heart, beloved male lovers, and many cherished male friends. When I began this work many years ago, I was certainly angry at men. I was afraid of men. I was hurt by men. I did not trust men. That's what rape does. It robs women of agency over our bodies. It destroys our fundamental belief in humanity. Rape lives forever in our cells, like plutonium, making trust and intimacy almost impossible. It creates despair, depression, bitterness, and rage. It destroys confidence and self-esteem. It makes us feel dirty and soiled. For many years I was simply a consequence of rape and violence—a walking violent outcome. I learned to anesthetize my feelings, shut down, and disassociate. It was a long hard road back. Then I began the work of V-Day, and turned my life toward ending rape and violence against women and girls.

I know all men are not rapists. It is actually a very small percentage of men who hurt, attack, rape women. The problem is that the large majority of *other* men—the men not perpetuating the violence—do not stand up and say or do anything about what is going on to their mothers, sisters, daughters, girlfriends, wives, grandmothers. They remain silent and passive. And that silence consolidates their loyalty and solidarity in the circle of men; it perpetuates their unspoken commitment to the practices and existence of patriarchy. To stand up as a man against violence against women is to break the "secret code of dudes." It is to go up against the essential dominant narrative. It is to exile yourself from the country of the father.

That narrative is the tyranny of patriarchy, which has been far more destructive to men than to women. Asked to supply a definition of manhood I recently heard a man say that men are essentially brought up "not to be a woman." So what does that look like? Men are brought up to disassociate from their hearts, to not be open, certainly to not cry or express what is called weakness. They are brought up to always act as if they know what's going on even if they don't. That would imply never asking questions, never allowing themselves to be lost, never admitting being afraid or full of doubt, never surrendering to the great mystery of life.

For eleven years I have traveled the planet. I have visited the rape mines of the world in more than sixty countries, the places where the worst atrocities toward women are happening and the places where the everyday abuses continue with hardly a whisper of outrage or intervention. I ask myself maybe ten times a day, "What allows a man to become so cut off he can watch a women squirm and beg him to stop and still continue to shove himself into her and tear her apart? What allows a man to undress a woman and stick himself into her when she is completely intoxicated with no ability to give consent or even know what is going on? What allows a man to rape a young girl with a group of other men as she screams out and begs for mercy? What allows a man to choke or punch or slap or shove or stab his beloved? What have we done to men that they can do this to women? How have we raised them? What have we taught them about manhood?"

Psychiatrist and writer James Gilligan spent years working with long-term male inmates who had committed violent crimes. In his book *Violence*, he documents how in almost every case a man who had murdered or raped had at some point in his life been greatly humiliated or shamed. This took the form of economic, racial, gender, and physical shaming. In the rehabilitation programs developed for these men he discovered that by helping men address these core humiliations they were able to begin to end the cycle of violence.

Two years ago, I had the privilege of meeting Dr. Denis Mukwege. He is a Congolese gynecologist and obstetrician who for the last 12 years has been sewing up women's vaginas in the Congo as fast as the militias are ripping them apart. Meeting and coming to know Dr. Mukwege changed my life. He is a great man, a man who cherishes women, who honors them, a man who has devoted his life to their healing and safety and empowerment and protection. Last February I had the privilege of traveling with him around America trying to wake this country up to the terrible atrocities being inflicted on women's bodies in the Congo in the fight for its economic resources. I watched the way he interacted with the public. I witnessed his modesty, humility, his fierceness (not aggressive, but determined), his commitment, which allowed for questions, uncertainty, his vision, which inspired collaboration.

We asked Dr. Mukwege if he would be the godfather of the V-Men movement and he said yes. What does a V-man look like? Careful, modest, brilliant, takes time. Asks questions, expresses sorrow, compassionate, connected to his heart, determined, humble, open. Mainly a V-man knows that being vulnerable is his greatest strength, and as Dr. Mukwege says, "Men's happiness is dependent on women's happiness." A V-man does not seek to hurt or punish, doesn't need to prove himself.

Since Dr. Mukwege's visit, in partnership with many amazing groups and individual men who have been working for years to shift this paradigm, V-Day launched the V-*Men* program. In recent months I have sat in rooms with extraordinary men, pioneers, radicals—men who have stepped outside the boundaries and definitions and safety; men who have made themselves vulnerable.

Which ones of you will be the next to join them, to leave your father's country? Who of you will be the willing and courageous refugees traveling with your sister refugees in search of the rising new paradigm? Which of you will bravely surrender the privilege and power of patriarchy to stand for your sisters, to protect life itself, to ensure the future? Which secure ones of you will say my manhood is based on my character and my actions, and not on posturing and lies? Which one of you will be willing to give up the keys to the kingdom in order to open the door to the new world?

My brothers, your sisters are counting on you to be that man. Will you stand up now if you are going to make that journey with us, if you are going to fight with your life to end violence against women and girls? Please stand up.

Baseball's Challenge: Teaching What Not to Hit
By Rob Okun
Summer 2006

I'm rooting for the day when enough men in this world so strongly condemn domestic violence that what happened in the shadow of Fenway Park on June 22nd never happens again. The time has long passed for us as men to remain silent when a man abuses a woman. That the accused is an alleged role model to children, Brett Myers, Philadelphia Phillies star pitcher, and the victim, Kim, is his wife, doesn't make it more important than other reprehensible assaults, but it does give the cause more visibility.

The police report and eyewitness accounts sketch out what happened: Myers and his wife were arguing on the street near their hotel in Boston's Back Bay after midnight when, Kim Myers said, her husband hit her twice in the face with his fist. Witnesses told police the Phillies' pitcher slapped his wife and pulled her to the ground by her hair. She was seen down on the sidewalk with a swollen face, crying. Read enough?

What was going in the minds of Philadelphia's management—not to mention Major League Baseball—that thirty-six hours after being accused of throwing his wife around that Myers was allowed to throw balls and strikes against the Red Sox in a nationally televised game? Apparently not much.

The club's empty-headed duck-and-cover statement read in part, "Out of respect for the privacy of both Kim and Brett Myers, the Phillies will not comment until the matter is resolved by the court." Translation: By our silence, we're saying we consider our economic investment in our prized pitcher more important than the health and well being of Kim, as a person, let alone the mother of the three-year-old child he fathered.

Wake up, Major League Baseball! In the wake of the steroid abuse investigation, how about creating a full-scale education campaign against domestic abuse? Don't get me wrong. Violence against women is an epidemic in society as a whole; no one is suggesting baseball or professional sports should be singled out.

But domestic abuse is a social crisis that ballplayers, as role models, have a special responsibility to speak out about. I propose baseball put the same attention on domestic violence that it so powerfully directed toward prostate cancer awareness just a few weeks ago. Why? Because both are men's issues.

The truth is the vast majority of ballplayers—just as most men in general—are good guys who want to do the right thing. What can baseball do to connect the dots from this teachable moment? Talk to Sox outfielder Gabe Kapler and his wife, Lisa. They set up a foundation to support the victims of partner abuse after Lisa went public two years ago that she had been physically and emotionally abused by her high school boyfriend. Talk to New York Yankees manager, Joe Torre, who established the Safe at Home foundation after acknowledging that he had grown up witnessing his father abuse his mother. If you think Joe Torre would have sent Brett Myers to the mound, think again.

Thankfully, progress is being made. The Sox have been working with a program out of Northeastern University's Center for the Study of Sport in Society called Mentors in Violence Prevention (MVP). They educate Sox minor league players about domestic violence at spring training. That's a start. (The New England Patriots also work with the program). But there's more to do. It is high time for baseball—and all professional sports—to recognize their critical responsibility to teach early about abuse—and respect—in relationships.

Before Father's Day a number of organizations nationally broadcast a series of television and radio PSAs, "Coaching Boys into Men." The brainchild of the Family Violence Prevention Fund, the ads feature a father and son playing sports together. "You've taught him how to hit the strike zone, a nine iron, the open man," the narrator says. "But have you taught him what not to hit?"

Apparently nobody taught Brett Myers that lesson. Maybe it's not too late for him. For the rest of us, we hope baseball's next play isn't to issue an intentional walk.

Sports & Hypermasculinity
Violence, Male Culture, and the Jovan Belcher Case
An Interview with Daryl Fort, senior trainer, Mentors in Violence Prevention
By Jackson Katz
Summer 2013

Just two weeks before the massacre at Sandy Hook Elementary School in Newtown, Connecticut, another high-profile murder-suicide dominated the 24/7 news cycle and—briefly—captured the public's imagination. On December 1, 2012, the news broke that 25-year-old Kansas City Chiefs linebacker Jovan Belcher had murdered his 22-year-old girlfriend, Kasandra Perkins, and then drove to Arrowhead Stadium where he committed suicide in front of his coach and other Chiefs staff. Until Newtown pushed that story off the front pages, there had been an outpouring of commentary from people in the gender violence prevention field, sports journalism, and the cultural mainstream.

Much of the conversation revolved around men's violence against women as an ongoing national tragedy, and the specific aspects of professional football culture and its unique and often combustible mixture of hypermasculinity, bodily self-sacrifice, and misogyny, along with the stark reality that the players—many of them young African-American men—are under intense pressure to perform in an industry where they can become famous and make a lot of money, but where their physical and emotional health takes a backseat to the demands of the business.

In the wake of this tragedy, many people in the gender violence prevention field called on officials of the National Football League to respond by increasing their efforts to provide counseling services to players and their families in need, as well as to provide training for team personnel in how to detect and intervene in potentially volatile situations, and to implement violence prevention programming league-wide.

The Mentors in Violence Prevention (MVP) Program, which I cofounded in 1993 at Northeastern University's Center for the Study of Sport in Society, has worked extensively with college and professional football players, coaches, and administrators for two decades. In addition, over the past decade MVP has also been called in to work with professional sports organizations after high-profile domestic violence, sexual assault, and sexual harassment incidents. Focused workshops at such "teachable moments" can help make future incidents less likely if the participants—individuals and organizations—are willing to forthrightly address some of the underlying causes.

Jovan Belcher's murderous actions formed one of those teachable moments. Since then, countless people inside and outside sports culture have been talking about domestic violence and asking: what can we do? To provide some badly needed context for the national conversation sparked by the Kansas City tragedy, Voice Male *agreed to provide a forum for me to engage in a dialogue with my friend and MVP colleague Daryl Fort. Fort has long been among the most senior trainers with MVP, and is one of the most experienced male gender violence prevention educators in the world. He has worked extensively with NFL players, coaches, and front office staff since 2006. A former senior adviser to the governor of Maine, Fort is a 1992 graduate of the University of Maine, where he played on the football team.*

Jackson Katz: You're a graduate of the same college football program as Jovan Belcher, although you're almost a generation older. That must have hit closer to home for you than it did for most of us. Can you talk about your initial thoughts and feelings when you heard that he had murdered his girlfriend and then took his own life?

Daryl Fort: Like many people around our former collegiate program and among his NFL peers, I felt a deep sadness. Personally, it struck a nerve that was already close to the surface, because a couple of weeks earlier, a former high school classmate of mine here in Maine had murdered his wife and committed suicide. On an almost annual basis, the majority of all homicides in this state (as in so many others) are domestic-violence related. And almost all of those murders are perpetrated by men against women. It is always disturbing when a man decides to externalize his own pain by lethally assaulting someone he purports to love and care about.

JK: There are hundreds of domestic violence murder-suicides in our society every year. But because this one was perpetrated by a professional athlete, people want to talk about how male sports culture—especially football culture—might be implicated. But as someone who has worked extensively in gender violence prevention with men inside and outside of sports, I was wondering if you could offer any observations about whether football players react similarly to or differently from other men with whom you've worked on these issues.

DF: The fact that an NFL player killed his intimate partner is why so many people are talking about this issue now. It's why many people want to read about it. What makes this a potentially important moment to talk more about these issues is that we know so much about the dynamics involved in the overwhelming majority of DV homicides, as well as the violent and abusive behaviors of many, many perpetrators. We need much more serious dialogue, asking some important questions such as: Why do many men use violence or the threat of violence to gain or maintain control within their intimate relationships? Why do so many people—from professional athletes to, say, mortgage brokers—choose not to "get involved" in the face of this abuse?

JK: It's important for people to know that in Mentors in Violence Prevention (MVP), or other programs that utilize the bystander approach, the kinds of abuses we talk about are generally not the sensational murders that happen periodically. Sexist attitudes and behaviors occur along a continuum, and MVP encourages men to interrupt and challenge each other in a range of ways. It's not just about helping guys know how to detect or what to do when their teammates or friends might be on the verge of killing someone.

DF: No question. At the end of the day, we're trying to get people to consider the connection between disrespectful, harassing, abusive attitudes and language and the violence and abuse most everyone agrees is unacceptable. We're looking at rape, murder, and domestic battering at the top of a pyramid of very destructive behavior. At the bottom of that pyramid lies the foundation for those almost universally denounced crimes, things like sexually bigoted "humor," sexist language, and objectification.

In a larger culture where sexist behavior and sexist media are considered edgy, marketable, and cool, it's a process to get guys to look past what feels normal and harmless to see the potential harm. Even for guys who are willing to recognize a lot of what they see and hear as abusive and disrespectful, it still takes courage to step into the social backlash they're likely to get from peers, teammates, and colleagues who are likely to tell them to lighten up for saying, "Hey man, why you gotta call women bitches all the time?"

But with the challenge there also lies an opportunity, when we're talking about engaging high-level athletes. On the one hand, we're talking about guys who in many ways are supposed to represent the edgiest, the coolest, and the most "manly." For them, there is some pressure to go along and uphold rather than buck that system. On the other hand, we are also talking about guys who stand on a cultural platform because of their status. For the many guys who take that responsibility seriously, it's about leaning hard into that desire to want to do the right thing by shifting the conversation about what "the right thing" is and challenging them to have the courage to take action.

JK: In the Belcher case, many people focus on the violent nature of football, or speculate about physiological factors that might have arisen from head injuries he sustained. I think it's comforting for many people to think that in cases of horrific violence, "something must have snapped." But in MVP sessions with men, we talk a lot about manhood and social norms, both in the larger society and in various subcultures. How do you see men responding to that discussion?

DF: Men's responses are basically the same whether we're working with college or professional football players, athletes of other sports, military personnel, or corporate professionals. There is almost always a cross-section of responses within football and non-football peer groups; some guys are reluctant—the discussion is especially challenging because of the degree to which some of them have invested in the gender stereotypes of how they are supposed to relate to one another as well as women. We offer an opportunity to have an unvarnished dialogue about these subjects, and guys are often quick and eager to engage.

Men who are reluctant participants at the outset often become the most enthusiastic proponents of taking positive action. For example, at the beginning of an MVP training on one of the largest military bases in the world, a master sergeant with 19 years' service in the Marine Corps made it clear that he had much more important things to do than talking about sexual violence and how to prevent it. He made everyone in the training aware that he was there because it was required. But by the second day, some junior noncommissioned officers were expressing doubts that they could leave the space and challenge their peers about abusive behavior toward women. The master sergeant firmly told them he didn't think they had the right attitude, and that *he* expected more of them.

JK: Many people imagine that football players—because they occupy such a hypermasculine and privileged space—would be particularly resistant to this kind of introspection about men's violence against women. Do you think that's the case?

DF: No. I find men want the opportunity to talk about relationships and the challenges that often surround navigating the expectations that the culture can impose on men—expectations to behave in certain ways and represent dominant, in-control roles in their relationships. Elite football players have many of the same issues about masculinity and relationships—and some of the same anxieties—as other guys. But many people see them as "alpha males" who have it all figured out. I believe some of the assumptions other people make about who we are and can be as men trouble NFL players as much as they do regular guys on the street. I've had many, many of these guys eager to talk about those pressures when they feel there is a safe environment to do so. Facilitating that space is a big part of my job. It can help when you're sitting in a locker room or meeting space that some of these guys spend more time in than they do their own homes. It's literally meeting them where they are.

JK: Some men can get very defensive when you try to strip away the tough exterior.

DF: Often we see an initial defensiveness regarding the subject; I once had a young college basketball player from a Division II school ask me before a session, "I'm from the Bronx, what can you teach me about violence?" Of course he was flexing a little bit, trying to let me know a classroom couldn't teach him anything of value about life "on the street." It's still a surprise to many who work with us that the "teaching and learning" isn't some kind of PowerPoint lecture. We want to have a conversation—one that is structured, yet open, honest, and frequently raw—and hopefully come to some often difficult and also empowering conclusions about our responsibilities as men to hold ourselves and each other accountable with courage and compassion.

Another assumption a lot of these guys make coming in is that we're going to point fingers at them and treat them all as potential perpetrators. For some, that has been their experience. For many others, it is a taught reflex in the wake of the media stereotype of "athletes behaving badly." Of course, a big part of the real message is that men's violence against women affects all of us, one way or another. What can we do as men, as brothers, fathers, uncles, cousins, teammates, friends, to be part of the solution? Once these guys see they have an opportunity to participate in an honest dialogue, to speak their minds, the introspection, the curiosity about one another's perspective, and their personal desire to talk about personal wants, needs, and challenges often takes over. Don't get me wrong—not everyone feels comfortable with the content of these conversations. Far from it. Especially since we focus on their responsibility to address these issues within their peer cultures and interrupt their teammates' or friends' sexist behaviors. For a lot of people that's anxiety-producing. Think about it: How do I tell my friend that taking that drunk woman home to try and have sex with her is a bad idea for him and her, when before we went out, his game plan was to get laid? How do I talk to my boss about how inappropriate and uncomfortable I think sexist banter around the office is when he/she's one of the participants? When we bring it down to those types of authentic and difficult circumstances, you can see the wheels turning in people's minds, because many of them have encountered those very situations. In terms of inspiring leadership, finger wagging won't get it done. But in a team/peer group concept we don't necessarily have to go it alone—we can "have each other's back." That's also part of the message.

JK: What's your strategy for motivating men as leaders in gender violence prevention?

DF: A way to do this is to get folks to see themselves as the friends, family, teammates, peers of both perpetrators and victims of abuse. We will ask directly what it might feel like to have a woman they care deeply about be the victim of violence or abuse. Too many don't have to imagine it—they already know. Others find it upsetting and infuriating. An important dynamic to consider is to ask ourselves how we would feel about someone or a group of people who had the opportunity to do something about stopping that abuse. In the end, most of us want those bystanders to find a way to help, whether they know our loved one or not. The next step is to figure out how individually and collectively we can develop and nurture the tools to actually help. But the opportunity to step up and make courageous choices here comes, in part, from recognizing how much influence we have over our peers' attitudes and behaviors on a daily basis already. We do it in positive ways and, unfortunately, in negatives ways as well. It is our choice to make.

JK: One particularly sensitive dimension of the Jovan Belcher case is his—and his victim's—race. Belcher was African American, as was Kasandra Perkins. I realize you did not know Belcher personally, and so you can't presume to know the dynamic of his, or their, relationship struggles, and how race did or did not play a critical role. But as a black man yourself, and one who has facilitated countless dialogues with men and women of color, as well as white men and women, can you talk about how race—and racism—plays a role in workshops devoted to men's violence against women? Do men ever talk openly about race?

DF: Like almost everywhere in our culture, it is often a challenge in MVP sessions to have a nuanced and honest discussion about the dynamics of race. It's woven through the fabric of American life. One of the issues is an old one: guys in a room mixed along racial lines are usually unwilling to speak to any conflicts over race. Ironically, this is also true within sports and military cultures, where over the years great strides have been made in this country in the ways that people work together across racial lines. You might think some of those bonds help create an environment where enough trust exists to have those difficult conversations. But as with gender, utopian dreams and some significant denial often overshadow our vision of reality.

Race is always a subtext to the work we do, but sometimes we make it visible and explicit. There may be 40 football players sitting in a stadium meeting room having a conversation and the split is 60/40 black-to-white. I've often asked a group of guys who have no issues referring to women as "bitches" how they would respond to a group of white guys using the term "niggers" to describe their teammates of color. Most groups consider the racially bigoted term unacceptable because, they will say, the word has a history and current meaning that is derogatory. It's degrading to black people. Well, doesn't the "B-word" carry the same derogatory status, both historically and in current times? Half may look at me like I'm crazy. Another quarter of the group may take on a contemplative disposition. The other quarter of the group may nod in agreement and challenge the rest to see their point of view. The personal challenge we're posing to each person in this instance is, "What is the difference between racial bigotry and gender bigotry—in principle? Just because we have normalized one form, does that make it right? And further, don't we all still make the choice to participate in and/or condone the use of bigoted language?" To be clear, it's not a magical spell that transforms everyone's opinion. But people are always engaged and you can clearly see some attitudes change.

JK: In an interview the day after the murder-suicide, Chiefs quarterback Brady Quinn said, "When it happened, I was sitting and, in my head, thinking what I could have done differently. When you ask someone how they are doing, do you really mean it? When you answer someone back how you are doing, are you really telling the truth?" Quinn was expressing what many people around perpetrators—and victims—often feel. Could I have prevented something terrible from happening if I knew more, and was willing to act? In MVP trainings we encourage men to speak up and support their teammates and friends when it's possible, or to interrupt their abusive behaviors—even if they merely suspect something might be going on. We make it clear that being an active bystander is an act not only of friendship but of leadership.

DF: This can feel like tricky and anxious territory for a lot of guys; how do I "get in his business," meaning issues about a teammate/friend's personal relationship or apparent depression. What it highlights is the limited emotional range of expression and means of support within which too many people—men in particular—operate. Sadly, in the sports culture, there seems to be even less support. Think about what Brady Quinn was suggesting, that locker room culture doesn't allow its male participants to ask for or offer certain types of emotional support. It's the type of support that is labeled "feminine," and that's the last thing many men want to have associated with their reputation—especially among other men. But think about it: if your teammate is reluctant to share with you problems he's having in his relationship for fear of being "clowned" as a punk or a "pussy," can you really say you've got his back?

VOICE MALE

A Vet for Peace: Recruiting One Soldier at a Time
By Eric Wasileski
Spring 2007

I am a Persian Gulf veteran of Operation Desert Fox, a divinity student at Andover-Newton (Mass.) Theological School as a Quaker, and I serve as president of the Wally Nelson Chapter of Veterans for Peace (veteransforpeace.org). I'm also the father of a two-year-old daughter.

I vigil for peace, never knowing the impact I might have on passersby or the effect they may have on me. In the nearly five years I have been vigiling I have seen the number of one-finger salutes (middle finger) go down dramatically, replaced by the two-fingers peace sign. But on Dr. Martin Luther King Jr.'s weekend recently, I didn't know what would happen at our weekly Saturday vigil in Greenfield, Massachusetts.

Because the banner I brought is too big to hold alone, I asked my friend "Ted" to help. We discussed Dr. King's tactics. As a pacifist, I see the world differently from those who believe peace can be achieved by force. As Ted and I talked, a uniformed Marine private walked by our vigil. I called out a hello to him, and then Ted yelled in his face: "Don't recruit anyone today!" The private replied defensively, "Thanks for supporting me" and continued on.

I was dismayed. I told Ted, "Listen, when you hold a Veterans for Peace banner you represent VFP. It is not okay to yell at active duty members while holding our banner." It is difficult for civilians to understand that once you've worn the uniform you always remember how it feels—in a sense, veterans never take theirs off. As a former GI, it is not possible for me to be "against" the troops.

Ted apologized; he told me his story. As a hippie riding a bus in 1968, his life was threatened by four service members on that ride, he said. He was petrified for the entire trip, and thankful when they got off at a stop before his.

Later, I was surprised to see the same Marine walking back past us, a brave young man. Before I could think better of it, I was chasing after him. I said, "Hey, Private, can I walk with you?" in a tone a sergeant would use. I fell into step beside him and pointed to the logo on my ball cap. I told him I was a Persian Gulf veteran and a member of Veterans for Peace. "I don't want you to be angry at the peace movement," I began. "That guy has other issues that have nothing to do with you." He eased his posture as he looked at my hat. He said his name was "Chris" and added he was just home from boot camp and doing recruiting work to save leave time (I had done this, too).

A block up the street, at the Veterans Memorial, we stopped to talk. Chris said, "People like your friend don't understand why I joined the military. I didn't join to kill; I don't want to kill. I joined to serve, get a career, and do something with my life. I needed to get out of this town—my friends are either working at McDonald's or are in jail. There is nothing here for me. I want something different."

"I thought the same things in 1991," I told him. "That's why I joined, too."

I pointed to the Gettysburg Address on the Civil War memorial in front of us, and we stood there reading silently together. I said, "It's the best *stay the course* speech ever written. It identifies with the victims of the war and says, 'Don't let them be sacrificed in vain.'" I looked at Chris and said, "Do we owe our allegiance to those who have already died, like those named here, whom we can't do anything for? Or do we owe our allegiance to those who are still alive, like you?

"People die in war," I continued. "I know what it is like to kill people, and it's not something you ever get over. You can learn to live with it, but you can't ever get over it. When you see war, after 10 minutes you realize it's horrible. There's nothing manly about war. Being a man is about being emotionally connected. I hope you will figure that out."

After a moment, Chris replied, "You know all this because you served. *You* did it. Why shouldn't I?"

I responded, "I wish I could go back and change what I did. I can't, but I can talk to guys like you." After a pause I said, "Look, as a Marine you will be going over in four-month rotations. Maybe on your second, third, fourth, or even your tenth time, if you reconsider, we will be here to support you. Veterans for Peace and this peace vigil will be here to support you."

Chris nodded. Then he said, "Thanks—for talking with me, I mean. You've given me something to think about when I'm over there."

I looked him in the eye and said quietly, "Remember your humanity."

Our conversation had lasted just 15 minutes but the impact on me was beyond measure. I wonder where Chris is, how he is doing. Also, I wonder what might have happened if a veteran had said something like that to me. Being a member of the current peace movement—and a veteran—I am a bridge between war and peace, between soldiers past and present and the peace movement. I believe as Americans we need to work together to move beyond our differences, for the good of our nation and the world. I pray that as civilized people we find our way.

When a Beloved Teacher Is Also a Rapist

By Sarah Buttenwieser

Summer 2012

This is the thing I don't want to say: My son's beloved community theater teacher raped one of his former students.

The reason I say raped, not "allegedly raped," is because he was convicted, and just last month, sentenced for having sex with a 14-year-old girl, a former student. Statutory rape. His conviction rattled me to the core. The experiences my son had under this theater teacher's supervision were hugely positive. He and his family are people I like. I still can't imagine he'd do something so terrible—and yet he did.

When he was arrested nearly two years ago, early June, the news hit me fist-in-stomach hard. On that very hot afternoon, I felt mostly for the teacher—and for my eldest son, who'd studied with him and worked on a couple of community productions as a stagehand. The teacher's accuser, a former acting student of his, had been just 14 at the time of the alleged crime—and I didn't want to think about her at all.

In a long, intense, teary conversation with our 12-year-old, my husband and I defined statutory rape. We explained that neither accusation nor arrest assured guilt. We said this wasn't black and white, right and wrong, necessarily. Our boy was scared and confused; we tried to allay his fears.

Privately we whispered that the best-case scenario was likely entirely gray. If he'd made the mistake of being alone in a building with a 14-year-old, that was a lapse in judgment, not a crime. Things couldn't be as bad as they seemed. Could they? We didn't want to believe someone we'd trusted, someone that cheery and that focused on a vision for the community, could be hurting a child in one of the worst ways imaginable. In my denial, I was too willing to cede all benefit of the doubt his way. I couldn't articulate it to myself then, but I didn't want to face the possibility that I'd put my son in harm's way.

In the days that followed we offered our concern to the teacher and his wife. From arrest to trial to sentencing, eighteen months lapsed. When I saw the teacher with his young son, he was a dad not unlike the other preschool dads, cheerful and patient and overtired. Up until the trial, I didn't let myself contemplate rape. It wasn't that I actively disbelieved his accuser—thought she was lying or consenting. I just told myself it was the jury's to decide. Although I am a feminist and mother to a daughter, I found the possibility of his guilt too disconcerting —and I willed it away. Or tried to will it away—what gnawed at me was that I let my fear and my loyalties place me on what I'd have generally imagined to be the wrong side of a rape trial. I'm ashamed that I couldn't take a real step toward having empathy for her because I was so afraid of how I'd feel if I believed her.

I read newspaper reports of the trial both reluctantly and avidly. The young woman's testimony and others' corroboration were compelling. His testimony that he hadn't been alone in the building was corroborated, too— but if I hadn't thought of him and his family as friends, I knew I wouldn't have believed him. The jury didn't: he was convicted of five counts of statutory rape. He was released on bail until sentencing.

I'm not sure why I was incredulous. I'd acknowledged that had he been a stranger I wouldn't have harbored doubt. I hadn't stopped liking him, though. To see him as a perpetrator remained too hard to imagine. Instead, I saw the father and the husband; I saw the son and the wife. Without hesitation I wrote a letter on his behalf to advocate that he serve time in the county jail closer to his son.

I should have let in the possibility of the young woman's truth so much sooner. Once I read newspaper reports of impact statements the accuser and her father both made during the sentencing hearing—her mother was too upset to speak—the walls I'd put up crashed down. Her anguish and her parents' grief propelled me to experience my own fear and anger at my son's vulnerability. I started shaking. Finally, way too late, I was scared. I was devastated for the victim. And I was ashamed I hadn't really worried about her before. That afternoon my son texted me: "Five to seven years." He was in stage-manager mode for the high school musical. I texted back: "I know. How are you?" He replied, "Fine." I knew we'd talk, eventually; I didn't know what I'd say.

That same night, at the show, I watched all those earnest performers, and my sense of violation, even at a remove, surprised me, like a rush of water I'd barely held at bay with a faltering dam that finally burst. I was flooded with sadness and fear for all the families who trusted this man, including us. I don't think my son wanted to imagine the teacher had done something so wrong—and I hadn't pushed him to do so.

In retrospect I fault myself for how little we discussed the victim, her violation, her feelings, her rights. I still don't know how I turned away from a whole side of a two-sided story. Or maybe I do, and that's the thing I feel worst about: that I didn't want to feel something terrible could occur so close to us, that it wasn't a stranger or a person I deemed unsafe for my son to learn from who was accused of this crime, so I held fast to my denial, some very washed-out gray.

But I only wanted the kind of gray that would let me be right about someone I'd trusted as a friend. This kind of gray—the kind that allows my trusted friend to also be the man who raped a girl barely older than my son, that allows me to have been so wrong, that leaves me both angry and fearful and grieving and somehow still caring—this is a gray I'd never imagined, and never imagined trying to navigate a child through. It's left me looking at myself in disbelief. That fist-in-my-stomach breathlessness isn't going away.

VOICE MALE

When Men's Violence is Missing in the News
By Jackson Katz
Winter 2010

Despite a generation of feminist activism that inspired changes in countless laws and social practices, in public life it is far from clear that women's experiences and voices count as much as men's. United States Supreme Court Justice Ruth Bader Ginsburg recently provided an inside look at how this works in the highest provinces of power, when she questioned her own influence at justices' conferences: "I will say something—and I don't think I'm a confused speaker—and it isn't until somebody else says it that everyone will focus on the point."

Ginsburg was too politically cautious—or polite—to note that the "somebody else" to whom she was referring was coded language for *a man*, whose opinion is deemed more valid by virtue of his sex. Men's expertise and opinions are routinely valued more than women's, here and around the world.

How ironic and revealing, then, that what came to be known in mainstream accounts as "The Exchange" between Secretary of State Hillary Clinton and a young man at a public event in Kinshasa during Clinton's visit to the Congo in the summer of 2009 overshadowed the substance of her trip, which shone the spotlight on the ongoing epidemic of sexual violence. Secretary Clinton, you may recall, testily responded to the student's question seeking "President Clinton's" opinion about a political issue. It turned out the student had misspoken, and had meant to ask about President Obama. Secretary Clinton was evidently irritated that once again, her own opinions and experience were seemingly being overlooked in favor of the sexist presumption that a woman leader is merely the mouthpiece for a more powerful man.

Why was so much media coverage devoted to *that* during her trip to Africa, when one of the secretary's goals was to use the power of her voice to highlight African women's lives? In particular, Clinton wanted to draw public attention to the ongoing tragedy of mass rapes of women, children, and men in the Congo. She was the first US secretary of state to travel to the war zone, and she announced a $17 million plan to fight sexual violence. Among other steps, the American government would train doctors, supply rape victims with cameras to document their injuries, and train Congolese law enforcement to crack down on rapists.

Corporate and independent media did cover this part of the story, although with nothing like the gusto with which they recounted Ms. Clinton's short-tempered response to the African student. Many American reporters in the ever-shrinking international press corps tried to convey the scope of the horrific suffering of women and children in the Congo, as well as communicate empathy with the emotional toll it all appeared to be taking on Ms. Clinton. "I was just overwhelmed by what I saw," she said. "It is almost impossible to describe the level of suffering." Several news accounts observed that Ms. Clinton seemed emotionally drained by the experience.

Unfortunately, however, the focus in news stories on the almost-unimaginable sexual violence in the Congo had an unintended effect. It pushed women's lives to center stage, which is appropriate, necessary, and represents a big step forward. At the same time, it kept men out of the spotlight—at just the wrong time. Male leaders often get too much credit, and our opinions are unfairly given a higher value than women's. But when it comes to being held responsible for the negative consequences of our behavior, including the widespread incidence of rape around the world, men are typically rendered *invisible* in the journalistic conversation.

Men's role in rape is characteristically hidden in mainstream journalism through a variety of linguistic conventions. One of the more significant of these is when writers and speakers use the passive voice—consciously or not—to talk about incidents of sexual violence (e.g., "200,000 women have been raped since the conflict began"). In addition, men's central responsibility for the rape pandemic escapes critical examination whenever writers and speakers use gender-neutral terminology to talk about perpetrators, who are overwhelmingly men. A *New York Times* article on August 12, 2009 reporting on Secretary Clinton's trip provides a good case study of these phenomena.

The article appeared beneath the fold on page A8, in the International section. It was headlined "Clinton Presents Plan to Fight Sexual Violence in Congo," by Jeffery Gettleman. The passive voice began in the first paragraph: "... Secretary Clinton ... met a Congolese woman who *had been gang-raped* while she was eight months pregnant." Passive sentence structures that hid male perpetration appeared in subsequent paragraphs: "... hundreds of thousands of women *have been raped* in the past decade." And "... countless women, and recently many men, *have been raped*." Then, "Hundreds of villagers *have been massacred*" and "The aid worker told Mrs. Clinton that an eight year-old boy who had strayed out of the camp *was raped* the other day."

This brief catalogue of passive sentences is not an attempt to single out the *New York Times* reporter for criticism. He was merely a vehicle for the transmission of the dominant ideology, which routinely obfuscates men's culpability for rape through both conscious and unconscious omissions. Victims themselves often use passive voice. Gettleman quoted one woman, Mrs. Mapendo, who said, "Our life is very bad. *We get raped* when we go out and look for food." Another woman said, "Children *are killed*, women *are raped* and the world closes its eyes."

In addition to the passive language, the photo accompanying the story showed Secretary Clinton in an outdoor meeting with a throng of Congolese women. There was not a man's face in sight. In fact, the only mention of the word "men" in the entire 1,029-word article was in reference to men as *victims* of rape. If it had not been for that (welcome) acknowledgment of men's vulnerability and victimization, a naïve reader might have inferred that there are no men in the Congo, only "women and children who are raped and killed."

The *New York Times* article was also suffused with gender-neutral language, particularly language that could have identified the gender of the individuals and groups responsible for sex crimes. For example: "Often the *rapists* are Congolese *soldiers*," or "... Congo ... has become a magnet for all the *rogue groups* in Africa." Secretary Clinton was quoted as saying the world needed to regulate the mineral trade to make sure the profits do not end up "in the hands of *those who fuel the violence*."

But while the gender of the perpetrators is obscured, the gender of the victims is stated plainly. The following sentence provides a clear illustration of this: "... an intensely predatory conflict driven by a mix of ethnic, commercial, nationalist, and criminal interests, in which various *armed groups* often vent their rage against women." This type of language usage is ubiquitous in contemporary journalism. When the perpetrators are men, their gender is not mentioned ("armed groups.") When the victims are women, their gender is in full view.

The result is that discussions about sex crimes, in the Congo and elsewhere, focus on what is happening *to women*, and not on *who is doing it* to them. In practice, this has obvious repercussions for so-called prevention efforts, which as a result of their focus on women, often amount to mere band-aid solutions. Of course rape victims and survivors need better medical and counseling services. But let's not mistake those services for prevention—which can only be successful to the extent that men and boys are a part of them.

The growing movement to engage men and boys in sexual and domestic violence prevention in the United States, sub-Saharan Africa, and around the globe—a movement *Voice Male* chronicles—faces an uphill climb in societies where cultural norms about masculinity both contribute directly to the violence *and* prevent women and men from speaking freely about men's responsibilities to end it.

This is not merely an academic debate about linguistic practices. Linguistic choices have practical consequences, especially in terms of what sorts of issues get discussed, and by whom, on main streets, in back rooms and in the shadowy corridors of power. As long as political leaders and policy makers—in national and international contexts—focus on rape primarily as a women's issue, strategies for addressing it will tend to emphasize services for victims and survivors, rather than accountability for perpetrators, or more critical attention to how we socialize boys.

Unfortunately, the failure of journalists and others to use active language to describe who is doing what to whom, as well as their hesitation to use gender-specific language to talk about men and boys as the perpetrators of sexual violence, make it next to impossible to hold male (and female) leaders accountable for addressing these problems forthrightly. As a result, the struggle to bring a critical mass of men into the social change process necessary to achieve significant reductions in gender-based violence continues. Women—along with a small number of male allies—continue to mourn the victims, care for the survivors, and pick up the broken pieces in the lives of their traumatized children. And across the world we lurch endlessly from one preventable tragedy to the next.

Pimps and Johns: Pornography and Men's Choices
By Robert Jensen
Spring 2005

There has been much talk about the need for men to love one another and be willing to speak openly about that love. That is important; we need to be able to get beyond the all-too-common male tendency to mute or deform our emotions, a tendency that is destructive not only to ourselves but to those around us. Many have spoken about our need to nurture one another, and that's important, too. But it's also crucial to remember that loving one another means challenging ourselves as well.

I would like to challenge us all—as men—on our use of pornography. In an unjust world, those of us with privilege must be harsh on ourselves, out of love.

This challenge is: *Can we be more than just johns?*

Let me start with a story that a female student at the University of Texas told me. She was riding to a football game on a bus chartered by a fraternity, on which many of the passengers were women. During the trip, someone put into the bus's VCR a sexually explicit video. Uncomfortable with the hardcore sexual images of women being used by men, the female student began a discussion with the people around her about it, and one of the men on the bus agreed that it was inappropriate. He stood up and said to the other men, "You all know me and know I like porno as much as the next guy, but it's not right for us to play this tape when there are women on the bus."

No doubt it took courage for that young man to confront his fraternity brothers on the issue, and we should honor that. But we should recognize that his statement also communicated to his male peers that he was one of them—"one of the guys" who, being guys, naturally like pornography. His objection was not to pornography and men's routine purchase and use of women's bodies for sexual pleasure, but to the viewing of it with women present. He was making it clear that his ultimate loyalty was to men and their right to use women sexually, though that use should conform to some type of code of chivalry in mixed company.

In doing that, he was announcing his own position in regard to sex. He was saying: *I'm just a john.*

Pimps and johns

A *john* is a man who pays another human being for sex. Typically that other human being is sold through an intermediary known as a *pimp.*

Pimps sell the bodies of other people (most typically, a male pimp selling a woman) to a third person (almost always a man). Men sell women to other men for sex: pimps and johns.

I want to concentrate here not on the pimps but on the johns, on the men who buy women for sex. I assume that many men reading this use, or have used, pornography. I assume that many men reading this masturbate, or have masturbated, to pornography. So I assume there are lots of johns and former johns reading this article.

I don't mean that most of us have necessarily bought a woman from a pimp in prostitution, though no doubt some have. I'm talking about the far more common experience of masturbating to pornography. In my childhood and young adulthood, I was sometimes a john. Virtually every man I know has been a john.

In pornography, the pimp is called a publisher or a video producer, and the john is called a fan or a pornography consumer. But that doesn't change the nature of the relationships: one person (usually a man) selling another person (a woman) to a third person (usually a man).

So pornography is pimps and johns, mass-mediated. When you masturbate to pornography, you are buying sexual pleasure. You are buying a woman. The fact that there are technologies of film or video between you and the pimp doesn't change the equation. Legally, it's not prostitution; legally, you're not in trouble—but you're still just a john.

The pornography that johns like

At this point, let me define a few terms. I'm using the term *pornography* to describe the graphic sexually explicit material that one finds in a pornographic video store that depicts primarily heterosexual sex and is consumed primarily, though not exclusively, by heterosexual men. Such material is also widely available on the Internet. There are, of course, other genres of pornography (such as gay or lesbian). But I'm speaking of the material that I suspect most men have used most routinely—those DVDs and videos that are the bulk of the commercial pornography market.

There are three consistent themes in that pornography:

1. All women want sex from all men at all times.

2. Women naturally desire the kind of sex that men want, including sex that many women find degrading.

3. Any woman who does not at first realize this can be turned on with a little force.

The pornography industry produces two major types of films, features and gonzo. Features mimic, however badly, the conventions of a Hollywood movie: minimal plot, character development, and dialogue, all in the service of presenting the sex. "Gonzo" films have no such pretensions; they are simply recorded sex, often in a private home or on some minimal set. These films often start with an interview with the woman or women about their sexual desires before the man or men enter the scene.

All these films have a standard series of sex acts, including oral, vaginal, and anal penetration, often performed while the men call the women "bitch," "cunt," "whore," and similar names. As they are penetrated, the women are expected to say over and over how much they like the sex. As pornography like this has become increasingly normalized—readily available throughout the country by increasingly sophisticated technology—pornographers have pushed the limits of what is acceptable in the mainstream. As one pornographic film director put it: "People want more ... Make it more hard, make it more nasty, make it more relentless."

In recent years, the pornography industry has produced about 11,000 new hardcore, graphic sexually explicit films a year. Estimates of the annual revenues of the pornography industry in the United States start at $10 billion. For comparison, the Hollywood box office was $9.5 billion in 2003.

That's a lot of johns, and a lot of profit for the pimps.

Men's choices and responsibility

We live in a world in which men sell women to other men directly. And men also sell women to other men through the mass media. These days, women are sometimes the buyers. And on rare occasions in recent years, women are the sellers. That is, there are women who consume pornography and a few women who make it. In this society, that's called progress. Feminism is advanced, we are told, when women can join the ranks of those who buy and sell other human beings.

All this is happening as a predictable result of the collaboration of capitalism and patriarchy. Take a system that values profit over everything, and combine it with a system of male supremacy: you get pimps and johns, and pornography that is increasingly normalized and mainstreamed, an everyday experience.

When confronted with this, men often suggest that because women in pornography choose to participate, there's no reason to critique men's use of pornography. We should avoid this temptation to take the easy way out. I'm going to say nothing in regard to what women should do, nor am I going to critique their choices. I don't take it as my place to inject myself into the discussions that women have about this. (The book, *Not for Sale,* has interesting insights into those questions: www.spinifexpress.com.au/Bookstore/book/id=109/)

I do, however, take it as my place to talk to men. I take it as a political/moral responsibility to engage in critical self-reflection and be accountable for my behavior, at the individual and the collective level. For men, the question is not about women's choices. It's about *men's* choices. Do you want to participate in this system in which women are sold for sexual pleasure, whether in prostitution, pornography, strip bars, or any other aspect of the sex industry? Do you want to live in a world in which some people are bought and sold for the sexual pleasure of others?

When we ask such questions, one of the first things we hear is: These are important issues, but we shouldn't make men feel *guilty* about this. Why not? I agree that much of the guilt people feel—rooted in attempts to repress human sexuality that unfortunately are part of the cultural and theological history of our society—is destructive. But guilt also can be a healthy emotional and intellectual response to the world and one's actions in it.

Johns *should* feel guilty when they buy women. Guilt is a proper response to an act that is unjust. Guilt can be a sign that we have violated our own norms. It can be part of a process of ending the injustice. Guilt can be healthy, if it is understood in political, not merely religious or psychological, terms.

Buying women is wrong not because of a society's repressive moral code or its effects on an individual's psychological process. It is wrong because it hurts people. It creates a world in which people get hurt. And the people who get hurt the most are women and children, the people with the least amount of power. When you create a class that can be bought and sold, the people in that class will inevitably be treated as lesser, as available to be controlled and abused.

The way out of being a john is political. The way out is feminism. I don't mean feminism as a superficial exercise in identifying a few "women's issues" that men can help with. I mean feminism as an avenue into what Karl Marx called "the ruthless criticism of the existing order, ruthless in that it will shrink neither from its own discoveries, nor from conflict with the powers that be."

We need to engage in some ruthless criticism. Let's start not just with pornography but with sex more generally. One of those discoveries, I think, is not only that men often are johns but that the way in which johns use women sexually is a window into other aspects of our sexual and intimate lives. For many men, sex is a place where we both display and reinforce our power over women. By that, I don't mean that all men at all times use sex that way, but that a pattern of such relationships is readily visible in this society. Women deal with it every day, and at some level most men understand it.

This is not just about pimps and johns and women who are prostituted. It's about men and women, and sex and power. If you've been thinking, "Well, that's not me—I never pay for it," don't be so sure. It's not just about who pays for it and who doesn't. It's about the fundamental nature of the relationship between men and women, and how that plays out in sex and intimacy.

And if you think this doesn't affect you because you are one of the "good men," think again. I'm told that I am one of those good men. I work in a feminist movement. I have been part of groups that critique men's violence and the sex industry. And I struggle with these issues all the time. I was trained to be a man in this culture, and that training doesn't evaporate overnight. None of us is off the hook.

What is sex for?

No matter what our personal history or current practice, we all might want to ask a simple question: What is sex for?

A male friend once told me he thought that sometimes sex can be like a warm handshake, a greeting between friends. Many people assert that sex can be a purely physical interaction to produce pleasurable sensations in the body.

At the same time, sex is said to be the ultimate act of intimacy, the place in which we expose ourselves most fully, where we let another see us stripped down, not just physically but emotionally.

Certainly sex can be all those things to different people at different times. But is that not a lot to ask sex to carry? Can one human practice really carry such a range of meanings and purposes? And in such a context, in a male-supremacist culture in which men's violence is still tacitly accepted and men's control of women often unchallenged, should we be surprised that sex becomes a place where violence and control play out?

This isn't an argument for some imposition of a definition of sex. It's an invitation to confront what I believe is a crucial question for this culture. The conservative framework, often rooted in narrow religious views, for defining appropriate sex in order to control people, is a disaster. The liberal/libertarian framework, avoiding questions of gender and power, has failed.

We live in a time of sexual crisis. That makes life difficult, but it also creates a space for invention and creativity. That is what drew me to feminism, to the possibility of a different way of understanding the world and myself, the possibility of escaping the masculinity trap set for me, that chance to become something more than a man, more than just a john—to become a human being.

VOICE MALE

Are Too Many on the Left Excusing Porn?
By Ben Barker

If the fight against pornography is a radical one, where are the radicals fighting against pornography?

In 2013, the 18th annual San Francisco Bay Area Anarchist Bookfair, an event that brings together radical activists from around the world, was held at the headquarters and production facility of so-called alternative porn company Kink.com (www.counterpunch.org/2013/02/08/anarchist-book-fair-porn).

Kink.com is known for its unique brand of torture porn. As longtime antiporn activist and writer Gail Dines reports, women are "stretched out on racks, hogtied, urine squirting in their mouths, and suspended from the ceiling while attached to electrodes, including ones inserted in their vaginas." But to grasp the agenda of Kink.com, we can just go to the source: founder Peter Acworth started the company after devoting his life to "subjecting beautiful, willing women to strict bondage."

When the Anarchist Bookfair announced its choice of venue, feminists were outraged. The few who were billed to speak during the event dropped out. But ultimately, the decision was defended, the outcry lashed back against, and the show went on.

Anarchists are my kind of people—or so I thought. When I first discovered the radical Left some eight years ago, I thought I'd stumbled upon the revolution. The rhetoric seemed as much: brave, refreshing demands for human rights, equality, and liberation; a steadfast commitment to struggle against unjust power, however daunting the fight.

It wasn't long, though, before my balloon of hope burst. To the detriment of my idealism and trust, the true colors of my radical heroes began to show.

Pornography was then and is now one such letdown. Over the years, I've bounced between a diversity of groups on the radical Left: punks, Queers, anarchists, and many in between. But wherever I went, porn was the norm.

Here's the latest in radical theory: "We're seventeen and fucking in the public museum. I'm on my knees with your cock in my mouth, surrounded by Mayan art and tiger statues. Our hushed whispers and frenzied breathing becomes a secret language of power. And us, becoming monstrous, eating-whole restraint and apology. The world ruptures as we come, but it isn't enough. We want it all, of course—to expropriate the public as a wild zone of becoming-orgy, and to destroy what stands in our way."[1] I'm sad to report that this quote, and the book it comes from, *Politics Is Not a Banana: The*

---

1 The Institute for Experimental Freedom. *Politics is Not a Banana: The Journal of Vulgar Discourse*

Journal of Vulgar Discourse, reflects one of the most increasingly popular of the radical subcultures.

Conflating perversion and revolution is nothing new. We can trace the trend all the way back to the 1700s in the time of the Marquis de Sade, one of the earliest creators and ideologues of pornography (not to mention pedophilia and sadomasochism). Sade was famous for his graphic writings featuring rape, bestiality, and necrophilia. Andrea Dworkin has called his work "nearly indescribable," writing, "In sheer quantity of horror, it is unparalleled in the history of writing. In its fanatical and fully realized commitment to depicting and reveling in torture and murder to gratify lust, it raises the question so central to pornography as a genre: why? why did someone do . . . this? In Sade's case, the motive most often named is revenge against a society that persecuted him. This explanation does not take into account the fact that Sade was a sexual predator and that the pornography he created was part of that predation." Dworkin also notes that, "Sade's violation of sexual and social boundaries, in his writings and in his life, is seen as inherently revolutionary."[2]

Despite all they seem to share in common, most of today's radicals actually don't revere the Marquis de Sade. Rather, they look to his followers; namely, one postmodern philosopher by the name of Michel Foucault, no small fan of Sade, whom he famously dubbed a "dead God." Foucault's ideas remain some of the most influential within the radical Left. He has catalyzed more than one generation with his critiques of capitalism, his rallying cries for what he calls "social war," and his apparently subversive sexuality. Foucault, who in fact lamented that the Marquis de Sade had "not gone far enough," was determined to push the limits of sexual transgression, using both philosophy and his own body. His legacy of eroticizing pain and domination has unfortunately endured.

So where are the radicals in this fight against pornography? The answer depends on whom we call radical. The word radical means "to the root." Radicals dig to the roots of oppression and start taking action there—except, apparently, when it comes to the oppression of women. How radical is it to stop digging halfway for the sake of getting off?

What is called the radical Left today isn't really that. It's radical in name only and looks more like an obscure collection of failing subcultures than any kind of oppositional movement. But this is the radical Left we have, and this one, far from fighting it, revels in porn.

Just as we need to wrest our culture from the hands of the pornographers, we need to wrest our political movements from the hands of the sexists. Until we do that, so-called radical men will continue to prop up sexual exploitation under the excusing banner of freedom and subversion.

---

2 Dworkin, Andrea. *Pornography: Men Possessing Women*

This male-dominated radical Left is expressly antifeminist. In a popular and obscene anarchist essay, "Feminism as Fascism," the author—who is male, need I mention—ridicules feminists for drawing any connection whatsoever between porn and violence against women. He concludes that feminism—rather than, say, the multibillion dollar porn industry—is a "ludicrous, hate-filled, authoritarian, sexist, dogmatic construct which revolutionaries accord an unmerited legitimacy by taking it seriously at all."

I've ceased to be surprised at the virulent use and defense of porn by supposedly radical—and even "antisexist"—men. The two have always seemed to me to go hand-in-hand. My first encounter with radicals was at a punk rock music show in the basement of a stinky party house. I stood awkwardly upstairs, excited but shy. Amidst the raucous crowd, a word caught my ear: "porn." Then, another word: "scat." Next, the guys were huddling around a computer. And I was confused… until I saw.

More sophisticated than the punks, the anarchist friends I made a few years later used big words to justify their own porn lust. Railing against what they deem censorship, anarchists channel Foucault in imagining themselves a vanguard for free sexual expression, by which they really mean men's unbridled entitlement to the use and abuse of women's bodies. And any who take issue with this must be, as one anarchist put it, "uncomfortable with sex" or—and I'm not making this up—"enemies of freedom."

The Queer subculture puts the politics of sexual libertarianism into practice. Anything "at odds with the 'normal' or legitimate" becomes fair game. One Queer theorist, Sandra Jeppesen, explained in specifics: "Sleaze, perversion, deviance, eccentricity, weirdness, kinkiness, BDSM and smut . . . are central to sex-positive queer anarchist lives," she wrote. As the lives of the radicals I once counted as comrades began to confirm and give testament to this centrality, I abandoned ship.

Pornography is a significant part of radical subcultures, whether quietly consumed or brazenly paraded. That it made me uncomfortable from the beginning did not, unfortunately, deter me from trying it myself. It seems significant though, that, despite growing up as a boy in a porn culture, my first and last time using porn was while immersed in this particular social scene. Who was there to stop me? With all semblances of feminist principles tossed to the wind, who was there to steer me from the hazards of pornography and toward a path of justice?

The answer is no one. Why? Because the pornographers control the men who control the radical Left. Women may be kept around in the boy's club—or boy's *cult*—but only to be used in one way or another; never as full human beings. How is it a male radical can look honestly in the face of a female comrade and believe her liberation will come through being filmed or photographed nude?

I have a dear neighbor who says, "There's nothing progressive about treating women like dirt; that's just what happens already." My neighbor has little experience in the radical Left, but apparently has bounds more common sense than most individuals therein. She, along with many ordinary people I've chatted with, have a hard time believing—let alone understanding—that people who think of themselves as radical could actually embrace and defend something as despicable as pornography. If the basic moral conscience of average people allows them to grasp the violence and degradation inherent in porn, we have to ask: what's wrong with the radical Left?

In a way, this letdown is predictable. From ideologues like Sade and Foucault, to the macho rebellion of punk bands like the Sex Pistols, to the anarchist-endorsed Kink.com, justice—for women and for all—has been a peripheral goal at best for countercultural revolutionaries. Of vastly greater priority is this notion of transgression, an attempt at "sexual dissidence and subversion which challenges the symbolic order,"[3] the devout belief that anything not considered "normal" is radical by default.

I can't speak for you, but there are plenty of things that I think *deserve* not to be seen as normal. Take Kink.com, for example. Despite the cheerleading of shock value crusaders, I don't really care how many cultural boundaries the company believes itself to be transgressing; tying up and peeing on another human being is simply wrong. If this sentiment gets me kicked out of some sort of radical consensus, so be it.

What is transgressive for some is business-as-usual oppression for others. As Sheila Jeffreys explains, "Transgression is a pleasure of the powerful, who can imagine themselves deliciously naughty. It depends on the maintenance of conventional morality. There would be nothing to outrage, and the delicious naughtiness would vanish, if serious social change took place. The transgressors and the moralists depend mutually upon each other, locked in a binary relationship which defeats rather than enables change." Transgression, she contests, "is not a strategy available to the housewife, the prostituted woman, or the abused child. They are the objects of transgression, rather than its subjects."[4]

Being radical is a process, not an outcome. To be radical means keeping our eyes on justice at every instance, in every circumstance. It means maintaining the agenda of justice when picking our issues and the strategy and tactics we use to take them on. Within a patriarchy, men cannot be radical without fighting sexism. This is to say that radical activism and pornography are fundamentally at odds. Where are the radicals fighting porn? The ones worth the name are already in the heat of battle, and on the side of justice, whether or not it gets us off.

---

3 Weeks, Jeffrey. *Making Sexual History*
4 Jeffreys, Sheila. *Unpacking Queer Politics*

PROGRESSIVE MEN *ARE* CONFRONTING PORNOGRAPHY

From the earliest days of feminist activism against the deep misogyny of the porn industry, a small but vocal number of men have joined with women not only to protest the harm porn culture causes women but to articulate the need for a radical critique of porn's role in shaping (heterosexual) men's sexuality in a way that reinforces men's dominance, power, and control over women. "The core of one's being must love justice more than manhood," said John Stoltenberg in 1994.

While the trend within a significant segment of the radical Left bends toward male entitlement and violation, there is more to the story. For some progressive men, humanity and justice have seemed the better choices.

Profeminist men—radicals in the most honest sense of that word—comprise a movement that should hearten men everywhere. Since the 1970s, both in and outside of the "organized" Left, they have supported feminist activism on a range of issues, including challenging the sexism of men on the Left. They have created organizations, organized conferences, written books, held trainings, participated in demonstrations, and taken legal action.

They have also produced works that explore the role of pornography in maintaining sexism, racism, and other systems of inequality, as well as its effects on men's lives, sexuality, and relationships. Books like Stoltenberg's *Refusing to Be a Man*, Robert Jensen's *Getting Off: Pornography and the End of Masculinity*, Michael Kimmel's *Men Confront Pornography*, and Jackson Katz's *The Macho Paradox* give me heart for men's role in this struggle. And organizations like the Stop Porn Culture, as well as periodicals like *Voice Male* illuminate the path toward gender justice, without which any sense of social justice is just empty rhetoric.

As for the rest, we're going to have to *make* them. As the current radical Left self-destructs under the crushing grip of misogyny—as it already is and inevitably will—it is up to us to gather from the rubble whatever fragmented pieces of good there are left. And it is up to us to forge those pieces into a genuinely radical alternative.

Women have been doing this work for a long time. But it is by and for *men* that women's lives are stolen and degraded through pornography. And it is by and for *men* that the radical Left colludes with this injustice. So it must now be *men*—the ones with any sense of empathy or moral obligation left—who take final responsibility for stopping it. Women have already mapped out the road from here to justice. Men simply need to get on board.

It's no easy task taking on the cult of masculinity from the inside, but it's a privileged position in comparison to being on the outside and, thus, its target. And this cult needs to be dismantled. Men need to take it down inside and out, from the most personal sense to the most global.

Men can start small by boycotting porn in our own lives, both for the sake of our individual sexualities and for the sake of the many women undoubtedly suffering for its production. Through images of dehumanized women, pornography dehumanizes also the men who consume those images.

Individually rejecting pornography is necessary, but social change has always been a group project. Men must put pressure on other men to stop supporting, and at the very least stop participating in, sexual exploitation. We can demand our movements and organizations outspokenly oppose it. We can disavow them if they refuse.

As it stands, it's hard to tell apart the radical Left and porn culture at large. Both are based on the same rotten lie: women are objects to be publicly used.

As it falls, the male-dominated radical Left can be replaced by something new and so desperately needed: a feminist, antipornography radical Left. Its goal: not the transgression of basic human rights, but the uncompromising defense of them.

The Rites of Manhood

Alden Nowlan
Winter 2003

It's snowing hard enough that the taxis aren't running.
I'm walking home, my night's work finished,
long after midnight, with the whole city to myself,
when across the street I see a very young American sailor
standing over a girl who's kneeling on the sidewalk
and refuses to get up although he's yelling at her
to tell him where she lives so he can take her there
before they both freeze. The pair of them are drunk
and my guess is he picked her up in a bar
and later they got separated from his buddies
and at first it was great fun to play at being
an old salt at liberty in a port full of women with
hinges on their heels, but by now he wants only to
find a solution to the infinitely complex
problem of what to do about her before he falls into
the hands of the police or the shore patrol
—and what keeps this from being squalid is
what's happening to him inside:
if there were other sailors here
it would be possible for him
to abandon her where she is and joke about it
later, but he's alone and the guilt can't be
divided into small forgettable pieces;
he's finding out what it means
to be a man and how different it is
from the way that only hours ago he imagined it.

Photo Chuck Stern

Gay, bisexual, transgender, and queer men speak out about their experiences within their own communities as well as the challenges and oppression they face within a broader homophobic culture. From stories of San Francisco in the heyday of its gay community to the devastating effects of AIDS, from facing blatant homophobia to coming out to loved ones and often finding support there, these men courageously articulate their experiences, joined and supported by women and heterosexual allies.

Finding Acceptance as a Transgender Man
By Dennis Bushey
Spring 2003

My name is Dennis. I was once very good at meeting the expectations of others, in order to gain their acceptance. Until one day I realized the only thing I actually got from it was criticism and a large sense of emptiness. I then began a journey, four years ago, to understand what it means to be true to myself. I started to put myself back together after thirty-five years of taking me apart.

This meant some significant changes. It started with a divorce and moved from Florida back to western Massachusetts. I moved in with family, back in the room I grew up in. I was literally starting over with no job, vehicle, or place of my own. I have a very independent nature and relying on family was very difficult for me, especially since among the first things I needed to do was deal with childhood issues.

Coming back to Massachusetts to do this had a benefit. There were resources here I needed to help me begin taking myself seriously. Once I started to do that, it was no small task for my family to do the same. I had come to terms with my gender identity and its expression. Since I had been born female, my parents had to cope with losing a daughter and my siblings with no longer having a sister. In the beginning the thought of gaining a son or brother was no comfort to them.

I was six months into a new job in the mental health field when I started the transition from female to male. Management was clueless about how to help, which meant most times they didn't. The clients we worked with had issues of their own. Trying to explain why their female staff member was now growing a beard seemed at times as challenging as being a high-wire performer in the circus.

In addition to this major transition, there was also my sexual orientation: I am attracted to men. I went from living a life as a straight woman to being a gay man. This shift was quite confusing for a lot of people. The idea that identity is separate from orientation was difficult for them to grasp. I had support for issues related to being transgender. Now I was at a point where I needed support for integration into a community of men, especially gay men.

I had always been in intimate relationships with men, but as a (very uncomfortable) female. It was well accepted to show affection to my mate in public. I could talk about my relationships openly. Now all that is different. How would I learn to navigate in a new world? Negotiate in a world with new prejudices?

Three years ago I decided to finally check out a gay/bisexual/transgender and questioning men's support group offered at the Men's Resource Center. It did list *T* for transgender, but was that only for male-to-female? Do they know about female-to-males? Many people don't. What about those who identify as gay? Would they take me seriously, as a gay man, or would they be like others I have met who thought, "Why change your sex if you're attracted to males?" Would I be looked at with disdain or would they laugh my butt right out of there?

Knowing all too well the stereotypical masculinity most men are indoctrinated with, one of my transgender (male-to-female) friends was certain they would reject me and was frightened on my behalf. But what if they didn't reject me? How would that feel? The only way I'd find out was to go.

I was nervous. I physically shivered the entire half-hour ride to the meeting. I thought to myself that I would just sit and listen. Maybe they won't be able to tell what I am. During the meeting, I was rather quiet. But the evening went smoothly. It wasn't so bad. I left thinking that if I just don't mention anything related to being "trans" I'll fit in.

The next week I returned. As men were talking, I found myself having to refrain from expressing my thoughts. In order for anything I had to say to make sense, I would need to disclose who I was. I realized that being "trans" was related to every aspect of my life.

Maybe this wasn't the place for me. How could I ever fit in?

As the meeting progressed I was struck by the way the men were talking. They were being honest about their feelings. The most amazing thing was that they were aware they *had* feelings! Let alone being able to articulate them as well as they did. This was new for me to experience among men. That night a discussion evolved that brought up some uncomfortable feelings for some group members. Even so, they conveyed their thoughts respectfully. They took ownership of their feelings and didn't place blame. I was inspired by their level of communication and by their honesty. I began to think that this was the kind of male mentoring I was looking for.

An opportunity presented itself for me to speak. I took the risk and disclosed who I was. The response was compassionate. They wondered if they could ask questions. I was the first female-to-male in this group and they wanted to know how to relate in a respectful way. They even thanked me for sharing. Whew! I had found a place to integrate. For the first time in my life, I felt at home among others. I now had many role models to help mentor me in a positive, unstereotypical masculinity. I began to believe I could sanely survive in a new world.

Since then, each week I have a place to go to process both the day-to-day stuff and the really big stuff. Now that my physical transition is over, things are less "trans" related and I feel more like an "average Joe." I love to meet new people. Since it's a drop-in group, there are often new people at the meeting. This can also be a frustration for me. Sometimes if there are new people and it involves my past, I don't say much. Those are times when I just don't feel strong enough to deal with explaining it or changing their image of me. Although it does not keep me away, it can make me acutely aware of my differences and cause a real struggle inside. Nevertheless, of all the groups I belong to, this is my main support; it's a place where I can bring *anything*.

The Men's Resource Center's mission of breaking down male stereotypes has created a safe space for me and provided an emotionally healthy atmosphere to grow in. I have gained more courage to integrate into the larger scale of life. I have had the chance to develop many profound friendships through the group. No question it has helped save my life.

The organization's dedication to overcoming violence has helped me become more conscious of how I speak. The more I am able to eliminate judgmental and angry language, the more peace of mind I find. I like that, and I'm glad I have a place that encourages my own personal growth on so many different levels.

The GBTQ group has seen me through my second adolescence and has been a large part of helping me grow into an active, confident, compassionate young man.

Who would've guessed having the courage to attend that first meeting would have been the catalyst for me to accomplish so much?

My Gay San Francisco
By Les Wright
Winter 2007

> *Richard Nixon was on nationwide television resigning the presidency on the day I was flying back to Germany, an avowed out-of-the-closet expatriate, writes Les Wight. "Five years later, in 1979, when I found myself repatriating to the States, I had become radicalized by the gay Left in Germany. When I arrived in San Francisco by Greyhound from*

Boston, I came looking for the grand experiment in gay community known as Castro Street. Like many gay pilgrims before and after," Wright recalls, *"once I got here, I abandoned myself to the city, and jumped into the never-ending party."*

The gay activist upstarts populating the Castro and led by Harvey Milk represented a very different kind of gay political vision from the one I had carried with me from Germany. They were mavericks even in 1970s gay boomtown San Francisco; a solidly established, if very quiet gay and lesbian community already had a long tradition of working within the political culture of the city.

By the time I arrived in August 1979, San Francisco was still in shock from the Jonestown mass suicide in Guyana (Jim Jones had moved his People's Temple there from San Francisco's poor black Fillmore neighborhood) and re-covering from the double assassination of city supervisor Harvey Milk (representing the gay Castro district) and Mayor George Moscone. That sum-mer Castro Street overflowed with young gay men, mostly buff, white twentysomethings in 501 jeans and flannel shirts. Gay bars had sprouted like mushrooms after a hard rain, all across the city. Bathhouse culture was in full swing. The leather scene centered around Folsom Street was thriving. The old gay commercial heart on Polk Street still thrummed. Hippie-bohemian Haight-Ashbury had plenty of gay commercial life as well. Discos and designer drugs were all the rage. Recent reformist gains for legal recognition of gays and lesbians had opened the floodgate of endless, exuberant celebration.

On the ground, life as I experienced it in those years, before and during AIDS, was larger than life. Every day I got up I felt, as many of us did, that I was participating in making history. This was the time when Armistead Maupin, then a local columnist, was writing twice-weekly columns called "Tales of the City." We read his installments as a kind of open collective journal.

In retrospect, it all seems heartbreakingly innocent and naïve. Even at the time, many of us were saying to one another, "This is too good to be true; something is going to happen." Even as "everyone" was being embraced, many people were feeling left out, invisible, or shunned. "Gay" began looking very white, male, and comfortably middle-class. And, just as sexual identity politics shifted focus to queer and multicultural, AIDS hit, and hit catastrophically hard. Castro Street was ground zero. An entire generation of gay men was fod-der for a precision-pinpointed genocide. Because San Francisco is a city of dense neighborhoods—and much smaller than L.A. or New York—the AIDS epidemic was inexorably palpable and ubiquitous.

Castro Street became a ghost town—many businesses and most bars folded overnight. I remember thinking that this is what the Black Death must have felt like. And for five years, Ronald Reagan could not even utter one word about AIDS. We in gay San Francisco lived with an acute awareness that the president's Republican regime clearly was waiting for all the fags to die. What had we been celebrating?

To give a more accurate personal account, I have to admit that I arrived in San Francisco a full-blown, raging alcoholic. I got sober two years later, initially through the assistance of Eighteenth Services, one of the first-ever alcohol and drug treatment facilities for gay men. I learned to appreciate much more keenly the vast scope of the gay community in San Francisco, as well as in the Bay Area and northern California more broadly. I even escaped a ghettoized existence of my own making.

In 1981 I got sober, became infected with HIV, and returned to graduate school, never expecting to survive to the end of my studies. In 1993, Ph.D. in hand, I accepted a teaching post in Boston, still not expecting to live much longer. When I moved back to San Francisco in 2005, after 12 years in Massachusetts, I discovered my crazy, wild, maddening, beloved city much changed. In fact, I had completely missed the dotcom boom-and-bust, one of the defining events of recent times here. And there were more ghosts waiting to haunt me than I could shake a stick at.

Returning to the Gay Capital of the World
By Les Wright
Spring 2007

It has been two years since I moved back to San Francisco. Living here now it is impossible, at least for me, to escape noticing the radical remaking of the world going on all around me. Post-dotcom-bust San Francisco is a boomtown again, reminiscent of post-Wall Berlin. An entirely new twenty-first-century urban high-density city is rising. Dire, street-survival poverty jostles up against an unprecedented exuberance of über-conspicuous consumption here. As gay community scholar Gayle Rubin remarked at a recent GLBT Historical Society presentation, our painted lady is being transformed into a "command city for the twenty-first century." Like Hong Kong or Dubai, it is a "desirable" place for the new global corporate elite to build their personal homes. This, I sometimes think, is what expansive Gilded Age Manhattan must have felt like.

We San Franciscans tend to forget this is a uniquely diverse, world-class metropolis. "Downtown," the vast, impenetrable center of bureaucracies and corporations, has made but shallow incursions into our sense of living in a small town, a social space of perhaps two degrees of separation.

And as cities have become desirable again, deeper-pocket interests have been gentrifying the gays out of their urban enclaves all across the country.

The Castro, our own homegrown "ethnically" gay neighborhood and symbolic (if less frequently visited) gay capital of the United States, suddenly looks like the last "traditional" gay neighborhood. As the Castro has been turning a bit seedy, local queer pride and, increasingly, the city planning and tourism boards see it as the Gay Capital of the World. Herein lies the ironic paradox today: as gay folk have been disappeared by AIDS or sucked into the queer diaspora, gays and straights alike see this newly "ethnic" community through gently softening lenses, engulfed in cloud-shrouded images of quaint, nostalgic, queer white-picket fences.

My return nearly two years ago, portending no such evolution, began very painfully. In 2005 I returned to the emotional scene as I had left it in San Francisco 12 years before—by 1993 I was subsisting on SSI, waiting to die of AIDS, with no future, nor even the capacity to dream of a future. Indeed, I had explicitly organized my life around not surviving. But I did; I completed a long doctoral program at UC Berkeley and was hired out of permanent disabled status into a tenure-track college teaching post in Boston.

I won tenure, settled down with a life partner, got a mortgage, and swiftly atrophied in this middle-class happily-ever-after. Then came a moment of clarity: the life I was living was not mine. It may have been someone else's, perhaps the dream of a much younger me. But the longer I willed myself to stay on this path, the more miserable, insane, isolated, and despairing I became. The last time I had seen my life, it was still in San Francisco, among the AIDS ghosts and other debris of living life messily.

Returning to San Francisco I found everything changed, and myself lost in a kind of time-and-space misalignment. My entire social reality had perished before I left in 1993, and now it was long forgotten. During my first six months back, I encountered the ghosts of my past at every turn. Old familiar places, sounds, and smells would trigger them, reminding me of the future that never happened. As I had encountered while teaching about Holocaust survivorship in my Death and Dying humanities course, I too had come back from a world history had forgotten.

Since then, I have sought out numerous support groups and fellow survivors. Recently I participated in a gay men's community meeting on the "poz/neg divide" in gay San Francisco today. Profound healing has occurred through reconnecting with my fellow survivors. But, as the meeting facilitator commented to me privately, it is still far too painful for the queer community at large to hear about or acknowledge our generation. Did you know, he asked me rhetorically, that when Holocaust survivors immigrated to Israel, they were asked to shut up about their experiences and get on with building a future?

I first found reengagement in the world by returning to the rooms of recovery. In this way I have been able to mourn and heal and move on. Like many gay men who unexpectedly survived the AIDS epidemic, I am now exploring my "middlessence"—how to be of service, to contribute meaningfully to the world, to earn a living again. Between the social services available to AIDS survivors returning to the workforce and the rich and diverse spiritual communities I participate in, I am reconnecting with my particular tribe.

Falteringly at first, struggling to overcome a by then paralyzing social anxiety, I found my way back. After recurrent respiratory illnesses landed me in the hospital in October 2005, I found my way to support services for long-term poz folks. The AIDS Health Project provided me with psychological support, while the Positive Resource Center helped with career change and employment retraining support. The State of California has deemed my choice of work as a grant writer supportable. I relish digging into my new field of employment, as a development specialist in the culture and arts nonprofit world.

I've taken two semesters of intensive Spanish, have screened and penned reviews of a couple hundred films, and recently joined a writers' group (all HIV-ers). I work daily with recovering alcoholics. The Bear History Project is rising from old cyber ashes. The Billy Club, a rural collective of socially engaged and spiritually awakened gay, bi, and queer men, has welcomed me with open arms. As I trudge my spiritual path, as ordinary and unconventional as it comes, I find the world makes sense when I live in San Francisco. I know that I am of this place.

Nobody Likes a Nelly Homo
By Mubarak Dahir
Spring 2006

No one likes a nelly homo. Least of all these days, other homos.

That fact is blatantly obvious in our own culture of desire, and I got a jolting reminder of it recently at a local pride celebration where I live, called Pridefest.

It was a perfect Florida day, sunny and warm without being too hot. There was almost no humidity.

The weather conditions ensured that scores of muscled men would turn out, pumped, to show off their own pride.

I parked myself between the concession stands and tents that housed the gay business booths. I stood there sipping a Diet Coke, admiring the sea of flesh and brawn. I had my focus on a particularly hunky group of hairy musclemen standing in a gaggle nearby.

I wasn't the only one marveling at them. They were the stars of the showcase of bare-chested beefcake.

As I stood watching, an effeminate man passed by and, like everyone else assembled on the grounds there, ogled the burly studs.

I figured the he-men should have been flattered. After all, they were showing off for the crowd. But they weren't pleased at all about this one particular admirer.

"Nelly faggot!" one said loud enough that I could hear him, and certainly so that the passerby could, too.

"Prissy queen," smirked another, and the whole group laughed together.

The blatant animosity toward men perceived as sissies is ubiquitous in gay culture. All you have to do is visit any gay cruising or dating site to find it in abundance.

Take, for instance, these real-life examples from the popular gay site Manhunt:

"MASCULINE GUYS ONLY!" screams one entry.

"No fems" is a common mantra.

"UB butch or UB gone," reads another.

"No girl acting guy," or, "You have a dick, act like a man," are just a couple of others in an endless stream of advertisements singing the praise of "manliness."

Some of these come with a veiled apology ("just my preference") but most are as unabashed as they are callous.

As I scrolled through the list of descriptions for butch, one particularly jumped out at me: "Normal and masculine only." Here, quite succinctly and bluntly, the author succeeded in equating masculine with "normal," suggesting, of course, that if you are a man who doesn't live up to his standard of masculine, you are not normal.

It hit me that this is exactly what our enemies in the heterosexual world have long done to us, as a way to stereotype us, humiliate us, put us down and demean us. As a way to make us less equal.

Now they don't need to anymore. Looks like we're doing a plenty good job of doing it to ourselves.

I understand the attraction of a manly man. I run around in the bear and leather crowds, two subgroups famous in the gay world for their almost fetish-like worship of masculinity. I have had a beard since I was 19, and I go to the gym and aim for the bulging biceps look like so many other gay men. When I go out, I am more likely to wear Wranglers than Ralph Lauren. You're not going to see me in anything that is frilly or shiny or gold lamé.

If I see a guy I like, and I get up the courage to say hello, I'm sure my voice drops half an octave. In the world of machismo, I can "pass."

But it wasn't always like that for me.

When I was a school kid growing up in central Pennsylvania, I was the classic sissy. I played violin. And clarinet. And piano. I was book smart. I even liked reading and math and history. I sucked at sports. In gym class, I was always the last one to be picked for a team. The only activities I was good at on the playground during recess were jump rope and dodgeball. The girl games. My older sister frequently used to have to protect me from bullies on the playground. Even girls would beat me up.

The reason I got picked on, of course, was that I was different. I was softer and gentler. I didn't exemplify the standard notion of what it meant to be a boy. And that obviously scared and threatened the other kids, who were already so well indoctrinated by society even at such an early age. So their reaction was to lash out and beat me up.

I thought about my playground days as I stood there at Pridefest and watched the group of burly "butch" men pick on the "nelly queen." It occurred to me the situation wasn't so different from my schoolyard days.

Luckily, no one was getting physically assaulted. But the burly men were definitely beating up on the guy who was less macho. They were picking on the man who was different, the guy who didn't exemplify the socially accepted notion of what it means to be "a man."

Why? He obviously threatened them. He made them nervous. He touched on their insecurities as gay men.

One of the great battle cries of the gay rights movement has been that our society should not only tolerate, but also embrace differences in people. Publicly, at least, we preach that diversity is what makes us, and our world, a more interesting, richer place.

And yet, ironically, within our own ranks, we reject that very premise when it comes to the issue of masculinity. There exists within the gay world a rigidly tiered system of superiority, with the butch men at the top of the food chain. The nelly queens are the bottom of the barrel. Manhunt profiles and the Pridefest incident are just two examples of a ubiquitous attitude that permeates contemporary gay male society.

Every gay man is, of course, free to choose whom he finds sexy and what image he wishes to personally portray. But in doing so, there's no need to denigrate those who don't want to follow the same path of what it means to be "a real man."

Indeed, it would be a real loss, to all of us, if nelly queens disappeared from our ranks. How dull gay life would be if we all showed up at Pride in Wranglers and work boots, and no one came in a wig or something tight and shiny and wonderfully outrageous.

Who would remind us how to laugh at ourselves, and the world around us? Who would show us the courage and strength it takes to defy the stiff molds of social expectation? And who would remind us all of our great sense of possibility?

I say thank goodness for nelly queens. Where would any of us be without them?

Gay and Queer: What's in a Name
By Michael Greenebaum
Fall 2001

I recently attended my (shudder) fiftieth high school reunion. It was good to see old friends. But it was strange to be "Mike" once again. "Mike" was a high school and college kid; somewhere along the line he became "Michael," more formal, more distant, more inward. Mike was out there, friendly, social. Michael is private. Mike was clueless; Michael has a clue. Mike was sexless; Michael is queer.

Was Mike queer, too? Not possible; queer didn't exist in the forties. Neither did "gay," for that matter. In the forties, those people (we?) were fairies or pansies. Those people walked with mincing gait, wore pink shirts, flitted about on Thursdays. And, of course, Mike did none of those things. It was not that girls, those formidable and exotic creatures, exerted any sexual attraction on Mike. He loved girls; he could talk about art and music and religion and world government with them. Girls had ideas, at least the girls who were his friends did. Boys exercised no sexual attraction on Mike, either. Mike solved the problem of sex by having none of it.

This little excursion into autobiography is really leading up to the question, What if the term "queer" had existed in the forties? What, even, if "gay" had been in use then? What, in other words, might have been the difference for me if affirmative, gutsy names for the confusing, alluring yearnings I suppressed had been available?

"Gay" has an equivocal history, and some straight people express regret that its original meaning of frivolous and weightless joy is no longer available to them. But that transformation is complete, and "gay" is now weighted with tremendous irony. Happiness and sadness seem irreparably linked by this label of choice. Being gay is both a burden and a joy; but then, so is life for most people. Burdens and joys are distributed without regard to sexual preference or sexual orientation. "Gay" and "straight" have become ways people describe themselves, without much emotional content or commitment. One does not seem to be affirming much of anything by claiming either of them.

That is why, for some gay men, the term seems a bit pallid in a society still cursed with individual and institutional homophobia. To be sure, sometimes we want to remind everyone that we are part of the human family, that orientation toward or preference for same-sex partners is parallel to orientation toward or preference for opposite sex partners. In these cases, "gay" is a convenient and often acceptable label. But sometimes, we (or at least some) want to be more assertive and affirming about our essential identities. We want to claim that just those things our haters use against us are the very things we assert and affirm.

Our sexuality is sometimes just one of those things, but at other times it is the central thing. For many, "queer" is the name that captures and identifies what we want to assert and affirm—that in spite of grief and oppression our sexuality is a source of pride and joy, as our local queer shop reminds us.

"Queer" is a tough, hard-edged, in-your-face identity. It is still used against us by those we discomfit. When we transform it into a positive and affirmative identity, we are part of a long historical tradition of oppressed groups who have challenged their oppressors by appropriating their labels of hate.

"Queer" has two other distinct virtues, at least to this queer man. First, it is inclusive. "Queer" is as much an umbrella as it is a label. Gay men, lesbians, bisexual men and women, and transsexuals are accommodated under its sheltering embrace. When I call myself queer, I am not only making a statement of identity but also a statement of affiliation. I am joining a community, and it is the community I prefer. It includes women, and for me life without women would be unfulfilled. One of the great joys of coming to terms with my sexuality later in life is that at last I don't have to be afraid of women; I don't have to worry about being in a false position when I am with them. I love women and I love being with them. The queer community includes women, and hurray for that! It includes transsexuals, who must be about the most courageous people I know. It includes drag queens and drag kings and other variations on the theme of gender bending. Thank you to all these queer people for transforming gender from a fixed to a fluid and nuanced notion. They have done a great service to all of us and enriched the ways we have of being human.

But there is another reason I am queer. For a number of years I answered to the label "bisexual." It felt antiseptic and clinical, but it was all we had. Like "homosexual," it seems off-putting, intrusive, and sloppy. "Bisexual" sounds like it is drawn from one of those huge medical tomes. It makes me feel like a scientific object, an example of a condition. "Bisexual" is intrusive since it implies something about my sexual activity, which is nobody's business.

"Queer" suits me fine. Often, when I call myself queer, people read that as gay. That's fine; often I feel gay. I love my gay friends; they are an important part of my life. But queer is what I am; the queer community is my community. It is inclusive, embracing, and affirming. Slowly but surely, Michael is introducing Mike to his new friends.

Men, Homophobia, and My Pink Helmet
By Pip Cornall
Winter 2006

I purchased a pink rafting helmet from a sporting goods store in Oregon when I first arrived in the United States. It was the only one left in my size.

The salesperson seemed surprised that I would take it, and I remember saying nonchalantly that it was as good as any other color.

Many years later, my pink helmet has stories to tell. It has received more uninvited comments from strangers than I could ever have imagined. Hardly a day has gone by on the river without someone letting me know his opinion. Not surprisingly, all of these comments were from men.

We were on a two-raft overnight camping trip on the Upper Klamath River in southern Oregon, along the California border. A man who was a client in another raft guided by my friend Bill called out to me in a mocking tone. In a faux feminine voice, he said he liked my attire of purple shorts, purple life vest, and pink helmet, and then he held up his arms letting the wrists go limp in a stereotyped gay simulation. Jokingly, but with a little sting behind my words, I called back that if he was homophobic I could have a chat with him at camp, since I taught classes in area schools for overcoming homophobia and could clue him in. He replied angrily that he was an ex-sheriff and that he shot gays! Shocked by his harsh response, I pulled my raft away downriver to breathe and regroup my thoughts.

In the calmer sections of the river, I watched my mind running through numerous scenarios and possible responses. I wondered about the feelings of the twelve people in our two rafts. What if some of them were gay or had gay family members, as I did? I wanted to ask the man: If I were gay, would he have run the rapids with me? Would he want to shoot my gay family member? Was he really dangerous, or just shooting his mouth off? However, I did not at the time reflect on his fear and pain or how he had become so hardened. All too soon the size and intensity of the rapids demanded my full focus, so I gladly put the incident aside.

I made a point to look him up that evening when the meal was over and tried to build some rapport with him. We chatted for a while, but after a few probing questions from me it was clear that he would not say any more about the topic. Perhaps he was embarrassed by the anger of his response, or at the idea of exposing his attitudes in mixed company. For my part I wondered whether, if I had not been such a smart guy when he first taunted me, we might have had a better dialogue. My initial response had simply polarized us more. I had training in nonadversarial communication skills and could have gently learned more about his stance rather than making him wrong for his beliefs. I wondered about my smug political correctness and regretted a missed opportunity for healing between two men whose emotional development had most likely been trashed during the long years in "male boot camp." That could have been our common bond.

Even some of my friends who were river guides working for other companies could not restrain themselves from commenting on my pink helmet. Their comments were made in good humor, and simply reminded me that different cultures have different attitudes and traditions. One day I heard the words "G'day, ponce" ring out across the river. The "g'day" greeting referred to my Australian identity, and "ponce" was a reference to a gay man. I looked up and saw Lou, a guide I liked very much but one who took pains to promote a strong masculine image.

There is no doubt that pink clothing or equipment worn by men pushed some of my friends' homophobic buttons. I had been an outdoor skills instructor in Australia for years without hearing comments about the colors I wore. I wondered if homophobia was bigger in the United States than in Australia, or whether it merely had a different emphasis. Whatever the case, these incidents illustrate men's conformity to norms learned through male socialization.

While I understand the reasons for the comments about my attire, I've always thought the whole male-conformity thing was rather silly. I mean, using the same logic, men would be prohibited from looking at sunsets or pink flowers because that would mean they were gay. And since nature contains every color known to man, could that mean God is gay? It's sad that a belief system would prevent a man from wearing a color he likes! I came to love my pink helmet and the opportunities it gave me to have some juicy discussions with complete strangers—and a chance to tease my American friends. Perhaps in the process, my pink helmet may even have helped a few men take some tentative steps toward gay equity and acceptance.

Sadly, however, I must report that my pink helmet is no more. When I recently returned to the United States after three years in Australia, I found the helmet had been stored too close to the heat of the garage roof and had split down the middle. I called all the rafting shops trying to get another, but could not find any in pink. So I have been borrowing helmets until I find another pink one. I know it's out there, somewhere.

On Being a Gay Father
By Allan Arnaboldi
Summer 2001

I can still recall many of the details of my daughter Dana's Lamaze delivery 31 years ago. I know many men have had similar experiences, but my path as a father diverged from theirs because I am a gay dad.

At that time, in the early 1970s, gay men and lesbians were just beginning to be more visible, but the lack of visible models of nonstereotyped gay people had led me to deny my sexuality. Growing up, I had helped to parent two much younger siblings, loved children, and as an audiologist (later an elementary school teacher) had chosen a career that put me in contact with kids a lot.

When I met a nonstereotypical woman who accepted me as a non-traditional male, it felt comfortable to marry and have a child. I loved being a father and sharing the responsibilities of parenting.

While I always knew I was different from most boys and men, I was successful at sublimating my need for emotional and sexual intimacy with a man in order to fit into society and continue my fulfilling father role. But as Dana became more independent, I started to tune into my needs. I joined my first men's group to find connections with other males, something I had never experienced growing up. I met my first two openly gay friends there and began to explore my repressed emotional side. While my wife and I had mutual love and respect, sadly, each of us felt a lack of deep intimacy in the relationship. When Dana was seven we decided to divorce, and she lived with each of us halftime during the week.

I then began my journey of self-discovery to find out what it means to be gay—and to be a gay dad. The negative images and stereotypes presented by society didn't fit with my self-perception, and there were no models for gay fathers. I decided to start a gay fathers' group because I didn't feel I fit into the "straight fathers" world anymore, nor the world of single gay men. I helped to create a diverse group that ran for about four years. I received much support and encouragement there and felt good about wanting to be an involved gay dad. I was also fortunate enough to have an ex-spouse who respected me as a father and as a gay man.

When Dana was twelve, I came out to her. Besides my ex-wife, I had already come out to my siblings, close friends, and a few coworkers, but not to my parents, so I was still closeted in many ways. I was not afraid of legal repercussions of my disclosure, but I did have concerns for my job, housing, and Dana's and my personal safety. Her mother and I worried about the reactions of her friends and their families once they knew. Although Dana seemed to take the news in stride, it was not an easy topic to discuss. While I had a community of supportive friends and was even able to be "out" in my work environment (an elementary school!), my daughter did not come out about me to anyone until her senior year in high school.

I regret the isolation Dana felt and some of my own self-imposed limitations. While I had a short-term relationship soon after I came out to her, he was not a dad and did not understand my needs as a father. For example, he didn't grasp my need to have regular contact with Dana and to experience her development and the major changes in her life. The complexities of living in two households and of trying to protect Dana's family image while developing my own positive, gay identity led to the decision, when she was 15, for Dana to live full-time with her mother and stepfather. That ranks as the most painful decision of my life; to this day I have incredible anger at the society that did not—and in many ways still does not—recognize our value as a family.

After that change, I did have a long-term, gay relationship. Eventually Dana and I felt comfortable and safe enough to be part of the "Love Makes a Family" exhibit, a collection of photographs and accompanying text about gay and lesbian families that continues to tour the US.

It allowed us to be the model that we never had. Along the way I have been able to openly support and speak out on behalf of the gay-parent families whose children I taught, and to develop and teach an inclusive families curriculum for first graders.

But it's not enough! Perhaps that's what has led me to work at the Men's Resource Center, where I hope to support all fathers (and those who serve in that role), particularly those who have or will come out as gay dads to their children, families, and larger communities. There are many gay men who have so much to offer to today's children. I hope organizations like the MRC can lead the way in providing ways for them to experience the joys and challenges of being nurturing, involved fathers.

Discovering Fatherhood as a Gay Stepdad
By Doug Arey
Winter 2006

When I was in my twenties and dealing with my identity as a gay man for the first time in a serious way, one of the issues staring me in the face was the belief that being gay meant I would have to forgo the chance of ever becoming someone's dad. I felt a lot of grief about this, and realized that many ideas I had about being a man had a Velcro-like attachment to the image of fatherhood. Letting go of that way of being a man seemed necessary at the time for me to form an acceptable new image for myself as a man who was gay.

Then, nine years ago, much to my surprise and delight, I met and fell in love with a man who had two beautiful teenage daughters from a marriage prior to his coming out. Through my work as a psychotherapist I have become acquainted with many gay men over the years who, like me, became involved with men who have children, and found themselves in stepparenting roles with their partner's kids. I know from talking with them, and now from my own experience, how challenging, fulfilling, and oftentimes confusing this can be. The first challenge I had to face was my ambivalence about revisiting what had seemed like a dead issue in the development of my sense of self.

Though my partner's children did not live with him, he was very much involved in their lives, and therefore they were a big part of our lives together. It felt strange to me to have the issue of fatherhood rise up again seemingly out of the ashes, suggesting that I undo all of my earlier grief work. It felt even stranger when I finally realized how different stepparenting was from being a parent, and had to let go of the fatherhood fantasies all over again.

What helped me most was accepting that I would not play a starring role in my stepdaughters' lives, and that I needed to focus instead on a hopeful nomination in the "best supporting actor" category. So much of good stepparenting, I've come to appreciate, is supporting our partners to be the best parents they can be. Resisting the temptation to step in and be the authority—even when you think you know the right thing to say and do—was (and still is at times!) very hard. Agreeing instead to follow and not lead in matters involving the kids is humbling, but is the right thing to do, and for this stepdad it has led to lots of wonderful opportunities I never imagined possible. Though it's very different from being their parent, my stepdad role allows me to be involved in the lives of these two remarkable young women and to be regarded as a trusted, valued, respected older person and confidant in their lives. Most days I feel that I got the better deal.

Trusting my partner and being willing to bow to his experience, I've found, is key. He had lots of history with his girls before I came into their family that informed his perspective and parental decision-making. Though I've seen him do many things differently than I would have, I almost always in retrospect have come to appreciate the wisdom I saw in his approach with his girls. He knows them in ways I never have and never will. Ultimately it has helped me deepen the respect, appreciation, and love I have for him to witness his gentle guidance, profound patience, tolerance, and sweet affection and consideration with them, even when I've had to observe it from across the room instead of next to them on the sofa. Knowing that I helped make it possible through my support of him to continue having those experiences with his daughters has been a great source of pride and accomplishment for me.

I think it's tough for anyone who signs on as a stepparent for a host of reasons, only a few of which are unique to the gay stepdad. I was lucky not to have been the first man my stepdaughters were introduced to as the lover and partner to their dad. For guys who are the first man their partner's kids meet to give a real face to their dad's homosexuality, I wish you lots of patience, understanding, and personal strength, because you'll need it to face the challenges ahead of you. For those of you who must interface with bigoted school officials, medical professionals, extended family members, and angry ex-wives in your attempt to help and show care for your stepchildren, my heart goes out to you. There are lots of good books on the topic of stepparenting that are very useful, even if they aren't written with same-gender partners in mind. Healthy stepparenting is a noble endeavor, and one that may need a lot of study and support to accomplish with grace and dignity.

My partner and I helped usher his daughters and my stepdaughters into young adulthood, and now we are joyously facing the next level of challenge.

Nine and a half months ago we were blessed to meet our first grandchild, and we learned this summer that we should prepare to meet another little being early in 2006. I have no words of wisdom yet to offer anyone on effective gay step-grandparenting, as I feel I'm still figuring it out myself day to day. I do know that I welcome this new challenge, and even find the diaper changing and staying up half the night with a cranky infant cutting his first teeth to be charming, in an odd way

To me stepparenting is not just the "next best thing" to parenting; it's a valuable thing on its own. One day Hallmark may get around to setting aside one Sunday a year and declaring it Stepparents Day; but we who are stepdads and feel that we perform our roles well don't need to wait for that particular stamp of legitimacy to validate our unique contributions. We can buy ourselves a tie.

Relationship to Deceased? "Partner."

By Thomas Ziniti
Winter 2003

By the time my partner died on June 14, 2002, I'd gotten used to people misunderstanding our relationship. Early Onset Alzheimer's Disease had aged Russ considerably beyond his years, although to me he always retained the large facial features of an exceptionally good-looking man, and the forehead of a great philosopher.

"Don't tell me!" a woman good-naturedly, but somewhat stridently, offered one day as she approached us in a Wal-Mart parking lot, "Father and son! Right?" Russ developed a lumbering gait in his last years, and I've always walked that way. Anyway, we looked alike; so I guess it was an understandable mistake for a stranger unused to considering a relationship between two men that was anything other than familial or platonic.

After Russ entered a nursing home, and later a hospital, we got the father-and-son question a lot. I always responded the same way. "He's not my father; he's my partner." Then I'd watch my words register on the surprised faces of nurses and aides. My quiet but determined declaration was almost always met with kindness, often warmth.

Once, though, an aide replied, "What kind of business were you in?" I, being for the moment as slow on the uptake as was she, stared blankly back, then when her meaning dawned said, "Oh no, not business partners, domestic partners." She was visibly shaken, yet struggled to maintain a casual air, and stammered weakly, "Oh. I know about that. There's some of that where I live." In a measured tone and being careful to smile, I relied, "Yes. There's a lot of *that* around." I suppose I could have offered her something enlightening in place of knee-jerk contempt, but she struck me as decidedly unreceptive and, besides, at the time I had more important things on my mind.

Hours after Russ died, I rushed to a funeral home with a close friend and my minister. I explained Russ's and my relationship to the funeral director (who, as it turned out, had once been Russ's student) and told him that I would be making all of the final decisions concerning Russ's remains and the service. His manner was personable and he appeared to take everything I told him in his stride.

But when it came time to talk about the obituary, he first asked me if I wanted to be mentioned at all, then when I said yes asked (although it struck me more like a suggestion) did I want to be mentioned as Russ's "friend"? Perhaps I should have stopped here to consider that, even though I was clear with this man about what Russ and I had been to each other, he might still have been unsure as to whether or not I wanted to go public. Instead I replied emphatically that no, I didn't want to be mentioned as Russ's friend; I wanted to be mentioned as Russ's partner of twenty-eight years.

A spouse in my situation would not be brought to the question that now distracts me from my grief: Who was that guy, anyway? Was he my friend, my boyfriend, my partner, my companion, my lover? What was he to me?

I like to refer to myself, facetiously, as a "post-Stonewall pansy" because I came out in the very early seventies, a time before commitment ceremonies and same-sex marriages, when gay couples lived together bravely as outlaws. In those days, those of us in relationships referred to our better halves as our *lovers*. I reminded a friend of that recently. He said, "True, but that makes it sound like the relationship is all about sex." I had to agree, but later wondered why when I realized that the literal meaning of the word *lover* is, simply, someone in love.

Therefore, I think it a great misfortune that Standard English usage propels the collective imagination directly into the bedrooms of gays, causing many heterosexuals to cringe a lot, and even some homosexuals to cringe a little. To me, *lover* is not only the most comprehensive term, but also the loftiest—although I admit it will probably never do for legally sanctioned relationships, such as civil unions.

I can just hear the official saying, "I now pronounce you lover and lover!" (If nothing else I suppose such a pronouncement would give new meaning to the expression "Until death do you part.") A week or two later a certified copy of a License to Love would arrive in the mail.

The first time I remember hearing the term *partner,* as it related to same-sex couples, was in the early nineties. Initially, at least, the word struck me not only as foreign but too palatable. It seemed to me at the time as though gays were saying that heterosexuals might accept us if we're partners, but never lovers.

As for friends, sure, Russ and I were friends—best friends. But for me to claim friendship as the be-all and end-all of our relationship would be, finally, to deny us and betray him. All of the other terms I could conjure to describe what we had together ("companion," etc.) strike me as equally euphemistic, and fall sadly short of the mark.

A week or so after the funeral, I opened a valise given to me by the funeral director, which contained a guest book, two laminated copies of the obituary, some thank-you cards, and six certified copies of the death certificate (the information for which I had provided to the funeral director, who in turn provided it to the town clerk). The death certificate contains information about Russ, including his last address, the cause of his death, his parents' names, and even (because the law requires it) the name of a woman to whom he had been married for two years some thirty-two years ago. The document further indicates that she was his wife.

I am mentioned too. At the bottom, the certificate reads, "Information provided by: Thomas Ziniti. Relationship to deceased: Friend."

With thanks to my friends inside and outside of the gay and lesbian community, who held me up with love during the most difficult time of my life, I am pleased to say that after the writing of this article and before its publication, I went to the town clerk and requested a change. The death certificate now reads, "Information provided by: Thomas Ziniti. Relationship to deceased: Partner."

Jan

By Eric Kolvig
Summer 1993

You were the best
teacher of all.

Empty-handed I entered this life.
Empty-handed I'll leave.
Between those two events
somehow these hands
got tangled in grasping.

Before I'd let them
cling to you,
I'd cut them away
with a blunt rusty knife
if nothing better came to hand –
first the right with the left,
then the left with my teeth.

Freedom moves closer
thanks to you,
its breath on my cheek
this clean fall day.

With silent lips
I press earth's seal
on your mouth and breasts,
run these empty hands
on the smooth, firm
beauty of your man's body,
bow three times in gratitude,

And pass along the way.

WHAT IS HEALTHY MASCULINITY?

When a "healthy masculinity summit" was held in Washington, DC, in October, 2012, part of an ambitious two-year project to "spread the message of nonviolent, emotionally healthy masculinity," *Voice Male* turned to several members of its national advisory board, and other colleagues and allies, to address in short essays their thoughts about the challenges inherent in trying to define the term "healthy masculinity."

Any Gender is a Drag

By Michael Kaufman

What is healthy masculinity? There's no such thing! After all, *masculinities* are social constructs, descriptions of the power relations between women and men and among men. Especially in their hegemonic versions, they are a set of stereotyped assumptions about what it means to be a man. They are systems of ideas—ideologies. But the thing is, masculinity doesn't exist, at least not as we think it exists, as a fixed or timeless reality or as a synonym (healthy or harmful) with being a male.

Years ago I described masculinity as a collective hallucination, as if we'd all taken the same drug and were imagining this thing actually existed in front of our eyes.

Couldn't, though, we speak of healthy versions of these assumptions and ideas?

True, there are healthier and less healthy brands of masculinity.

However, by prescribing and proscribing certain behaviors, having definitions of gender (even healthy ones) limit us as human beings to a code that supposedly comes with our biological sex.

Ultimately, I think what is important is to encourage healthy *men*, healthy in the physical and emotional sense. That has a wide range of meanings (which I hope other, more clever, contributors are enumerating!) but perhaps which boil down to men who were raised to be nurturers, that is nurture others, nurture the planet, and nurture themselves.

I look forward to the day when the gender terms "masculinity" and "femininity" in either the singular or plural, healthy or harmful, are seen as quaint old terms. I'll always be a fan of rocker Patti Smith who said, "Any gender is a drag."

VOICE MALE

Loving, Passionate, and Grounded
By Juan Carlos Areán

I'll be totally frank. I understand the label of "healthy" when we talk about masculinity, relationships, communities. In fact, it's in the name of the very network I lead. However, I don't like to stop there. When I die, I'd hate to be remembered only as a "healthy" man in a "healthy" relationship or as a "responsible" father. I want my family (and others) to think of me as a loving, passionate, grounded, joyful man and father (who also happens to be healthy and responsible).

So, for me, a loving, passionate, grounded, joyful man is someone who lives his life leading with love and not fear; who values integrity and leads by example; who puts the welfare of his family at the top of his priorities; who stands by his word and his vows; who rejoices in his intimate partner's and children's dreams and works hard at helping them achieve them; who understands an intimate relationship as a partnership, not with identical responsibilities but with complementary strengths; someone who takes care of his own physical, emotional, and spiritual health; who doesn't depend on his partner for all his emotional needs; who is real with other men (and women) and is not afraid of showing his feelings and vulnerability, when appropriate; someone who loves other men (and women and children) so much that he is willing to help them stop hurting themselves and others.

This is the kind of man I aspire to be.

Democratic Manhood
By Michael Kimmel

In the twenty-first century I believe we need a different sort of manhood, a "democratic manhood." The manhood of the future cannot be based on obsessive self-control, defensive exclusion, or frightened escape. We need a new definition of masculinity in this new century: a definition that is more about the character of men's hearts and the depths of their souls than about the size of their biceps, wallets, or penises; a definition that is capable of embracing differences among men and enabling other men to feel secure and confident rather than marginalized and excluded; a definition that is capable of friendships based on more than common activities (what among toddlers is called "parallel play") or even common consumer aesthetics; a definition that centers on standing up for justice and equality instead of running away from commitment and engagement.

We need men who truly embody traditional masculine virtues, such as strength, a sense of purpose, a commitment to act ethically regardless of the costs, controlled aggression, self-reliance, dependability, reliability, responsibility—men for whom these are not simply fashion accessories but come from a deeply interior place. But now these will be configured in new and responsive ways. We need men who are secure enough in their convictions to recognize a mistake, courageous enough to be compassionate, fiercely egalitarian, powerful enough to empower others, strong enough to acknowledge that real strength comes from holding others up rather than pushing them down and that real freedom is not to be found in the loneliness of the log cabin but in the daily compromises of life in a community.

Men Are Human First
By Robert Jensen

The list of traits we claim to associate with being a man—the things we would feel comfortable telling a child to strive for—are in fact not distinctive characteristics of men but traits of human beings we value, what we want all people to be. The list of understandings of masculinity that men routinely impose on one another is quite different. Here, being a man means not being a woman or gay, seeing relationships as fundamentally a contest for control, and viewing sex as the acquisition of pleasure from a woman. Of course that's not all men are, but it sums up the dominant, and very toxic, conception of masculinity with which most men are raised in the contemporary United States. It's not an assertion about all men or all possible ideas about masculinity, but a description of a pattern.

If the positive definitions of masculinity are not really about being a man but simply about being a person, and if the definitions of masculinity within which men routinely operate are negative, why are we holding onto the concept so tightly? Why are we so committed to the notion that there are intellectual, emotional, and moral differences that are inherent, that come as a result of biological sex differences?

It's obvious that there are differences in the male and female human body, most obviously in reproductive organs and hormones. But how we should make sense of those differences outside reproduction is not clear. And if we are to make sense of it in a fashion that is consistent with justice—that is, in a feminist context—then we would benefit from a critical evaluation of the categories themselves, no matter how uncomfortable that may be.

VOICE MALE

Escaping the Man Box
By Ted Bunch

Men must challenge our views and beliefs about one another. A major obstacle will be to confront our traditional male socialization and how it limits us and boxes us in. We must get out of the socially defined roles that sexism, patriarchy, and male privilege provide for us. In addition, we must end our collusion with the violence, objectification, and demeaning thoughts and behaviors that we as men engage in toward women. This will require that we address our fears and anxiety about stepping out of our—often harmfully—defined roles and challenge the traditional images of manhood. The fear of being perceived as "soft" or "weak" is an obstacle for many men that stops them from challenging sexist attitudes and behaviors, the hallmarks of male dominance. Social change requires courage, integrity, accountability to women, and consistency through action. What is needed from men is to act in appropriate and respectful ways toward women. That will be the day when men, along with our sisters, have redefined manhood so that violence is not a part of being a man. As we promote and work to increase healthy and respectful manhood, we also prevent and work to decrease violence and discrimination against women and girls.

Healthy Males, Healthy Females
By E. Ethelbert Miller

The term "healthy masculinity" seems somewhat problematic to me. Is there a bar or level of measurement we should all attempt to reach? Should masculinity even be linked to topics or issues of health? Are we looking at our actions, thoughts, or simple conditioning? Is this a term that's now a part of our vocabulary because of how men wrestle with their identity and the handling of power in this society? Social change often demands a realignment of power relationships between groups. As women become more empowered, does it threaten male privilege? Do men respond by showing "unhealthy" manners and behavior? Do they become violent toward women and other men? If we turn our attention to young males during a time of transformation in our society, how do we raise them to have a "new" idea of what masculinity might mean? Can a society have a healthy male without a healthy female? This is not a Zen koan but instead a serious way of "interpreting" healthy masculinity. Do we need an "other" to determine how we behave and think? The term is perhaps linked to what we want best for our society. It could be connected to the pursuit of the common good and citizenship with purpose; how we live and love will determine our health as well as our vision.

What is Healthy Masculinity?

Irreconcilable Concepts
By Jackson Katz

"Healthy masculinity" incorporates two distinct but nonetheless intertwined concepts: "health," which suggests a biological perspective, and "masculinity," which is a social construct.

This interplay between the biological and the societal represents one of the great dialectics of our time, and raises a fundamental question: What does it mean to be a "healthy" man, when the very idea of what it means to be a man is so contingent on the maintenance of an economic and social order in which men are arranged hierarchically in relation to one another, and as a group are in a position of dominance over women?

If we can speak of healthy masculinity, can we speak about "healthy whiteness" or "healthy heterosexuality?"

There's another catch. The very act of deconstructing the term "healthy masculinity" in a brief essay—rather than exploring some of the physical, emotional, or relational aspects of being a man—repeats the familiar pattern of a man staying in the more "masculine" intellectual realm and neglecting the more "feminine" realms of emotions and relationship.

We do need to explore the meanings that underlie our use of terms like "healthy masculinity" if we want to help build better and more life-sustaining institutions. But we're also embodied animals who experience pleasure, pain, and love, and are around for a preciously brief time. We might be able to envision democratic futures in which there is such thing as "healthy masculinity," but in the meantime we still have to hug our children, laugh and cry, and share our lives with others.

Men's Existential Vulnerability
By Charles Knight

Men's health suffers from anxiety associated with deeply felt needs to control the world. Boys, much more than girls, are taught to seek power over things and relationships. Many men sense that control is a male privilege and feel that control should be within their reach.

In reality most men have little effective control over the world or their relationships. Other men control many aspects of their lives, and as a result there is a persistent orientation toward anxious competition and too often doubts about self-worth.

Beneath this social level there is the existential vulnerability of living creatures, which no one, even the most powerful alpha males, can escape. Those who deny vulnerability often seek to dominate others and the natural world in order to escape the anxiety.

The best we can do as humans is to increase our odds of health and happiness; we do not control outcomes. Men's understanding of strength must be repositioned to mean living well with the acceptance of vulnerability. Men who learn to accept vulnerability and are relieved of the desperate need to control will be much less likely to resort to violence in their relationships with others. And they will have happier lives.

A Thousand Points of Light or One Definition?
By Patrick McGann

A year ago when I typed into a Google search bar "defining healthy masculinity," one of the first links to appear was "Choosing Healthy Masculinity and What That Means" on the website of the organization where I work, Men Can Stop Rape. I thought, "Oh, good. Maybe we've already defined it." Joe Samalin, my former colleague who wrote the piece in 2009, characterizes healthy masculinity as "a group of high school boys volunteering at a local domestic violence shelter … or, straight and cisgendered college men partnering as allies with LGBTQ student organizations … and, the enlisted men and officers in the Air Force who come to [our organization] for training on how to create safer workplaces." But when it comes to defining it, he claims "there is no single definition or ideal of healthy masculinity—there are as many definitions as there are men."

Here's a definition with the caveat that it's very much a work in progress. Healthy masculinity:

• involves the ability to recognize unhealthy aspects of masculinity—those features that are harmful to the self and others

• leads to the replacement of harmful, risky, and violent masculine attitudes and behaviors with empathetic behaviors and attitudes that benefit men's mental, emotional, and physical well being and increase their ability to role-model nonviolence

• is based on supporting gender equity and other forms of equality

• includes social and emotional skills used to positively challenge in yourself—and in others—unhealthy masculine attitudes and behaviors that harm the self and others

I've tried to combine two related sides of the healthy masculinity coin: those of us who use healthy masculinity as a means of engaging men in preventing gender-based violence, and those who use it to advance men's emotional and physical health. A definition like this could be culturally manifested in multiple ways. (Healthy masculinity in India, for example, might look different than in Australia, but the general principles would be the same.) So, in this sense, a definition of healthy masculinity might result in healthy *masculinities*. I am beginning to think that maybe a single definition and a thousand points of light can coexist peacefully.

The Courage to Grow
By Tom Gardner

"What are you afraid of?" That was a question I wanted to put to a young friend whom most would define as courageous—a man's man. He never flinched from tough, physical sports like ice hockey, or dangerous assignments connected with his work abroad. But he seemed to be running from something more challenging: a committed relationship.

Mind you, relationships are not for the spineless. They take a lot of work, and, most threatening of all, they require looking inward. They may require even reconsidering everything you thought you knew about being a male in this world. Why are men not well prepared for this challenge? Because traditional notions of courage that society associates with masculinity are not the kind we need in relationships. The flip side of tough is obstinate, and that makes it difficult to hear another person's needs or pains. The tough-minded also have trouble hearing or voicing their own needs and pains. We are told that denial and stoicism are so much more functional when faced with threats and challenges. Vulnerability only creates an opening for defeat. Press on. Stuff it. We fear emotion because it may show weakness.

These standard notions of masculinity do not serve us well in the most important arena of our lives: relationships with others, especially close, intimate relationships with significant others.

One thing I have learned about relationships is that one must dig deep for the courage to grow as a person, to admit you don't have the answers. You must open yourself to a vulnerability that says to your partner, "I want to grow with you." Healthy masculinity rejects the superficial social construction of physical courage (though, at times, it may be necessary to draw on it) and replaces or supplements it with a deeper, riskier, but much more rewarding form of courage: the courage to examine oneself and grow. Committing to a healthy, loving relationship is a path to healthy masculinity and, more important, healthy humanity.

Humanity Beyond Boxes
By Paul Kivel

Describe a healthy masculinity. Sounds easy at first glance. But the word *masculinity* immediately calls up feelings and thoughts—from cultural meanings and practices the word has accumulated—almost none of which seem healthy either to the bearer or those around them. A certified masculinity and its benefits were the devastating "rewards" that male-socialized people were given for colluding with ruling elites and carrying out their violence. My colleagues and I have long invited men to step out of the "act like a man" box that glorifies certain attributes and calls them "true" or "successful" masculinity. Do we really want to create another box that claims to describe a healthy one?

There are many masculinities, femininities, and transsexual, transgender, and gender queer identities that people claim. None are easily described. All vary widely based on class, race, culture, sexual orientation, and a variety of other factors. Some people, ignoring the hierarchies of power connected to particular masculinities, want to default to a nongender-specific concept of "humanness." But does everyone in the world share certain qualities? Would it be "healthy" if they did? Would it be appropriate to their circumstances and their other identities? I'm inherently distrustful of any attempt to create new social expectations for people to aspire to or new boxes for people to put themselves into. For me the relevant questions are:

- What gender identity do you feel, experience, and live?

- What attitudes, circumstances, and practices are healing, healthy, and sustainable for you and your family, friends, communities, and the natural environment you are immersed within?

- What can you do to subvert the gender identity and other hierarchies that so many people are forced to live inside of?

Healthy Masculinity Is Oxymoronic
By Allan Johnson

The idea of a "healthy masculinity" is oxymoronic, because what patriarchy takes from both women and men is the fullness of our humanity, which is the only valid standard against which to measure the health of a human being. I can think of no positive human capability that is best realized by being culturally assigned to one gender or another, nor can I imagine a truly healthy way of life that does not include the work of understanding and embodying what it means to live as a full human being.

To ask what constitutes a healthy masculinity affirms the patriarchal principle that gender is the indispensable core of human identity and that men and women are distinct kinds of human beings, each with their own standard of well being. It is a separation that forms the basis for the elevation and dominance of men over women and the Earth.

Trying to identify a "healthy" masculinity is a distraction because it encourages us to focus on issues of personality rather than the patriarchal system's destructive patterns of privilege and oppression. In this way, we are kept from the real challenge before us, which is to confront the patriarchal worldview that splits humanity into masculine and feminine and assigns the former an obsession with control that threatens both the well being of women and men and the Earth itself.

Finding the right answers begins with asking the right questions, and what constitutes a healthy masculinity is not one of them.

Healthy Masculinity is a Collective Journey
By Steven Botkin

Healthy masculinity is remembering and reclaiming a caring, loving, and sensitive self from the dominant legacies of patriarchy. Even as the boy grows to be a man, learning each gesture of domination or control, he is also searching for ways to express his inherent, healthy desire for connection and natural capacity for compassion.

Healthy masculinity is men respecting, and being respected for, the full range of our feelings, no longer denying our pain, our fear, our anger, or our joy. It is men from different backgrounds, lifestyles, and communities learning to feel safe with, listen to, and care for one another. It is men creating a culture where we can practice understanding rather than winning, communication rather than fighting, sharing rather than defending. We inhabit our homes and families, remembering the delights of nurturing relationships, seeking out close, loving companionship with other men and women.

Healthy masculinity means learning how to recognize, take responsibility for, and change our individual and collective patterns of hurtful behavior. Men find ways to take actions that challenge cultural and institutional systems of domination and control, and give voice to our caring and our commitment. Homophobia, violence against women, and war—the ultimate weapons of gender conformity—disappear, no longer needed to prove and protect "manhood."

Healthy masculinity is a collective journey of men and women joining together to find the courage to stand and face the dominant culture, saying with determination and pride: *We refuse to be rigidly boxed into masculinity by seductive promises of power or intimidating threats of violence.* Men identify as allies with women, learning how to work collaboratively and developing shared power and leadership. Together, we are creating a new culture where being a healthy man is an open-ended, ever-expanding expression of possibilities.

Healthy masculinity means hope for the world in places where we have long felt only hopelessness.

A FAREWELL TO ARMS: MANHOOD AFTER NEWTOWN

Photo: Samart Booyang

Ernest Hemingway, after whose acclaimed novel *A Farewell to Arms* this section is named, has long been touted as a "man's man." Today, fewer and fewer people accept that description as the pinnacle of manhood. On the pages that follow, a chorus responds with a shared message: move manhood and masculinity from the periphery to the center of the national conversation about gun violence.

Fatal Distraction: Manhood, Guns, and Violence
By Allan Johnson
Winter 2013

As I write this, it's been only a few weeks since the mass murder of children and staff in Newtown, Connecticut, less than 50 miles from my home. I have grandchildren of the same age as the children who were killed and find it especially difficult to listen to the latest national conversation about gun violence, because, like all the others, it's being conducted in a way that guarantees that such violence will continue.

The problem is not what we talk about—guns and the media in particular—even though both are important. The real problem is what we don't talk about, for we are once again allowing ourselves to be distracted from the underlying cause of this epidemic of violence, and with fatal consequences.

In the aftermath of the mass murder in Aurora, Colorado, for example, I watched the PBS *Newshour* display photographs of the four most recent shooters as the moderator posed to a team of experts the question of what the perpetrators all had in common. They looked at the photos and shook their heads. "Nothing," they said, going on to explain that there were no significant overlaps in the men's psychological profiles. All men, with nothing in common.

I watched again after the massacre in Newtown as a PBS moderator expressed her exasperation at the steady stream of killings that seem to defy explanation, adding to her earnest question, *Why is this happening?* What seemed to her almost an afterthought—that all of the shooters are young men—might this hold a clue? The expert replied as if he hadn't heard, and she did not bring it up again.

I pick on PBS only because they are so enlightened and serious compared with all the rest, and if they can't see what's right in front of them, then I don't know who among the media can.

But, of course, the thing is, they do. I used to think they actually didn't see on account of ignorance—fish not noticing the water because it's everywhere. I don't believe that anymore. They have eyes that see and they're not stupid. We know this because if you point out to them that all the shooters are male, they don't say, "They *are?*" They know what they're looking at, and, even more, some feel moved to ask about it. So why, then, do they—and just about everyone else of consequence, it seems—act as if they don't, as if the question isn't worth the asking, not to mention a serious reply?

Many are in a state of denial, or the willful ignorance that Martin Luther King saw as the greatest threat. But denial and willful ignorance are used for self-protection, which raises the question of what these educated, sensitive shapers of public policy and opinion are so afraid of.

The most immediate reason not to ask about the connection between men and violence is, quite simply, that men won't like it if you do. We are a nation tiptoeing around men's anger, men's ridicule, men's potential to withhold resources (such as funding for battered women's shelters and sexual assault programs), men's potential for retaliation, violent and otherwise, men's defensiveness, and the possibility that men might feel upset or attacked or called out or put upon or made to feel vulnerable or even just sad. In other words, anything that might make them feel uncomfortable *as men*.

I have seen this again and again over the years that I've worked on the issue of men's violence. Whether testifying before a governor's commission or serving on the board of a statewide coalition against domestic violence or consulting with a commissioner of public health, when I point out that since men are the perpetrators of most violence, they must be included in naming the problem—as in *men's* violence against women—the response has been the same: *We can't do that. Men will get upset. They'll think you're talking about them.*

Even when children are gunned down at school—shot multiple times at close range so as to be rendered unrecognizable to their own parents—people in positions of influence and power show themselves all too willing to look into the camera and act as if they cannot see and do not know.

As a result, when men engage in mass murder, the national focus is on the murder but not the men, beginning with a nationwide outpouring of broken hearts and horror and disbelief that this is happening yet again. All of this is undoubtedly heartfelt and sincere, but it gives way all too quickly to this country's endless debate about controlling guns. Yes, we must talk about guns, because they do kill people in spite of what their defenders say. Killing someone (including yourself) with a gun is far easier and quicker (harder to change your mind) and more certain and therefore more likely than is killing someone with a baseball bat or a knife. The rest of the industrialized world shows clearly how limiting access to guns lowers rates of murder and suicide. So, yes, we must talk about guns. And we must also talk about violence in the culture, from movies to video games. Even the

National Rifle Association wants to talk about that.

But those debates are endless precisely because they are such effective distractions from what just about everyone is working so hard to ignore, which is the obvious connection between men and guns and violence. It is much easier to argue the fine points of the First and Second Amendments than to take seriously the question of what is going on with men. Such distractions enable us to avoid talking about the underlying reality that is driving it all, which, strangely enough, isn't strictly about guns or even violence. Or even, in a way, just about men.

Guns and violence are not ends in themselves. People are not attached to guns *because* of guns. Nor is violence glorified for itself. Guns and violence are *used* for something, a means to an end, and it is from this that they acquire their meaning and value in the culture. It is that end that we must understand.

Guns and violence are instruments of *control*, whether used by states or individuals. They otherwise have no intrinsic value of their own. Their value comes from the simple fact that violence *works* as a means to intimidate, dominate, and control. It works for governments and hunters and police and batterers and parents and schoolyard bullies and corporations and, by extension, anyone who wants to feel larger and more powerful and in control than they otherwise would. The gun has long been valued in this culture as the ultimate tool in the enforcement of control and domination, trumping all else in the assertion of personal control over others. Can anyone forget the scene in *Indiana Jones* when "our hero" is confronted with the huge man wielding an equally enormous sword, and the white man unholsters his gun and the crowd roars its approval as he calmly shoots the other man down? The gun is the great equalizer with the potential to elevate even the most weak, shy, or timid above anyone who lacks equivalent firepower. What this makes clear is that violence in this country is not an aberration or a simple product of mental illness. It is an integral part of the American story and the American way of life.

The key to understanding gun violence and the fact that all these shooters are men is this: An obsession with control forms the core of our cultural definition of what it means to be a real man. A real man is one who can demonstrate convincingly an ability always to be in control. Because violence is the ultimate and most extreme instrument of control, then the capacity for violence—whether or not individual men may actually make use of it—is also central to the cultural definition of manhood.

Every man and boy faces the challenge of signaling either their own capacity for violence or their support if not admiration for that potential in other males, if for no other reason than to solidify their standing as real men (or boys), if not to deter acts of violence and ridicule directed at them. It is a dynamic that begins early—in locker rooms and schoolyards—and extends in one form or another throughout men's entire lives. However men and boys choose to deal with it as individuals, deal with it they must.

No one, no matter how powerful, is immune to this imperative of manhood as defined in this culture. Every presidential candidate must first and foremost demonstrate their qualifications to be the nation's commander in chief, which is to say, their willingness and readiness to make use of and direct the US military's massive capacity for violence in the overriding interest of controlling what happens in other countries. The record is clear, for example, that Lyndon Johnson kept us in the Vietnam War long after he knew it was unwinnable, for the pathetically simple reason that he was afraid of being seen as a president who could not control the outcome of that war. The horrific cost of protecting his manhood and the nation's identification with it was not enough to keep him from it. The choices he made have been repeated by every president since, with the electorate's enthusiastic support, right down to the present day where drone strikes routinely take the lives of innocent women, children, and men who happen to be in the wrong place at the wrong time, including weddings, family gatherings, and schools.

Men's acceptance of the cultural association of manhood with control makes them complicit in its consequences, including the use of violence. Acceptance need not be conscious or intentional. Individual men need not be violent themselves. Mere silence—the voice of complicity—is enough to accomplish the effect and to connect them to the violence that other men do. When a young man who is feeling wronged or is insecure in his manhood straps on body armor and takes up a gun, he is pursuing by extreme means a manhood ideal of control and domination that has wide and deep support in this society, including among men who would never dream of doing such a thing themselves. That our culture is saturated with images of violence—from television and video games to the football field—is not the work of a lunatic fringe of violent men. Nor is the epidemic of actual violence. All of it flows from an obsession with control that shapes every man's standing as a real man in this society.

It would be a mistake to end the analysis here, as if the problem of violence was simply a matter of men and manhood. The Newtown murderer, after all, used weapons belonging to his mother, which she had taught him how to use. She would not be the first woman attracted to guns because they made her feel powerful and in control and safe. It might seem that this would nullify the argument about manhood, control, and violence. But, in fact, the involvement of women merely extends the argument to a larger level. The argument, after all, is not that men's violence is caused by something inherently wrong with men, but that such behavior is shaped and promoted by a social environment that includes women.

A patriarchal society—which is what we've got—is, among other things, male-identified, which means that men and manhood are culturally identified as the standard for human beings in general. Consider, for example, the routine use of "guys" to refer to both men and women, even though the word clearly and unambiguously points to men. (If you doubt this, ask a crowd of people to raise their hand if they're a guy and see how many women you get.) Or that for years, medical research on heart disease focused only on men, based on the (false) assumption that the male body could serve as the universal standard for the human being.

In a male-identified world, what works for men, what is valued by men, is generally assumed to work for and be valued by human beings in general. So if the obsession with control associated with true manhood includes defining power and safety in terms of domination and control and, therefore, the capacity for violence that comes with owning a gun, then this is seen as not merely manly but as universally human. Cultural ideas that would preclude women being both feminine and interested in guns have been a device for excluding and marginalizing women and keeping them dependent on men for protection (from other men). As such limitations have been broken down by the women's movement, it is inevitable that many women will adopt male-identified ideals about power and control as their own.

But the analysis of violence rooted in an obsession with control must go further still, beyond issues of gender, because the obsession shapes every social institution, from economics and politics to education, religion, and health care. Our entire history has been inseparable from a continuing story of control and domination directed at the Earth and its nonhuman species, at Native Americans, at enslaved Africans and other people of color, at those who resist the building of the American empire and its exercise of global power, at workers, at immigrants. As Richard Slotkin argues in his brilliant history of the making of American mythology, violence has played a central role in that history. Although the heroes of that mythology have always been men, the larger idea of America shaped by it—of American exceptionalism and superiority, and liberty as the right to dominate and act on others without restraint—is about more than manhood. It has become the heart of who we think we are as a society and a people.

Which may be why we are so ambivalent about guns and violence, and why we would rather focus on a few crazy individuals than on what this is really about, which is ourselves and an entire worldview that informs our lives, with cultural ideals about manhood at the center. The national silence about manhood and violence is about much more than either. It is about protecting a way of life even if it means failing to protect our children.

Any society organized in this way is a frightening place to be—people afraid to go to the movies unless they're packing heat, parents afraid to send their kids to school. And the solution offered by that same society is, of course, still more control. If someone has a gun, get your own. Arm the teachers. Arm yourself. Arm your kids.

But every crisis is also an opportunity. Here we are once again. The prohibition against talking about violence and manhood in the same breath puts us in a state of paralysis, which is where we find ourselves today. And it is where we will find ourselves when this happens again, as it's all but certain to do if it hasn't already.

Unless we do something to break the silence. History is full of examples of the power of ordinary citizens speaking out—on slavery and race; on the rights of working people, gays, immigrants, Native Americans, and women; on the exploitation and abuse of children; on the degradation, exploitation, and destruction of the Earth and its species; on capitalism and the power of the wealthy. We have done it before and we can do it again.

Newtown is Not New
By E. Ethelbert Miller
Winter 2013

In a free society, some are guilty; all are responsible.

—Abraham Joshua Heschel

Newtown is not new. What is old is our failure to change the American narrative. Is anyone describing the incident in Connecticut as one of domestic terrorism? How many parents are now afraid to send their children to school? How many of us will pay more attention to the quiet kid who has few friends?

We keep asking ourselves... why? How could so many young children be murdered by a lone gunman?

Why did Adam Lanza go on a rampage? Before we begin with the tragedy at the Sandy Hook Elementary School, we should turn our attention to Lanza's first victim. *Adam Lanza shot and killed his mother.* This is another case of domestic violence. Man against woman. Why did Adam kill her?

Every house is a house of secrets. Our struggle to find a narrative is dependent on finding "clues" and evidence that will help us build a story. If there are no letters, suicide notes, diaries, then we might have to fall back on the guns themselves. Lanza's mother was the owner of the guns her son committed his crimes with. What would these guns say if they could talk?

The hands that held them first belonged to a woman not a man. Many woman love guns, too. How many of us remember Annie Oakley? With a gun was how the West was won. All hands today still remain on the trigger.

VOICE MALE

Why White Men Keep Mum about the White Maleness of Mass Shootings
By Charlotte Childress and Harriet Childress
Summer 2013

The national conversation that followed the Boston Marathon bombing demonstrates again how important it is to continue to write about the effects of white male culture on violence. Despite the Tsarnaev brothers being immersed in US white male culture for 10 years, virtually all discussion about their actions focused on their religion. The suspects were clearly white men of European descent. Nevertheless, the overwhelming response to what happened dismissed their race. Many conservative commentators said essentially the men weren't white; they're Muslim.

When we published a column in the *Washington Post* about white males and mass shootings two weeks *before* the tragedy in Boston, it caused a firestorm of protests from Fox News, Rush Limbaugh, and the *Wall Street Journal*. Most of the tens of thousands of comments that followed, and the response found on 300 websites and on talk radio revealed no logical conversation about solving the violence problem, just comments from what appeared to be white males whose primary goal was to shift accountability away from their group and their leaders.

Threats, bullying, lies, ridicule, insults, and listing of statistics of other groups were common tactics. There were so many nasty rants that a *Washington Post* editor wrote a follow-up article describing them as "vile, racist, and sexist." We were pleased our column helped hierarchical conservatives act out for a wide audience. So consider another way to approach this story.

Imagine if African American men and boys were committing mass shootings month after month, year after year. Articles and interviews would flood the media, and we'd have political debates demanding that African Americans be "held accountable." Then, if an atrocity such as the Newtown shootings took place, and African American male leaders held a news conference to offer solutions, their credibility would be questionable. The public would tell these leaders they need to focus on problems in their own culture and communities.

But when the criminals and leaders are white men, race and gender become the elephant in the room.

Nearly all of the mass shootings in this country in recent years—not just Newtown, but Aurora, Tucson, and Columbine—have been committed by white men and boys. Yet when the National Rifle Association (NRA), led by white men, held a news conference after the Newtown massacre to advise Americans on how to reduce gun violence, its leaders' opinions were widely discussed.

Unlike other groups, white men are not used to being singled out. So we expect that many of them will protest that it is unfair if we talk about them. But our nation must correctly define their contribution to our problem of gun violence if it is to be solved.

When white men try to divert attention from gun control by talking about mental health issues, many people buy into the idea that the United States has a national mental health problem, or flawed systems with which to address those problems, and they think that is what produces mass shootings.

But women and girls with mental health issues are not picking up semi-automatic weapons and shooting schoolchildren. Immigrants with mental health issues are not committing mass shootings in malls and movie theaters. Latinos with mental health issues are not continually killing groups of strangers.

Each of us is programmed from childhood to believe that the top group of our hierarchies—and in the US culture, that's white men—represents everyone, so it can feel awkward, even ridiculous, when we try to call attention to those people as a distinct group and hold them accountable.

For example, our schools teach American history as the history of everyone in this nation. But the stories we learn are predominantly about white men. To study the history of other groups, people have to take separate classes, such as African American history, women's history, or Native American history. And if we take "Hispanic American History," we don't expect to learn "Asian American History," because a class about anyone but white men is assumed not to be inclusive of anyone else.

This societal and cultural programming makes it easy for conservative, white-male-led groups to convince the nation that an organization led by white men, such as the NRA or the tea party movement, can represent the interests of the entire nation when, in fact, these groups predominately represent only their own experiences and perspectives.

If life were equitable, white male gun-rights advocates would face some serious questions to assess their degree of credibility and objectivity. We would expect them to explain:

- What facets of white male culture create so many mass shootings?

- Why are so many white men and boys producing and entertaining themselves with violent video games and other media?

- Why do white men buy, sell, and manufacture guns for profit, attend gun shows, and demonstrate for unrestricted gun access disproportionately more than people of other ethnicities or races?

• Why are white male congressmen leading the fight against gun control?

If Americans ask the right questions on gun issues, we will get the right answers. These answers will encourage white men to examine their role in their own culture and to help other white men and boys become healthier and less violent.

Letter to Adam Lanza
By Phap Luu
Winter 2013

Dear Adam,

Let me start by saying that I wish for you to find peace. It would be easy just to call you a monster and condemn you for evermore, but I don't think that would help either of us. Given what you have done, I realize that peace may not be easy to find. In a fit of rage, delusion, and fear—yes, above all else, I think, fear—you thought that killing was a way out. It was clearly a powerful emotion that drove you from your mother's dead body to massacre children and staff of Sandy Hook School and to turn the gun in the end on yourself. You decided that the game was over.

But the game is not over, though you are dead. You didn't find a way out of your anger and loneliness. You live on in other forms, in the torn families and their despair, in the violation of their trust, in the gaping wound in a community, and in the countless articles and news reports spilling across the country and the world—yes, you live on even in me. I was also a young boy who grew up in Newtown. Now I am a Zen Buddhist monk. I see you quite clearly in me now, continued in the legacy of your actions, and I see that in death you have not become free.

You know, I used to play soccer on the school field outside the room where you died, when I was the age of the children you killed. Our team was the Eagles, and we won our division that year. My mom still keeps the trophy stashed in a box. To be honest, I was and am not much of a soccer player. I've known winning, but I've also known losing, and being picked last for a spot on the team. I think you've known this too—the pain of rejection, isolation, and loneliness. Loneliness too strong to bear.

You are not alone in feeling this. When loneliness comes up it is so easy to seek refuge in a virtual world of computers and films, but do these really help, or only increase our isolation? In our drive to be more connected, have we lost our true connection?

I want to know what you did with your loneliness. Did you ever, like me, cope by walking in the forests that cover our town? I know well the slope that cuts from that school to the stream, shrouded by beech and white pine. It makes up the landscape of my mind. I remember well the thrill of heading out alone on a path winding its way—to Treadwell Park! At that time it felt like a magical path, one of many secrets I discovered throughout those forests, some still hidden. Did you ever lean your face on the rough furrows of an oak's bark, feeling its solid heartwood and tranquil vibrancy? Did you ever play in the course of a stream, making pools with the stones as if of this stretch you were king? Did you ever experience the healing, connection, and peace that comes with such moments, like I often did?

Or did your loneliness know only screens, with dancing figures of light at the bid of your will? How many false lives have you lived, how many shots fired, bombs exploded and lives lost in video games and movies?

By killing yourself at 20, you never gave yourself the chance to grow up and experience a sense of how life's wonders can bring happiness. I know at your age I hadn't yet seen how to do this.

I am 37 now, about the age my teacher, the Buddha, realized there was a way out of suffering. I am not enlightened. This morning, when I heard the news, and read the words of my shocked classmates, within minutes a wave of sorrow arose, and I wept. Then I walked a bit farther, into the woods skirting our monastery, and in the wet, winter cold of France, beside the laurel, I cried again. I cried for the children, for the teachers, for their families. But I also cried for you, Adam, because I think that I know you, though I know we have never met. I think that I know the landscape of your mind, because it is the landscape of my mind.

I don't think you hated those children, or that you even hated your mother. I think you hated your loneliness.

I cried because I have failed you. I have failed to show you how to cry. I have failed to sit and listen to you without judging or reacting. Like many of my peers, I left Newtown at seventeen, brimming with confidence and purpose, with the congratulations of friends and the approbation of my elders. I was one of the many young people who left, and in leaving we left others, including you, just born, behind. In that sense I am a part of the culture that failed you. I didn't know yet what a community was, or that I was a part of one, until I no longer had it, and so desperately needed it.

I have failed to be one of the ones who could have been there to sit and listen to you. I was not there to help you to breathe and become aware of your strong emotions, to help you to see that you are more than just an emotion.

But I am also certain that others in the community cared for you, loved you. Did you know it?

In eighth grade I lived in terror of a classmate and his anger. It was the first time I knew aggression. No computer screen or television gave a way out, but my imagination and books did. I dreamt myself a great wizard, blasting fireballs down the school corridor, so he would fear and respect me. Did you dream like this too?

The way out of being a victim is not to become the destroyer. No matter how great your loneliness, how heavy your despair, you, like each one of us, still have the capacity to be awake, to be free, to be happy, without being the cause of anyone's sorrow.

You didn't know that, or couldn't see that, and so you chose to destroy. We were not skillful enough to help you see a way out.

With this terrible act you have let us know. Now I am listening, we are all listening, to you crying out from the hell of your misunderstanding. You are not alone, and you are not gone. And you may not be at peace until we can stop all our busyness, our quest for power, money, or sex, our lives of fear and worry, and really listen to you, Adam, to be a friend, a brother, to you. With a good friend like that, your loneliness might not have overwhelmed you.

But we needed your help too, Adam. You needed to let us know that you were suffering, and that is not easy to do. It means overcoming pride, and that takes courage and humility. Because you were unable to do this, you have left a heavy legacy for generations to come. If we cannot learn how to connect with you and understand the loneliness, rage, and despair you felt—which also lie deep and sometimes hidden within each one of us—not by connecting through Facebook or Twitter or e-mail or telephone, but by really sitting with you and opening our hearts to you, your rage will manifest again in yet unforeseen forms.

Now we know you are there. You are not random, or an aberration. Let your action move us to find a path out of the loneliness within each one of us. I have learned to use awareness of my breath to recognize and transform these overwhelming emotions, but I hope that every man, woman, or child does not need to go halfway across the world to become a monk to learn how to do this. As a community we need to sit down and learn how to cherish life, not with gun-checks and security, but by being fully present for one another, by being truly there for one another. For me, this is the way to restore harmony to our communion.

The Unbearable Whiteness of Suicide-by-Mass-Murder
By Cliff Leek and Michael Kimmel
Winter 2013

If your only sources were Facebook and Fox, tabloids and TV, you'd likely think that guns, mental illness, and violent media were the only things worth talking about to explain the horrific massacre at Sandy Creek Elementary School. Of course, any rational approach to this problem would indicate that these three factors are important.

Surely, guns played some role in this. Although guns, by themselves, are not the cause of the rampage, they can help explain its horrific scale, its terrible scope. Consider two of our closest allies. In 1996, in Dunblane, Scotland, a single gunman killed sixteen children and one adult in an affluent suburb before taking his own life. That same year, a gunman killed thirty-five people and wounded twenty-three more in a Tazmanian resort town; it was Australia's worst mass shooting ever. Both countries immediately passed tough gun controls, making it effectively illegal to own a handgun in the UK. And there hasn't been another school shooting since in Britain; in Australia, homicides by firearms have declined by about 60% over the past fifteen years.

And yes, we believe Adam Lanza was mentally ill. Perhaps he was on the autism spectrum, he was perhaps manic-depressive. Pop psychologists will never have the opportunity to properly diagnose him (but that won't stop them from trying). We do not know enough and he left few clues, but it is safe to say that he was mentally ill. And just as surely, the overwhelming majority of mentally ill people do not hurt other people (and the majority of violence is performed by people who would test as fully rational.)

And yes, of course, our violent media culture, of apocalyptic action movies and glorified graphic violence and first-person shooter video games has to have some cognitive impact. Even though the overwhelming majority of game players and media consumers will never commit a violent act in our lives, most research indicates that media images have some effect on our behavior. (Had they no effect, the entire advertising industry would collapse!)

But these three factors are simply not enough. We need to broaden the conversation. Other elements must be considered. There are at least two more elements of this equation of what can only be described as "suicide by mass murder" that have to be weighed judiciously alongside guns, mental illness, and violence in media. These often unspoken elements are gender and race.

The biggest surprise in the deluge of punditry about Sandy Hook is the sudden visibility of gender. The utter maleness of these mass murders is no longer being ignored (61 of the 62 perpetrators of mass murders in the United States in the last 30 years have been men). We are finally questioning how using violence to retaliate against nearly any perceived slight is accepted, and even encouraged, for men in our society. Righteous retaliation is a deeply held, almost sacred, tenet of masculinity: if you are aggrieved, you are entitled to retribution. American men don't just get mad, we get even.

Both of us have been writing and researching this lethal equation of masculinity and righteous resort to violence for years, so we weren't surprised that it plays a role in these events. But we were surprised to see a gender analysis becoming one of the central framing themes in the media coverage. It is long overdue.

But a deeper, and perhaps more controversial issue is race—or, rather the combination of race and class and gender. (We academics call it "intersectionality"—the way that race or class or gender are not separate categories but rather intersect with one another in constantly shifting patterns). Even as gender is finally making headlines in relation to this horrible violence, race and its intersection with class and gender has been left behind.

Newtown is a white, upper- and upper-middle-class suburb. Think of the way we are describing those beautiful children—"angels" and "innocent"— which they surely were. Now imagine if the shooting had taken place in an inner city school in Philadelphia, Newark, Compton, or Harlem. Would we be using words like "angels"? We don't know the answer, but it's worth asking the question. It is telling though that we do not see a national outcry over the far too frequent deaths of black- and brown-skinned angels in our nation's inner cities.

Now let's talk about the race and class of the shooter. In the last thirty years, 90 percent of shootings at elementary and high schools in the US have been perpetrated by young white men. And 80 percent of the thirteen mass murders perpetrated by individuals aged twenty or under in the last thirty years have also been committed by white men. There is clearly something happening here that is not only tied to gender, but also to race.

This new phenomenon of suicide-by-mass-murder has emerged as a corollary to the earlier suicide-by-cop as a phenomenon of those whose real goal is, at least in part, to kill themselves—and to take out as many of "them" as possible on the way. And this seems to be an entirely white male thing.

In urban settings, when young men of color experience that same sense of aggrieved entitlement—that perception of victimhood despite everything men expect for themselves—they may react violently, and even with lethal violence. But the victims of their violence are usually those whom the shooter believes have wronged him and the unintended and accidental victims caught in the line of fire. And it rarely ends with his suicide.

White men, on the other hand, have a somewhat more grandiose purpose: they want to destroy the entire world in some cataclysmic, video game- and action movie-inspired apocalypse. If I'm going to die, then so is everybody else, they seem to say. Yes, of course, this is mental illness speaking, but it is mental illness speaking with a voice that has a race and a gender.

One must feel a sense of aggrieved entitlement to pick up a gun and go on a rampage, yes. But that sense of aggrieved entitlement must also be grandiose if you are going to make them all pay.

Even as we challenge ourselves to see the racial difference in perpetration, we must not ignore the way that our response to this kind of violence is also shaped by race. When we hear of a rampage shooting by a white guy, we immediately claim it is a result of individual pathology—mental illness.

The problem is "him," not "us." When we hear of a rampage or gang murders in the inner city, we assume it is the result of a "social pathology"— something about the culture of poverty, the legacy of racism, or some intrinsic characteristics of "them" or "those people." This difference in treatment allows us to avoid talking about what whiteness might have to do with the violence, while always talking about what blackness or brownness has to do with it.

In both cases, though—individual mental illness or social pathology— it is not "our" story, but "their" story. And thus we miss the other variables in this equation—how the shooter is, indeed, one of us—shaped in the same culture, fed the same diet of images and ideas about the legitimacy of righteous rage, and given access to the same guns, subject to the same poorly diagnosed and undertreated mental illnesses, regardless of their cause.

Just as those innocent angels (no quotations marks this time, as they surely are that) are "ones of us," so, too, is Adam Lanza. We, the authors, speak inside that frame; we, too, are white and male, and have drunk from the same glass of aggrieved entitlement. Unless we address all the elements of the equation in his horrific act, including race and gender, our nation will continue to produce Adam Lanzas, Dylan Klebolds, James Holmeses, Jared Loughners, arm them with a small arsenal, and then inspire them to explode.

Also, a friend of mine who works with folks with mental disabilities pointed out that autism is *not* a mental illness, but rather is a developmental disability and that is an important distinction for us to respect. Perhaps all we need to do is add "or developmentally disabled" to the end of the first sentence of the paragraph on mental illness.

Message to the Media: It's About Manhood More than Guns and Mental Illness
Jackson Katz
Winter 2013

Many of us whose work touches on the subject of masculinity and violence have long been frustrated by the failure of mainstream media—and much of progressive media and the blogosphere as well—to confront the gender issues at the heart of so many violent rampages like the one at Sandy Hook Elementary School in Newtown, Connecticut.

My colleagues and I who do this type of work experience an unsettling dichotomy. In one part of our lives, we routinely have intense, in-depth discussions about men's emotional and relational struggles, and how the bravado about "rugged individualism" in American culture masks the deep yearning for connection that so many men feel, and how the absence or loss of that can quickly turn to pain, despair, and anger. In these discussions, we talk about violence as a gendered phenomenon: how, for example, men who batter their wives or girlfriends typically do so not because they have trigger tempers, but rather as a means to gain or maintain power and control over her in a (misguided) attempt to get their needs met.

We talk among ourselves about how so many boys and men in our society are conditioned to see violence as a solution to their problems, a resolution of their anxieties, or a means of exacting revenge against those they perceive as taking something from them. We share with each other news stories, websites and YouTube videos that demonstrate the connection between deeply ingrained cultural ideas about manhood and individual acts of violence that operationalize those ideas.

And then in the wake of repeated tragedies like Newtown, we turn on the TV and watch the same predictable conversations about guns and mental illness, with only an occasional mention that the overwhelming majority of these types of crimes are committed by men—usually white men. Even when some brave soul dares to mention this crucial fact, it rarely prompts further discussion, as if no one wants to be called a "male basher" for uttering the simple truth that men commit the vast majority of violence, and thus efforts to "prevent violence"—if they're going to be more than minimally effective—need to explore why.

It is still too early to say, but the Newtown massacre might mark a sea change. Maybe the mass murder of young children will come to be seen as the tipping point that sparked a more honest national dialogue about the underlying causes of violence. Prompted by Newtown, maybe the ideological gatekeepers in mainstream media will actually agree to pry open the cupboards of conventional thinking long enough to have a thoughtful conversation about manhood in the context of our ongoing national tragedy of gun violence. Then again, maybe not. Initial signs are not particularly promising. In the months since the shooting, some op-eds and blog posts have spoken to the gender dynamics at the heart of this and other rampage killings. But despite voluminous coverage and commentary in print, TV, and online, most mainstream analysis has continued to steer clear of this critical piece of the puzzle. This lack of a gender analysis was certainly the case when, almost four months to the day after Newtown, another violent incident shocked the nation and dominated the news for several weeks: the Boston Marathon bombing.

In this discussion, the usual focus on guns and mental illness as explanatory factors was replaced by a fixation on the ethnicity and religious beliefs of the suspects. Even if this explanation was insufficient, it was understandable, as the bombing seemed to be a more explicitly political act than, say, a school shooting or murderous rampage at a movie theater.

But in the rush to blame jihadism or Islamist radicalism, another ideology was once again overlooked. It is the ideology of a certain type of manhood that links acts of violence to masculine identity. It is the idea that committing an act of violence—whether the precipitating rationale is personal, religious, or political—is a legitimate means to assert and prove one's manhood. Its roots are planted as firmly in domestic soil as they are in that of foreign countries.

The idea that these violent incidents represent individual performances of manhood, rather than the enactment of specific religious or political ideologies, can partially be summed up by the headline of a *New Republic* article: "Boston: More Like Sandy Hook Than 9/11." The article, written by John Judis, quoted the author Olivier Roy, a professor at the European University Institute in Italy, explaining why the motivation in these types of bombings is not primarily religious:

"They want to make headlines," Roy said. "That's the point. They want to become a hero. It's why I compare them with many of the guys who did the Columbine sort of terrorist attacks against a school. They were very young guys, probably loners and slightly suicidal. They want to end in beauty, they want to do something extraordinary."

What Roy did not say explicitly is that they want to assert their manhood in the most dramatic way possible: through a display of violence. Investigators of terrorist incidents employ computer models to look for patterns: traits, experiences, contacts shared by individuals and organizations that are involved in these types of incidents, in the hope that this knowledge can contribute to greater understanding of the methods—and motives—of perpetrators. But the one overarching pattern that is often overlooked is the gender of the perpetrators. In Boston, as with the vast majority of mass killings, the most important characteristics of the murder suspects is that they are young *men* whose psychological and identity needs for some reason require them to perpetrate violence.

What follows is a brief list of suggestions for how journalists, cable hosts, bloggers, and others who write and talk about these unbelievable tragedies can frame the discussion not only about Newtown and Boston, but also the tragic mass killings that—sadly—everyone knows are going to continue.

1. Make gender—specifically the idea that men are gendered beings—a central part of the national conversation about rampage killings. Typical news

accounts and commentaries about school shootings and rampage killings rarely mention gender. If a woman were the shooter, you can bet there would be all sorts of commentary about shifting cultural notions of femininity and how they might have contributed to her act, such as discussions in recent years about girl gang violence. That same conversation about gender should take place when a man is the perpetrator. Men are every bit as gendered as women.

The key difference is that because men represent the dominant gender, their gender is rendered invisible in the discourse about violence. So much of the commentary about school shootings, including the one at Sandy Hook Elementary, focused on "people" who have problems, "individuals" who suffer from depression, and "shooters" whose motives remain obtuse. When opinion leaders start talking about the *men* who commit these rampages, and ask questions like: "why is it almost always men who do these horrible things?" and then follow that up, we will have a much better chance of finding workable solutions to the outrageous level of violence in our society.

2. Use the "M-word." Talk about masculinity. This does not mean you need to talk about biological maleness or search for answers in new research on brain chemistry. Such inquiries have their place. But the focus needs to be sociological: individual men are products of social systems. How many more school shootings do we need before we start talking about this as a social problem, and not merely a random collection of isolated incidents? Why are nearly all of the perpetrators of these types of crimes men, and most of them white men? (An article by William Hamby, "Connecticut Shooting, White Males, and Mass Murder," published just after Newtown is a step in the right direction.)

What are the cultural narratives from which school shooters draw lessons or inspiration? This does not mean simplistic condemnations of video games or violent media—although all cultural influences are fair game for analysis. It means looking carefully at how our culture defines manhood, how boys are socialized, and how pressure to stay in the "man box" not only constrains boys' and men's emotional and relational development but also their range of choices when faced with life crises. Psychological factors in men's development and psyches surely need to be examined, but the best analyses see individual men's actions in a social and historical context.

3. Identify the gender subtext of the ongoing political battle over "guns rights" versus "gun control," and bring it to the surface. The current script that plays out in media after these types of horrendous killings is unproductive and full of empty clichés. Advocates of stricter gun laws call on political leaders to take action, while defenders of "gun rights" hunker down and deflect criticism, hoping to ride out yet another public relations nightmare for the firearms industry. But few commentators who opine about the gun debates seem to recognize the deeply gendered aspects of this ongoing controversy. Guns play an important emotional role in many men's lives, both as a vehicle for their relationships with their fathers and in the way they bolster some men's sense of security and power.

It is also time to broaden the gun policy debate to a more in-depth discussion about the declining economic and cultural power of white men, and to deconstruct the gendered rhetoric of "defending liberty" and "fighting tyranny" that animates much right-wing opposition to even moderate gun control measures. Unfortunately, even with broad public support, President Obama failed in his attempt to push background checks and other commonsense gun policy reforms through Congress in the aftermath of Newtown. Most commentary about this political defeat focused on the continued electoral muscle—real or imagined—of the National Rifle Association and the extremism and intransigence of the contemporary Republican Party. Relatively little attention was paid to the cultural forces at work just beneath the surface of political debate—especially the gender subtext. Looking forward, if journalists and others in media are able to create space for a discussion about guns that focuses on the role of guns in men's psyches and identities, and how this plays out in their political belief systems, we might have a chance to move beyond the current impasse.

4. Consult with, interview, and feature in your stories the perspectives of the numerous men and women across the country who have worked with abusive men. Many of these people are counselors, therapists, and educators who can provide all sorts of insights about how—and why— men use violence. Since men who commit murder outside the home more than occasionally have a history of domestic violence, it is important to hear from the many women and men in the domestic violence field who can speak to these types of connections—and in many cases have firsthand experience that deepen their understanding.

5. Bring experts on the air, and quote them in your stories, who can speak knowledgeably about the link between masculinity and violence. After the Jovan Belcher murder-suicide, CNN featured the work of the author Kevin Powell, who has written a lot about men's violence and the many intersections between gender and race. That was a good start. In the modern era of school shootings and rampage killings, a number of scholars have produced works that offer ways to think about the gendered subtext of these disturbing phenomena.

Examples include Rachel Kalish (logicalliving.blog.com/files/2011/04/Suicide-Ten.pdf) and Michael Kimmel's piece "Suicide by Mass Murder: Masculinity, Aggrieved Entitlement and Rampage School Shootings"; Douglas Kellner's "Rage and Rampage: School Shootings and Crises of Masculinity" (www.huffingtonpost.com/douglas-kellner/rage-and-rampage-schools_b_1449714.html?); and a short piece that I cowrote with Sut Jhally after Columbine, "The National Conversation in the Wake of Littleton is Missing the Mark" (www.jacksonkatz.com/pub_missing.html).

There have also been many important books published over the past fif-teen years or so that provide great insight into issues of late-twentieth- and twenty-first-century American manhood, and thus provide valuable context for discussions about men's violence. They include *Real Boys*, by William Pollack; *Raising Cain*, by Michael Thompson and Dan Kindlon; *New Black Man*, by Mark Anthony Neal; *Why Does He Do That?* by Lundy Bancroft; *Dude You're a Fag*, by C.J. Pascoe; *Guyland*, By Michael Kimmel; *I Don't Want to Talk About It*, by Terrence Real; *Violence*, by James Gilligan; *Guys and Guns Amok*, by Douglas Kellner; *On Killing*, by David Grossman; and two docu-mentary films: *Hip-Hop: Beyond Beats and Rhymes*, by Byron Hurt; and *Tough Guise*, which I created and Sut Jhally directed. (Not to mention this magazine, which has been chronicling the transformation of masculinities for decades).

6. Resist the temptation to blame this shooting or others on "mental ill-ness," as if this answers the why and requires no further explanation. Even if some of these violent men are or were "mentally ill," the specific ways in which mental illness manifests itself are often profoundly gendered. Consult with ex-perts who understand the gendered features of mental illness. For example, conduct interviews with mental health experts who can talk about why men, many of whom are clinically depressed, comprise the vast majority of perpe-trators of murder-suicides. Why is depression in women much less likely to contribute to their committing murder than it is for men? (It is important to note that only a very small percentage of men with clinical depression commit murder, although a very high percentage of people with clinical depression who commit murder are men.)

7. Don't buy the manipulative argument that it's somehow "antimale" to focus on questions about manhood in the wake of these ongoing tragedies. Men commit the vast majority of violence and almost all rampage killings. It's long past time that we summoned the courage as a society to look this fact squarely in the eye and then do something about it. Women in media can initiate this discussion, but men bear the ultimate responsibility for addressing the masculinity crisis at the heart of these tragedies. With little children being murdered en masse at school, and innocent children and others killed at peace-ful sporting events, for God's sake, it's time for more of them to step up, even in the face of inevitable push back from the defenders of a sick and dysfunc-tional status quo.

The Tears of the Sandy Hook Fathers
By Rob Okun

> *There's something happening here*
> *What it is ain't exactly clear*
> *There's a man with a gun over there*
> *Telling me I got to beware*
> *I think it's time we stop, children, what's that sound*
> *Everybody look what's going down*

> —"For What It's Worth," Stephen Stills (Buffalo Springfield, 1966)

Less than a week after Adam Lanza murdered his mother in her bed and then killed twenty-six students and staff at Sandy Hook Elementary School on December 15, 2012, I wrote a column, "Moving Beyond Men's Killing Fields." In it, I talked about the need to establish a broader set of measures by which we define manhood and suggested ways we could more safely raise the next generations of boys. What follows are some recommendations and observations that seem like an apt afterword for this book.

Let's begin by cultivating boys' emotional intelligence, making it as high a priority as is teaching math and reading. In our roles as fathers and mentors, coaches and clergy, teachers and community leaders, men can play an important role in this kind of a sea change.

Let's bring together gun control advocates and those working to redefine masculinity to create a new coalition that recognizes the irrefutable, longstanding relationship between men and guns, men's mental health, and men and power.

Let's stop kidding ourselves that we can ignore men underreporting their depression, and their aversion to mental health checkups (*all* health checkups, for that matter). Too many men are at risk to themselves and others, their pain masked by a toxic rage.

In the wake of Newtown the president established a commission on gun violence. Now is the time for him to use his office to promote a national program to train early childhood educators and care providers, as well as elementary school teachers, to create curricula that emphasize boys' emotional well being—from training in mediation to practicing meditation.

Let's put men's mental health on the docket, too; the Centers for Disease Control and Prevention are well equipped to coordinate a national campaign to raise awareness about mental health and males, including creating treatment plans tailored to reach troubled men. The families of the Sandy Hook School shooting victims deserve nothing less. As do those affected by the Boston Marathon bombing and the mass shootings at Aurora, Colorado, Oak Creek, Wisconsin, and Tucson, Arizona, for example—not to mention the loved ones of the more than 5,000 persons killed by guns in the first six months after Newtown (ironically, an average of twenty-seven a day, the same number killed at Sandy Hook, including the murderer's mother).

In the struggle to replace conventional expressions of manhood with a profeminist vision, there's a simultaneous cultural truth at play as we fishtail along the slippery road of gender justice. On the one hand are men like Wayne LaPierre of the NRA still attracting followers despite the disdain with which his tone-deaf analysis of how to prevent gun violence is being received by a growing number of citizens. On the other are men, say, like Jason Collins—the National Basketball Association player who announced he was gay in a *Sports Illustrated* cover story in April 2013. Mr. Collins was an unlikely counterpoint to Mr. LaPierre. Still, as "man's man" sports figure, his moment on the national stage spotlighted a different expression of manhood and helped unlock the door for younger males—gay young men, of course, and many, many others—hungry for a way out of the "man box" that seeks to constrain them.

In the years ahead I believe Mr. LaPierre will be seen as a throwback to a bygone era. I know, I know; we're not there yet. Sooner than later though, he will be marginalized as a credible voice representing the will of the American people, replaced perhaps by the eloquent and passionate voices of the heartbroken fathers of Sandy Hook. In those grief-stricken men is another example of a still under-the-radar expression of conventional manhood eroding. Let me explain.

There was a time when we didn't hear at all from men suffering a heart-wrenching family tragedy. ("He's the silent type," a female relative might offer. "He just keeps his feelings bottled up inside," she'd explain about another stoic man unable to find and shed his tears.) Well, the Sandy Hook dads are different. Alongside their wives they are leading the way in a cultural shift Mr. LaPierre and his NRA backers in the US Congress have heretofore never seen. The tears of fathers are mixing with the fierce determination of mothers to create a tribe of new social justice change agents: activist parents. This is a good sign for those who support their promise to continue lobbying Congress until substantive gun reform legislation is passed (www.sandyhookpromise.org).

Beyond that pledge, though, must come another declaration to urge—no, demand—that Congress, the White House, and the media make gender a central part of the national conversation about mass shooting violence. As has been well documented in the essays and reflections in the final section of the book, we need only look at the deadly Boston Marathon bombing to notice that gender, specifically white maleness, was once again absent from the discussion.

For white males in particular this is a perfect moment to leverage whatever privilege and influence our status affords to add white maleness to a conversation now too narrowly focused on guns. It won't be easy to make the change; there are a lot of forces against us—powerful, white male forces. If we are to accelerate the pace of change in redefining manhood then we have to expose its dangerous conventional white male expression at every possible moment. And we must simultaneously encourage one another to spotlight expressions of egalitarian, profeminist manhood whenever and wherever we see them. (To get started, turn to the organizations and groups listed in the Resources section.)

In the next stage in "one of the most important social justice movements you've never heard of," profeminist men and our allies must amplify our voices to tell our side of the story. For too long, we've ceded the stage to men like Mr. LaPierre and his ilk. Those days have to come to an end. The time to begin is now.

RESOURCES

For Young Men

Advocates for Youth
Helps young people make informed and responsible decisions about their reproductive and sexual health
www.advocatesforyouth.org

Amplify Your Voice
A youth-driven community working for social change
www.amplifyyourvoice.org

Boys to Men
Initiation weekends and follow-up mentoring for boys 12–17 to guide them on their journey to manhood
www.boystomen.org

The Brotherhood/Sister Sol
Provides comprehensive, holistic, and long-term support and rites of passage programming to youth ages 8–22
www.brotherhood-sistersol.org

YCteen Magazine
A magazine written by New York City teens that helps marginalized youth reach their full potential through reading and writing
www.ycteenmag.org

Rites of Passage

A sampling of rites of passage opportunities for teenage boys in the United States:

Wilderness (nondenominational)

Rites of Passage Journeys, Seattle, WA riteofpassagejourneys.org
School of Lost Borders, Big Pine, CA schooloflostborders.org
Wilderness Reflections, Fairfax, CA www.wildernessreflections.com
Stepping Stones, Mill Valley, CA www.steppingstonesproject.org
Men's Leadership Alliance, Boulder, CO www.mensleadershipalliance.org

African American and African-centric

Rites of Passage Institute, Cleveland, OH eenh.org
Oriki Theater, Mountain View, CA www.oriki.org
Vision Quest Intl., Atlanta, GA visionquestinternational.org

Native American

Ed Featherman, Kyle, SD
Buffalo Visions, MT www.visionsserviceadventures.com
Youth Struggling for Survival, Chicago, IL
  tekpatzin.proboards.com/index.cgi
La Plazita Institute, Albuquerque, NM laplazitainstitute.org

Christian

Passage to Manhood, Peregrine Ministries, Colorado Springs, CO
  www.peregrineministries.org
Band of Brothers, Colorado Springs, CO www.bandofbrothers.org
Passage, Arcata, CO www.passage.org

Jewish

(Rabbis reinvigorating the bar/bat mitzvah with an emphasis on initiation)
Rabbi Goldie Milgram, Philadelphia, PA www.aleph.org/teacher_
  milgram.htm
Rabbi Stephen Booth-Nadav, Denver, CO
Rabbi Mendel Dubrawsky, Dallas, TX
Rabbi Steven Gross, Houston, TX
Rabbi Gary Gerson, Oak Park, IL

Weekend Workshops (nondenominational)

Rite of Passage Experience, Glastonbury, CT www.rope.org
Rites of Passage VisionQuest www.ritesofpassagevisionquest.org
Boys to Men, San Diego, CA www.boystomen.org
Young Men's Ultimate Weekend, San Rafael, CA www.ymuw.org
Spiritual Warfare Effectiveness Training, Philadelphia, PA www.swet.org

Public School Programs (nondenominational)

Challenge Day, San Rafael, CA www.challengeday.org/
Lifeplan Institute, Tiburon, CA www.lifeplaninstitute.org/
Community Matters, Santa Rosa, CA www.community-matters.org/

Freelance Initiators of Boys:

Luis Rodriguez—luisrodrigues.com/
Malidoma Some—malidoma.com/main/
Michael Meade—www.mosaicvoices.org/
Orland Bishop—www.globalonenessproject.org/people/orland-bishop

Imam Dawud Walid—dawudwalid.wordpress.com/
John Eldredge—ransomheart.com/
Dr. Maka'ala Yates—www.manalomi.com/
Kalani Souza—www.youtube.com/watch?v=am7-OGnGhis
Aaron Ortega—www.facebook.com/pages/Indigenous-
Insights/318517958176419

On Masculinity

American Men's Studies Association
Advancing the critical study of men and masculinities
www.mensstudies.org

EME
CulturaSalud blog dedicated to social research and development, programs, and networks on issues of masculinity and gender equity. In Spanish
www.eme.cl

EngagingMen
A public resource for anyone committed to gender justice and overcoming violence against women
engagingmen.net

ManKind Project
New Warrior training weekends
www.mkp.org

Masculinidades
Profeminist blog about the anthropology of masculinity. In Spanish
masculinidades.wordpress.com

Menstuff: The National Men's Resource
National clearinghouse of information and resources for men
www.menstuff.org

Men's Resources International
Trainings and consulting on positive masculinity, especially on the African continent
www.mensresourcesinternational.org

The Men's Bibliography
Comprehensive bibliography of writing on men, masculinities, gender, and sexualities listing 14,000 works
www.mensbiblio.xyonline.net

The Men's Story Project
Resources for creating public dialogue about masculinities through local storytelling and arts
www.mensstoryproject.org

The Takeback
> *Meditations on masculinity, politics, and culture by a collective of pro-feminist, male liberationist men*
> thetakeback.com

XY
> www.xyonline.net
> *Profeminist men's web links (more than 500 links):*
> www.xyonline.net/links
> *Profeminist men's politics, frequently asked questions:*
> www.xyonline.net/content/frequently-asked-questions-about-pro-feminist-men-and-pro-feminist-mens-politics
> *Profeminist e-mail list: www.xyonline.net/content/profem-mail-list*
> *Homophobia and masculinities among young men:*
> www.xyonline.net/content/homophobia-and-masculinities-among-young-men-lessons-becoming-straight-man

For Men of Color

100 Black Men of America, Inc.
> *Chapters around the US working on youth development and economic empowerment in the African American community*
> www.100blackmen.org

2025 Network for Black Men and Boys
> *Working toward the creation of a society with new social and economic realities that inspire ambition and hope among African descendant males*
> 2025bmb.org

Asian & Pacific Islander Institute on Domestic Violence
> *A national resource center on domestic violence, sexual violence, trafficking, and other forms of gender-based violence in Asian and Pacific Islander communities*
> www.apiidv.org

Concerned Black Men
> *A national organization providing mentors and programs that fill the void of positive black role models and provide opportunities for academic and career enrichment*
> www.cbmnational.org

Institute on Domestic Violence in the African American Community
> *Working to enhance society's understanding of and ability to end violence in the African American community*
> www.idvaac.org

National Compadres Network
Reinforcing the positive involvement of Latino males in their lives, families, communities, and society
www.nationalcompadresnetwork.com

National Latin@ Network for Healthy Families and Communities
A project of Casa de Esperanza and a national institute on domestic violence focusing on Latin communities
www.nationallatinonetwork.org

For Fathers

About Dads Radio
A podcast series focused on loving and committed fathers and the impact they have on children
www.k-state.edu/wwparent/aboutdads/Welcome.html

At Home Dad
A website for and collection of blogs about stay-at-home fathers
www.angelfire.com/zine2/athomedad/index.blog

Dad Man
Consulting, training, speaking about fathers and father figures as a vital family resource
www.thedadman.com

Dads and Daughters
A blog of thoughts and reflections on father-daughter relationships by Joe Kelly
dadsanddaughters.blogspot.com

Fathers with Divorce and Custody Concerns
Looking for a lawyer? Call your state bar association lawyer referral agency.
Useful websites include:
www.divorce.com
www.divorcecentral.com
www.divorcehq.com
www.divorcenet.com

Collaborative Divorce
www.collaborativealternatives.com
www.collaborativedivorce.com
www.collaborativepractice.com
www.nocourtdivorce.com

Fathers and Family Law: Myths and Facts
Debunking common myths regarding fathering and family law and providing facts directly from the research
www.thelizlibrary.org

Feminist Fathers
Resources for dads seeking to raise fully realized human beings with a mindfulness to how gender socialization affects parenting and children
feministfatherhood.com

National Fatherhood Initiative
Organization improve the well being of children through the promotion of responsible, engaged fatherhood
www.fatherhood.org

National Latino Fatherhood and Family Institute
Addresses the needs of Latino communities by focusing on positive Latino identity while addressing issues faced by Latino fathers, families, and communities
www.nlffi.org

Men and Feminism

Finally, A Feminism 101 Blog
An information resource, for both feminists and those questioning feminism
finallyfeminism101.wordpress.com

Guys' Guide to Feminism
Explores men's and women's perspectives on feminist issues and antiviolence.
guysguidetofeminism.blogspot.com

Guy's Guide to Feminism
Website companion to a book by Michael Kimmel and Michael Kaufman that illustrates how supporting feminism enriches men's lives
guysguidetofeminism.com

National Organization of Men Against Sexism (NOMAS)
Profeminist, gay-affirmative, antiracist activist organization supporting positive changes for men
www.nomas.org

Men's Health

American Journal of Men's Health
A peer-reviewed quarterly resource for information regarding men's health and illness
jmh.sagepub.com

International Society for Men's Health
Prevention campaigns and health initiatives promoting men's health
www.ismh.org

Malecare
Volunteer men's cancer support group and advocacy national nonprofit organization providing resources in multiple languages
malecare.org

Male Health Center–Lewisville, TX
Provides men with an integrated system of care that addresses all their needs
www.malehealthcenter.com

Men's Health Network
National organization promoting men's health
www.menshealthnetwork.org

Prostate Health Guide
Offers a guide to the prostate and various conditions that can affect men's health
www.prostatehealthguide.com

World Health Organization HIV/AIDS
Provides evidence-based technical support for comprehensive and sustainable responses to HIV/AIDS
www.who.int/hiv/en

Male Survivors of Sexual Assault

1in6
Provides resources for male sexual abuse survivors and their family members, friends, and partners
1in6.org

Black Sexual Abuse Survivors
A national online support system for African Americans
www.blacksurvivors.org/home.html

Giving and Receiving Guidance and Hope
A page of brief stories written by men who were sexually abused
www.jimhopper.com/hope

Just Detention International
A health and human rights organization that seeks to end sexual abuse in all forms of detention, by advocating for the safety and well being of inmates
www.justdetention.org

MaleSurvivor
National organization overcoming sexual victimization of boys and men
www.malesurvivor.org

Men Thriving
A peer resource offered to male survivors by male survivors
www.menthriving.org/forum

Stop It Now!
An organization dedicated to preventing the sexual abuse of children by providing support, information, and resources to keep children safe and create healthier communities
www.stopitnow.org

Overcoming Domestic Violence & Sexual Assault

1in4: The Men's Program
Offers workshops that educate men in women's recovery and lowers men's rape myth acceptance and self-reported likelihood of raping
www.oneinfourusa.org/themensprogram.php

A Call to Men
Trainings and conferences on ending violence against women
www.acalltomen.org

Coalition Against Trafficking in Women
An organization that works to end human trafficking and the commercial sexual exploitation of women and children worldwide
www.catwinternational.org

Emerge
Counseling and education to stop domestic violence; comprehensive batterers' services
www.emergedv.com

Equality Now
An organization that works with grassroots women's and human rights organizations and individual activists to document violence and discrimination against women and mobilize international action to support efforts to stop these abuses
www.equalitynow.org

Founding Fathers
A group of men of all ages working in partnership with women to create a new society where violence is no longer part of the human condition
www.founding-fathers.org

VOICE MALE

Futures Without Violence

Working to end violence against women globally; programs for boys, men, and fathers
www.futureswithoutviolence.org
Resources for mentoring young men on respect and healthy relationships and choices. Especially aimed at athletic coaches:
www.futureswithoutviolence.org/content/features/detail/811/

Gloucester Men Against Domestic Abuse

Gloucester, Mass., volunteer advocacy group of men's voices against domestic abuse and sexual assault
www.strongmendontbully.com

Healthy Dating

Sexual assault prevention
www.canikissyou.com

Hollaback

A movement to end street harassment powered by a network of local activists around the world, advocating the use of smartphones to document, map, and share incidents of street harassment
www.ihollaback.org

Men for Gender Equality

A Swedish NGO engaging men and boys in gender equality and violence prevention through focusing on social norms of masculinities. In Swedish
www.mfj.se

Mending the Sacred Hoop

Works to end violence against Native American women and to strengthen the voice and vision of Native peoples
www.mshoop.com

MenEngage Alliance

An international alliance promoting boys' and men's support for gender equality
www.menengage.org

Men Against Sexual Violence (MASV)

Men working in the struggle to end sexual violence
www.menagainstsexualviolence.org

Men Against Violence

UNESCO program advocating for education, social and natural science, culture, and communication as the means toward building peace
www.unesco.org/cpp/uk/projects/wcpmenaga.htm

Men Against Violence
Yahoo e-mail list
groups.yahoo.com/group/menagainstviolence

Men Can Stop Rape
Washington, DC-based national advocacy and training organization mobilizing male youth to prevent violence against women
www.mencanstoprape.org

Men's Initiative for Jane Doe, Inc.
Statewide Massachusetts effort coordinating men's antiviolence activities
www.mijd.org

Men's Nonviolence Project
Texas Council on Family Violence
www.tcfv.org/our-work/the-men's-nonviolence-project

Men Stopping Violence
Atlanta-based organization working to end violence against women, focusing on stopping battering and ending rape and incest
www.menstoppingviolence.org

Mentors in Violence Prevention
Gender violence prevention education and training
www.mvpnational.org
The MVP-National Facebook page:
www.facebook.com/mvpnational?ref=ts&fref=ts
Also, www.mvpstrategies.net
Educational outreach in the Greater Boston area:
www.northeastern.edu/sportinsociety/leadership-education/mvp

National Center for Children Exposed to Violence
Provides education and public awareness of the effects of domestic violence, especially on children
www.nccev.org/violence/domestic

National Center on Domestic and Sexual Violence
An organization that helps professionals who work with victims and perpetrators. Their resource list includes info about male victims of domestic and sexual violence
www.ncdsv.org

National Coalition Against Domestic Violence
Provides a coordinated community response to domestic violence
www.ncadv.org

National Domestic Violence Hotline
Provides 24-hour support, offering advocacy, safety planning, crisis intervention, information, and referral to victims of domestic violence, perpetrators, friends, and families
www.thehotline.org
800-799-SAFE (7233) or 800-787-3224 (TTY)
Advocates who are deaf are available Monday to Friday, 9 a.m. to 5 p.m. (PST):
Videophone: 855-812-1001
Instant messenger: DeafHotline
E-mail: deafhelp@thehotline.org

National Sexual Violence Resource Center (NSVRC)
A national information and resource hub related to all aspects of sexual violence
www.nsvrc.org

National Resource Center on Violence Against Women
An online collection of searchable materials and resources on domestic violence, sexual violence, and related issues
vawnet.org

One in Four
An all-male sexual assault peer education group dedicated to preventing rape
www.oneinfourusa.org

PreventConnect
Uses online media to build community among people engaged in efforts to prevent sexual assault and relationship violence
preventconnect.org

Promundo
Brazilian NGO seeking to promote gender equality and end violence against women, children, and youth
www.promundo.org.br/en

Prostitution Research & Education (PRE)
An organization dedicated to abolishing prostitution, that conducts research on prostitution, pornography, and trafficking, and offers education and consultation to researchers, survivors, the public, and policy makers
www.prostitutionresearch.com

Rape Abuse and Incest National Network (RAINN)
A national antisexual assault organization
www.rainn.org

Sexual Violence Prevention 101
Sexual assault and domestic violence prevention workshops
www.olywa.net/tdenny

Sonke Gender Justice (South Africa)
*A nonpartisan, nonprofit organization using a human rights frame-
work to build the capacity of government, civil society organizations
and citizens to achieve gender equality, prevent gender-based violence
and reduce the spread of HIV and the impact of AIDS*
www.genderjustice.org.za

Stop Porn Culture
*A group for those willing to question and fight against pornography and
porn culture*
www.stoppornculture.org

Students Active For Ending Rape
*Organization dedicated to fighting sexual violence and rape culture by
empowering student-led campaigns to reform college sexual assault policies*
www.safercampus.org

V-Day
*Global movement to end violence against women and girls; includes
V-men, male activists in the movement*
www.vday.org

Voices of Men
*Ben Atherton-Zeman's theatrical sketches advocating ending men's violence
against women*
www.voicesofmen.org

White Ribbon Campaign
International men's campaign decrying violence against women
www.whiteribbon.ca

LGBTQQIAA Resources

Ambiente Joven
*An advocacy project and LGBTQ community for Spanish-speaking
LGBTQ youth*
www.ambientejoven.org

Beyond Masculinity
Collection of essays by queer men on gender and politics
beyondmasculinity.com

COLAGE
National movement of people with one or more lesbian, gay, bisexual,

transgender, or queer parent working toward social justice through youth empowerment, leadership development, education, and advocacy
www.colage.org

Gay and Lesbian Alliance Against Defamation (GLAAD)
Works to combat homophobia and discrimination in television, film, music, and all media outlets
www.glaad.org

Gay Men's Domestic Violence Project
Provides crisis intervention, support, and resources for victims and survivors of domestic abuse
gmdvp.org/gmdvp

GenderTalk Transgender Resources (and More)
A directory of prescreened resources on transgender, GLBT, and progressive issues
www.gendertalk.com/info/resource/index.shtml

Hear My Voice
Educates and engages young people in the LGBTQ community to create safe, healthy relationships, and connects victims of dating abuse to help and legal services
hearmyvoice.breakthecycle.org

Human Rights Campaign
Largest GLBT political advocacy in the US
www.hrc.org

Interpride
Clearinghouse for information on pride events worldwide
www.interpride.net

Intersex Society of North America
Devoted to systemic change to end shame, secrecy, and unwanted genital surgeries for people born with an anatomy societally deemed not "standard" male or female
www.isna.org

National Gay and Lesbian Task Force
National progressive political and advocacy group
www.ngltf.org

National Resource Center on LGBT Aging
Resource center improving service and supports for LGBT older adults
www.lgbtagingcenter.org

Oasis Magazine
A writing community for queer and questioning youth

www.oasisjournals.com/magazine

Parents and Friends of Lesbians and Gays
Promotes well being of LGBTQ persons, and their parents, friends, and families
www.pflag.org

Straight Spouse Network
Provides personal, confidential support and information to heterosexual spouses/partners, current or former, of GLBT individuals
www.straightspouse.org/home.php

Survivor Project
A nonprofit organization dedicated to addressing the needs of intersex and trans survivors of domestic and sexual violence
www.survivorproject.org

Transgender Resources
Dedicated to educating those unfamiliar with or curious to learn more about the transgender community
www.glaad.org/transgender

Men's Resource Centers

Austin Men's Center—Austin, TX
Provides counseling, psychotherapy, and classes helping men with their lives, relationships, health, and careers
austinmenscenter.com

Males Advocating for Change—Worcester, MA
Center with groups and services supporting men and challenging men's violence
www.malesadvocatingchange.org

Men's Resource Center for Change—Amherst, MA
Model men's center offering support groups for nonabusive men and trainings and consulting on a range of issues addressing men and masculinities
www.mrcforchange.org

Men's Resource Center of West Michigan—West Michigan
Consultations and training in helping men develop their full humanity, create respectful and loving relationships, and caring and safe communities
www.menscenter.org

Redwood Men's Center—Santa Rosa, CA
A mythopoetic gathering dedicated to filling the need for men to come together in community healing
redwoodmen.org

Saskatoon Men's Center—Saskatoon, Saskatchewan, Canada

Profeminist, male-positive, gay-affirmative center dedicated to offering a safe environment where men may explore their true natures and improve their health

www.saskatoonmenscenter.com

Twin Cities Men's Center—Minneapolis, MN

Provides resources for men seeking to grow in mind, body, and spirit, and advocates for healthy family and community relationships

www.tcmc.org

ACKNOWLEDGMENTS

By its nature, an anthology is the result of the contributions of many, beginning with the writers. So I first want to appreciate each of them and their dedication to the issues found in this book. Their rich and varied voices make up this profeminist chorus and their stories are stronger in the company of one another.

Since the book grew out of the magazine that grew out of the newsletter that grew out of the Men's Resource Connection three decades ago, I want to acknowledge the early stewards of *Valley Men* who helped edit, produce, and distribute the publication BIE (Before the Internet Era). Deep appreciation to: Bill Payne, Dave Beauvais, Donald (Gopi Krishna) Shelton, Frank Hannigan, John Breckenridge, Mark Nickerson, Rafael Bradley, Rick Morton, Russell Bradbury-Carlin, Seth Fischer, Steven Botkin, and Tom Schiff.

As managing editor of *Voice Male* for a decade beginning in 1998 (and since then as its chief copy editor), Michael Burke's many gifts include wry humor and impeccable editing. If that weren't enough, drawing on intimate moments from his life as a son and a father, he contributed several poignant stories. In the transition from *Valley Men* to *Voice Male,* Michael Dover's sharp eye as a copy editor and clear voice as a writer helped to strengthen the publication. Former circulation coordinator Read Predmore, who showed up one day with an open-ended offer to help, managed the publication's database for five years with an unflappable demeanor, a perfect antidote to a sometimes-frantic editor on deadline.

As *Voice Male* art director since 2007, Lahri Bond not only completely redesigned the magazine, his inspired covers and interior page design just scrape the surface of what this kindhearted artist, writer, and musician has to offer.

The genesis for this book goes back several years, when a talented then-high school intern, Remer Rietkerk, started compiling a decade's worth of my op-eds and commentaries. Other enthusiastic interns continue to help *Voice Male* today. In summer 2011 and 2012 two worked almost exclusively on the book, Chelsea Faria and Maia Mares. Both Chelsea's painstaking research and Maia's insights and organizational skills were an enormous help. In addition, three other interns—Tim Boateng, Ethan Corey, and Arjun Downs—demonstrated not only a sophisticated understanding of the ideas in the book but also great skill in devising strategies to more widely broadcast them. Jeff Roth-Howe is the kind of dedicated volunteer every organization needs.

When I began this effort a number of people offered important support including James Baraz and Shoshana Alexander. James offered friendship and wise counsel in the early going, and like many writers before me, I greatly benefited from Shoshana's considerable editorial expertise. My compadre Paul Gorman has always been ready with a wealth of ideas, support, and friendship; and Bernice Gordon has singlehandedly become *Voice Male*'s ambassador-at-large in New York City.

Mary Hale, Johnny Lapham, and Anna Markus have been stalwarts, their support for my work longstanding and wholehearted. I have been the grateful recipient of their insights over many long lunches, and all have been unflagging in their belief in *Voice Male*'s mission. As have generous supporters Jack Hornor, Malcolm Jones, Jim Levey, and Sandy Pearson; I am grateful to all of them. Gladys Miller Rosenstein and Perry Rosenstein have long and enthusiastically supported my work as founders of the pioneering Puffin Foundation, unwavering in expressing its belief in projects that wed art and social justice. I also want to express my thanks to Sara Elinoff Acker and the Hyman Foundation for a long history of generosity and friendship.

Longtime friend—and sister—Peggy Gillespie, a founder of Family Diversity Projects, has been more than the fiscal sponsor for *Voice Male*. Her personal and professional support has been immeasurable. For the past five years, *Voice Male* has been fortunate to have its offices at the PDF Center for Peace & Justice, where we share space with other activist organizations including the Peace Development Fund (PDF), Earth Action & 20/20, the Prison Birth Project, and a field office of the International Center on Nonviolent Conflict. I've been privileged to engage in many enlightening conversations with my colleagues, in the early days especially with former PDF staffer Tony Rominske and, over the years, with PDF's Paul Haible, Ray Santiago, Kathy Sharkey, and Arlean Solis; Lois Barber at Earth Action & 20/20; Lisa Andrews, Marianne Bullock, and Marissa Pizii at Prison Birth Project, and especially my friend Hardy Merriman from the International Center on Nonviolent Conflict.

Much of this book took shape while I was on retreat at the Rowe Conference Center in the foothills of the Berkshires, where executive director Felicity Pickett —and codirectors emeriti Doug Wilson and Prue Berry—always welcomed me to my home away from home. And generous friends Barry Elson and Vicki Elson time and again demonstrated their support, extending me use of their cozy lake house.

I am grateful also to dear friend Sylvia Staub, a pioneer practitioner of feminist therapy, for testing my assumptions and always asking probing questions. Members of my manuscript group, Connie Griffin, Dusty Miller, and Janine Roberts—who regularly offer incisive comments on chapters from a memoir—welcomed me into a supportive writers' sorority. Equally helpful have been friends Donna Jenson, Oran Kaufman, and Joan Tabachnick, the other members of the "Gang of Four," a sounding board collective supporting one another's work life. My friends and colleagues at the Media

Acknowledgments

Education Foundation—particularly Sut Jhally, Kendra Hodgson, Jeremy Earp, Loretta Alper, and Alex Peterson—have long been staunch allies and I value each of them for all they do. Among colleagues and friends who ask challenging and important questions about profeminist men's work I particularly value those of change agent and acclaimed filmmaker Frederick Marx.

It is my good fortune the book landed at Interlink, where publisher and editor Michel Moushabeck and his staff have been publishing scores of critically important books for three decades. I am especially grateful to Pam Fontes-May for her design work, and David Klein for his skillful editing. If there are errors in the book, they are my fault alone.

In the preface I referred to the special connection I had with the men and women I worked with at the pioneering Men's Resource Center (MRC). Of my many friends and allies there I want to especially thank those with whom I worked longest and most closely: Steven Botkin, Russell Bradbury-Carlin, Aaron Buford, Malcolm Chu, Sara Elinoff Acker, Juan Carlos Areán, Steve Jefferson, and Steve Trudel. We worked shoulder to shoulder for years to build a unique organization to both support men and challenge men's violence. I also want to extend my appreciation to many other longtime members of the MRC family: Allan Arnaboldi, Michael Burke, Paula Chadis, Michael Dover, Jan Eidelson, Carl Erikson, Tom Gardner, Scott Girard, Nancy Girard, Karen Fogliatti, Joy Kaubin, Yoko Kato, Peter Jessop, Dot LaFratta, Bob Mazer, and Barbara Russell.

I am privileged to have an extraordinary national advisory board, all gifted members of the *Voice Male* chorus. They include: Juan Carlos Areán, John Badalament, Eve Ensler, Tom Gardner, Byron Hurt, Robert Jensen, Sut Jhally, Allan G. Johnson, Bill T. Jones, Jackson Katz, Joe Kelly, Michael Kimmel, Charles Knight, Don McPherson, Mike Messner, Ethelbert Miller, Craig Norberg-Bohm, Judy Norsigian, Chris Rabb, Haji Shearer, Joan Tabachnick, Shira Tarrant, and Miriam Zoll.

I want to cite several members in particular. Eve Ensler became an enthusiastic supporter from the moment she first encountered *Voice Male* and has extended herself on my behalf time and again. Her work as an artist, ally, and activist, remains as an inspirational guiding light. Likewise, Judy Norsigian began demonstrating fierce support as soon as she started reading *VM*, once digging out back issues from her car's trunk in a snowstorm to bring to a rally. Craig Norberg-Bohm and Haji Shearer regularly blanket New England with the magazine and have long demonstrated an unflagging friendship. Mike Messner and Shira Tarrant have for years championed the magazine as *VM* ambassadors in Southern California, as has Michael Kaufman, north of the border in Toronto.

Charles Knight, whose path briefly crossed mine when we were both young magazine publishers more than three decades ago, is the kind of grounded, easy-to-talk-to friend everyone deserves. He has offered important counsel and support when it's been sorely needed. Even from afar Ethelbert Miller has demonstrated a quality of friendship that reminds me how close men are capable of becoming. The same can be said about dear brother Allan Johnson, whose editorial suggestions immeasurably improved the first chapter.

My friendships with Michael Kimmel and Jackson Katz have long been twin beacons illuminating the path to gender justice. Michael has opened his Brooklyn home to me many nights over the years, offering an editor from New England—a Red Sox fan no less—safe haven in Yankees country. Besides his enormous accomplishments in profeminist men's work, Michael walks his talk. Witnessing him in his roles as a husband and father brings the work from the theoretical to the practical. His wife, Amy Aronson, and son Zachary know what I'm talking about. My heart is always lighter after spending time with all of them.

Similarly, Jackson Katz has long been a friend, passionate ally, and a major force in our movement. If any one person can be credited with promoting the idea for this anthology it is Jackson, and he has never wavered in his belief in this book. Our marathon phone conversations from one time zone to another are legendary in our respective households. They always begin or end with what's happening with my family and his—his wife, Shelley Erickson, and son Judah. I look forward to breaking gluten-free bread with them again soon.

Speaking of family, I want to thank my brother Stuart Okun, and brother-in-law, Peter Valentine, for their enduring love and support. And, I am blessed with four amazing children—Aviva, Jonah, Amber, and Lani. Their adventurous spirits, zany humor, and many acts of kindness nourish me whether they are near at hand or far away. They are my home base. Everything I do in the world comes from the love I feel for them and for my sons-in-law, Laney and John James. And there's one more. As I was laboring to deliver the manuscript of this book, Lani was delivering a boy, Tennessee James, born in New Orleans on June 18, 2013. FTF, Tenn.

How to thank my wife and best friend, Adi Bemak? Her love is the deep well from which I drink and that sustains me. She has read and edited nearly all of my columns and essays and my work is always better because of her. Of all her considerable skills and talents in the world, what I value most is her unwavering demand that I walk my talk. She is my true north.

CONTRIBUTOR BIOS

Mumia Abu-Jamal is an award-winning journalist and author of two best-selling books, *Live From Death Row* and *Death Blossoms*. In 1981 he was elected president of the Philadelphia chapter of the Association of Black Journalists. His 1982 murder trial and subsequent conviction has raised considerable controversy and criticism for alleged constitutional violations and other improprieties. In spite of his more than three-decade-long imprisonment on death row, Abu-Jamal has fought for his freedom and for his profession. He holds a B.A. from Goddard College and an M.A. from California State University, Dominguez Hills.

Sara Elinoff Acker is a longtime activist in the movement to end domestic violence who for many years directed the Men Overcoming Violence partners' program at the Men's Resource Center for Change, where she facilitated batterer intervention groups. Her book *Unclenching Our Fists,* about perpetrators who've become nonviolent, was published in 2013. A psychotherapist in private practice, she lives with her husband and daughter in Pelham, Massachusetts.

Juan Carlos Areán has worked since 1991 to engage men across different cultures to become better fathers, intimate partners, and allies to end domestic violence and achieve gender equity. A trainer who has led hundreds of workshops and presentations throughout the United States, as well as in Mexico, Chile, Brazil, Russia, Austria, Sweden, Bermuda, Canada, the US Congress, and the United Nations, he has worked at Futures Without Violence (formerly Family Violence Prevention Fund), the Men's Resource Center for Change, and Harvard University. He is currently the director of the National Latin@ Network for Healthy Families and Communities, a project of Casa de Esperanza.

Doug Arey, LICSW, has maintained a psychotherapy practice for two decades focusing on helping male survivors of childhood abuse, as well as addressing gender and sexuality issues with men and women. He lives with Mark, his partner and husband of 17 years, and is stepdad to Lindsey and Carly, and step-granddad to Logan and Madeline.

Alan Arnaboldi was the director of support programs and youth education supervisor for the Massachusetts-based Men's Resource Center for Change. A former audiologist, preschool and elementary school teacher, he is currently a life coach. He and his husband divide their time between western Massachusetts and Palms Springs, California.

VOICE MALE

John Badalament is program director of the Fatherhood Project at Massachusetts General Hospital in Boston. He is the author of *Modern Dad's Dilemma: How to Stay Connected with Your Kids in a Rapidly Changing World* and director of the PBS documentary *All Men Are Sons: Exploring the Legacy of Fatherhood.* His work has been featured on ABC News, NPR, and in the *Los Angeles Times* and Huffington Post. He was named a "hero" by Futures Without Violence (formerly Family Violence Prevention Fund) for his commitment to ending violence against girls and women. He speaks and consults with schools, parent groups, government agencies, nonprofit, and private-sector organizations both in the US and abroad.

Lundy Bancroft is the author of *Why Does He Do That? Inside the Minds of Angry and Controlling Men.* He is an activist for the custody rights of battered women.

Ben Barker is a writer and community organizer from West Bend, Wisconsin. A member of the Deep Green Resistance organization, he is currently writing a book about toxic qualities of radical subcultures and the need to build a vibrant culture of resistance. benbarker@riseup.net

Laura Barron is a flutist, writer, and community artist who uses the arts as an educational tool to empower people to become instruments of transformative change in their own lives. Former faculty at the universities of Oregon and Wisconsin, she now runs Instruments of Change, a nonprofit dedicated to interdisciplinary, arts-based community development. She has been published in *Cure* magazine and *Flutist Quarterly*; is the author of the travel blog Sans Souci; teaches creative writing to elementary school students; and is completing her first novel, *Mosquito Chronicles.*

George Bilgere's most recent book of poetry includes "Imperial" and "The White Museum," chosen by Alicia Ostriker for the 2010 Autumn House Poetry Series. He received the Cleveland Arts Prize in 2003, a Pushcart Prize in 2009, and the May Swenson Poetry Award in 2006 for *Haywire.* Former US Poet Laureate Billy Collins has called Bilgere's work "a welcome breath of fresh, American air in the house of contemporary poetry." His poems are heard frequently on Garrison Keillor's *The Writer's Almanac,* and he has also appeared on *A Prairie Home Companion.*

Dr. Steven Botkin has been leading men's groups for more than 30 years, conducting trainings for men and women, consulting to national and international organizations, and promoting a global movement to transform masculinity. As the founder and executive director of Men's Resources

International and cofounder and emeritus executive director of the Men's Resource Center for Change, he has been instrumental in the formation of the Rwanda Men's Resource Centre, the Congo Men's Network, and the MenEngage Alliance. He developed a tool kit for organizing "Masculinity Reflection Groups" for men and women with CARE International in Mali and Niger; a model for women and men as partners in peace building in the Central East African Great Lakes Region; a Healthy Manhood curriculum for the YMCA in the United States; and a male involvement initiative for Concern Worldwide in Liberia.

Russell Bradbury-Carlin directed the Moving Forward batterer intervention program at the Men's Resource Center for Change and served as MRC associate director during his 15 years with the organization. Currently, he works with immigrants and refugees in his capacity as executive director of Center for New Americans. He lives with his wife and son in western Massachusetts. Russellbradburycarlin.com

Willow Brocke is a social worker, writer, researcher, public speaker, and a director in a large Canadian health care organization. She is passionate about the relationship between the practice of compassion and capacity building in individuals, organizations, and communities. She lives in Calgary, Alberta, Canada, with her fabulous husband of twenty-two years, who is also her best friend.

Ted Bunch is co-founder of A CALL TO MEN: The Next Generation of Manhood. He is recognized both nationally and internationally for his expertise in organizing, educating and training men to work to end violence against women. He is former senior director and co-creator of the domestic violence accountability program for Safe Horizons in New York City. United Nations Secretary General Ban Ki-moon appointed him to UNiTE, an international network of male leaders working to end violence against women. In addition to conducting trainings at scores of colleges and universities throughout the country, he has been a guest presenter for the UN's Commission on the Status of Women and has conducted trainings and made presentations in Israel, Suriname, South Africa, Ghana, and Brazil.

Michael Burke, former *Voice Male* managing editor, is a freelance book and magazine editor, writer, and marketing consultant. He lives in western Massachusetts.

Dennis Bushey is a tool designer, fiber artist, and a member of the Radical Faerie community at Faerie Camp Destiny in Vermont. He has been attending a GBTQ support group for more than a decade.

Sarah Werthan Buttenwieser is a freelance writer whose work has appeared in the *New York Times, Brain, Child* magazine, and Salon, among others. Her essays have appeared in anthologies including *The Maternal Is Political* and the forthcoming *The Good Mother Myth.* A longtime political activist and community organizer, she's also a mother to four. Twitter account: @standshadows

Lacey Byrne is the artistic director of Salix Productions, which creates collaborative performances that illustrate women's experiences while inspiring change. She has taught women's studies at the University of Connecticut. A dancer and choreographer, she lives in northwestern Connecticut with her husband and daughter. www.salixproductions.com.

Charlotte and Harriet Childress are consultants, authors, and college faculty who have researched, written, and spoken about issues related to social and political change for more than three decades. They are authors of the book *Clueless at the Top: While the Rest of Us Turn Elsewhere for Life, Liberty, and Happiness.* They live in the Pacific Northwest. www.cluelessatthetop.com.

Pip Cornall is director of the Grace Gawler Institute on the Gold Coast, Queensland, Australia, where he combines his outdoor educator skills with yoga therapy in his work with prostate cancer patients. Founder of "Prostate Mates: Let's Talk About it Outdoors" and "Male Challenge: Helping Boys Become Fantastic Men," Pip has been a physical education teacher in Australia and a raft guide and ski instructor in the US. He has served as a mediator in the juvenile justice systems in Oregon and Australia and is the author of books on men's emotional health including *Sustainable Masculinity* and *Kicking a Goal for Masculinity.* www.malechallenge.com; www.prostatemates.com; www.germancancertreatments.com

Mubarak Dahir is a freelance writer and editor living in Florida.

Gail Dines is a professor of sociology and women's studies at Wheelock College in Boston, where she is also chair of the American studies department. She has been researching and writing about the pornography industry for more than 20 years. She is coeditor of the best-selling textbook *Gender, Race and Class in Media* and has written numerous articles on pornography, media images of women, and representations of race in pop culture. She is a recipient of the Myers Center Award for the Study of Human Rights in North America. Her latest book is *Pornland: How Porn Has Hijacked Our Sexuality.* Featured in a number of documentary films on gender, she is a founding member of the activist group Stop Porn Culture.

Michael Dover, Ph.D., is a retired environmental scientist who spent much of his career working on environmental policy development and support. After retiring, he worked in various capacities at the Men's Resource Center for Change (formerly the Men's Resource Center of Western Massachusetts), including chair of the board and interim coexecutive director. More recently he has served on the board of the Hitchcock Center for the Environment in Amherst, Massachusetts. He is coordinator and coeditor of "Earth Matters," a biweekly column on nature and the environment, which appears in the Northampton, Massachusetts, newspaper the *Daily Hampshire Gazette*.

Paul Ehmann is an essayist, real estate broker, and a survivor. He lives in Albany, New York, and can be reached at etrain@nycap.rr.com

Nathan Einschlag currently works as a junior high school ESL teacher and lives in New York City.

Randy Ellison is a child sexual abuse victim's advocate who has written extensively on the subject. Author of *Boys Don't Tell; Ending the Silence of Abuse*, he is president of the board of the Oregon Abuse Advocates and Survivors in Service (OAASIS) and a member of the Oregon attorney general's sexual assault task force.

Aviva Okun Emmons, a registered nurse at Duke University Hospital in Durham, North Carolina, holds a bachelor's of arts in psychology from Goucher College and a bachelor's of science in nursing from Duke University. She resides in Hillsborough, N.C., with her husband—who treats her with kindness and respect.

Eve Ensler is the Tony Award-winning playwright, activist, and author of many works including *The Vagina Monologues, The Good Body, I Am an Emotional Creature,* and her 2013 critically acclaimed memoir *In the Body of the World*. She is also the founder of V-Day, the global movement to end violence against women and girls, and initiator of the One Billion Rising Campaign.

Carl Erikson is former business manager and support group leader for the Men's Resource Center of Western Massachusetts. Since retiring, he has expanded his activities as a visual artist, writer, and theater stage manager and director.

Martín Espada is a poet and professor at the University of Massachusetts, Amherst, who has published several award-winning collections of poetry, including *The Trouble Ball* (2011), which received the Milt Kessler Award, a

Massachusetts Book Award, and an International Latino Book Award, and *The Republic of Poetry* (2006), which received the Paterson Award for Sustained Literary Achievement and was a finalist for the Pulitzer Prize. His work has been translated into several languages, and his collections of poems have been published in Spain, Chile, and Puerto Rico. His collection of essays on Latino identity, *Zapata's Disciple*, has been banned in Arizona as part of the Mexican-American Studies Program outlawed by the state legislature.

Chelsea Faria, a student at Yale Divinity School, is interested in the intersection between spirituality and politics. An antiwar activist and a lover of astrology, she was an intern at *Voice Male* in 2011.

Randy Flood is cofounder and director of the Men's Resource Center of West Michigan and coauthor (with Charlie Donaldson) of *Stop Hurting the Woman You Love*. A psychotherapist and consultant, he has created specialized counseling programs for men and offers workshops and trainings for professionals on the social construction of masculinity and its consequences on men's healthy development. www.menscenter.org.

Jane Fonda is an actor and activist who has won two Academy Awards, an Emmy, and three Golden Globes. She is the author of a memoir, *My Life So Far*.

Daryl Fort is among the most senior trainers with Mentors in Violence Prevention and is considered one of the most experienced male gender violence prevention educators in the world. He has worked extensively with NFL players, coaches, and front office staff since 2006. A former senior adviser to the governor of Maine, Fort is a 1992 graduate of the University of Maine, where he played on the football team.

Rus Funk is the founder and executive director of MensWork: Eliminating Violence Against Women based in Louisville, Kentucky. He has been active in working to combat violence against women for 30 years. Rus currently serves on the boards of directors of the Indiana Coalition Against Domestic Violence, the National Center for Sexual and Domestic Violence, and the Association of Community Organization and Social Administration. He is on the global advisory committee of Mobilizing Men for Violence Prevention and on the steering committee of the North American Men Engage Network and the Interpersonal Violence Prevention group. He lives in Louisville with his partner and their child.

Tom Gardner, Ph.D., teaches communication law, public relations, and journalism at Westfield State University in Massachusetts. He is former managing director of the Media Education Foundation where he was producer and interviewer for the film *Framing an Execution: The Media and Mumia Abu-Jamal.*

Dr. Richard Gartner is the founding director of the Sexual Abuse Service at New York's William Alanson White Institute where he serves on the faculty and is training and supervising analyst. The author of *Betrayed as Boys: Psychodynamic Treatment of Sexually Abused Men* (1999, 2001) and *Beyond Betrayal: Taking Charge of Your Life after Boyhood Sexual Abuse* (2005), he is a cofounder and past president of MaleSurvivor.org. (www.richardgartner.com)

Doug Ginn is a cheesemaker and part owner of an artisanal creamery in - upstate New York. The father of twin baby boys, Olin and Ryan, he works from home as business consultant to the food industry in order to spend time with his two little lions. He was a volunteer facilitator at the Men's Resource Center while a student at the University of Massachusetts-Amherst.

Michael Greenebaum has been a school administrator, professor, and conductor of youth orchestras and light operas. Since his retirement he has been active in Learning in Retirement.

Patrick D. Higgins, author of *Some America,* is also a musician. He lives in Brooklyn, New York.

Richard Hoffman is the author of five books, *Half the House: A Memoir;* the poetry collections *Without Paradise, Gold Star Road,* and *Emblem;* and *Interference and Other Stories.* He is senior writer-in-residence at Emerson College in Boston.

Byron Hurt is an award-winning documentary filmmaker, writer, and anti-sexism activist. Hurt is also the former host of the Emmy-nominated series *Reel Works with Byron Hurt.* His documentary, *Hip-Hop: Beyond Beats and Rhymes*, premiered at the Sundance Film Festival and broadcast nationally on the PBS Emmy-Award winning series *Independent Lens.* His film *Soul Food Junkies* won the CNN Best Documentary Award at the American Black Film Festival and best documentary at the Urbanworld Film Festival in New York City, and also aired on *Independent Lens.* www.bhurt.com.

Robert Jensen is a professor in the School of Journalism at the University of Texas at Austin and board member of the Third Coast Activist Resource Center in Austin. He is the author of *Arguing for Our Lives: A User's Guide to Constructive Dialogue* (City Lights, 2013); *All My Bones Shake: Seeking a*

Progressive Path to the Prophetic Voice (Soft Skull Press, 2009); *Getting Off: Pornography and the End of Masculinity* (South End Press, 2007); and *The Heart of Whiteness: Confronting Race, Racism and White Privilege* (City Lights, 2005).

Mark Jimerson, LICSW, is the director of the Massachusetts Society for the Prevention of Cruelty to Children's western Massachusetts office. A cofounder of CrossPoint Clinical Services, Inc., he is a past recipient of a Supporting Fathering Award from the New England Fathering Conference.

Allan Johnson is a nonfiction author, novelist, sociologist, public speaker, and workshop presenter who has devoted most of his working life to understanding the human condition, especially in relation to issues of social justice rooted in gender, race, and social class. His nonfiction books include *The Gender Knot: Unraveling Our Patriarchal Legacy* and *Privilege, Power, and Difference*. His work has been translated into several languages and excerpted in numerous anthologies. His first novel, *The First Thing and the Last*, a story of healing and redemption in the aftermath of domestic violence, was recognized by *Publishers Weekly* as a notable debut work of fiction. His second novel, *Nothing Left to Lose*, the story of an American family in crisis during the Vietnam War, was published in 2011.

Charles Johnson is a scholar, novelist, short story writer, and essayist who addresses a broad range of issues related to African American life. His first novel, *Faith and the Good Thing*, was published in 1973, and he is known for several other novels including *Middle Passage* and *Dreamer*.

Jackson Katz, Ph.D., is an internationally recognized educator, author, filmmaker, and cultural theorist who is a pioneer in the fields of gender violence prevention education and critical media literacy. He is cofounder of Mentors in Violence Prevention, whose signature "bystander" program is widely used in sexual and domestic violence prevention initiatives in college and professional athletics, and in the US. military. He is the creator of popular educational videos including *Tough Guise: Violence, Media and the Crisis in Masculinity*, and is author of *The Macho Paradox: Why Some Men Hurt Women and How All Men Can Help* and *Leading Men: Presidential Campaigns and the Politics of Manhood*. He lectures widely in the US and around the world on violence, media, and masculinities.

Michael Kaufman, Ph.D., has worked for more than 30 years as an educator and a writer focused on engaging men and boys to promote gender equality and end men's violence against women. He has worked in 45 countries, including extensively with the United Nations. He is the cofounder of the White Ribbon Campaign and the author or editor of seven books on gender issues, democracy, and development studies, as well as an award-winning novel. His articles have been translated into 15 languages. Married with two children, he lives in Toronto, Canada. www.michaelkaufman.com @GenderEQ

Joe Kelly is a fathering educator and author of 10 books on family life, including the best-seller *Dads & Daughters*. A longtime advocate for healthy masculinity, he speaks often on how to see men in families as a valuable natural resource. Joe lives close to his adult daughters and grandson near Oakland, California. thedadman.com

Michael Kimmel, Ph.D., has been a leading researcher and writer on men and masculinity for more than three decades. Having written or edited more than 20 books, he has helped build the subfield of masculinity studies with works including *Changing Men: New Directions in Research on Men and Masculinity* (1987), *Men Confront Pornography* (1990), *The Politics of Manhood* (1996), *The Gender of Desire* (2005) and *The History of Men* (2005). His best-known works are *Manhood in America* (1996) and *Guyland* (2008), and *The Guy's Guide to Feminism* (coauthored in 2011 with Michael Kaufman). He also founded and edits *Men and Masculinities*, the field's premier scholarly journal and is Distinguished Professor of Sociology and Gender Studies at Stony Brook University in New York.

Paul Kivel, a social justice educator, activist, and writer, has been an innovative leader in violence prevention for more than 35 years. He is an accomplished trainer and speaker on men's issues, racism, challenges of youth, teen dating and family violence, raising boys to manhood, and the impact of class and power on daily life. A cofounder of the Oakland Men's Project, he is the author of numerous books and curricula, including *Uprooting Racism, Men's Work, Boys Will Be Men*, and *Helping Teens Stop Violence, Build Community and Stand for Justice*. His most recent book is *Living in the Shadow of the Cross*. www.paulkivel.com.

Charles Knight is senior fellow at the Project on Defense Alternatives, an organization he cofounded in Cambridge, Massachusetts in 1991. While there he authored or coauthored numerous articles and reports that appeared in publications including *Defense News, American Sentinel, Boston Review, Bulletin of Atomic Scientists, Social Policy, International Security, Dissent, Time,* and the *Boston Globe*. He has made numerous presentations on peace and security issues before governments and NGOs. Between 1994 and 1996 he consulted with the African National Congress and the South African Ministry of Defense on security options for southern Africa. A fellow at the Institute for Peace and International Security, he is the former publisher of *Working Papers* magazine and current editor of the blog OBRM: Other and Beyond Real Men.

Stephen Koenig is an economics and anthropology double major at Amherst College. He was an intern at *Voice Male* magazine in 2011 while a member of the Amherst College football team.

Eric Kolvig has been teaching meditation in the Vipassana Buddhist tradition since 1985. He leads retreats and gives public talks around the United States with a particular interest in "grassroots dharma"—building spiritual community in democratic, non-authoritarian ways. Eric also leads retreats in the wilderness as part of his interest in the value of spiritual practice in the natural world.

David Kundtz has written six books including *Nothing's Wrong: A Man's Guide to Managing His Feelings*. His most recent book is *Coming To: A Biomythography*. He lives in Berkeley, California.

Michele Landsberg is a journalist and author who for 25 years was Canada's leading feminist columnist, writing in the *Toronto Star*, the country's largest newspaper. Her activist journalism earned her two National Newspaper Awards, five honorary degrees, and, in 2006, the Officer of the Order of Canada. Her latest book, *Writing the Revolution*, came out in 2012.

Cliff Leek is a Ph.D. student in sociology at Stony Brook University, Stony Brook, New York. His studies focus on the intersections of whiteness, masculinity, and violence prevention.

Sean Casey LeClaire is a speaker, writer, and coach who assists individuals and organizations in increasing their capacity for engagement, inspired performance, and inner peace. Founder of a leadership development and coaching process called Timeless Wisdom at Work, which combines business principals with the ethical discipline and openheartedness of monks, he currently serves as president of the SCL Group. He lives in Westborough, Massachusetts with his son Beau.

Mike Lew, M.Ed., a psychotherapist, cultural anthropologist, and group leader, is codirector of the Next Step Counseling and Training Center in Brookline, Massachusetts. A leading expert on recovery from sexual child abuse, particularly issues surrounding adult male survivors, he frequently lectures and provides professional training and workshops for survivors worldwide. He is author of *Victims No Longer: The Classic Guide for Men Recovering from Sexual Child Abuse* and *Leaping Upon the Mountains: Men Proclaiming Victory over Sexual Child Abuse.*

Erica Little-Herron is a nomadic Alaskan freelance photographer and poet. Formerly a sex advice newspaper columnist, she is a vocal advocate for sex-positive education who is currently working to earn a doctorate in gender and sexuality. She lives in Baltimore, Maryland.

Jeff Kelly Lowenstein is database and investigative editor at *Hoy*, the Chicago Tribune company's Spanish-language newspaper and immediate past president of the Dart Society, an organization of journalists dedicated to covering issues of trauma and violence with compassion and sensitivity. He received a 2012 Society for News Design award of excellence and has participated in national and international fellowships, including the 2011 Climate Change Media Partnership Fellowship. He is author of *On My Teacher's Shoulders: Lessons Learned Along The Way,* a memoir about learning from his fourth grade teacher and was named a 2013 Fulbright scholar at the University of Diego Portales in Santiago, Chile. He and his wife, Dunreith, live in Evanston, Illinois. Their son Aidan is entering his junior year at Tulane University.

Phap Luu (né Douglas Bachman) grew up in Newtown, Connecticut. A Zen monk teaching applied ethics and the art of mindful living to students and schoolteachers, he lives at the Plum Village monastery in Thenac, France, founded by Buddhist monk Thich Nhat Hanh.

Bruce MacMillan founded the legendary Broadside Bookshop in Northampton, Massachusetts, in 1974. A force for literacy and civility in the community, he died in 2001.

Freya Manfred's sixth collection of poetry, *Swimming with a Hundred Year Old Snapping Turtle,* (www.reddragonflypress.com), won the 2009 Midwest Bookseller's Choice Award for Poetry. Her seventh collection is *The Blue Dress,* 2012. Her poetry has appeared in more than 100 reviews and magazines and more than 40 anthologies. Novelist Philip Roth says, "Freya Manfred always startles me by how close she gets to everything she sees. That's her tough luck, but it makes her a wonderful poet." She lives half an hour east of the Twin Cities with the screenwriter Thomas Pope. Their sons, Nicholas Bly Pope and Ethan Rowan Pope, have illustrated some of her poetry.

VOICE MALE

Maia Mares is a women's and gender studies major at Amherst College and a former intern at *Voice Male*.

George Marx created and maintains Amensproject.com, which features more than 2,400 Internet listings for boys and men in North America in support of positive masculinity. He cofounded Men Stopping Rape in Madison, Wisconsin, in 1983.

Stephen McArthur is a victim/survivor advocate for Circle, the domestic violence agency serving Washington County, Vermont. He is also a violence prevention educator with students kindergarten through college, and a community workshop and training facilitator on issues ranging from bullying to dating and domestic violence, sexting, gender stereotypes, and the culture of male violence, consent, and cyberbullying. He served on the Vermont Sexual Violence Prevention Task Force and is a member of the Washington County Domestic Violence Coordinated Community Response team. In his spare time, he writes.

Patrick McGann is director of strategy and planning at Men Can Stop Rape in Washington, D.C. where he has worked since the organization was founded in 1997. Coauthor of a comprehensive sexual assault prevention strategy for the Department of Defense, he has overseen the creation the organization's "Where Do You Stand?" bystander intervention training and its highly regarded Young Men of Strength social marketing campaign.

Vernon McLean is a retired college professor and former chair of the department of African-American and Caribbean studies at a public university in New Jersey. A Fulbright scholar and the author of several anthologies on racism, sexism, and homophobia, he has written for the *New York Times,* the *Chronicle of Higher Education,* the *Western Journal of Black Studies,* and the *Society for the Psychological Study of Men and Masculinity*, among many other publications.

Michael Messner is professor of sociology and gender studies at the University of Southern California. His books include *King of the Wild Suburb: A Memoir of Fathers, Sons and Guns* and *It's All for the Kids: Gender, Families and Youth Sports.* In 2011 he received the Pursuit of Justice Award from the California Women's Law Center for his support of girls and women's sports. The American Sociological Association awarded him the 2012 Jessie Bernard Award in honor of a career of research and teaching that expands scholarly and public understandings of women's lives.

Contributors

E. Ethelbert Miller is a literary activist. He is the board chair of the Institute for Policy Studies, a progressive think tank in Washington, DC. He has published several collections of poetry and is the author of two memoirs. His writes a popular blog called E-Notes (www.eethelbertmiller1.blogspot.com).

Richard Jeffrey Newman writes about the impact of feminism on his life as a man and that of classical Persian poetry on our lives as Americans. His books include *The Silence of Men*, a volume of poetry, and *The Teller of Tales: Stories from Ferdowsi's Shahnameh*, a translation of part of the Iranian national epic poem. He curates the First Tuesdays reading series in Queens, New York, and is on the board of directors of Newtown Literary Alliance, a Queens-based literary nonprofit. He is professor of English at Nassau Community College in Garden City, New York. www.richardjnewman.com.

Alden Nowlan was a Canadian poet who worked as a newspaperman and published poetry, plays, short stories, and novels. His collection *Bread, Wine and Salt* won the Canadian Governor General's award in 1967.

Rob Okun, editor of this book and editor and publisher of *Voice Male* magazine, has for more than a quarter century addressed issues of gender equality, fathering, and men overcoming violence in his speaking, activism, and widely published writing. The former executive director of the Men's Resource Center for Change, he is a member of the board of the New England Learning Center for Women in Transition and the steering committee of North America MenEngage. His book *The Rosenbergs: Collected Visions of Artists and Writers* was made into the award-winning film, *Unknown Secrets: Art and the Rosenberg Era*. www.robokun.net

Brian Pahl worked for 11 years to prevent sexual assault and dating violence, first at Western Washington University and then at Rape Trauma Services of San Mateo County in the San Francisco Bay area. In 2008, 16 years after his battle with stage 2 testicular cancer, he became a daddy to Luna. Baby Grace followed in 2011. He currently is a facilitator of learners in the fourth grade in Bellingham, Washington.

Jan Passion has worked in the field of peace and nonviolence for more than 30 years. He was a founding member of the Nonviolent Peaceforce working in Sri Lanka, West Africa, and Palestine/Israel. His peace-building experience also includes work in the US, Macedonia, Colombia, Thailand, Israel, Kenya, Sierra Leone, India, Ecuador, the former USSR, Guinea, Ghana, South Africa, and Cyprus. For a decade he was a psychotherapist in northern Vermont working with perpetrators and victims of various forms of violence and trauma.

Tal Peretz, a doctoral candidate in sociology and gender studies at the University of Southern California, endeavors in his research and activism to engage men in ending sexism. For the past decade he has volunteered with domestic violence shelters, rape crisis hotlines, and men's groups working to end sexual violence and promote healthy masculinities. His dissertation uses an intersectional analysis to investigate how social location affects black, Muslim, and gay/queer men's gender justice groups.

Imani Perry is a professor in the Center for African American Studies at Princeton University. She is the author of *Prophets of the Hood: Politics and Poetics in Hip Hop* and *More Terrible and More Beautiful: The Embrace and Transcendence of Racial Inequality in the U.S.* www.imaniperry.com.

Tony Porter is cofounder and codirector (with Ted Bunch) of A CALL TO MEN: The Next Generation of Manhood. Author of *Well Meaning Men Breaking Out of the Man Box: Ending Violence Against* Women, he works with a wide array of domestic and sexual violence programs, the National Football League, other professional sports teams, and the United States military. A State Department lecturer in the Democratic Republic of Congo, he has been a guest presenter for the United Nations Commission on the Status of Women, and works closely with A Call to Men UK to provide training and support for the British organization.

Elias Sánchez-Eppler is pursuing a master's degree in public and international affairs at Princeton University and working at the State Department on US policy in Latin America.

Tom Schiff has worked with men and boys for more than 30 years. He is the director of Phallacies (www.phallacies.org), a profeminist, male-positive men's health dialogue and theater program that provides leadership development, health education, and violence prevention training for men. He is also an adjunct professor in the social justice education and public health programs at the University of Massachusetts, Amherst, and lives in western Massachusetts with his wife and two beautiful stepdaughters.

Haji Shearer has facilitated hundreds of groups for fathers. Director of the Fatherhood Initiative at the Massachusetts Children's Trust Fund, he founded the fathers' program at the Family Nurturing Center in Dorchester, which continues to provide groups for men in Boston's urban communities. His writing has appeared in the *Boston Globe* and the anthology *Men Speak Out: Views on Gender, Sex and Power*. He has facilitated men's healing circles, boys to men rites of passage, and couples workshops. Haji and his artist-wife are the parents of two young adult children.

Ethan Smith is the pen name of a 2004 graduate of the University of Massachusetts at Amherst. In his senior year he worked as an intern at the Men's Resource Center and *Voice Male*, where he made an excellent start in changing the world.

Jason Sperber is a writer, the stay-at-home-dad of two daughters, and the husband of a family physician in Bakersfield, California. He writes the blog daddyinastrangeland.com, cofounded the group blog by Asian American Dads, RiceDaddies.com, and is a member of the collectives at Daddy Dialectic and Dadcentric. His work has been published in the anthology *Rad Dad*.

Jacob Stevenson is the pseudonym of a writer and survivors' advocate who was instrumental in establishing programs and services for male survivors at men's centers and elsewhere.

Brendan Tapley is a writer whose essays have appeared in the *New York Times,* the *New York Times Magazine*, the Daily Beast, the *Los Angeles Times,* Slate, and the *Boston Globe*, among many others. He lives in New England.

Donald N. S. Unger is the author of *Men Can: The Changing Image & Reality of Fatherhood in America*. He has been writing and lecturing on issues relating to gender, media, and representation for more than 15 years. His work has appeared in the *Boston Globe*, the *Philadelphia Inquirer*, and the *Village Voice* among other publications; he has been a commentator for a local NPR affiliate and has had both short fiction and poetry published in journals in the US, Canada, and Europe. He lives in central Massachusetts with his wife and daughter.

Eric Wasileski, M.Div., is a veteran of Operation Desert Fox, a Quaker minister at Smith Neck Friends Meeting in Dartmouth, Massachusetts, and a charter member of Veterans for Peace, chapter 95. He does preenlistment and welcome-home counseling for returning veterans.

Tom Weiner is author of the book *Called to Serve: Stories of Men and Women Confronted by the Vietnam War Draft*, which has been made into a play entitled *The Draft*. He is father of four children, 22 to 42, a grandfather of three, and has been teaching sixth grade and mentoring student teachers at the Smith College Campus School in Northampton, Massachusetts, since 1976.

Les Wright founded the Bear History Project and edited two academic books on early gay bear culture. He is a former professor of humanities and English. Although currently living in Palm Springs, California, his goal is to retire permanently in upstate New York.

Tom Ziniti is a freelance writer. His work has been broadcast on New England Public Radio and has appeared in *Bay Windows, Out in the Mountains,* and *The People's Voice.* He has been a public school elementary reading and math teacher since 1998. He lives in Orange, Massachusetts, with his partner, Doug, and their dogs, Jazz and Rufus.

Joe Zoske is an administrator at Siena College in Loudonville, New York, where he teaches health care communication skills courses. He lectures on men's health and gender issues at Siena, the University of Albany's School of Public Health, and Empire State College.

The following articles first appeared in these print publications and on these websites:

Boys to Men
"Searching for a New Boyhood" by Michael Kimmel (Winter 2000) appeared in different form in *Ms.* (October–November, 1999). Used with permission.

"Leaving the Team, Becoming a Man" by Nathan Einschlag (Winter 2007), appeared in the anthology *Men Speak Out: Views on Gender, Sex and Power*, edited by Shira Tarrant, (Routledge, 2008, 2013). Used with permission.

"Men's Tears" by Freya Manfred appears in the author's collection *My Only Home* (Red Dragon Fly Press, 2003). Used with permission.

Changing Men
"The High Cost of Manliness" by Robert Jensen (Winter 2007) first appeared on Alternet, September 7, 2006. Used with permission.

"The National Conversation about Masculinity" by Michael Kimmel (Winter 1998) is adapted from remarks the author delivered in the fall of 1997 at Hobart and William Smith Colleges in Geneva, N.Y. Used with permission.

"Male Student Athletes: Profeminism's Newest Allies" by Rob Okun (Summer 2013) appeared as the Father's Day column for V-Men at Vday.org. Used with permission.

"Looking at (White, Male, Straight, Middle-Class) Privilege" by Michael Kimmel (Spring 2003) was excerpted and adapted from *Privilege* (Westview Press, 2003), coedited by the author and Abby Ferber. Used with permission.

"Poisoned Privilege: The Price Men Pay for Patriarchy" by Jane Fonda (Fall 2003), is excerpted from a speech the author delivered on June 12, 2003, to the National Women's Leadership Summit in Washington, DC. Used with permission.

"What Kind of Man Am I?" by Jason Sperber (Spring 2012) appeared in different form at daddyinastrangeland.wordpress.com. Used with permission.

"Hanna Rosin and the End of (Middle Class Straight White) Men," by Michael Kimmel (Fall 2012) was excerpted from remarks delivered by the author at Boston University Law School, October 5, 2012. Used with permission.

"The Coming Masculinity" by Brendan Tapley (Winter 2010), first appeared in the *Bay Area Reporter*, San Francisco, August 6, 2009. Used with permission.

"Men Come in the Room" by Sean Casey LeClaire (Spring 2004) appears in his book *Hug an Angry Man and You Will See He Is Crying*, (Red Spiral Books, 2003). Used with permission.

"The After Hours Crowd" by Patrick D. Higgins (Winter 2009) first appeared in *Some America*. Used with permission.

Color Lines
"A 'Precious' Paradox" by Imani Perry (Spring 2010) first appeared on the website Afronetizen.com. Used with permission.

"Barack Obama and the Mythology of Black Men" (Fall 2011) by Dr. Charles Johnson first appeared in E. Ethelbert Miller's *E-Channel*. Used with permission.

"A 'Good' White Man" by Robert Jensen (Winter 2005) is excerpted and adapted from his book the *Heart of Whiteness: Confronting Race, Racism, and White Privilege*, (City Lights, 2005). Used with permission.

"Macho, Mongo, and the Men's Movement" by Martín Espada (Winter 1999) is excerpted from his essay "The Puerto Rican Dummy and the Merciful Son," in the author's collection *Zapata's Disciple* (South End Press, 1998). Used with permission.

"Father Hunger" by Mumia Abu-Jamal (Winter 1999) originally appeared in his book *Death Blossoms: Reflections from a Prisoner of Conscience*, (Plough Publishing House, 1997). Used with permission.

"Fathering Your Father" by John Badalament (Spring 2010) is excerpted from his book *The Modern Dad's Dilemma: How to Stay Connected to Your Kids in a Rapidly Changing World* (New World Library, 2010). Used with permission.

"The Last Hunt" by Michael Messner (Spring 2011) is excerpted from his book *The King of the Wild Suburbs* (Plainview Press, 2011). Used with permission.

"After the Funeral" by Richard Jeffrey Newman (Summer 2011) appears in his book *The Silence of Men* (CavanKerry Press, 2006). Used with permission.

Male Survivors
"Finding the Child Within" by Mike Lew (Summer 2004) is excerpted from his book *Victims No Longer: The Classic Guide for Men Recovering from Sexual Child Abuse* (HarperCollins/Quill, 2004). Used with permission.

"Betrayed as Boys" by Richard Gartner (Winter 2002) is excerpted from his book *Betrayed as Boys* (Guilford Press, 1999). Used with permission.

"The Taste of a Little Boy's Trust" by Richard Jeffrey Newman (Summer 2013) appears in his book *The Silence of Men* (CavanKerry Press, 2006). Used with permission.

Men and Feminism
"A Feminist Wife Embracing Men's Work" by Willow Brocke (Fall 2001) first appeared in somewhat different form in the Canadian magazine *Synchronicity*. Used with permission.

"An Open Letter to Gentle Men" by Erica Little-Herron (Spring 2007) was first published in *The Picket News* in Hagerstown, Maryland, in November 2006. Used with permission.

"Pop Culture and Pornography" by Gail Dines (Spring 2007) is based on remarks the author made at an antipornography conference at Wheelock College in Boston, March 2007. Used with permission.

"Canadian Feminists' Uneasy Alliance with Men Challenging Violence" by Michelle Landsberg (Spring 2000) first appeared in *The Toronto Star*. Used with permission.

Men's Health
"I Don't Know What I'm Feeling" by David Kundtz (Spring 2004) was adapted from his book *Nothing's Wrong: A Man's Guide to Managing His Feelings* (Conari Press, 2004). Used with permission.

Overcoming Violence
"The Macho Paradox" by Jackson Katz (Spring 2006) is excerpted from his book *The Macho Paradox: Why Some Men Hurt Women and How All Men Can Help* (Sourcebooks, 2006). Used with permission.

"Breaking Out of the Man Box" by Tony Porter (Spring 2009) is excerpted from his book *Breaking Out of the Man Box* (ACT Men, 2009). Used with permission.

"Man to Man: A Community Letter" by Paul Kivel (Fall 2007) appears in the articles section of the author's website (paulkivel.com/resources/articles/23-article/65-man-to-man). Used with permission.

"Challenging Rape Culture" by Robert Jensen (Winter 2003) appeared in different form in the *Free Lance-Star*, Fredericksburg, Va., September 2002. Used with permission.

"Breaking the Secret Code of Dudes" by Eve Ensler (Summer 2009) is adapted from remarks the author prepared for a conference, "Men and Women as Allies in Violence Prevention," organized by Men Can Stop Rape, Washington, DC, April 2009. Used with permission.

"When a Beloved Teacher Is Also a Rapist" by Sarah Buttenwieser (Summer 2012) also appeared in *Motherlode*, the parenting blog of the *New York Times* (parenting.blogs.nytimes.com). Used with the permission.

"When Men's Violence Is Invisible in the News" by Jackson Katz (Winter 2010) appeared in slightly different form in the *Huffington Post* in December 2009. Used with permission.

"Pimps and Johns: Pornography and Men's Choices" by Robert Jensen (Spring 2005) is excerpted from a talk the author delivered to the Conference on the College Male, Saint John's University, Collegeville, Minn., in February 2005. Used with permission.

VOICE MALE

OutProud: GBTQ Voices
"Nobody Likes a Nelly Homo" by Mubarak Dahir (Spring 2006) first appeared in *Express Gay News* in Ft. Lauderdale, Fla., April 2006. Used with permission.

What Is Healthy Masculinity?
"Democratic Manhood" by Michael Kimmel (Fall 2012) is adapted from a passage on page 284 in his book *Manhood in America* (Oxford University Press, 2006). Used with permission.

A Farewell to Arms: Manhood After Newtown
"Suicide-by-Mass-Murder" by Cliff Leek and Michael Kimmel (Winter 2013) first appeared in the *Huffington Post* on December, 23, 2012. Used with permission.

"The Game Is Not Over Though You Are Dead" by Phap Luu (Winter 2013) appeared in different form as a blog in *Patheos*, December 28, 2012. Used with permission.

"Message to the Media: It's About Manhood More Than Guns or Mental Illness" by Jackson Katz (Winter 2013) first appeared in the *Huffington Post* on December, 18, 2012. Used with permission.

INDEX

Page numbers in italic indicate photograph locations.

VOICE MALE

"box" of conformity, 33–35, 44–45, 57–59, 120–21, 366, 370
boys
  boy crisis, 52–54
  in "man box" for survival, 33–34
  patriarchy's toll on, 99, 196–97
  privileges of "man box," 57–59
  rules to survive (black boys), 139–40
  socialization of, 100, 120, 393
  See also masculinity; socialization; sports culture; vulnerability
Boys to Men Rites of Passage retreat, 136–37
Boys Will Be Boys (Miedzian), 53
Boys Will Be Men (Kivel), 54
Brace Center for Gender Studies, 91
Brannon, Bob, 17, 41–42
breast cancer, in men, 271, 273–77
Briggs, Jimmie, *40,* 40–41
Bro Code, The (documentary), 87–90, 234
Brod, Harry, 3
Brownmiller, Susan, 7, 228
Bunch, Ted, *33,* 34–35, 366
b word *versus* n word, 320–21
Byrne, Lacey, 231–34
bystander(s), 25–26, 28, 34, 234, 317

California Coalition Against Sexual Assault (CALCASA), 46
A Call to Men (organization), *33*–35
Campaign for Healthy Families, 235–37
Campus Men of Strength Club, 31
cancer, psychological effects of, 267–71
capitalism, 22, 101, 212, 331
Carlin, Kathleen, *14*–15
the Castro, 345–47
Catholic Church, 195–97
CDC (Centers for Disease Control and Prevention), 31
Center for the Study of Men and Masculinities, 5
Center for the Study of Sport in Society, 314, 315
Centers for Disease Control and Prevention (CDC), 31

Challenging Macho Values (Salisbury and Jackson), 54
change agents, men as, 55–57
Changing Men (magazine), 22–*23*
childcare, during men's retreats, 244, 246
child sex abuse. *See* sexual abuse / trauma
Christeson, Bill, 29
class
  black middle and elite, 129
  invisibility of, 94–98, 386
  and mass shootings, 386–87
  therapists' obliviousness to, 53
  See also invisibility; privilege
Clinton, Hillary and "The Exchange," 326
Coach for America, 46
coaching youth sports, 66–70
Collins, Jason, 394
Common Ground Collective, 76–77
Community Dialogue Series, 29
competition
  anxiety of, 367–68
  as dominance ideology, 80–82, 93, 197
  for jobs, against women, 216
  white men's, 131, 133
  in youth sports, 68–69
  See also control; masculinity
Congo, Clinton's visit to, 326–28
CONNECT (antiviolence organization), *28*–29
"Connecticut Shooting, White Males, and Mass Murder" (Hamby), 390
Connell, R. W., 97
conscientious objection, 102–105
control
  as core definition of manhood, 376–79
  guns/violence as instruments of, 376
  lack of, 367–68
  need for, 388
  US obsession with, 378
  See also masculinity
Conway-Long, Don, 11–12
cosurvivors, 190–95, 294–95
Courage to Raise Good Men, The (Silverstein and Rashbaum), 53
Creighton, Allan, *8, 210*

Index

Index

Index

Index